COASTAL
NATURE,
COASTAL
CULTURE

environmental
history
and the
american
south

COASTAL NATURE, COASTAL CULTURE

Environmental Histories of the Georgia Coast

EDITED BY Paul S. Sutter
AND Paul M. Pressly

Published in association with Georgia Humanities

The University of Georgia Press
Athens

© 2018 by the University of Georgia Press
Athens, Georgia 30602
www.ugapress.org
All rights reserved
Designed by Kaelin Chappell Broaddus
Set in 11/13.5 Garamond Premier Pro
by Kaelin Chappell Broaddus

Most University of Georgia Press titles are available
from popular e-book vendors.

Printed digitally

Library of Congress Control Number: 2018937915
ISBN 9780820351872 (hardcover: alk. paper)
ISBN 9780820353692 (pbk.: alk. paper)
ISBN 9780820351889 (ebook)

To the late Mark Finlay, professor of history at
Armstrong Atlantic State University
(now Georgia Southern University–Armstrong Campus),
a passionate scholar and devoted teacher whose
leadership guided the first steps toward this book

CONTENTS

ILLUSTRATIONS

SIDEBARS

ACKNOWLEDGMENTS

Many individuals deserve recognition for their efforts in bringing about *Coastal Nature, Coastal Culture: Environmental Histories of the Georgia Coast.* First are members of the group of people who came together in 2014 to envision a symposium and lay the groundwork for a book. The committee, which first met at historic Wormsloe, included the late Mark Finlay, Armstrong Atlantic State University; John Inscoe, University of Georgia; Paul Sutter, University of Colorado Boulder; Dorinda Dallmeyer, University of Georgia; Sarah Ross, Wormsloe Institute; Chris Curtis, Armstrong Atlantic State University; Stan Deaton, Georgia Historical Society; Elizabeth DuBose, Ossabaw Island Foundation; and me, Paul Pressly.

The Ossabaw Island Foundation played a critical role in putting the many pieces together. A different planning committee, chaired by Lisa White and drawn from the trustees of the foundation, raised the necessary funds to underwrite the cost of both the symposium and the book. Elizabeth DuBose, executive director, and Robin Gunn, program coordinator, handled the logistics. It would be easy to underestimate their considerable efforts over two years unless one had the opportunity of watching it unfold as I did. Robin tirelessly worked to ensure that each step along the way lived up to her high standards of excellence. Throughout the project, I served as director of the Ossabaw Island Education Alliance, a partnership between the Board of Regents of the University System of Georgia, the Georgia Department of Natural Resources, and the foundation. That position offered me the running room to create the framework for this extended effort.

Paul Sutter provided the critical vision that pulled the many chapters together around common themes. His insistence on originality and big ideas as well as his attention to detail ensured the quality of the final manuscript. Without his investment of time and creative energy, our project would never have come to fruition in its present form. Tremendous credit also goes to the authors of the main essays in this volume, who not only produced excellent papers for the symposium but also worked diligently on revising them for publication. Caroline Grego provided critical support at the manuscript preparation stage.

I would like to thank the contributors of the sidebars for their selfless spirit. Many of them are historians in their own right or professional naturalists who stopped to take the time to help our project. I also thank the many photographers and artists who willingly shared their images for this publication in the spirit of promoting the unique qualities of the Georgia coast.

The Georgia Humanities Council made a generous contribution to the publication of this book. The council deserves special thanks for its continuing efforts to realize its mission of "sharing stories that move us and make us."

Finally, the enthusiasm, encouragement, and remarkable patience of the staff at the University of Georgia Press made this publication possible. Thanks go to the press's Lisa Bayer, director; Mick Gusinde-Duffy, executive editor for scholarly and digital publishing; Bethany Snead, assistant acquisitions editor; the remarkable design and production staff; and Jim Giesen, editor for the Environmental History and the American South book series; as well as the anonymous reviewers.

Paul M. Pressly
Coeditor
Director emeritus,
Ossabaw Island Education Alliance

Coastal Nature, Coastal Culture had its origins in a well-received symposium on the environmental history of the Georgia coast that took place in Savannah during 2016. Scholars from around the United States made presentations on topics that ranged from Native Americans on barrier islands to the struggle over groundwater in the twentieth century. The organizers of the event were expecting a solid turnout but were surprised when over four hundred people showed up for the first presentation on a Thursday afternoon. It was an even greater surprise when most stayed until the closing at noon on Saturday.

Georgians are fascinated by a coast where nine of the thirteen barrier islands are undeveloped and five unconnected to the mainland by bridge. In the whole of the Eastern Seaboard from Maine to Miami, the Georgia coast stands out today as atypical, a stretch where relatively few lights interrupt the blackness of night. However, that appearance can be deceptive. Over the centuries, the human presence has led to successive transformations of land and landscape in ways that raise multiple questions. The assumption that nature's course is a progression from pristine to despoiled proves to be simplistic.

The symposium took aim at building a bridge between current scholarship on the history of the American South and the booming field of environmental history. The first comprehensive environmental history study of the Georgia coast came at a relatively late date—the publication of Mart Stewart's *"What Nature Suffers to Groe": Life, Labor, and Landscape on the Georgia Coast, 1680–1920* (University of Georgia Press, 1996). Today Stewart's volume remains the foundation for all subsequent studies. The chapters in *Coastal Nature, Coastal Culture* continue his work of exploring how successive communities of Native Americans, British imperialists, planters and enslaved people, lumbermen, wage-earning freedmen, vacationing industrialists, truck farmers, and river engineers developed distinctive relationships with the environment and produced distinctive coastal landscapes.

It took two years of effort to bring the conference about. The original idea lay with Mark Finlay, an environmental historian at Armstrong Atlantic State University, who secured the backing of the Ossabaw Island Foundation, Armstrong Atlantic State, and the Wormsloe Institute of Environmental History. After the first meeting, Dr. Finlay was killed in an automobile accident while returning from a history conference. The symposium was dedicated to his memory.

The sponsors of the symposium and of this book represent important forces in the preservation and conservation of the coast. The Ossabaw Island Foundation promotes and manages educational, cultural, and scientific programs on Ossabaw, the third largest island off the coast of Georgia. It does so in partnership with the Georgia Department of Natural Resources. Armstrong State University, renamed Georgia Southern University–Armstrong Campus, located in Savannah, has created a growing role for itself in environmental matters. The Wormsloe Institute, located at the site of one of Georgia's oldest land grants and now a part of the University of Georgia, conducts interdisciplinary research across a wide range of fields, including ecology, geography, archaeology, and history.

Standing behind this project were Lisa Bayer, director of the University of Georgia Press, and Mick Gusinde-Duffy, senior editor of the press. It is fortunate that Paul Sutter, a major figure in environmental history, agreed to be the editor of this volume. He served as the founding editor of the University of Georgia Press's Environmental History and the American South book series while on the faculty at the University of Georgia and is now in the middle of a productive and busy career teaching and publishing at the University of Colorado Boulder. I had the pleasure of a ringside seat watching his careful editing of the chapters as they came from the authors, and I appreciate his remarkable skill at shaping themes.

Our hope is that *Coastal Nature, Coastal Culture* will provide a fresh perspective on the history of the Georgia coast and a meaningful framework for discussion about its future.

Paul M. Pressly
Coeditor

COASTAL NATURE, COASTAL CULTURE

The History of Conservation and the Conservation of History along the Georgia Coast

PAUL S. SUTTER

In the March 27, 1971, issue of the *New Yorker*, John McPhee published the second in a triptych of essays on postwar conservation icon David Brower. Brower was the John Muir of his time, an unyielding champion of the American wilderness and a leading voice in the then-cresting environmental movement. As the executive director of the Sierra Club from 1952 to 1969, Brower had led the battle against the construction of a dam at Echo Park in Dinosaur National Monument and then fought for almost a decade to secure passage of the Wilderness Act of 1964. In the process, he built the Sierra Club into a formidable political force. After the club's board ousted him in 1969, for financial mismanagement and general defiance, Brower immediately founded Friends of the Earth, and a year later he founded the League of Conservation Voters. By 1971 Brower was one of the leading voices of the modern environmental movement as well as one of its great institution builders. Hence McPhee's interest in him.

Rather than writing a conventional profile of Brower, McPhee used each of his three essays to situate Brower with an ostensible adversary in a place of environmental controversy and to report the ensuing conversation. A week earlier, on March 20, McPhee's first installment had featured Brower and a mining geologist named Charles Park on a backpacking trip into the Glacier Peak Wilderness in Washington's North Cascade Mountains. Beneath Glacier Peak sat a lode of copper that the Kennecott Copper Company hoped to exploit by using the mining exception to the Wilderness Act. The third and most memorable installment in the series, which appeared on April 3, recounted a float trip down the Colorado River with legendary commissioner of the Bureau of Reclamation and arch dam builder Floyd Dominy, with whom Brower had repeatedly clashed during his conservation career. Sandwiched between these stories about the fate of two majestic western wilderness landscapes—a mountain and a river—was the shortest and least assuming of the three pieces, which featured Brower in conversation with a real estate developer named Charles E. Fraser over the fate of an island—Georgia's Cumberland Island. Fraser considered himself a conservationist too, but he likened strict preservationists such as Brower to modern "druids" for their apparent preference for unspoiled nature over the needs of people. McPhee adapted and amplified this epithet as the title for his series and for the book that followed, *Encounters with the Archdruid.*[1]

Today Charles Fraser is best known for two signature resort developments that bookend and set off the Georgia coast—Sea Pines Plantation on Hilton Head Island in South Carolina and Amelia Island Plantation on Amelia Island in Florida. As large-scale residential and recreational developments go, they have their virtues. Both have been lauded as models for design in harmony with nature. Fraser clustered homes to minimize the footprint of his communities, and he kept them away from beaches and other fragile habitats, which allowed him to preserve large portions of these properties in their natural states. Fraser also blended his architectural and landscape designs with the local environment, and he made aggressive use of restrictive deeds and covenants to achieve conservation goals and aesthetic uniformity within his planned communities. He hoped most of all to avoid the crass commercialism that had come to define so much coastal development. In 1968, Fraser purchased three thousand acres on Cumberland Island, the largest and southernmost of Georgia's barrier islands, and he was planning a similar resort development there, to be called Cumberland Oaks, when McPhee arranged for he and Brower to meet.[2]

At the time of the Fraser-Brower encounter, Cumberland Island had only eleven permanent residents and the East Coast's longest undeveloped beach, which made it attractive to both preservationists and developers. (Cumberland had also attracted the federal government's attention; it had been the runner-up to Cape Canaveral as the site for a major NASA launch facility for the U.S. space program in the early 1960s.) As significantly, the almost century-long reign of the Carnegie family as the primary stewards of the island was beginning to fray. Fraser had acquired his Cumberland Island real estate from three descendants of Andrew Carnegie's brother Thomas, who, with his wife, Lucy, had purchased most of the island in the early 1880s. By the late 1960s, the financially stressed Carnegie heirs, freed from a restrictive trust that Lucy had put on the property, were divided over how, and even whether, to main-

FIGURE Int.1. Charles Fraser, the developer of Sea Pines
and Amelia Island Plantations, circa 1962.
Courtesy of the Charles Fraser Estate.

tain the island as a family retreat. It was a familiar dynamic that had played out and would play out on many of Georgia's other barrier islands.[3]

The Carnegie heirs and some of Charles Fraser's other opponents viewed him as an arriviste threat to the patrician conservation regime that had prevailed on Cumberland Island since the end of Reconstruction, but the Fraser family had deep Georgia roots. The first Frasers had landed in New England with the Puritans, but they soon drifted south, and by the early nineteenth century they were one of Georgia's largest slaveholding families. According to McPhee, Fraser liked to remind the critics of his proposed Cumberland development that his family had been substantial landowners in the state well before the Carnegies had even migrated to the Americas. Charles was himself a product of coastal Georgia, even though his most important work would be done at its edges. He was born in 1929 in Hinesville, the seat of Liberty County, which sat in the piney woods just back of the coast. The Hinesville of Fraser's childhood was a quiet town, although that changed in 1940 when the U.S. military purchased 280,000 adjacent acres and turned it into Fort Stewart, which quickly became a vibrant mustering ground for the American invasion of Europe. This was but one example of the strong role that the military—and military considerations—would continue to play in coastal Georgia's environmental history. Fraser's father, General Joseph B. Fraser, was himself a military man, but he was also a successful lumber merchant, timber being another industry that had a profound impact on the region. From the end of Reconstruction until about World War I, the timber industry cut the region's longleaf pine forest in a fit of activity that remade an entire bioregion. And thanks in part to the pioneering work of Savannah resident Charles Herty, the young Charles Fraser witnessed a new chapter in the region's forest history: the rise of the pulp and paper industry that would again transform the region's environment after World War II.[4]

Charles Fraser would make his mark by taking his father's timber business in an entirely different direction. Joseph Fraser and several Hinesville partners had formed the Hilton Head Company in 1949 and soon purchased most of Hilton Head Island, just across the state line from Savannah, with plans to cut its timber, much of it second-growth. At the time, the island had several hundred residents, most of them African American descendants of former slaves who had either worked the island's antebellum Sea Island cotton plantations or had fled to the island during the Civil War.[5] Hilton Head was a key site for the Port Royal Experiment, an ambitious but short-lived program that the historian Willie Lee Rose famously called a "rehearsal for Reconstruction." The Port Royal Experiment involved the Union Army and northern philanthropists resettling freedpeople on former plantation lands, restoring plantation production with wage labor, and creating schools, churches, hospitals, and even housing for freedpeople. In fact, Union general Ormsby Mitchel oversaw the creation of an entire town for resettled freedpeople on Hilton Head, called Mitchelville in his honor. It came complete with rectilinear streets, quarter-acre lots, modest wooden homes, civil and religious institutions, rules about community behavior and sanitation, and democratic self-governance. While the Port Royal Experiment did not survive the end of the war, and Mitchelville suffered when the Union Army left a few years later, the town lasted until the late nineteenth century, and a remnant settlement lingered into the early twentieth century.[6] By the time that Charles Fraser encountered Hilton Head and first began to imagine a different kind of planned community for the southern end of the island, Mitchelville had ceased to exist, but it deserves a place of primacy in the history of Hilton Head real estate development. Charles Fraser, in other words, was not working with a blank slate.

Fraser knew that Hilton Head had a history, but he also saw a region poised on the edge of substantial change, and he was ready to push the island in a new direction. Fraser's father and the other Hilton Head Company partners soon divided their holdings, with Joseph getting the southern portion of the island. Meanwhile, after he finished an undergraduate degree at the University of Georgia, Charles Fraser headed to Yale Law School, where he mastered the legal tactics that he later used to shape and control his resort developments. Fraser then purchased his father's portion of the island, and beginning in 1957 he set about developing Sea Pines Plantation. In its mixture of golf and other active recreation with residential real estate, Sea Pines spawned numerous imitators along the southern coast during the postwar years. More importantly, it was but one example of how postwar coastal development overwrote landscapes with deep and complex environmental histories.[7]

Sea Pines emerged at a moment of reckoning for many of the Lowcountry's barrier islands and their residents, when the heirs of wealthy industrial families and the descendants of slaves were both struggling to retain their legal, historical, and cultural claims to the islands, and when new economic forces like the postwar timber boom, the industrialization of the South, the incipient Sunbelt migration, the rise of automobility, the growth of southern tourism, and new forms of residential development threatened to transform landscapes that had slowly re-naturalized over the previous three-fourths of a century.

By the time Charles Fraser purchased his Cumberland Island acreage a decade later, an additional force had entered the mix—the modern environmental movement, embodied by David Brower. In building Sea Pines, Fraser had operated largely unencumbered by organized environmental opposition, but he would not be so lucky on Cumberland Island. Brower, it turns out, was the least of his problems. In McPhee's profile, Brower seemed at once immune to Fraser's provocations and amenable to his vision for a contained and responsible resort. If a portion of the island was inevitably going to be developed, then Brower agreed that Fraser was the person to do it. McPhee had to throw in an additional character—Sam Candler, scion of the Coca-Cola founders, whose family owned the northern tenth of Cumberland Island—to give voice to the strict preservationist position to which Candler and a number of the Carnegie heirs still adhered. It was a position that, in the absence of sustaining family wealth, had come to rest on the prospect of National Park Service stewardship for the island. As McPhee made clear, vast industrial profits had made possible the "beautiful and fragile anachronism" that was Cumberland Island at the beginning of the 1970s. It was a place whose private seclusion and rustic comforts he enjoyed guiltily, knowing that, no matter who prevailed in the battle over the island's future, Cumberland was going to change.[8]

Charles Fraser never developed Cumberland Oaks. Environmentalists, including the local chapter of the Sierra Club, and Carnegie heirs, whose cooperation was essential to Fraser's development plan, offered so much opposition that Fraser eventually sold his property to the National Park Foundation, which then transferred the land to the federal government. Most of the island's other residents agreed to sell out as well, though they retained certain exclusive property rights for several generations into the future. In 1972 Congress created Cumberland Island National Seashore from these consolidated properties, a decidedly happy ending for the archdruid and his followers. Ten years later Congress designated almost ten thousand acres of Cumberland Island National Seashore as wilderness.[9]

Cumberland Island's public protection came amid a punctuated flurry of environmental activism and state and federal environmental legislation that birthed the modern environmental movement. The environmental movement, in turn, gave new meaning to the Georgia coast. At the state level, the Coastal Marshlands Protection Act of 1970 limited development in the hundreds of thousands of acres of marsh that sat between Georgia's barrier islands and its mainland, an achievement made possible in part by the research of ecologists such as the University of Georgia's Eugene Odum. While the poet Sidney Lanier had sung the praises of the aesthetics of Georgia's coastal marshes almost a century earlier, it took the insights of modern ecosystem ecology to create an ironclad case for their economic and environmental value. In the process, the Georgia coast became a vital center for research in coastal ecology and oceanography. The many federal environmental achievements of this period, from the Wilderness Act of 1964 through the Endangered Species Act of 1973, also shaped the Georgia coast. To give just one example, the Environmental Protection Agency, created in 1970, banned DDT in 1972, assuring that coastal visitors for generations to come would enjoy the aerial grace of brown pelicans gliding in formation above the strand. (Despite their current ubiquity, it is worth remembering that the Fish and Wildlife Service removed brown pelicans from the Endangered Species List only in 2009.) The late 1960s and early 1970s were thus pivotal years in the protection of Georgia's coastal nature, and nothing better symbolized that than national park status for Georgia's largest barrier island. More than that, though, John McPhee's choice to include the Cumberland story in his profile of David Brower reminds us of the Georgia coast's quiet but important place in the rise of the larger environmental movement.[10]

The story of Cumberland Island National Seashore's creation is only one among many such stories—each unique but all of a sort—that help to explain a distinctive and defining feature of Georgia's barrier islands: most of them, to this day, remain undeveloped, and many of them enjoy formal conservation status of one sort or another. Blackbeard, Wolf, and Wassaw Islands are all national wildlife refuges managed by the U.S. Fish and Wildlife Service. All of Ossabaw Island and most of Sapelo Island is owned by the State of Georgia and managed by the Georgia Department of Natural Resources. Ossabaw is a heritage preserve, the first of its kind in the state, and public use is limited to scientific, cultural, and educational activities. Much of Sapelo is protected as a national estuarine research reserve, a designation overseen by the National Oceanic and Atmospheric Administration. Jekyll Island is a state park, owned by the State of Georgia but managed by an independent authority—the Jekyll Island Authority—that oversees the island and provides a mix of preserved and developed tourist landscapes. A few of Georgia's other barrier islands, including St. Catherines and Little St. Simons, are protected in private ownership, with almost no development. Aside from portions of Jekyll, only Tybee Island, St. Simons Island, and Sea Island are substantially developed. Surely this happy state of affairs, this distinctive conservation patchwork, can be classed as a victory for environmentalists.

Environmentalism, however, is always more complicated than it seems. At the very moment that John McPhee was chaperoning the encounter between David Brower and Charles Fraser and listening in on their conversations about the future of Cumberland Island, Fraser was deeply embroiled in another environmental controversy—one that McPhee only briefly mentioned in his profile. In 1969 the German chemical company BASF, lured by the state of South Carolina's aggressive recruiting efforts, announced plans to locate a major manufacturing facility on Victoria Bluff, overlooking Port Royal Sound, just inland from Hilton Head Island. Strong opposition to the plan emerged quickly, and the fight against the BASF facility soon gained considerable national attention. It helped that the controversy reached its peak just as millions of Americans celebrated the first Earth Day in April 1970. Barry Commoner, the man who *Time* magazine had just called the "Paul Revere of Ecology," was enlisted in the fight. But anchoring the opposition to BASF's plans were residents of Hilton Head's exclusive resort communities, including Sea Pines, and Charles Fraser emerged as one of their most vocal leaders. While Fraser and many of the other well-connected Hilton Head residents who organized and bankrolled the campaign against BASF resisted calling themselves "environmentalists," and while some professed environmentalists involved in the campaign felt uneasy about their alliance with wealthy resort developers and privileged homeowners, the advocacy of Fraser and his allies nonetheless illustrated the role that

FIGURE Int.2. African American protesters marching in favor of the proposed BASF plant that would have been built near Hilton Head Island and to which Charles Fraser led the opposition. The photo was published May 7, 1970, in the Beaufort Gazette (Bluffton, SC). Photo by Bessie Hookstra/Beaufort Gazette.

these new coastal residents, most of whom had moved to the region for its environmental amenities, would play in defining the importance of coastal environmental protection and even what counted as environmental protection. By pitting Fraser against Brower and preservation against development, McPhee's piece had missed how vital Fraser and his constituents were to setting the modern coastal environmental agenda. Environmental protection and real estate development had a more complicated relationship than McPhee let on, and the BASF controversy made that plain.[11]

The BASF controversy also illustrated some of the racial complexities involved in the environmental politics of coastal protection circa 1970. For their part, BASF and its allies in the state's political and business communities insisted that the plant would play a major role in alleviating the region's poverty, particularly in providing employment to African Americans, and they portrayed Fraser and his allies not as selfless protectors of coastal nature but privileged defenders of their wealthy enclaves. How African Americans felt about the proposed facility was a little more complicated. While a group of African American commercial fishermen allied themselves with the anti-BASF forces, concerned that pollution from the plant would affect the productivity of coastal waters, NAACP members and many African American activists demonstrated in favor of the plant and the jobs it would bring. But again the environmentalists prevailed, and this time Charles Fraser was on the winning side. In January 1971, just two months before McPhee's article on Brower and Fraser appeared, BASF abandoned its plans for the Victoria Bluff site and located its facility instead in a part of the new industrial South where environmental opposition was less well-heeled: a highly industrialized stretch of the lower Mississippi River in Louisiana, between Baton Rouge and New Orleans, that soon became known as Cancer Alley.[12]

One of the central story lines in the environmental history of the Georgia coast is that real estate developers such as Charles Fraser, as a rule, have *not* prevailed there. To a great degree, this collection of essays and the vibrant symposium in Savannah in February 2016 that made it possible grew from a realization that coastal Georgia's unique history of conservation helps to make the region distinctive and anchors a sense of place that many coastal Georgians carry with them. That an academic conference drew an audience of more than four hundred people, and that that audience remained admirably engaged through almost two days of presentations in a windowless auditorium, speaks to this acute sense that the nature of the coast matters to local residents. But another central story line in the environmental history of the Georgia coast can be found precisely in Charles Fraser's own history of environmental advocacy and in the sorts of divides about what constitutes coastal conservation and who benefits from it, which the BASF controversy laid bare. While environmental historians often celebrate the victories that conservationists have won over the forces of concentrated economic power, they also have made it clear that when environmental advocates speak for nature they are usually also speaking for themselves and that appeals for environmental protection often shroud other ideologies and interests. This does not mean that calls for environmental protection are always sullied by ulterior motives, but it does mean that we need to interrogate the power dynamics of environmental activism and who benefits when nature is saved.[13]

Once we recognize this double-edged nature of environmental advocacy, the question for the Georgia coast and its residents becomes this: how do we value and protect this place in ways that all of its residents can find meaning and satisfaction in? To answer this question well, we need to pay as much attention to culture as we do to nature, and we need to recognize that we do not save nature *from* history but *in* history. Beneath the patina of wildness—and in the case of Cumberland Island, even designated wilderness—that has come to characterize most of Georgia's barrier islands, there are complex and contested environmental histories that need to be part of any conservation vision for the region. If one of the most important tasks of the field of environmental history is to bring historical perspectives to contemporary questions about environmental protection, the Georgia coast is a fruitful place to do so.

The Savannah symposium that gave birth to this book was the brainchild of the late Mark Finlay, a professor at Armstrong Atlantic State University who was working on a book on the preservation of Georgia's barrier islands, with a focus on Ossabaw Island, when he died in 2013. Mark had approached Paul Pressly of the Ossabaw Island Foundation to float the idea of a conference in the wake of a successful symposium that Paul had organized on African American life in the Georgia Lowcountry, a gathering that also resulted in an excellent edited collection.[14] Mark and Paul both recognized that scholars and others interested in the Georgia coast would profit from environmental approaches to its history and that environmental historians had much to learn from studying the Georgia coast. In many ways, the inspiration for this volume was Mark's unfinished history of Georgia's coastal preservation.

Yet celebrating the diverse ways in which Georgia's coastal nature now enjoys protection functions only as the entry point for this volume, which also contends with deep veins of history and culture in the region. One only needs to examine Cumberland Island, with its rich historical stratigraphy and the management challenges that come with preserving much of it as a "wilderness," to see the confounding ways in which the Georgia coast's past has complicated what conservation means in the present. While environmental historians are keen to reveal the role and place of nature in history and to show that environmental entities and forces have mattered in the course of human events, an equally important task on the Georgia coast is to reveal the place of history in what we would otherwise recognize as nature. The essays in this volume work in sophisticated ways at this intersection of nature and culture, and they warn us that, even as we do the important work of protecting and finding meaning in nonhuman nature, we ought not to let the natural grow over and engulf the cultural or to bulldoze history in the name of wildness. On the Georgia coast, the history of conservation is inextricable from the conservation of history.

The following essays also point out that the environmental history of coastal Georgia has necessarily occurred in larger regional, national, and global contexts that deserve our careful attention. Indeed, the coast's conservation success stories are implicated in other social and environmental histories,

MAP Int.1. The Georgia Coast

some of which we might not want to treat in quite so celebratory a fashion. How, for example, are we to judge the conserving work of the Carnegies, Coffins, Candlers, Reynoldses, and other wealthy families when we consider the larger environmental implications of the steel, automobile, soft drink, and tobacco-processing industries from which they made the vast fortunes that helped to buffer Georgia's coast against development? When we ask that kind of question, we realize that the conservation of the Georgia coast is really only a single entry on a much larger balance sheet. Indeed, a myopic focus on the Georgia coast itself can obscure the more expansive and interconnected histories that give the coast its meanings as a place. Another great achievement of this volume, then, is to provide us with some intriguing ways of thinking about how to define and bound the Georgia coast and how to situate it in the larger world.

The Georgia coast is defined by its barrier island geography. It is not unique in being fronted by such islands, which extend north into North Carolina and south into Florida, but it is certainly coherent as such. Behind those islands are hundreds of thousands of acres of tidal marsh, another unifying physiographical feature of the coastal region. Flowing through and beyond those islands and marshes are innumerable veins of tidal influence that pull the coast, as the meeting place of ocean and land, farther inland. If we consider not just the present edges between land and ocean but past ones as well, the Georgia coast becomes a more expansive region, one that has stretched, in a deep history, from fall line to continental shelf. But coastal Georgia cannot be defined by geography and environment alone. As a place, as a landscape, it is the product of human-environmental interactions and transformations and of human thought and feeling across centuries. It is a place defined by culture as much as by nature, by human presences and practices, from distinctive native lifeways to the tidal-flow rice culture that defined the coast as a nineteenth-century place, and from the persistence of culturally resilient African American communities to the region's emergent resort complex and conservation regime. The essays in this volume do not hew to a strict definition of the Georgia coast as a region, but they all home in on the same place and sense of place.

Coastal Nature, Coastal Culture begins with an essay by Mart Stewart, a revised version of the keynote address that he delivered at the 2016 symposium. Stewart was an obvious choice for the keynote since his 1996 book *"What Nature Suffers to Groe": Life, Labor, and Landscape on the Georgia Coast, 1680–1920* has long been the definitive environmental history of the region.[15] Stewart's book did many things well, but I want to highlight three of its achievements. First, it provided a rich rendering of the tensions during

Georgia's early English settlement between the formal landscape that James Oglethorpe and his followers envisioned for the place and the impromptu vernacular landscape that they created, suggesting that, from the very beginning of English settlement, the coastal environment reshaped settlers' land use practices and mental maps. Second, Stewart's analysis of tidal-flow rice cultivation and the human and nonhuman energies that made it work continues to be, two decades later, the state of the art for environmental histories of slavery and systems of plantation production. To those who might see the absence of an essay focused on coastal Georgia's rice landscapes as a glaring omission in this volume, I can only implore you to read Stewart's treatment of the subject. Finally, Stewart's portrait of the post-plantation transformation of the Georgia coast in all of its myriad forms—not only the slow fadeout of the engineered landscapes of rice production but also the rise of aristocratic landscapes of conservation and recreation, the impacts of industrial timbering, the rise of market gardening, and the persistence of African American communities and environmental lifeways—has served as a starting point for many of the essays in this volume.

Stewart's essay in this volume builds on many of those themes, but he also provides us with an essential meditation on the place of coastal Georgia in the larger world. He does so by focusing first on the dominance of islands in our sense of the place, and on the rich cultural history of islands and how we have thought with them. Islands have always been places for imagining bounded utopias; they have been retreats and preserves that we have kept separate from the mainland of human experience, with important implications for environmental thinking. Stewart shows that all sorts of people have dreamed on and with Georgia's barrier islands, and that those dreams are essential to the place and our sense of it even today. Stewart also defines the Georgia coast as a place of edges, particularly ecological ones. The coast may be where land meets sea, but what make the Georgia coast distinctive are its more specific kinds of edginess. Much of the coast is estuarine, where saltwater and freshwater meet and mix in a riot of biological productivity. The coast's marshes are themselves edgy places, swinging between land and water with the tides and fronting gallery forests in ways that produce their own edge effects. The coast edges into the coastal plain in ways that have been vitally important to the region's history, and human land uses have created new edges both productive and disruptive. On the Georgia coast, ecotones set the tone. Stewart ends, appropriately, by noting some of the coast's global dimensions. Its ecology has always been particularly cosmopolitan, its economy has always been one of Atlantic and global connections, and its future is now tied up in incipient global environmental changes that may rewrite the coast's entire geography. As powerful as island idylls have been to a sense of place along the Georgia coast, Stewart insists that these islands have always been integrated into the mainstream and moving in a sea of change.

That this volume then turns to an essay by David Hurst Thomas seems apropos, for no one has done more to enlighten us about the deep human history that necessarily defines the Georgia coast. Thomas, an archaeologist with the American Museum of Natural History, is best known for the excavations he has led on St. Catherines Island, where, almost forty years ago, he and a team discovered the long-lost site of the Spanish mission Santa Catalina de Guale.[16] Thomas's contribution to this volume provides a deep historical baseline against which to measure more recent change over time. He reminds us that the coast in its current form is only five thousand years old and that it has some unique biogeographic features that shaped early human history in the region. He also shows us the formative role that Native peoples—the Guale and Timucuan peoples—played in shaping coastal environments over several thousand years and how their lives on these resource-rich islands could never be entirely separated from a larger, continental Native American history. Finally, Thomas reminds us of the formative Spanish era in the coast's environmental history, an era that predated the arrival of the British by two centuries but is too often ignored in Anglocentric renderings of early Georgia's history. Part of the problem, as Thomas suggests, is the scant textual evidence for the Native American and Spanish periods, an absence that makes the work of archaeologists so important to chronicling the coast's early environmental history and integrating it with later periods that have more robust archives. While St. Catherines Island, the focus of Thomas's essay, is today remarkably undeveloped, in large part because of its archaeological importance, Thomas reminds us that the island was once thoroughly transformed by Native peoples and then Spanish missionaries, and that its landscape remains the most important archive for understanding that history of transformation.

When we think of the early history of the Georgia colony, the first image that probably pops into our minds is Peter Gordon's famous and much reproduced 1733 view of early Savannah's grid, an imagined space of urban order hemmed in by endless forest. As Max Edelson aptly puts it, "Perhaps no other picture of British colonization represents its fundamental ethos more clearly." Gordon made his sketch at another watershed moment in the history of the Georgia coast, when Oglethorpe and his followers were busy establishing the city of Savannah and other gridded town settlements as places where England's poor could remake their lives by transforming a wilderness into an ordered agrarian society. Historians have often rendered the story of Savannah's early settlement and the Georgia colony's development as a cautionary tale about the inevitable disconnections between imperial longing and environmental reality, a tale that ends in the 1750s when slavery and plantation agriculture undid the colony's early utopian aims. In his essay on early British cartographic visions of the Georgia coast, Edelson reminds us how important a range of maps were to early imaginings of coastal Georgia as a discrete place and to its evolving function in the larger empire. He also shows us how we can read maps as evidence of the Georgia colony's drift away from ordered colonization and control and toward a plantation society where the placement of rivers, swamps, and soils mattered more than abstract grids. Edelson insists that eighteenth-century maps were not merely ways of spatially illustrating what we now know as the Georgia coast. Rather, they were evidence of, and arguments for, how coastal colonization was to be organized and whether it would serve expansive territorial sovereignty or limited settlement. In Edelson's skillful hands, eighteenth-century maps emerge as both sources and forces, as documents that illustrate growing environmental knowledge and as texts whose ideologies shaped environmental transformation in the new world.[17]

Another distinctive feature of the Georgia coast, as we have already seen, is the presence of the Gullah Geechee people and culture. Certainly one of the most important nature-culture tensions in contemporary coastal conservation has to do with balancing the protection of nature with recognition of the distinctive history of coastal African Americans in what has come to be known as the Gullah Geechee Cultural Heritage Corridor, which stretches along the coast from southern North Carolina to northern Florida. In her contribution to this volume, Edda Fields-Black takes on the central question of how we are to understand Gullah Geechee identity by interrogating an environmental narrative that she believes has distorted our understanding of the nature, the dynamism, and even the geographical expansiveness of that identity. In the late nineteenth and early twentieth centuries, many came to understand the Gullah Geechee as people whose distinctive culture, one shaped by African cultural persistence, was the result of their isolation on island environments that history had left behind. Implicitly taking on this kind of geographical determinism, Fields-Black instead argues that it would be better to see the Gullah Geechee as "Lowcountry creoles," people whose distinctive identities predated their supposed island isolation and whose culture was more than the stuff of static African retention and survival.

Tiya Miles begins her essay with a cruel irony: Dunbar Creek, on St. Simons Island, the site of an uprising of Ibo slaves against their captors in 1803 that shaped a regionally distinctive myth of flying Africans, is today the dumping ground for treated effluent from the water pollution control facility that serves the residents of St. Simons and Sea Island. The creek is hemmed in by high-end residential development, and the site of the uprising remains unmarked to this day—except, perhaps, by the supernatural chanting and moaning that some say emanates from the haunted creek. Here is a potent metaphor indeed for how the African experience on the coast has been both obscured and degraded by the forces of development. Miles uses that vignette as a launching pad for her own rich analysis of the myth of flying Africans, the larger African American "story-world" that it represented, the importance of coastal waters and other aspects of the coastal environment to that story-world, and the surprising place of the Ebo Landing uprising, as it came to be known, in contemporary ghost tourism on the coast.[18] Indeed, Miles suggests that this story-world is a distinctive feature of the Georgia coast, and she intimates that the coast will remain a haunted place until we confront the structural inequalities that have shaped African American experiences in the region. Miles powerfully concludes with a call for a new "eco-cultural consciousness that should motivate habits of preservation along the Georgia coast." Miles's essay, then, is not only a powerful object lesson about what happens when we fail to honor particular peoples and their stories, but also a call to link environmental and historical preservation in innovative ways.

Drew Swanson shifts our attention from the ghosts of the slave trade to another kind of dark tourism that sharply redefined the Georgia coast in the late nineteenth and early twentieth centuries: a growing aesthetic and touristic fascination with the ruins of the plantations that once dominated coastal Georgia and the regeneration of a distinctive coastal nature that became a paradise for sportsmen. In Swanson's telling, the antebellum plantations of the Georgia coast represented, in the minds of the planter class, the apotheosis of human and environmental mastery, a plantation model that stood in stark contrast to the disorderly, itinerant, and brutal cotton frontier of the Old Southwest. That mastery quickly came unraveled at the end of the Civil War when coastal planters lost their most essential resource—the coerced labor of slaves. Swanson then shows how, after the war, prominent visitors to the region, almost all northern and white, came to find aesthetic pleasure in the picturesque ruins they found along the coast, developing what he calls a "rhetoric of ruin" that was the genesis of Lowcountry tourism. As plantation agriculture receded from the region and its infrastructure slowly crumbled, northerners found romance in ruination both because it expressed the righteousness of the Union cause and because such landscapes stood in stark contrast to the increasingly industrial nature of much of the rest of the nation. At a time of immense change, history seemed to be running in reverse along the Georgia coast. One benefit of this natural regeneration swallowing a ruined civilization was that many coastal landscapes became rich in fish and game, paradises for wealthy sportsmen and poor freedpeople alike. As Swanson powerfully shows, this story of coastal tourism's origins in dynamics of architectural ruin and ecological regeneration defines the affinity of both tourists and conservationists for the Georgia coast to this day, and he insists that we understand the post–Civil War conditions that gave rise to this particular worldview.[19]

The next several essays in the volume look at the environmental history of the Georgia coast as it entered the urban-industrial age, and each engages a different set of environmental geographies. Albert Way examines the industrial cutting of longleaf pine during the last several decades of the nineteenth century, providing an innovative analysis of how the timber resources of Georgia's inland coastal plain funneled through the coast and then on to the rest of the industrial world. Just as the idylls of ruin and regeneration that Drew Swanson described were redefining American understandings of the Georgia coast, the great cut of longleaf pine was also transforming certain portions of the coastal landscape—places like Darien, St. Simons Island, and even the Altamaha River. But Way does not stop there. Instead, he conceptualizes the coast as a "geographical fulcrum" where "Georgia's natural resources entered the broader world of valuable commodities." We know something about the environmental impacts that the industrial timber-cutting era had on the South's massive longleaf pine eco-region, but Way insists that we pay attention to where all that timber went. He reminds us that most mature coastal longleaf was cut down before the Civil War, and he notes that part of what made the longleaf resources of the inland coastal plain so valuable in the late nineteenth century was timing: the industrial world needed timber, and the South had it. But it was the specific qualities of longleaf timber that made it essential to the second industrial revolution, and these qualities, Way demonstrates, were products of longleaf's historical and evolutionary ecology. It was their very nature that made longleaf pine trees as indispensable to industrial culture as coal and steel. Way keeps the environmental qualities of longleaf alive even in its dead commodity form, and this allows him to connect the natural history of the inland coastal plain with the human history of the industrial Atlantic world. Coastal Georgia, in Way's telling, served as an entrepôt that linked diverse natural and industrial ecosystems.[20]

William Boyd's essay examines the next chapter in the history of the South's timber industry and its impacts on the Georgia coast: the rise of the pulp and paper industry beginning in the 1930s. Boyd gives us a glimpse at some of the expansive geographies of this particular industrialization of nature, a process that reached deep inland for the timber resources of the South's "second forest," transformed them into pulp and paper in massive new coastal manufacturing plants, and then sent finished products out to the world.[21] For the better part of a century, the sights and smells of papermaking have been defining features of coastal Georgia. But Boyd focuses on the invisible resource of the Floridan Aquifer, which proved as essential to pulp and paper manufacturing as it was difficult to conceptualize and regulate. The massive Floridan Aquifer extends well beyond the Georgia coast, but it was vital to coastal Georgia's pulp and paper production because of that industry's huge demand for inexpensive and clean water. The result, in a classic case of the tragedy of the commons, was creeping groundwater depletion that threatened to ruin the resource by allowing saltwater intrusion into the aquifer. Part of Boyd's story here focuses on the efforts of scientists to "see" the subterranean geography of this invisible resource, but ultimately he is interested in how industrial groundwater depletion has intersected with modern environmental law and politics on the Georgia coast. Particularly important here was the arrival of James Fallows (now an esteemed journalist) and his group of "Nader's Raiders," who came to Savannah in 1970 to sound the alarm about the pulp and paper industry's insatiable demand for water and the threat it posed to the region. Their pioneering study *The Water Lords* appeared in 1971, the same year that McPhee's *Encounters with the Archdruid* highlighted the battle over Cumberland Island and that Hilton Head's wealthy residents, led by Charles Fraser, were battling BASF.[22] The next year, in 1972, the State of Georgia finally began to create a regulatory regime for managing the use of the aquifer with the Groundwater Use Act of 1972, another formative environmental development. But, as Boyd makes clear, that act was a relatively weak one, groundwater withdrawals have continued at an unsustainable pace, and the problem will only become more complicated as climate change affects the region's groundwater resources.

Christopher Manganiello provides us with another story of the State of Georgia developing the regulatory capacity to protect and manage another of its critical coastal resources: its 378,000 acres of tidal marsh. Manganiello's essay is a political and environmental history of the passage of Georgia's pioneering Coastal Marshlands Protection Act and the "Sunbelt environmentalism" that made it possible. The South has long had a reputation for lagging behind the rest of the nation in its environmental politics, but Manganiello's essay suggests that, at least for Georgia, such an assessment is unfair. More than that, he gives us the detailed history of how a particular industrial threat—the desire of Kerr-McGee Corporation to mine phosphates from tens of thousands of acres of coastal marshland and then use the spoil to build up islands into "bulkhead communities"—led to the organization of a diverse group of statewide activists, in a variety of new organizations, to first oppose Kerr-McGee's plans and then create a regulatory structure for protecting and managing the state's marshlands as public property. His is a story of activist success in part because of the diverse coalition that came together to defend marshlands from industrial transformation. Manganiello concludes his essay with two important points. The first is that Georgia's marshlands remain vulnerable, increasingly to less obvious threats coming from up the watersheds that feed freshwater and sediment to coastal marshes. The second is his recognition of the powerful role of the sciences and particularly the arts in giving the coastal marshes a set of meanings to which Georgians attach their affinities. The cultural redefinition of wetlands is one of the great environmental stories of the last century, and Manganiello argues that without the work of Sidney Lanier and his celebration of the "Marshes of Glynn," Georgians, who knew the poem well, might not have been as eager to protect their coastal marshes in the ways that they did. These marshes were a cultural resource as well as an environmental one, and poetry mattered to the cause.

Coastal Nature, Coastal Culture concludes with an essay by the acclaimed nature writer Janisse Ray, who focuses on this very point of how writers have helped to make the coast and its landscapes meaningful. Ray provides a personal tour of the literature of the Georgia coast and the role that it has played in building a sense of place for her and other coastal Georgians. More than that, her essay is a manifesto about the importance of attaching oneself to a particular place and deepening one's appreciation of it. For Ray, place is "the experience of a human body in a landscape," it is "space with a story." The great environmental writer Aldo Leopold once noted, "Our ability to perceive quality in nature begins, as in art, with the pretty. It expands through successive stages of the beautiful to values as yet uncaptured by language."[23] Ray suggests a similar trajectory for thinking about the literature of place on the Georgia coast, a literature that has moved from early settler accounts of the scenery to deeper understandings of nature and history in the region. Ray cleverly uses William Bartram's invocation of the "majestic scene east-ward," which he marveled at when he first arrived at the Georgia coast, as a contrast to the westward-leaning American frontier tradition of itinerancy and detachment from place. For Ray, turning east, facing the coast, and settling in place is a defiant gesture that runs against the American grain. Such attachment to place, to its nature, to its literature, and to its histories, Ray argues, is a necessary precondition for proper conservation.

When David Brower and Charles Fraser met almost a half a century ago to argue over the fate of Cumberland Island, they did so at a moment when a new environmental regime was coming to redefine the coast. A half a century into that regime, many of the traditional threats to coastal nature remain, despite significant conservation victories, and new, confounding challenges are arising as the global environment increasingly becomes an artifact of human activity. At the same time, environmental historians and other environmental humanists have raised major challenges to some of environmentalists' reigning ideas, like wilderness, and they have insisted that we recognize that even the most natural of landscapes are usually full of history, of land-use legacies, and of culture and stories. Nature thus can be a fraught place. But the idea of nature has at its core another quality to which we have paid less attention: a sense of the public good in a world of transformative private actions. Even if, in the past, nature has been a realm in which the powerful have often acted against the powerless, it is also, by its very definition, a public realm that we can all make claims on. This is a part of its appeal. The challenge for residents of the Georgia coast and those who care about it is to imagine a nature that makes a place for all interests and all histories, a nature that is itself a vital public sphere for working out differences while also recognizing that the world we inhabit is more than a human one. We cannot hope to do that well—to achieve the kind of "eco-cultural consciousness" that Tiya Miles refers to in her essay—without a critical understanding of the region's environmental history.

NOTES

1. John McPhee, "Encounters with the Archdruid I: A Mountain," *New Yorker*, March 20, 1971, 42–91; McPhee, "Encounters with the Archdruid II: An Island," *New Yorker*, March 27, 1971, 42–80; McPhee, "Encounters with the Archdruid III: A River," *New Yorker*, April 3, 1971, 41–93. These three profiles were published together as a book that same year: John McPhee, *Encounters with the Archdruid* (New York: Farrar, Straus, and Giroux, 1971). McPhee has since written about the history and structure of this piece in "Progression: How and What?" *New Yorker*, November 14, 2011, https://www.newyorker.com/magazine/2011/11/14/progression, and "Structure: Beyond the Picnic-Table Crisis," *New Yorker*, January 14, 2013, https://www.newyorker.com/magazine/2013/01/14/structure.

2. McPhee, "Encounters with the Archdruid II," 45–47; "Charles E. Fraser, 73, Dies; Developer of Hilton Head," *New York Times*, December 19, 2002.

3. McPhee, "Encounters with the Archdruid II," 47–50; Lary M. Dilsaver deals with the Carnegie family and their history on Cumberland Island in chapters 2 and 3 of his *Cumberland Island National Seashore: A History of Conservation Conflict* (Charlottesville: University of Virginia Press, 2004). The NASA reference is from Dilsaver, *Cumberland Island National Seashore*, 63.

4. McPhee, "Encounters with the Archdruid II," 47–50, 69; "Charles E. Fraser, 73, Dies"; "Hinesville," *New Georgia Encyclopedia*, www.georgiaencyclopedia.org/articles /counties-cities-neighborhoods/hinesville.

5. McPhee, "Encounters with the Archdruid II," 45; "Charles E. Fraser, 73, Dies"; Michael N. Danielson, *Profits and Politics in Paradise: The Development of Hilton Head Island* (Columbia: University of South Carolina Press, 1995), 13.

6. On the Port Royal Experiment, see Willie Lee Rose, *Rehearsal for Reconstruction: The Port Royal Experiment* (Indianapolis: Bobbs-Merrill, 1964). On Mitchelville's history, see the National Register of Historic Places Registration Form, South Carolina Department of Archives and History, State Historic Preservation Office, http://www.nationalregister.sc.gov/beaufort/S10817707033/S10817707033.pdf; "The Mitchelville Story," Hilton Head Island-Bluffton Chamber of Commerce, http://www.hiltonheadisland.org/gullah/the-mitchelville-story; Mitchelville Preservation Project, http://exploremitchelville.org/history.

7. McPhee, "Encounters with the Archdruid II," 44–45; "Charles E. Fraser, 73, Dies."

8. McPhee, "Encounters with the Archdruid II," 53, 60–63, 80.

9. Ibid.," 80; Dilsaver, *Cumberland Island National Seashore*, 76–110.

10. On the Coastal Marshlands Protection Act, see Christopher Manganiello's essay in this volume; on the story of brown pelicans, see McPhee, "Encounters with the Archdruid II," 80.

11. My rendering of the BASF battle is entirely indebted to Will Bryan's wonderful article on the subject: Bryan, "Poverty, Industry, and Environmental Quality: Weighing Paths to Economic Development at the Dawn of the Environmental Era," *Environmental History* 16, no. 3 (July 2011): 492–522. See also McPhee, "Encounters with the Archdruid II," 71–72.

12. Bryan, "Poverty, Industry, and Environmental Quality," 492–522.

13. On the conference, see Coastal Nature, Coastal Culture: Environmental Histories of the Georgia Coast, www.gacoast2016.org/.

14. Philip Morgan, *African American Life in the Georgia Lowcountry: The Atlantic World and the Gullah Geechee* (Athens: University of Georgia Press, 2010).

15. Mart Stewart, *"What Nature Suffers to Groe": Life, Labor, and Landscape on the Georgia Coast, 1680–1920* (Athens: University of Georgia Press, 1996).

16. See David Hurst Thomas, *St. Catherines: An Island in Time* (1988; repr., Athens: University of Georgia Press, 2011).

17. Edelson's analysis here is part of a larger book project, *A New Map of Empire: How Britain Imagined America before Independence* (Cambridge, Mass.: Harvard University Press, 2017).

18. For Miles's larger study of ghost tourism, see *Tales from the Haunted South: Dark Tourism and Memories of Slavery from the Civil War Era* (Chapel Hill: University of North Carolina Press, 2015).

19. Drew Swanson, *Remaking Wormsloe Plantation: The Environmental History of a Lowcountry Landscape* (Athens: University of Georgia Press, 2012).

20. This essay builds upon Way's book *Conserving Southern Longleaf: Herbert Stoddard and the Rise of Ecological Land Management* (Athens: University of Georgia Press, 2011).

21. Boyd's *The Slain Wood: Papermaking and Its Environmental Consequences in the American South* (Baltimore: Johns Hopkins University Press, 2015) deals with these dimensions of the pulp and paper story in great detail.

22. James M. Fallows, *The Water Lords: Ralph Nader's Study Group Report in Industry and Environmental Crisis in Savannah, Georgia* (New York: Grossman Publishers, 1971).

23. Aldo Leopold, "Marshland Elegy," in *A Sand County Almanac and Other Writings on Ecology and Conservation*, ed. Curt Meine (New York: Modern Library of America, 2013), 86.

CHAPTER I

Islands, Edges, and Globe

The Environmental History of the Georgia Coast

MART A. STEWART

What is "place," and how was it created? Environmental historians and environmental storytellers in general have often sought to answer this question and see it as fundamental to the understanding of how humans have lived with nature. And why is it important? If you have to ask, the residents of a place suggest, you are not likely going to understand. But historians can identify the contours of a place, both as it has been lived in by residents and as it has been perceived by observers who visit or argue with the place rather than deeply root themselves in it. These are the first questions that need to be posed about coastal Georgia and its environmental history: what is this place, coastal Georgia, and why should we consider it a geographical and historical place of significance beyond our appreciation of it?

We know from cultural geographers that the physical characteristics of a place are always interwoven with how people live in it or even visit it. These features are not just shaped, and sometimes wrenched, into another form by agriculture, forest exploitation, or the manipulation of the place for leisure purposes (by causeways, roads, hotels, or water parks) but also by how people see and experience them and by the language they use to explain those perceptions and experiences. At the same time, environmental historians have never lost their grasp on the material and ecological reality of place, of how landforms encourage cultural possibilities or how soils and climate and the flow of water, for example, limit or define the human experiences with that place. There is a *there* there. And even if we are ultimately suspended in a web of our own creation and are limited by our own understandings and our language for expressing them, this *there* can be gotten at, at least in the outline. We can brush up against it if not clearly define it. And one of the best ways to do this is to look at a place in the long term, to see what emerges as relative constants in the experience of humans with that place. Looking at how humans historically used the soils of the coastal islands and river floodplains, how they extracted both ocean and freshwater resources from the tidal and estuary swirl of energy in the intercoastal waterways, and how they have explained both hurricanes and salt marsh sunrises, for example, tells us something enduring about this place.

Just what constitutes a temporal and spatial unit of meaning for the study of the history of place in the long term is not constant and uniform. Historical time does not tick off in exact and even units, and any moment of time intersects with other ones, as well as with undulating rhythms of meaning. As Michel Serres has observed about historical events, "[A historical] circumstance is thus polychromic, multitemporal, and reveals a time that is gathered together, and with multiple pleats." One might say the same about place and how humans create different and often overlapping units of space in tandem with undulating pulses of time—and the study of both space and time together. Historians have to make choices about which moments of time will yield the most significant meaning and at the same time be aware of the "multiple pleats" that intersect in those moments. Although historians are time specialists, environmental historians have also had to take seriously the problem of spatial scale—with the understanding that meaningful historical space is also a combination of different spaces at different scales, each contributing to the meaning of the place at the core of them. Again, historians have to make choices about what units of time and space—and what places—will yield the most profound historical meaning.[1]

So what is coastal Georgia? What is, in broad outlines, the environmental history of this place, and what choices might be the best ones for discerning this place in the long run? The essays in this volume collectively provide one answer. By way of introduction to all of these, we also might think about coastal Georgia in terms of islands, edges, and the globe and what they can tell us about the place that is coastal Georgia. Islands, interacting with them and thinking with them both, have been relative constants in the environmental history of this region. Edges, whether ecotones or meaningful geographical markers, have been particularly intense sites of meaning in this history and also yield useful clues about how to analyze that history. Human action has become increasingly global in the last half-century, and environmental changes in particular locales are often connected to changes on a much larger scale. By looking at the Georgia coast in a global context, we can not only see past connections with the Atlantic world or with global markets that have been important in driving environmental change in this particular region but also acquire insights into the future environmental history of coastal Georgia and some clues about how to tell stories about it.

Thinking about coastal Georgia in terms of islands, edges, and globe also allows us to understand it in terms of different scales of time and space, of the fluid interaction between local, regional, national, transnational, and global and of the daily, diurnal, seasonal, yearly, or longue durée, depending on the question we are asking. Even natural processes that shape the Georgia coast have operated on larger scales beyond the immediate environments of the coast, as well as on scales more minute than those picked up by the historian's radar—for example, climate patterns that are rooted in changes in the global atmosphere as well as the movements of sands up and down island coasts. Looking at how islands, edges, and the globe have structured the environmental history of this region allows us to peel back the layers of meaningful time and scale and understand the human actions that have created them. All in the interest of coming to an understanding, for those outside the region as well as those deeply rooted in it, of what this place called coastal Georgia might be.

ISLANDS

Coastal Georgia is, first of all, a string of islands—islands just off the coast and at the edge of a continent. These are islands of a particular kind; they are separated enough from the rest of the coast to be genuine islands but close enough to share an identity with the tidewater coast. Indeed, the tides that sweep up and into coastal rivers and define the tidewater are themselves shaped by these islands. But islands are always different than the main—they are bounded, discrete, easy to mark out, and separate. They are not only places that favor retreat and preservation but have also historically been good to dream with, to think with, to ask questions with. Coastal Georgia and its islands have had a material reality that has anchored human interactions with the region, but they have also inspired and continue to inspire island dreams.

We do not know enough about the Natives who lived there when Europeans first arrived to easily speculate about how they perceived and reckoned with the coastal islands, except in material terms. The Guale and Timucuan people left shell middens on many of the islands, some of them extensive enough to be woven into the subsequent material life of the area, in the tabby houses that island planters later built for their slaves. These speak to a history of oyster feeds that in sheer volume alone tell us something about how the Guale used the islands. But the records archaeologists and historians have uncovered or re-created tell us little about whether their geography of islands had any relationship to ours—aside from a shred of information here and there in the historical record, which is more an elaboration of European cultural mores and perceptions than of Native ones. The Europeans who began to establish beachheads along the Georgia coast in the sixteenth century were another matter. As many scholars have pointed out, the idea of islands as well as the fact of them, as Europeans moved around the globe (always by water, of course), has had a powerful history.

Though the Franciscans who established missions on Georgia's barrier islands appreciated the strategic value of island locations, these locations reinforced their insular millenarianism. An ideology that they hoped would eventually transform not just collected legions of unbaptized souls but indeed the world and create a new Christian paradise on earth was also served well and realized in earthly terms by the island missions on which they hoped to "reduce" Natives to better versions of humans. These missions, beginning with a settlement at St. Augustine in 1565, collected the Natives of Florida and up the coast in what is now Georgia into communities that were themselves islands in the wilderness. The Franciscans' intent was not only ultimately to make good Catholics out of them but also to settle them into established communities supported by agriculture and to reduce them to images of the missionaries themselves. The Spanish relationship with Natives up and down the coast was one fraught with complex reciprocity, but it began with a colonizing vision for the development of insular integrity. We know more about the complexities of this relationship and about the reciprocity that was required of both parties than about the persistence of the original vision of islands of Christian "reduction." But this was the first time Europeans used islands to think with in the history of this region.[2]

For Robert Montgomery, the Scottish nobleman who in the early eighteenth century conceived and promoted the Margravate of Azilia, an overdetermined design for a perfect community in Georgia, the coastal islands were "Golden Islands," lodestars for social perfection. In 1717 Montgomery proposed a colony of some four hundred square miles between the Savannah River and the Altamaha River in a tract titled *A Discourse concerning the Design'd Establishment of a New Colony to the South of Carolina, in the Most Delightful Country of the Universe.* The tract was a prospectus, but also served as an application for a grant of land from the Lords Proprietors of Carolina. Montgomery's fanciful description of the land is as enthusiastic as his plans for a colony:

> That nature has not blessed the world with any tract which can be preferable to it; that Paradise, with all her virgin beauties, may be modestly supposed at most but equal to its native excellencies. It lies in the same latitude with Palestine herself, that promised Canaan, which was pointed out by God's

own choice, to bless the labors of a favorite people. It abounds with rivers, woods and meadows. Its iron, and even gentle hills are full of mines, lead, copper, some of silver. 'Tis beautiful with odoriferous plants, green all the year. Pine, cedar, cypress, oak, elm, ash or walnut with innumerable other sorts, both fruit or timber trees, grow every where so pleasantly, that though they meet at top, and shade the traveller, they are, at the same time, so distant in their bodies, and so free from underwood or bushes, that the deer and other game, which feed in droves along these forests, may be often seen near half a mile between them.[3]

Montgomery got nowhere with his plan, and it was largely forgotten until historians recovered it in the nineteenth century and proclaimed it a curiosity (noted in the *Savannah Republican* and then the *New York Times* in 1869). But the plan for the Margravate of Azilia was just an initial exhalation of tidy English enthusiasm for islands of social perfection in this part of the world. Montgomery's appellation "Golden Islands" has since then been preserved by way of three centuries of island wilderness exaltation.[4]

In the meantime, the British Trustees who founded the first colony of Georgia in 1732 took a larger step onto the mainland, with an enterprise that was more at the edge of a sea than the edge of a continent. In their vision, the islands were important for strategic purposes, as barriers against threats from the Atlantic. But in fact the Georgia Plan itself was an expression of insularism and was rooted in some of the same idealism that had inspired Montgomery's proposal. Much has been written about this, but the characterization of colonial schemes in Georgia by historian Daniel Boorstin about a half-century ago is still the best general one: "Something about the fabled lushness and tropical wealth of Georgia inspired both extravagance and rigidity in the plans of those who wished to develop it. The supposed prodigality of the land seduced men to believe that they could cut the colony to their own pattern. These early planners combined a haziness about the facts of life in Georgia with a precision in their schemes for that life."[5]

This mix of haziness and precision also had a utopian component, where dreams that required insularity and clearly marked boundaries found a geography with which they meshed. And this reinforced what historian John Phelan has called "romantic insularism" among European colonizers, "a drive for control, a European *imperium*, a universalizing Christian cosmology and a planetary geo-strategic discourse." Europeans sought the kind of control that would strengthen ideological impositions and also secure their colonies. Island geography gave them this. At the same time, Europeans dreamed with islands. Phelan explains: "From the thirteenth century on, it was commonly believed that the most spectacular marvels and the most exotic lands were on far-off and mysterious islands." As Europeans began to establish colonies, islands retained an otherworldly character as potential terrestrial paradises, but they also became places where Europeans imagined societies that were perfect alternatives to the troubled ones in which they lived. The most famous ideal commonwealths of the Renaissance, it is sufficient to note—those of More's *Utopia* and Bacon's *New Atlantis*—were envisaged as mythical islands.[6]

Insular dreams about the potential of the Georgia coast faltered when they came up against the physical reality of coastal geography. The Georgia Plan failed partly because it was an unrealistic imposition on the geography of the region—the soils and climate did not turn out to be the blank but prodigiously productive slate that Oglethorpe and the Georgia planners believed it was. The first years of the colony were never as substantive as the Trustees dreamed they would be. As Paul Pressly has pointed out, Georgia in its first two decades was not an integrated colony with Savannah as its capital. It was a fragile archipelago of three small outposts—Savannah, Frederica, and Augusta—subsisting separately while connected to different parts of the larger Atlantic economy and to different imperial aims.[7]

The Georgia coast continued to be attractive to dreamers. Coastal geography provided a footing for the attempts of early nineteenth-century planters to assert control over people and place on coastal plantations. Even those residents who had to tangle regularly with the un-dreamlike realities of changing weather and difficult soils were encouraged by coastal Georgia geography in social visions that emphasized bounded communities of enduring balance. The plantation, one of the most significant social and economic units in the antebellum South, was conceived in general by planters as insular at the same time that plantations relied upon a larger capitalist economy for their survival and success. Plantations were small dominions for planters and intense nuclei of surveillance in the larger carceral system of slaveholding in the American South. Sea Island cotton planters on the islands and rice planters in the tidewater all sought control and more control—over the humans who labored for them, over wind and water and weather—in visions of absolutism on the one hand or of beneficent patriarchy on the other. Pierce Butler, whose estranged wife, the famous British stage actor, Fanny Kemble, once accused him of wanting to be the emperor of his rice plantation domain on Butler's Island in the Altamaha estuary in the 1830s, was a good example of the former.

Sea Island cotton planter William Hazard of St. Simons Island was a good example of the latter, of kindly but stern paternalism. Hazard wrote in the

Southern Agriculturist in 1828 about his dream of recovering a traditional past on his island plantation, of relative self-sufficiency and autonomy, affluence, and family—in a dream of recovering a dream:

> If family and custom and traditions that kept plantation society on the islands strong in "times past" were no longer vital, [it was because of] prodigality and bad management; it was because our fathers neglected to plant Corn, Peas, Potatoes, and Pumpions. Our forefathers had always raised enough of them on their plantations for all domestic purposes, without sacrificing their Indigo crops to buy these essentials at an exorbitant price, when they were most needed, as our fathers often did afterwards, in bartering their Cotton for Corn. I have it from a Planter in Liberty County, that thirty thousand dollars has been paid out of that county, in one years, for the article of Corn alone!

By "family" he meant just about everyone: "Of which I am speaking, tradition tells us, it was considered [neither] unfashionable nor stupid, to cousin the third and fourth generation of those who esteemed you as such." Planters who promoted this vision of plantation success also included slaves in their calculations of households, and they sought to claim the obligations of slaves to their master much as patriarchs sought to force the obedience of other family members. This was another note in the antebellum plantation imaginary, that self-sufficiency, rooted in plantation household relations, promoted economic success in the market as well in the plantation. Even while entangling themselves ever more inextricably in a capitalist economy that was their bread and butter as well as their reason for being, some planters espoused a balance of autarky and market dependency, as a mode of control but also as a defense against outside cultural and economic influences, especially as the threat of these intensified in the years just before the Civil War.[8]

Planters of Sea Island cotton and rice also sought mastery by developing systematic methods for growing them. The story of rice growing in the tidewater has attracted enough historians that it does not need to be explained again except to recall that the construction of extensive systems of ditches, drains, canals, dikes, and embankments required enormous investments of labor to build and to maintain and required an extraordinary level of control. Rice plantations were empires of mud and water, deeply rooted in the tidewater, and shored up by human hands. Sea Island cotton was a more graceful crop and for a while was the backbone of the Lowcountry plantation belt economy, just after the Revolution. The filaments of the Sea Island cotton were longer, more elastic, stronger, and silkier than the staple of the "green-seed," short-strand cotton and were much preferred by spinners for the ease with which it could be spun into cotton thread. From the beginning, planters invested the culture of this high-quality fiber with associations that gave it more than economic value, that wove the crop into ideas about honor and reputation that reinforced planter dominion. Sea Island cotton plantations thus marked distinctive features of the coastal island culture and coastal island geography.

Expressions of ideal practices for growing Sea Island cotton, as published in the *Southern Agriculturalist* and elsewhere, operated in the same way as the memoranda planters circulated on cotton and rice growing. They were statements of ideals and thoughtful wishes about agriculture. In practice, some planters (like James Hamilton Couper on St. Simons Island) sometimes came close to those ideals. When the harvest didn't match ideals, they increasingly told each other the kinds of stories that created the illusion that they had, especially in regard to rice growing. This was a cultural form—a kind of agrarian utopianism—that departed from the actual experience of mucking around in the Lowcountry environment but that was also deeply rooted in it.

Sea Island cotton, like wet-culture rice, would grow in a wide range of conditions. But just as production of rice in a specific environment greatly improved yields, so the production of this cotton in a specific locale greatly improved its quality. Sea Island cotton grew prolifically on sandy pine barrens soils. Most of Georgia's post–Civil War long-strand cotton crop, produced for a booming market in sewing machine thread, was grown on small farms on the upper coastal plain. But the best and silkiest long-strand cotton fibers could be produced in environmental conditions found only on the Sea Islands and a strip of land along the coast. There the moisture-laden sea breezes—what Thomas Spalding on Sapelo Island called an "elastic" atmosphere—made the staple longer, silkier, and glossier. Planters also credited the saline quality of the air (and sometimes of the soil) with improving the staple. The best staple was produced on the islands, and the best staple on the islands was produced in those fields having an ocean exposure. The plant required a long season, 260 frost-free days, which also made the coast an ideal environment. Sea Island cotton, then, was woven into the fabric of coastal planter society, but it was also a commodity that could be grown best only in particular island environments. Sea Island cotton was not just a successful commodity crop in a particular environmental region but was threaded through dreams planters had about themselves. It helped to define the Georgia coast and coastal islands at a moment in time. On Sea Island plantations, a social vision of the family gathered around planters in a bounded unit that was both self-sufficient and protected from the corruption of the world beyond, or a vision that exalted the planter as the lord of his domain, or both, converged with plans for a perfect crop grown in the felicitous conditions of Sea Island environments. But the transformation of this vision to reality was utterly dependent on the labor of slaves and inextricably linked to and dependent on the vagaries of the market. Like other dreams of perfection on the Georgia coast, these silky cotton utopias were compromised by their unavoidable connections to the main.[9]

Islands have always been retreats, places of restoration, and sanctuaries, as well as sites of discovery and reinvention. Daniel Defoe's *Robinson Crusoe* (1719) was the arch-expression of this island experience. The marooned Crusoe was the First Man—isolated, lonely, and occupying a place before the beginning of time. But he was also the namer and remaker of all things on his small domain. Islands have been good to dream with, but they have also been good to regress into. They can be places where one can return to a prelapsarian innocence, to childhood—J. M. Barrie's Neverland was an island. No one wrote a Crusoe account of the Georgia islands, or an account styled on the Crusoe version for the bourgeoisie, Johann David Wyss's *Swiss Family Robinson* (1812). But the notion of islands as retreats is part of the long history of the Georgia coast. And we do have a novel by a coastal Georgia author that takes place on an island off the coast of Florida, close enough that we might claim it as Georgia's Crusoe tale and appreciate it for what it tells us about this place. This is Francis Robert Goulding's novel for young readers, *Robert and Harold; or, The Young Marooners on the Florida Coast*, first published in 1853 and then in many editions afterward.[10]

Goulding was born and grew up in Liberty County, and after graduating from the University of Georgia he became a minister in Augusta and wrote novels for boys. In *Robert and Harold*, these two brothers, their younger brother Frank, their sister Mary, and their canine companions Fidelle and Mum—Fidelle a bit of a parlor dog, at least at first, and Mum, a dog raised in the Georgia pine barrens and exceptionally adept at running deer and other animals and, as Goulding makes clear, "no common dog"—are marooned on an island after a giant manta ray tows their boat out to sea.[11] This little group of marooners make a home on their island, build a raft, and fortuitously discover a wrecked pirate's vessel that supplies them with adzes, drawknives, augers, chisels, planes, saws, a square and compass, an oilstone, a box of sperm candles, a box of soap, three cutlasses and a rapier, four pikes, four pairs of pistols, three rifles, two muskets, gunpowder, a keg of rice and another of flour, a firkin of butter, two cheeses, six loaves of sugar, a grindstone, a box of tobacco, several hams, a table and leaves, six chairs, a sofa, five mattresses, silk dresses for Mary, a looking-glass, and an abundance of other tools and articles.

So they can live off the land. The boys shoot just about everything that moves and eat some of it. (Going back to nature in the South has usually been accompanied by guns.)[12] After one "abundant marooning dinner," Robert proclaims, "I doubt whether our old friend Robinson Crusoe fared better than we." After Robert, Harold, Frank, and Mary are rescued, their parents are greatly moved by the character their children have acquired. Goulding makes clear in the closing of the novel that such a return to an Edenic innocence both tests and builds character, especially in southern boys of a certain class:

> As they passed down the river, a gentle gale came from the woods, loaded with the perfume of flowers. Harold pointed [out] to his mother the tall magnolias on the riverbank, which had been to him a Bethel; (Genesis xviii. 16–19) it was now in bloom, and two magnificent flowers, almost a foot in diameter, set like a pair of brilliant eyes near the top, looked kindly on him, and seemed to watch over him until he had passed out of sight. The live oak, under whose immense shade their tent had been first pitched, was the last tree they passed; a nonpareil, hidden in the branches, sat whistling plaintively to its mate; a mockingbird was on the topmost bough, singing with all its might a song of endless variety; and underneath a herd of shy, peeping deer had collected, and looked inquisitively at the objects moving upon the water. It seemed to the young people as if the whole island had centered itself upon that bluff, to reproach them with ingratitude and protest against their departure. But their resolution could not be changed; the prow of their vessel held its way. *The Marooning Party was Over.*

But every elite white boy in the South should have one.[13]

Another character in this "marooning party" needs to be noted. A little over a third of the way into the tale, the group of marooners is joined by their parents' slave Sam, who himself had been marooned while looking for them. With a set of conventions that had deep roots in the American experience with slavery and race in the South, Goulding's African American character is represented as somewhat pathetic, childlike, and superstitious but certainly loyal. He is also adept at woodcraft and survival skills and represents a closer-to-nature type that shows up in several guises in some of Goulding's other stories as well. White Americans well into the twentieth century often perceived Native Americans and African Americans as more akin to nature than themselves (indeed sometimes indistinguishable from nonhuman animals) and having superior knowledge of the natural environment, especially plants and pharmacopeia.[14]

This notion of an animal-like closeness to nature, or at least an aptitude for woodcraft, was one of the components of racism in colonial America and in

FIGURE 1.1. "The Abduction." The party was marooned after being towed out
to sea by a giant manta ray (the "devil fish" of Lowcountry sporting lore).
From F. R. Goulding, *Robert and Harold; or, The Young Marooners on
the Florida Coast* (Philadelphia: William S. Martien, 1853).

the nineteenth-century South that was also intertwined with environmental
relations.

At the same time, some African Americans had a relationship to natural
environments that was often as tangible as these unreflective representations
suggested. They were Crusoes of a different sort, not marooned, but often ma-
roonagers. African Americans removed themselves, if not to islands, to isolated or hidden places beyond the bounds of plantations on which they were
enslaved. Here they lay out for a while to worship or to forage and hunt for
the food that sustained both bodies and community. This was not a return to
childhood or a reinvention of character but a ploy for survival and space for
community. The repressive surveillance of planters, overseers, and slave pa-
trols with horses and dogs meant that whatever environmental spaces African
Americans who were slaves were able to create for themselves were often also
confined spaces in the larger carceral landscape of slavery. These spaces were
also always negotiated ones, where African American environmental knowledge gave slaves a crucial weapon of resistance. The importance of this knowledge was sharply illuminated when the oppressive spaces of slavery began to
disintegrate during the Civil War. As the usually reserved coastal Georgia minister and planter Charles Colcock Jones shrieked about the neighborhood

slaves in 1862, "They know every road and swamp and creek and plantation in the country." Slaves not only ran away easily (and freed themselves) when Union troops were in the region, they also sometimes came back as guides to those troops: "They are traitors who may pilot a enemy into your *bedchamber*!" Jones added.[15] Enslaved African Americans were indeed often adept at woodcraft but in a different and far more discrete way than depicted in Goulding's and others' caricatures. On islands and on the main, in spite of the systems of surveillance and control to which they were subject, they knew their way around.[16]

After the Civil War, islands for freedpeople on the Georgia coast were sites where this antebellum experience with retreat was for a very short while rendered visible. "The great cry of our people is for land," said Tunis Campbell, the leader of a social experiment with former slaves on St. Catherines and Ossabaw Islands. After Sherman captured Savannah in December 1864 and issued the field order that appropriated lands along the southeastern coast for redistribution to freed slaves, and after Congress set up the Freedmen's Bureau in March 1865, Campbell was appointed by the bureau to supervise land claims and resettlement on five Georgia islands: Ossabaw, Delaware, Colonels, St. Catherines, and Sapelo. There freed slaves built community, grew provisions, and established schools, a dramatic if short-lived manifestation of yet another, and perhaps one of the more durable, no matter how briefly expressed, of island dreams. (Georgia planters received pardons from U.S. president Andrew Johnson and regained control of these islands in 1866.) Georgia's coastal islands for a time became the site of what Campbell called "separatism with strength," a vision for black community that was anchored by land ownership. This flew in the face of the Crusoe and Goulding fantasies that had been projected onto islands that were unoccupied and, more importantly, positioned in a world in which white people ruled and could move freely. The African American communities on St. Catherines and Ossabaw were double sanctuaries: they were autonomous, outside of white supervision, but also sanctuaries for African Americans that had the political protection of legal title, at least for a while.[17]

After the federal government returned coastal Georgia to white control, another kind of ownership and island retreat came to the islands in the next two decades. By the 1880s the islands had been discovered by northern industrialists who purchased land and established estates there, with all the amenities that enormous wealth could then provide. These island retreats would give them an insular retreat from the intensifying tumult of industrializing America—a counterpoint to the world that they had played major roles in creating.

The consequence was an almost absurd arrangement that only an insular geography might make comfortable—one of servants from the locale, the heirs of slavery, tending the pets, clipping the golf greens, and shining the shoes of visiting northern industrialists, the heirs of Union victory.

Some of the islands became healthful places where townspeople of a more general sort could "take the salts," socialize and rest, hunt, fish, dance, bathe, bicycle, and restore the "inner man" for life in the town or city. Some tourists also came for the scenery, both natural and historical, to drink in the atmosphere of seashore and old oaks and mosses, or to gaze at the ruins of past landscapes. By the 1890s, several of the islands, especially Tybee, St. Simons, and Cumberland, had become busy retreats, where harried businessmen from Savannah or Brunswick could commute for a day of rest or middle-class Georgians from Atlanta and Macon could vacation.

The imagery that local newspaper editors used to celebrate the islands both reflected and hawked the qualities that were attractive to these visitors. The island landscape was no longer a pleasant and passive backdrop for the leisurely activities of Lowcountry society but acted upon visitors with a restorative force. The islands provided a site of therapeutic immersion for visitors "unchained from business and social environments," a "haven of rest for the overworked professional man," and a "cool retreat from the burning heat of the interior." Sapelo Island was so healthy that "but for the death penalty imposed upon all mankind for the disobedience of Adam and Eve, no one could ever feel the pangs of death [there]." Though the recreation of visitors was often relatively passive, they participated in an active exchange with the environment. The "salts" and natural beauty and serenity of the islands were said to aid urban professionals, middle-class vacationers, and the convalescing alike, infusing them with energy and health and the "zest and buoyancy of a new found life."

But other islands were taken up entirely by wealthy families or groups that wanted a permanent private retreat. Ossabaw and St. Catherines again became hunting islands, owned by the Wanamakers of Philadelphia and the Rauers of Savannah, respectively, who created game reserves for private use. The Detroit automobile capitalist Howard Coffin purchased Sapelo Island in 1912 and re-created an aristocratic landscape, with a new mansion and elegant gardens, miles of shell roads, and enough cattle and cultivated fields to make the whole a model country estate. Thomas Carnegie bought most of Cumberland Island in 1882 and built an ostentatious gabled and turreted mansion, which he called Dungeness after its antebellum predecessor. The Carnegie family installed a golf course, riding trails, a formal garden, a kennel where Russian bear hounds and mastiffs were kept, and amenities necessary to keep themselves and their guests in comfort and pleasure. Here and elsewhere, the islands became nicely bounded reserves of wealth and privilege.

The largest and most significant appropriation of a Georgia Sea Island—and representative of others—occurred on Jekyll Island. In late 1885, an heir of the Du Bignon family—once prominent Sea Island cotton planters—joined with family members and wealthy business and social associates, many of them from New York, for the purpose of constructing on Jekyll a comfortable refuge from northern winters. The membership of the Jekyll Island Club included some of the most powerful men in American business circles, among them J. P. Morgan, William Vanderbilt, Joseph Pulitzer, and Marshall Field, who were accustomed to shaping their surroundings on a grand scale.

By 1900 Jekyll Island had become an insulated preserve, where club members could avoid icy New York, Philadelphia, and Chicago winters, play golf and tennis, go sporting and sea-bathing, and, after splendid meals of local game and fish prepared by European chefs, strengthen contacts and deliberate on deals that shaped the nation's economy. These wealthy islanders also engaged in rudimentary kinds of conservation to ensure a steady supply of game for their hunts but also to preserve species deemed essential to the island dream they sought to install. But the real protected species were the members of the club. Progressive reformers regarded some of them as predators, but a more generous appraisal came from a tutor to the Everit Macy family, who in 1917 described the Jekyll Island nabobs as "*a rare collection of very high bred and exclusive animals.*" On Jekyll this select club created a "gilded cage" for themselves and made the natural environment an ornament of wealth.[18]

In the twentieth century, the islands were not just refreshing retreats but once again became golden, as boosters and more formal apologists alike asserted the values that had attracted wealthy industrialists and middle-class tourists in the late nineteenth century—salubrious airs, beaches, boundedness. Montgomery's distant perception of Georgia's barrier islands as "golden islands" acquired a permanent status as a discursive trope in explanations of these islands as places to retreat to, sites of restoration and renewal, places outside of history, and always as "golden." This word continues to show up in representations of the islands in popular literature and in the rows of tourist brochures that greet travelers at coastal Georgia visitor centers and hotels and the Savannah airport. Georgia's "golden" islands have become coastal Georgia's wilderness, a universalized "nature" that accomplishes many of the fundamental requirements for the wilderness ideal in the United States. They are touted as pristine and relatively undisturbed places that step outside of time and history and are yardsticks of the natural. Tourists are incited repeatedly in the advertisements of coastal tourist vendors to enjoy pristine white beaches, salt marsh vistas, quiet retreats on islands unhitched from the main, close encounters with marsh tackies, sea turtles, and bottlenose dolphins, and timeless (except for a few well-marked ruins) places of natural beauty. The islands have continued to be what they became after the Civil War—places of hope and expectation—but mainly for the affluent.[19]

One of the final scenes in Ross McElwee's 1986 indie classic (filmed in 1981), *Sherman's March: A Meditation on the Possibility of Romantic Love during an Era of Nuclear Weapons Proliferation*, provides a timely and ironic comment on the history of the islands as prelapsarian and Edenic wilderness retreats. McEllwee intended at first to make a documentary film about Sherman's destructive March to the Sea, but he changed his mind when a personal break-up as well as a very tight budget encouraged him to make a film about the women in his life—as he traveled south on the Sherman trail. His film documents a march that left gently ruined relationships in its wake; it adds notes from the history of Sherman's March to anchor the wry melancholy of the main narrative of the film. When McElwee got to Savannah and (almost) the sea, he received permission to visit Ossabaw Island and the Genesis Project—the retreat established in 1970 for artists and researchers and supported by Ossabaw Island matriarch Sandy West. While he was there, he basked in a ruminative and idyllic extended conversation with Wini Wood, a linguist who, when not sunbathing or milking the Genesis Project cow, Daisy, was writing her dissertation. McElwee proclaimed that he had "stumbled into Eden." He left for a while to take a job in Boston, and, when he returned, Wini had taken up with someone else, with another one of the peregrinating Ossabaw Island recluses. And that was the wry and melancholy end of that.[20]

McElwee did not mean to make a romantic film about nature on a coastal island, but this episode and his perambulating handheld camera style, against the soft natural backgrounds of Ossabaw, create a perfect comment on the dialogue between imperfect and worldly encounters with human relationships and the evocation and reification of a romantic idea of Edenic nature. His is not the usual wilderness experience. Wini Wood the linguist, the Genesis Project cow, Ossabaw landscapes, and a narrative line that depends more on extended conversations than on quiet evocations of the sublime makes this part of the film an unusual mash. When McElwee leaves and when he comes back his coastal island wilderness changes. He stumbled into Eden and fell in love (maybe), but then Eden refused to stand still for him while he was away. His wilderness experience, like those of even more hapless tourists who think they're stepping out of time, has its ruins—but they are ruins that are very much a matter of history and reflection about it. Without meaning to, this odd film about the Georgia coast captured one of its enduring myths and at the same time subverted it, and it did this at about the same time that the wilderness idea in general in the United States accomplished its apotheosis and began to be questioned by both activists and scholars.[21]

Georgia's coastal islands have become attractive to those who would not just imbibe the natural landscapes of the coast but also more actively study them as relatively bounded sites for the analysis of coastal ecosystems and of ecosystem dynamics. Islands in general have been crucial to our understanding of evolution and the interaction of biological systems. In the nineteenth century, Alfred Wallace, Joseph Hooker, and Charles Darwin—the latter especially on the Galapagos—created the cornerstone for the modern discipline of ecology by analyzing and mapping out island biogeography. These scientific practices continued to develop throughout the twentieth century and arrived at a turning point in a substantive small volume titled *The Theory of Island Biogeography*, by Robert MacArthur and Edward O. Wilson, published in 1967. The book merged biogeography with ecology and added scientific rigor to both fields. Science journalist David Quammen explains, in *Song of the Dodo: Island Biogeography in an Age of Extinction*, that "islands have been especially instructive because their limited area and their inherent isolation combine to make patterns of evolution stand out starkly. . . . Islands give clarity to evolution. . . . Generally you will find fewer species and therefore fewer relationships among species, as well as more cases of species extinction. . . . [Consequently] islands have served as the Dick-and-Jane primers of evolutionary biology, helping scientists master enough vocabulary and grammar to begin to comprehend the more complex prose of the mainlands."[22]

Most of Georgia's coastal islands are partly owned or managed by public agencies that conduct scientific research, either as part of management plans or for a full range of dedicated ecological research projects. The research projects on Ossabaw alone have left records that fill many boxes at the Georgia Historical Society archives in Savannah, and some of them are now model research programs. The long-term research program on coastal ecology at the University of Georgia Sapelo Island Marine Institute is one such project. Sited on the eighty-seven-hundred-acre Sapelo Island National Estuarine Research Reserve, it links variables in the physical environment with changes in flora and fauna, showing nuance and commitment that bely Quammen's characterization of island research as Dick-and-Jane stuff. Modern ecologists are also discovering that while islands have important biogeographical boundaries that "give clarity to evolution," they are also places where the richness and fluidity of "invasion" and adaptation can also be observed with clarity.[23]

In general, coastal Georgia geography reaffirmed the visions and projects that successive generations of missionizers, colonists, creators of plantations and communities, resort impresarios, and scientists have brought to the region. Visions of bounded places and bounded experiences have been assented to by the boundedness of the region's geography, of islands and tidewater hemmed in by pine barrens. Coastal geography has always been a destination for dreams, has often given them safe haven for a while, but has seldom provided a permanent home for them. While island dreams have been rooted in and are even extensions of the messy world for which they provide conduits of escape, the realization of any perfect community also requires the perfectly unreal accomplishment of stepping outside of history. On the Georgia coast, history has instead often interrupted the hopes of dreamers, but each new tide of change has also brought refreshing possibilities. Coastal Georgia's islands, real and imaginary, have provided an archipelago of possibilities, and the history of this *place* is deeply anchored in the history of its islands.[24]

EDGES

If islands have been good to dream with, edges have been fertile sites of productivity and understanding. Coastal Georgia has had some prominent ones. The most important of these acknowledge the simple fact of ecotones—transition areas between two biomes, where two ecological systems meet and integrate and that provide a mix of vegetation and abundant opportunities for certain species (especially mobile ones). Ecologists call these opportunities, and the profusion of life because of them, edge effects. An ecotone may be narrow or wide, and it may be local (the zone between a field and forest) or regional (the transition between forest and grassland ecosystems). Ecotones are, quite simply, rich overlapping edges of activity and meaning. Coastal Georgia has been a place of enormous ecological productivity, renowned ecologist Eugene Odum once observed, because of the movement of natural energy throughout the region, but also because of these edges.[25]

These edges show up in the environmental history of coastal Georgia in ways that tell a larger story. When Quaker naturalist William Bartram made his famous walk through the Southeast and up across the Georgia coastal plain in the early 1770s, he noted a series of "steps" or "ascents," with accompanying changes in vegetation, with a brief speculation that they registered an ancient past history with the ocean. His account of the marked variations in the coastal plain, on up to the fall line, also noticed the relatively permanent variations in the geography of coastal Georgia as well as its geological origin.[26]

A more practical acknowledgment of the importance of ecotones was made in the eighteenth century by German-born Lutheran minister Martin Johann Bolzius, leader of the Salzburger community of German-speaking Georgia colonists at Ebenezer, just up the river from Savannah. Bolzius wrote many times of the turkeys that he and his Salzburg flock harvested from new edges in the neighborhood—edges that had been developed by creating fields for the community's crops. American turkeys thrived in the edge environments that the Salzburgers made when they carved fields out of forests in the area around Ebenezer. Given the frequency with which he mentions them (and they are mentioned in other accounts of the early days of the Georgia colony), they were a welcome addition to the sometimes scant provisions of the colonists. They were large and fat, Bolzius reported, and were reasonably easy to kill. And for a time they were made more plentiful by the agriculture of the Salzburgers. This edge story is not a singular one. Humans have again and again created or modified ecological edges, and these have in turn yielded changes in coastal Georgia flora and fauna that have sometimes had a larger significance. Ecotones, quite literally, have been sites of rich historical meaning.[27]

More important to the long story of environment and humans on the Georgia coast have been those edges between biological systems that have been driven by and yielded enormous quantities of ecological energy and that have provided a hospitable habitat for marine species. The rich currents of energy that swirl in the estuaries and intercoastal waterways of coastal Georgia have created a landscape that defies the conventional wisdom that diversity is directly proportional to topographic relief, Eugene Odum explained. Odum used this insight and studied this landscape to develop a pathbreaking understanding of the energy flows of ecosystems. At the same time, his understanding of the turbulent environments of salt marshes and what they were between has confirmed a larger understanding of the region as a place not only of beauty but also of ecological health. The "marsh was meshed with a million veins," the anoxic poet Sidney Lanier observed early in the last century in the ur-poem about the natural environment of coastal Georgia, "The Marshes of Glynn." The salt marshes have produced enormous biodiversity and energy, and they have been the source of understandings of ecosystem dynamics that have had a global influence. They also inspired some of the earliest environmental legislation in Georgia. In the late 1960s, when land developers and a mining firm threatened the survival of the state's coastal wetlands, Odum participated in a University of Georgia Save Our Marshes Committee by educating citizens about the economic value of the wetlands to the state—mainly by noting the value of the marshes as a nursery for the juvenile of marine species crucial to Georgia fisheries. This committee, with Odum's eloquent testimony, was successful in persuading the Georgia legislature to pass the Coastal Marshlands Protection Act in 1970.[28]

Another important edge in the history of coastal Georgia has been the one between saline and fresh water, an edge that moves. Studying this edge is currently fundamental to an important long-term research project poised against the promise of substantial environmental change in the next century. The Georgia Coastal Ecosystems Long Term Ecological Research site, established by the National Science Foundation in 2000, encompasses three adjacent sounds (Altamaha, Doboy, and Sapelo) on the coast and includes upland (mainland, barrier island, marsh hammock), intertidal (fresh, brackish, and salt marsh), and submerged (river, estuary, continental shelf) habitats. The flow of energy and organisms varies spatially and temporally in this environment, and by tracking these complex flows over time—and linking them to variations in the interaction between saline water and fresh—scientists hope to gain understandings that will help them prepare for future environmental change. In the coming century the Georgia coast is expected to experience substantial changes due to climate change and concomitant sea-level change as well as ongoing human alteration of the landscape. According to the project's website, it seeks "to understand the mechanisms by which variation in the quality, source and amount of both fresh and salt water create temporal and spatial variability in estuarine habitats and processes, in order to predict directional changes that will occur in response to long-term shifts in estuarine salinity patterns." Here a longitudinal study of the edge between saltwater and freshwater as it moves through this environment will be key to understanding a complex mesh of other ecological relationships and how all of these will respond to long-term environmental change.[29]

An earlier understanding of the importance of this gradient between saltwater and fresh—a crucial one for the productivity of tidewater rice plantations—was applied when planters, quite likely with the help of leading slaves, identified sites for installing rice fields and their infrastructure. A good site required adequate freshwater to flood the fields and to submerge the heavier mass of saltwater that was pushed up the estuary twice a day by high tides. Too close to the sea, and all that might be available to flood the fields was brackish water. Too far up the river, and the power of tides to raise the level of the river water to a level that made it available for rice field flooding was lost. What planters called the tidal "pitch"—freshwater flow from the river, tides from the sea, and the changing edge between them—had to be calculated carefully, or the enormous investment of labor that went into creating a rice plantation in the first place would be misplaced.

Planters and their slaves read vegetation to find the right site. Salinity levels in tidewater estuaries markedly affect plant distribution in marshes and swamps along the shores. Cattails, for example, which can grow in saline conditions, thrive profusely as salinity decreases. Wild rice is more common in freshwater marshes than in salt or brackish marshes. Dense stands of giant cutgrass signal tidal freshwater conditions. Freshwater wetlands also engender a greater diversity of plants in general. The sequence of plant species from season to season is more obvious in freshwater habitats, but the distinction between different vegetation zones (between high marsh and low marsh, for example) is not as pronounced as in brackish and saltwater wetlands. More significantly, a characteristic growth of water-loving trees, dominated by bald cypress, red maple, ash, black gum, and tupelo, marked the lands best suited for rice production in the swamps landward of the tidal freshwater marshes. What planters called black rush also signaled good conditions for growing rice. When planters or their slaves looked at a strong growth of "swamp maples" or saw a thatchy growth of black rush and identified the best land for growing rice, they read the tidewater flora to find the right soil, the right water, and the right tidal pitch for growing rice.

The stakes were very high. Constructing a tidewater rice plantation required prodigious investments of labor: an eighth-square-mile plantation, when it was completely "improved," had two and a quarter miles of exterior, interior, and "check" banks and twelve or thirteen miles of canals, ditches, and quarter-drains. In other words, slaves working with hand tools had to move well over thirty-nine thousand cubic yards of fine-grained river swamp muck to construct an eighty-acre plantation, this in addition to clearing the land and leveling the ground in the fields. Finding the right pitch required a shrewd, nuanced, and high-stakes reading of the complex edge between freshwater and saltwater. This was an edge that had to be read, analyzed, and then worked with to create a rice plantation that would be a productive one.[30]

When a plantation economy took root in the Lowcountry, it was successful because of how it was positioned at another resonant edge, this one more social and economic than ecological. The insular sites of production that planters dreamed about were linked inexorably to an Atlantic highway for goods and bodies, as part of a larger Atlantic economy. Both islands and edge were necessary, Daniel Defoe declared in 1713, about England's dependence on its Caribbean "sugar islands": "No Sugar no Islands, no Islands no Continent, no Continent no Trade."[31] As many scholars have pointed out, most recently Philip Morgan, Georgia at first was one of those figurative "islands" on the edge, linked more to the British West Indies and the larger Atlantic world than to other parts of North America. Morgan explains that the first long-strand cotton came from the Bahamas, the deforested West Indian islands provided a market for Georgia's forest products and beef exports, and Georgia's small nineteenth-century sugar industry was imported from Jamaica, as was the model for Georgia's 1765 slave code. The links were strong. Morgan concludes: "While lowcountry Georgia possessed the territorial extent of a mainland colony, it bore many of the features of a Caribbean island." And as Paul Pressly has now definitively explained, the larger Atlantic economy markets for cotton, indigo, and rice were essential for the development of plantations here on the edge, as were the flow of slave bodies throughout this economy. Coastal Georgia was perched on the edge of North America, more prominently on the edge of a constellation of island colonies to the south, and in the other direction on the edge of an Atlantic commercial economy that was essential to its economic survival.[32]

This geography shifted only slowly—the Atlantic connections continued to be crucial in the shaping of environmental energy on the coast throughout the antebellum period. Coastal Georgia rice and Sea Island cotton exited almost entirely out of coastal ports, with Savannah as the hub. The balance shifted substantially only after the Civil War, as the tidewater became a backwater—as gradually rice plantations were mostly abandoned, at least for the production of rice, and as sea islands became colonies of leisure for wealthy tourists from the interior. Still, much of the longleaf pine harvested on the coastal plain in the late nineteenth century was shipped from Georgia through coastal ports (the harvesting of which created a new edge, as Piedmont cotton agriculture moved into the deforested coastal plain). Tiny Darien for a while became a humming international timber entrepôt for lumber milled from yellow pine that was rafted down the Altamaha River and then transported by sea out to the world. Here and elsewhere in the history of coastal Georgia, whether a

A Georgia Salt Marsh Primer

All U.S. coastal states contain salt marshes, but along Georgia's hundred-mile-long shoreline the vast wetlands reign supreme. Like endless meadows of waving grass, the marshes stretch four to eight miles between barrier islands and the mainland, covering a giant swath of nearly four hundred thousand acres—a third of all the tidal marshes along the East Coast.

The vastness is awe-inspiring. For legions of people, it is a landscape of superb beauty and inspiration. Poets and artists strive to portray the natural splendor: breathtaking sunsets over a marsh extending to the far horizon; sparkling tidal creeks twisting and turning through the flat, grassy plain; swirl-ing flocks of shorebirds settling onto a creek bank to feed; oyster reefs and mud flats glistening at low tide.

Natural grandeur aside, the salt marshes have an even greater distinction—an astounding ability to produce. Georgia's salt marshes yield nearly twenty tons of biomass per acre, four times the output of the most carefully cultivated farmland and equal to the productivity of a tropical rainforest.

The pulsing tides are the reasons for the marshes' great fertility and, indeed, for their very existence. Twice a day, Georgia's tides rise and fall six to nine feet, alternately flooding and draining the marshes each

Marsh view on Ossabaw Island. Courtesy of Ossabaw Island Foundation.

time. Few ecosystems on the planet are as dependent on these daily, predictable inundations as salt marshes.

The rising tides shove saltwater into the estuaries around the barrier islands, where it mixes with freshwater flowing from mighty rivers that begin in distant mountains and foothills. The mixing traps sediments and nutrients, which the incoming tide, via tidal creeks, delivers to the salt marshes, fertilizing their lush expanses of *Spartina alterniflora*, or cordgrass.

The cane-like, salt-tolerant *Spartina* is by far the most abundant and important plant of the salt marsh. In Georgia, *Spartina* covers 90 percent of the salt marsh landscape. When it dies in autumn, it decomposes into ultra-tiny pieces collectively known as detritus. The bits and pieces are then colonized by microbes that become the nutritious staple of coastal food webs. Ultimately the detritus of salt marshes gives sustenance to untold numbers of shrimp, blue crabs, clams, oysters, all manner of finfish, birds, and other animal species.

But the marshes' ecological and economic benefits don't end there. The great swards of grass serve as nurseries, sheltering the teeming young of marine creatures from hungry predators. Salt marshes protect the mainland from storm surges, filter out pollutants, and maintain the physical integrity of the barrier islands.

The loss of salt marshes would have horrendous consequences—disappearance of entire fisheries, horribly eroded seashore, and magnificent natural beauty gone forever. That is why we must be forever vigilant in their protection.

CHARLES SEABROOK

consequence of ecotones, political boundaries, or economic exchanges, edge effects have yielded an important environmental story.[33]

GLOBE

Continental coasts and river estuaries have often been linked to larger cultural streams and have even been the source of them. Anthropologist Alfred Kroeber once pointed out that historically the interaction of water and land in watersheds and river deltas have made them rich environments for humans as well as other organisms, and places where water meets land have often been powerful sites of human culture as well. Coastal Georgia has historically been enmeshed in global flows of organisms and commodities by way of colonization, the slave trade, and successive export economies. In the century after the first colonial settlements were established in the Southeast, the region was the crossroads for Guale, Timucuan, and other Native peoples, along with various Spanish, French, and English imperial agents. Islands and coasts are also places where ecological energy has been concentrated and where larger ecological changes have registered their effects. Coastal Georgia has always been linked to the globe and has always been cosmopolitan.[34]

In the last half-century, coastal Georgia has become connected to global environments more intricately than ever before because of global climate change. Scientists project an increase in the movement of sand along the seaward side of the Sea Islands and intensified beach erosion. Estuaries all over the world, including those on the Georgia coast, are vulnerable to the sea-level rise that global warming will continue to cause. Coastal Georgia will also be increasingly vulnerable to the kinds of storms that rice planters worried so much about, when high tides and fall storms off the Atlantic converged, but that are now joined by higher sea levels as well. Even normal high tides will pose a challenge to low-lying areas. Some areas that previously were above sea level on Tybee Island are now flooded by king tides (see figure 1.2), for example. A recent study has noted that Fort Pulaski on Tybee Island has experienced nine inches of sea-level rise since 1935, and another argues that in the next century all of coastal Georgia will have another diurnal meter of sea come ashore (and 420 additional square miles of coastal Georgia underwater). In general, coastal Georgia is no longer simply at the edge of the continent or of the Atlantic world but is a nerve center for global environmental change. And visions of this place in the future, if not of the past, will be shaped by understandings that are more global in scale.[35]

Coastal Georgia, which has often been a preserve of nature and even a place where island dreams have marked the beginning of nature, may also in the future be a place to measure the end of it. The stories we tell about it may as a consequence become global in scale. How modern environmentalists mark the trajectory by which human impacts on the environment have decisively changed nature—all of it—is part good science and part old-fashioned jeremiad. Both are represented in *The End of Nature*, the 1989 tocsin by environmental journalist Bill McKibben. This book was an early account of global warming for the general reader and expressed a set of ideas that began to gain traction with the American public in the 1990s. McKibben's argument is simple: that evidence of anthropomorphic change of the upper atmosphere, with a change in climate as a consequence, means that no part of earth remains untouched by human action and influence—hence the end of nature. The envi-

FIGURE 1.2. Flooding on Highway 80 to Tybee Island as a result of a king tide.
As sea levels rise, this kind of flooding will become more common.
Photo courtesy of Stephen B. Morton/*New York Times*.

ronment we live in is now entirely human-shaped, and there is no longer any "nature" without us.[36]

The "end of nature" narrative has had two main effects on stories that environmental historians now tell. First, the scale at which environmental stories were conceived by historians has now shifted to include the global. This is not simply a matter of acknowledging and including the global scale of environmental change but also of learning how to tell stories, no matter the particulars, that take place in global spaces. This shift in environmental narratives has had a complex origin—but one major source has been an awareness of this environmental problem of our time, global warming, which has and will have specific local manifestations but that is a global phenomenon. Now that nature has ended, historians have also interrogated ideas of the pristine, of the "wild," a discussion that has converged with a scholarship questioning the cultural and political origins of twentieth-century American ideas about the wild, about wilderness, and about the divide between culture and nature. The consequence has been new narratives of nature in which the lines between culture and nature are much more porous (and sometimes dissolved altogether) and that acknowledge wilderness as, at the most, *relatively* pristine rather than untouched by human hands. The end of nature has been accompanied by a more profound understanding of the action in nature of human history. And historical narratives are now more profoundly shaped by the acknowledgment of this global event, "the end of nature."[37]

One of the ways that environmental historians have conceptualized this "end" is by appropriating the concept of the Anthropocene from its yet uncertain scientific context and using it to explain our modern relationship with nature. The Anthropocene is a proposed epoch that begins when human activities started to have a significant global impact on earth's geology and ecosystems. Neither the International Commission on Stratigraphy nor its parent body, the International Union of Geological Sciences, has yet officially approved the term as a recognized subdivision of geological time. (It would be demarcated from the currently officially recognized epoch, the Holocene.)[38] But this has not deterred scholars and activists who want to emphasize that humans have reached the point where we are living on the earth in a new way. The value of the "Anthropocene" as a framing concept is that it not only marks decisively the end of nature but also, for some, encourages an understanding of the emergence of a new nature, one that does not avoid history and that also hopes for strategies for adaptation in the future. Some see "Anthropocene" as an unnecessary and clunky and perhaps distracting concept that nonetheless in shorthand reminds us that we now live on a different planet than before—or another island, if you will—and it doesn't look good. Some celebrate a full embrace of the Anthropocene in a kind of neoliberal ecstasy that throws out even a qualified idea of wilderness, that turns its back on conservation efforts, and that also assumes that we can engineer and manage environments as adeptly as we have exploited them. Others among the more conservation-minded resign themselves to an acceptance of the Anthropocene and hope for whatever can be salvaged from the destruction of nature that it identifies. They fully acknowledge that history is embedded in nature but express a vision of history and the future that is shadowed by apocalypse. Others reject the new framing entirely and remain committed to what they believe to be more genuine or authentic ways for humans to live in and preserve what might remain of nature. And some see the frame of the Anthropocene as a sober recognition of what humans have done to the planet but one that encourages us to hope for and adapt to emergent ecosystems that transcend human conceits about ending them.[39]

When environmental storytellers follow through on a full commitment to "the end of nature" (and the possible beginning of another one) or to thinking in general about nature in the Anthropocene, the "globe" becomes not just a spatial scale in which environmental action happens. It is also an important narrative frame and one that has embedded in it an understanding that humans and nature everywhere are fully intertwined. How we tell stories about the environmental history of coastal Georgia, of any place, will be more fully shaped by an understanding of the global dimension of history and by the realization that the line we might try to draw between culture and nature has blurred or disappeared altogether.

As we move into an uncertain future that is also most certainly one where humans and environments will continue to interact on a global scale, we will need to meet the challenges of the Anthropocene in our storytelling. Writing history in the Anthropocene, as historian Dipesh Chakrabarty has explained, might encourage "species history," and much larger temporal and spatial scales will be necessary to capture meaning. Critics of Chakrabarty note that vigorous questions about human agency cannot be erased, as they might be in an emphasis on history at the species level, and that some humans—poor people who live on low-elevation islands or on tropical river deltas, for example— are more in the Anthropocene than others. This criticism will be particularly important to historians of coastal Georgia, where the history of multiple perspectives, human agency, and environmental justice have been fundamental. Critics also point to humans' quotidian and local experience of nature—not a global one—as the experience that is usually the source of ideas as well as feelings about history and nature. Strategies for adaptation and environmental activism often gestate in the everyday experience with nature. But the argument that Chakrabarty and other Anthropocenic historians have made about the importance of understanding history on a global scale, in order to encourage both meaningful political engagement and realistic strategies of hope, is one that environmental storytellers will likely want to consider.[40]

Thinking about nature as fundamentally always in flux, as something always emerging, rather than something either stable and healthy or in decline, opens the door to a new kind of hope—hope with many weeds in it, but more viable than hope (or despair) that idealizes pristine and utopian islands as a measure of what is right and what is not about how we live in nature. Envisioning coastal Georgia as a particularly dynamic environment and a window into the environmental history of the globe in general brings us full circle to the possibility of thinking with islands. But it does so in a way that allows us to imagine a world that does not reject either nature or history but negotiates the best we can manage with both. Studying the particular features of the extraordinarily dynamic environments of coastal Georgia at different temporal and spatial scales but with a sense of the global as a frame is not just a matter of identifying the correct spatial scale for historical action. It is also a matter of creating an environmental history narrative for the future and generating a new kind of hope.

Whatever the scale at which we imagine or the edges we use to analyze coastal Georgia, the old notion of islands as utopia—places of reserve and retreat, where one can recover as well as reinvent, awash in a golden haze of the perennially perfect (albeit with lots of ruins and ghosts)—seems distant from current environmental realities. Images of coastal Georgia and its islands as potentially perfect places force history to stand still in the same way that hazy notions of the pristine extract nature from human history and freeze it in time and place. The dream of islands that are "golden" nonetheless continues to have a strong hold on the imaginations of both residents and visitors. It is not going to disappear and has stoked some important environmental protection initiatives. And it may be necessary, in counterpoint to environmental depredations elsewhere on the coast and on the globe. Current conceits of the abundant coast and the golden islands will not acquire any more stability in the future than they have in the past, but they are a part of the identity of this place, and we may need them. As long as we keep in mind that when we dream too forcefully about islands or structure too forcefully the streams of energy that move around them, we are going to be disappointed. The dreams about coastal Georgia that have endured and that have defined this place have been those that have stayed the tide, that have flowed with history rather than against it. The hopes we have for the future integrity of coastal Georgia that will endure will be those that will be in history at the same time that they angle at it, that are forged by experience and lifted up by both investigation and self-knowledge, and that will provide us with new islands of possibility in a stream of change. In this *place*, coastal Georgia.

NOTES

My thanks to Paul Pressly, Paul Sutter, and the reviewers of this volume for their comments on previous drafts of this chapter.

1. The Michel Serres quotation, from his *Conversations on Science, Culture, and Time*, is in Jonathan Gil Harris, *Untimely Matter in the Time of Shakespeare* (Philadelphia: University of Pennsylvania Press, 2009), 3. For explanations of the volatility of almost any spatial unit and from a variety of disciplinary perspectives, see, for example, James Clifford, *Routes: Travel and Translation in the Late Twentieth Century* (Cambridge, Mass.: Harvard University Press, 1997), esp. chap. 3; James S. Duncan, Nuala C. Johnson, and Richard Schein, *A Companion to Cultural Geography* (Oxford: Blackwell, 2004), pt. 5 ("Landscapes"); and Don Mitchell, *Cultural Geography: A Critical Introduction* (Oxford: Blackwell, 2000), pt. 2 ("The Political Landscape").

2. John Leddy Phelan, *The Millennial Kingdom of the Franciscans in the New World: A Study of the Writings of Gerónimo de Mendieta (1525–1604)* (Berkeley: Uni-

versity of California Press, 1970). On the complex reciprocity of Spanish relationships with the Guale and Timucuan and others, see Amy Turner Bushnell, "'These
people are not conquered like those of New Spain': Florida's Reciprocal Colonial
Compact," *Florida Historical Quarterly* 92 (2014): 524–53. On the earlier history of
the Franciscan island missions, see David Hurst Thomas's chapter 2 in this volume.

3. Sir Robert Montgomery, *Discourse concerning the Design of a New Colony to
the South of South Carolina* (London, 1717), 12. Montgomery used the term "golden
islands" in subsequent publications that also promoted Azilia. See Montgomery and
John Barnwell, *A Description of the Golden Islands: With an Account of the Undertak-
ing Now on Foot for Making a Settlement There* (London: J. Morphew, 1720).

4. See Mart A. Stewart, *"What Nature Suffers to Groe": Life, Labor, and Landscape
on the Georgia Coast* (Athens: University of Georgia Press, 1996), chap. 1.

5. Daniel Boorstin, *The Americans: The Colonial Experience* (New York: Vintage,
1964), 265.

6. Phelan, *The Millennial Kingdom of the Franciscans*, 70–73. On islands, colonial-
ization, and the European imagination, see Leo Marx, *The Machine in the Garden*
(Oxford: Oxford University Press, 2000), chap. 1, esp. 32–33; Frank E. Manuel and
Fritzie P. Manuel, *Utopian Thought in the Western World* (Cambridge, Mass.: Belknap
Press, 1979), 117–204; Richard H. Grove, *Green Imperialism: Colonial Expansion,
Tropical Island Edens and the Origins of Environmentalism, 1600–1860* (Cambridge:
Cambridge University Press, 1995), 13. See also Stewart, *What Nature Suffers to Groe*,
chap. 1.

7. Paul M. Pressly, *On the Rim of the Caribbean: Colonial Georgia and the British
Atlantic World* (Athens: University of Georgia Press, 2013).

8. For a powerful exploration of plantation as private dominion in the slavehold-
ing South, see Drew Faust, *John Henry Hammond and the Old South: A Design for
Mastery* (Baton Rouge: Louisiana State University Press, 1985). See also Walter John-
son, *River of Dark Dreams: Slavery and Empire in the Cotton Kingdom* (Cambridge,
Mass.: Belknap Press, 2013), and Edward Baptist, *The Half Has Never Been Told:
Slavery and the Making of American Capitalism* (New York: Basic Books, 2014). The
Hazard quotation is from W. W. Hazard, "Hints, at Some of the Causes of Those
Evils Young Planters Complain of, and a Remedy Proposed," *Southern Agriculturist* 1,
no. 6 (June 1828), 252–77. For change and continuity in the plantation imaginary, see
Drew Swanson's chapter 6 in this volume.

9. Stewart, *What Nature Suffers to Groe*, 116–22. For a comprehensive discussion
of the history of Sea Island cotton in South Carolina, Georgia, and Florida, see Richard Dwight Porcher and Sarah Fick, *The Story of Sea Island Cotton* (Layton, Utah:
Gibbs Smith, 2005). For an explanation of Couper's "green paternalism" and ideal
planting practices, see Stewart, *What Nature Suffers to Groe*, 182–87; and Stewart,
"Plantations, Agroecology, Environmental Thought, and the American South," in
Comparing Apples, Oranges, and Cotton, ed. Frank Uekötter (Frankfurt, N.Y.: Campus Verlag, 2014), 33–40.

10. F. R. Goulding, *Robert and Harold; or, The Young Marooners on the Florida*

Coast (Philadelphia: William S. Martien, 1853). See also Goulding, *Marooner's Island; or, Dr. Gordon in Search of His Children* (Philadelphia: Claxton, Remsen & Haffelfinger, 1876); *Nacoochee; or, Boy-life from Home* (Philadelphia: Claxton, Remsen & Haffelfinger, 1871); *Sapelo; or, Child-life on the Tide-water* (Macon, Ga.: J. W. Burke, 1870); and *Adventures among the Indians* (London: George Routledge and Sons, 1871).

11. This is the "Devil Fish" of William Elliott's classic collection of Lowcountry hunting tales, *Carolina Sports: Carolina Sports by Land and Water: Including Incidents of Devil-Fishing, Wildcat, Deer and Bear Hunting, etc.* (New York: Derby and Jackson, 1859), originally published as a series of sketches in a Charleston, South Carolina, newspaper.

12. Hunting and stories about hunting have played a prominent role in the history of human encounters with nature in Georgia and the South. See, for example, Stewart, *What Nature Suffers to Groe*, 178–79; Nicholas Proctor, *Bathed in Blood: Hunting and Mastery in the Old South* (Charlottesville: University of Virginia Press, 2002); Scott Giltner, *Hunting and Fishing in the New South: Black Labor and White Leisure after the Civil War* (Baltimore: Johns Hopkins University Press, 2008). Hunting remains an important activity, even in coastal wildlife refuges, where a few hunters can assist wildlife managers in "harvesting" surplus populations of white-tailed deer and feral hogs. See, for example, "Hunting," Savannah National Wildlife Refuge, https://www.fws.gov/refuge/Savannah/Visit/Visitor_Activities/Hunting.html.

13. Goulding, *Robert and Harold*, 105 (Crusoe reference), 422 (Bethel quotation). In *Genesis* 28:16–19, Bethel was a sanctuary and the House of God.

14. See Susan Scott Parrish, *American Curiosity: Cultures of Natural History in the Colonial British Atlantic World* (Chapel Hill: University of North Carolina Press, 2006), chaps. 6 and 7. See also Sharla Fett, *Working Cures: Healing, Health, and Power on Southern Slave Plantations* (Chapel Hill: University of North Carolina Press, 2001).

15. Rev. C. C. Jones to Lt. Charles C. Jones Jr., July 10, 1862, in Robert Mansom Myers, ed., *The Children of Pride*, vol. 1: *The Edge of the Sword* (New York: Popular Library, 1972), 930.

16. See Mart A. Stewart, "Nature, Negotiation, and Community: Slavery and the Origins of African American Environmentalism," in *"To Love the Wind and the Rain": Essays in African American Environmental History*, eds. Dianne Glave and Mark Stoll (Pittsburgh: University of Pittsburgh Press, 2006); Anthony Kaye, *Joining Places: Slave Neighborhoods in the Old South* (Chapel Hill: University of North Carolina Press, 2007); Stephanie M. Camp, *Closer to Freedom: Enslaved Women and Everyday Resistance in the Plantation South* (Chapel Hill: University of North Carolina Press, 2004); Johnson, *River of Dark Dreams*. Though scholarly meditations on African Americans and the geography of slavery have continued to develop (see Johnson, *River of Dark Dreams*), these still do not fully acknowledge the importance as well as the specific content of African American environmental knowledge as a weapon of resistance. Instead of the "geography of resistance," we need more schol-

arship on the specific ways that this geography was negotiated and that examines these in relationship to the environments in which slaves actually lived rather than an abstract carceral meta-environment. See Mart A. Stewart, "Walking, Running, and Marching into an Environmental History of the Civil War," in *The Blue, the Gray, and the Green: Toward an Environmental History of the Civil War*, ed. Brian Drake (Athens: University of Georgia Press, 2014), 214–17. The spiritual meaning of places and of landscape for African Americans in the South Carolina and Georgia Low-country has been difficult to discover but of course shaped more visible behavior. See Ras Michael Brown, *African-Atlantic Cultures and the South Carolina Lowcountry* (Cambridge: Cambridge University Press, 2012) and Tiya Miles's chapter 5 in this volume. For an analysis of slavery that uses Michel Foucault's concept of biopower to illuminate the control of slave bodies by slave masters, at least as it is represented in Frederick Douglass's *Narrative*, see Colleen Glenney Boggs, "Bestiality Revisted: The Primal Scene of Biopower (Frederick Douglass)," in *Animalia Americana: Animal Representations and Biopolitical Subjectivity* (New York: Columbia University Press, 2012), 77–108.

17. See Allison Dorsey, "'The great cry of our people is land!' Black Settlement and Community Development on Ossabaw Island, Georgia, 1865–1900," in *African American Life in the Georgia Lowcountry: The Atlantic World and the Gullah Geechee*, ed. Philip Morgan (Athens: University of Georgia Press, 2010), 224–52; and Russell Duncan, *Freedom's Shore: Tunis Campbell and the Georgia Freedmen* (Athens: University of Georgia Press, 1986).

18. Most of this discussion comes from Stewart, *What Nature Suffers to Groe*, 216–24. See this for a full discussion of this chapter in the history of the islands and for notes on quotations. For a discussion of ruins in the cultural history of the Georgia coast, see Drew Swanson's essay in chap. 6 of this collection.

19. For those who cannot visit but want a virtual taste of an island wilderness experience, it can be had on *Jekyll Island: An Ambient Safari* (2009), DVD. This section comes from a collection of coastal Georgia tourist brochures (1992–2016) in the author's possession.

20. Edward Copeland, "Burning a Path of Destruction—through Relationships," *Edward Copeland's Tangents*, http://eddieonfilm.blogspot.com/2010/09/only-important-things-in-life-are.html; Scott MacDonald, *American Ethnographic Film and the Personal Documentary: The Cambridge Turn* (Berkeley: University of California Press, 2013), 205–7. See also Ann Foskey, *Ossabaw Island* (Charleston, SC: Arcadia, 2001): 93–106.

21. The notion that North America was once wilderness before Europeans mucked it up and that certain kinds of protected areas (many of them on islands) could be returned to a pristine state has had an enduring history in the United States. It began to be interrogated and destabilized in the 1980s and 1990s. The literature on this is now substantial, but for the core debate, see William Cronon, in "The Trouble with Wilderness; or, Getting Back to the Wrong Nature," in Cronon, ed., *Uncommon Ground: Rethinking the Human Place in Nature* (New York: W. W. Norton, 1996),

24–37; and the response to this essay in George Sessions, "Reinventing Nature: The End of Wilderness? A Response to William Cronon's 'Uncommon Ground,'" *Wild Duck Review* 2 (November 1995): 13–15, 21. Also see a recent comprehensive update to the debate on the meaning of "wilderness" in Michael P. Nelson and J. Baird Callicott, eds., *The Wilderness Debate Rages On: Continuing the Great New Wilderness Debate* (Athens: University of Georgia Press, 2008). See also Paul Sutter's discussion of John McPhee's *Encounters with the Archdruid* in the introduction to this volume.

22. David Quammen, *Song of the Dodo: Island Biogeography in an Age of Extinction* (New York: Scribner, 1997), 17–114, quotation from p. 19.

23. See the Sapelo Island University of Georgia Marine Institute website for brief explanations of research projects and a searchable archive of scientific publications: http://ugami.uga.edu/. See also Evelyn Sherr, *Marsh Mud and Mummichogs: An Intimate Natural History of Coastal Georgia* (Athens: University of Georgia Press, 2015).

24. The term "archipelago" here is used in the sense, "a sea in which there are islands" (*Oxford English Dictionary* [1971], s.v. "archipelago").

25. On ecotones and the concept of the edge effect, see R. L. Smith, *Ecology and Field Biology* (New York: Harper & Row, 1974), 333; Paul G. Risser, "The Status of the Science Examining Ecotones," *BioScience*, 45 (May 1995), 318–19; Paul G. Risser et al., "Special Issue: Ecotones," *Ecological Applications*, 3 (August 1993), 367–445.

26. Stewart, *What Nature Suffers to Groe*, 12–20.

27. These same fields also fed an expanding squirrel population, which sometimes ended up in Salzburger pots. See Stewart, *What Nature Suffers to Groe*, 78–79, for a full discussion of the Salzburger experience and for the many citations of primary sources for this story.

28. Personal conversation between the author and Eugene Odum. See also Chris Manganiello's chapter in this volume.

29. Georgia Coastal Ecosystems LTR, http://gce-lter.marsci.uga.edu/.

30. Stewart, *What Nature Suffers to Groe*, 99–104. For another kind of attention to the crucial edge between saltwater and freshwater, see the discussion of saltwater incursions into the water table in coastal Georgia, because of the large volume of water used by modern pulp mills, in William Boyd's chapter 8 in this volume. People on the coast have expressed different understandings of this edge. See Tiya Miles's chapter 5 in this volume. The understanding of the differences between environments close to the sea and those adjacent to freshwater was reflected in the distinction coastal Geechees made between "saltwater Geechee" and "freshwater Geechee."

31. Quoted in David Lowenthal, "Islands, Lovers, and Others," *Geographical Review* 97, no. 2 (April 2007): 203–4.

32. Philip Morgan, *African American Life in the Georgia Lowcountry*, 26; Pressly, *On the Rim of the Caribbean*. See also Edda L. Fields-Black, *Deep Roots: Rice Farmers in West Africa and the African Diaspora* (Bloomington: Indiana University Press, 2008) and her chapter 4 in this volume. The link between the experience of African American slaves and the African continent was also preserved in their belief in flying back to Africa. See Tiya Miles's chapter in this volume. We can see this edge repre-

sented powerfully in the eighteenth-century English maps of this region showing a coast that turned outward to the sea much more profoundly than to the developing links with the interior. See Mart A. Stewart, "William Gerard De Brahm's 1757 Map of South Carolina and Georgia," *Environmental History*, July 2011, 524–35, and Max Edelson's chapter 3 in this volume.

33. Stewart, *What Nature Suffers to Groe*, 197–216. See also Albert Way's chapter 7 in this volume.

34. See Alan Burdick, *Out of Eden: An Odyssey of Ecological Invasion* (New York: Farrar, Straus, and Giroux, 2005), esp. ch. 21; and Eben Kirksey, *Emergent Ecologies* (Durham, N.C.: Duke University Press, 2015).

35. "Sea Level Rise," Marine Extension and Sea Level Grant, University of Georgia, http://marex.uga.edu/sea-level-rise-in-georgia/; Gillam Campbell et al., *Tracking the Effects of Sea Level Rise in Georgia's Coastal Communities* (Atlanta: Georgia Institute of Technology, School of City and Regional Planning, 2012), https://smartech.gatech.edu/handle/1853/48711. The National Oceanic and Atmospheric Administration has sited several climate-monitoring stations, part of a global network, on coastal Georgia islands. To view the consequences of future sea-level rise, see Georgia Coastal Hazards Portal, Skidaway Institute of Oceanography, http://gchp.skio.uga.edu/. The Tybee Island City Council has recently acknowledged sea-level rise with Georgia's first sea-level adaptation plan: "Community Resilience: Tybee Island Creates Georgia's First Sea Level Rise Plan," National Oceanic and Atmospheric Administration, Sea Grant, May 18, 2016, http://seagrant.noaa.gov/News/FeatureStories/; and Jason M. Evans et al., "Tybee Island Sea-Level Rise Adaptation Plan, Final Report," April 2016, https://www.researchgate.net/publication/289999590_Tybee_Island_Sea-Level_Rise_Adaptation_Plan.

36. Bill McKibben, *The End of Nature* (New York: Random House, 2006).

37. See note 21 above.

38. Historians have been divided in their acceptance of the Anthropocene. For an exemplary view, see "Interview—John McNeill," *E-International Relations*, October 27, 2015, http://www.e-ir.info/2015/10/27/interview-john-r-mcneill.

39. For a meditation on the rapidly growing literature on the Anthropocene as well as on the terms "Anthropocene" and "Generation Anthropocene," see Robert Macfarlane, "Generation Anthropocene: How Humans Have Altered the Planet Forever," *Guardian*, April 1, 2016. Macfarlane's assessment of the challenge to narrative forms by the acknowledgment of the Anthropocene is especially noteworthy. See Burdick, *Out of Eden*, for an eloquent meditation on "invasion," how new systems emerge out of old ones, and the role of "invading" species in system change as organisms become more processes than objects. See also Lesley Head, *Hope and Grief in the Anthropocene* (Abingdon: Routledge, 2017), especially chapter 7, "Living with Weeds." The idea of Earth as island has a complicated history, but it was profoundly shaped by the Apollo 17 photographs of Earth from space. See Denis Cosgrove, "Contested Global Visions: One-World, Whole-Earth, and the Apollo Space Photographs," *Annals of the Association of American Geographers* 84, no. 2 (1994): 270–94.

40. See Dipesh Chakrabarty, "The Climate of History: Four Theses," *Critical Inquiry* 35 (Winter 2009): 197–222; and Robert Emmert and Thomas Lekan, eds., *Whose Anthropocene? Revisiting Dipesh Chakrabarty's "Four Theses,"* Rachel Carson Center Perspectives: Transformations in Environment and Society (Munich: Rachel Carson Center, 2016) See also Rob Nixon, "The Anthropocene: Promise and Pitfalls of an Epochal Idea," *Edge Effects*, November 6, 2014, http://edgeeffects.net /anthropocene-promise-and-pitfalls.

CHAPTER 2

Deep History of the Georgia Coast

A View from St. Catherines Island

DAVID HURST THOMAS

The Georgia coastline is unique in the world, and so are human adaptations to it. Georgia's Golden Isles were created by a one-of-a-kind combination of island-building processes including shifting sea levels, variability in tidal sediment loads, shifting ocean currents, and highly charged deepwater hydrology. The resulting coastal geomorphology is a rich tidal and subtidal marshland juxtaposed with a diverse matrix of terrestrial ecosystems blessed with an abundance of artesian freshwater. This delicate environmental balance, hundreds of thousands of years in the making, is remarkably fragile and vulnerable to irreversible change through human intervention.

Focused through the lens of St. Catherines Island, this essay will explore the deep environmental and cultural histories of the Georgia coastline, from the birth of the Sea Islands through the establishment of the Georgia colony by James Edward Oglethorpe in 1733. This is the coastal Georgia landscape I know best and a place where multiple marshland lifeways have played out over five millennia.

Three episodes of island history will be covered: the appearance of the first St. Catherines Islanders, the first attempt at Spanish utopia in North America, and the unique Franciscan and Native American alliance that played out in the Spanish missions of the Georgia coast. Each of these carries lessons in human-environment interaction and demonstrates the potential of directed archaeological and paleoenvironmental inquiry to generate new and richer understandings of Georgia's Sea Islands past and present.

GEORGIA'S BARRIER ISLANDS

Nearly twenty-two hundred barrier islands protect the margins of every continent on the globe except Antarctica, covering about 15 percent of the world's coastlines.[1] Hundreds of barrier islands ring the North American shoreline, but the number remains fluid because these nearshore islands are constantly appearing, disappearing, reappearing, and reinventing themselves. Although the western shoreline of North America hosts several "barrier beaches," true barrier islands are absent there.

Most barrier islands are simple beach ridges—long, linear, wave-built barriers punctuated by the occasional tidal inlet and separated from the mainland by broad, shallow estuaries.[2] The Outer Banks islands of the Carolinas, for instance, are typically thin, longish island isolates maintaining a migratory equilibrium—moving back and forward, up and down—keeping pace with sea level, the variable sources of sand supply, wave energy, and storm overwash. Onshore winds blow tons of airborne sand across the beach-ridge barrier islands, and dune vegetation traps the sand necessary to stabilize the dune ridge. The unconsolidated and poorly developed soils generally foster stunted vegetation, which is subject to severe impacts from ocean winds, salt spray, and sometimes massive damage from tropical storms and hurricanes. Terrestrial productivity is generally quite low, and the available food resource patches are universally small. From an aboriginal foraging perspective that spans five millennia, the typical barrier island commanded little interest. It was the mainland coast that provided primary access to the resource-rich estuaries, salt marshes, flowing freshwater, and swamps.

Georgia's "Fake" Barrier Islands

St. Catherines Island and the other Golden Isles of Georgia are not typical barrier islands—they are too rich, too stable, too luxuriant, and too well watered. Each hosts a rich maritime forest, producing acorns and hickory nuts in great abundance. White-tailed deer populations have long attracted hunters from across the country.

Writing about the "false" barrier islands of the Georgia coastline, geologist Orrin Pilkey sees a place where "things aren't what they seem to be." The Georgia "composite" islands are "fakes"—looking to the world like standard-issue barrier islands, but in reality they are something quite different.[3] Georgia's Sea Islands are unique accidents of sea-level history and differ remarkably from typical beach-ridge islands around the world.[4]

The most ancient portion of Georgia's Sea Islands was left behind when Ice Age seas peaked and then subsided. Sea level eventually rose again to create a chain of paired barrier islands—an old one and a recent one—that overlapped in exactly the same place. These large "composite" islands protect enormous estuarine salt marshes, initially formed during the Pleistocene and flooded again during the Holocene sea-level rise.[5]

Modern St. Catherines and the other Sea Islands were born about five thousand years ago when sea levels rose enough to isolate the ancient Ice Age island core from the mainland.[6] These composite islands of coastal Georgia rank among the broadest and most resource-rich barrier islands in the world. Although only one hundred miles long, the Georgia coastline protects one-third of all salt marshes in eastern North America—some of the world's richest habitats and several times more productive than America's most fertile farmland.[7]

Georgia's Sea Islands are uniquely configured and define a *place* (in the sense described in Mart Stewart's chapter in this book), with qualities that have shaped their human history for millennia.

Sea Island Hydrology

In 1753, South Carolina–born colonist Jonathan Bryan called St. Catherines Island "one of the most pleasant and agreeable Place[s] in all Georgia" and wrote in his journal, "Shaded by fine spreading Live Oaks, the middle of the island appears a perfect Meadow being a large Savanna of about a Mile or Mile and half wide and four or five Miles long, and finely water'd with Springs… the cristial [crystal] Streams in winding rills proceeds the rising Mounts and flow the verdant meads."[8] Bryan's meadow that once dominated the central reaches of St. Catherines Island disappeared in the 1930s when it was drained by dragline ditches. But the extent of this large freshwater lagoon can be clearly delimited in aerial photographs, earlier topographic maps, and geomorphic clues still preserved on the Ice Age core of the island.[9]

Why was there so much water? The answer is the Floridan Aquifer—one of the most productive groundwater reservoirs in the United States—that extends from South Carolina to Florida and reaches inland as far as Alabama. Near Brunswick, Georgia, these sedimentary strata are nearly two thousand feet thick below ground, deeply buried beneath more than five hundred feet of sand and clay.[10] This sloping underground landscape created artesian conditions—meaning that the recharge and discharge of the aquifer system remained nearly in equilibrium so long as the Floridan Aquifer was recharged by rainfall in the interior, where it lay near the ground surface. Because the aquifer was confined under "artesian" conditions, water flowed naturally to the surface in springs (with characteristic domes of yellow sand) and seeped to rivers, ponds, wetlands, and other surface-water bodies throughout most of coastal Georgia.[11]

On St. Catherines Island, several cracks in the deeply buried Floridan Aquifer propelled groundwater to the surface with an artesian water pressure of thirty-four feet above sea level. Even in places where surface water was unavailable from the deep aquifer, a relatively shallow well could tap the surficial reservoir of non-artesian rainwater. This means that—at least prior to the early or mid-twentieth century—freshwater was available almost everywhere in low-lying locales on the island (and most of the other Sea Islands), further adding to the foraging potential of this "false" barrier island.

THE FIRST ST. CATHERINES ISLANDERS

Mart Stewart's chapter in this book aptly highlights the "edge effect" as a window for understanding the greater environmental history of coastal Georgia as place. Probing into deep time, I think this historical sketch can readily be expanded well beyond the bounds of William Bartram's famous tramp across Georgia in the 1770s and the Sea Island cotton plantations.

The first human footprint on St. Catherines Island appeared about 2700 BC, almost immediately after rising sea levels had separated the island from the mainland. This was no coincidence. The first humans were drawn to the Sea Islands by a newly emergent, mid-Holocene ecotone that married the enormously productive estuarine marshland resources to a stable, well-watered, terrestrial ecosystem. With the newly stabilized sea level, more than 80 percent of the maritime forest margin on St. Catherines Island fronted directly on salt marsh, creating a classic example of an ecological "edge effect."[12] The first foragers here discovered that within a five-mile radius they could harvest massive tracts of prime maritime forest, rich salt marsh flats, deep waters of the sounds, seaside shorefront, and the gradually sloping continental shelf of the Atlantic Ocean.

Acutely sensitive to edge effects, the earliest St. Catherines Islanders deliberately built their most important settlements along the freshwater-saltwater ecotone separating estuarine from terrestrial resource bases. So long as they lived on that ecotone, these foragers could walk or paddle anyplace on the island and return home that night. More than four decades of archaeological fieldwork clearly demonstrate how this baseline shellfishing economy evolved and persisted, with some local impacts on estuarine resource patches, feeding the next two hundred generations of St. Catherines Islanders without detectable changes in diet.

This is how a working appreciation of edge effects and ecotones does indeed open windows to understanding coastal Georgia as place—now viewed across millennia.

Hardscrabble Foragers or Fortunate Beachcombers?

But questions remain: Were the prehistoric St. Catherines Islanders hardscrabble foragers barely getting by on emergency, starvation rations of the marshland? Or were they fortunate beachcombers privileged to exploit the essentially inexhaustible resources of Georgia's Golden Isles?

Anthropologists and archaeologists have debated this for decades. Some have underestimated the role of marine resources and shellfishing in past human diets. In 1907 German archaeologist Max Uhle expressed the belief that the "manner of procuring the essentials of life by collecting shells in itself indicates a low form of human existence. In all parts of the world, even today, people may be seen by the shore at low water, collecting for food the shells uncovered by the retreating tide. . . . These people always belong to the lower classes of society, and lead in this manner a primitive as well as simple life."[13] Others argued, as Alan Osborn did seventy years later, that shellfish collecting is an excessively labor-intensive strategy: "Not only does the food item contain less 'optimal' amounts of protein, but also producers in the society would have to spend an inordinate amount of time each day or so collecting food for dependents."[14] So viewed, shellfish becomes an "emergency" or "starvation" food— small, costly to harvest and process, nutritionally poor, unreliable, requiring high technological investments (boat transportation) to access, and vulnerable to storm and potentially lethal red tide events.

Others believed just the opposite, that shellfishing can anchor an extraordinarily productive way of life. Betty Meehan's research on Australia's Anbarra people convincingly confirms shellfishing as their most dependable source of food, vastly more reliable than fishing.[15] Investigators emphasized that nutrient-rich tidal estuaries—such as those surrounding St. Catherines Island—host mollusk populations concentrated in great abundance, providing compact resource clusters of high-quality animal protein, easily and predictably procured, and available throughout most, if not all, of the year. Shellfish potentially provide a high-quality, predictable protein source that contains all essential amino acids and compares favorably with other animal species.[16] If so, foragers working such oyster beds are virtually assured of meeting subsistence requirements, even in lean times. Whereas terrestrial hunters might need to travel far afield, shellfish remained available locally, thereby ensuring a stable level of protein intake. And whereas hunting is failure-prone, the failure rate for pursuing stationary shellfish approaches zero.

Shell Midden Archaeology

Speaking of Australia's Anbarra foragers, Betty Meehan once remarked that shellfish were there for them "for the taking, like the food on a supermarket shelf."[17] St. Catherines Island archaeology has today proven that the shelves of Georgia's barrier islands have been amply stocked for millennia. Beyond all doubt, the first St. Catherines Islanders were fortunate beachcombers indeed.

More than seven hundred archaeological shell middens survive today on St. Catherines Island, with eastern oyster being the most common taxon found within them, regardless of time period. Hard clams, whelk, stout tagelus, sea catfishes, mullets, killifishes, drums, diamondback terrapins, and white-tailed deer also show up in the earliest shell mounds, defining a pattern that carried into the Spanish contact period.[18] These aboriginal middens contain an extraordinary number of small-bodied, mass-capture fishes that demonstrate the long-term importance of salt marsh fishing. The middens also showed that white-tailed deer provided a considerable portion of the vertebrate biomass, augmented by large-bodied fishes such as red drums, sharks, and stingrays. Other fishes, marsh gastropods, crustaceans, small birds, small mammals, and turtles were also eaten, in smaller numbers. No new taxa were added to the diet over the millennia, but sea level changes could have markedly shifted encounter rates of specific shellfish taxa.[19]

Particularly striking is the remarkable size change of white-tailed deer on St. Catherines Island. The earliest middens contain deer bones from adult males averaging, it is estimated, about 165 pounds live weight. This is slightly larger than modern white-tailed deer on the South Carolina mainland, but adult deer living on Ossabaw Island today average only 75 pounds. The first St. Catherines Islanders stalked white-tailed deer that were twice the size of those hunted during the mission period.[20]

Why did St. Catherines Island deer shrink to half their size? This is an excellent example of the so-called island syndrome: over time, larger-size mammals (like deer) get smaller, while smaller-size mammals (like rabbits and carnivores) get larger.[21] The study of island biogeography has helped ecologists to understand the complex mix of processes involved with deficient food resources and selective factors involving habitat fragmentation. In effect, smaller island creatures get larger when predation pressure is relaxed (because some mainland predators are absent), and larger organisms get smaller due to the limited island food resources (because of the land area constraints).

Human occupation of the Georgia coast was disrupted beginning about 2300 BC, as seas dropped more than six feet over the next seven centuries.[22] This turn of events dramatically shrank the estuarine marshland, if it survived at all. St. Catherines Islanders were forced to move off-island until sea levels began rising again about 1600 BC (at a rate of roughly four inches per year). Returning St. Catherines Islanders practiced almost exactly the same mix of terrestrial hunting, shellfishing, and estuarine fishing strategies as before.

Several burial mounds were constructed on St. Catherines Island around this time, and the archaeology of those mounds holds clues to the social organization of the period. Three thousand years ago, St. Catherines Islanders lived fundamentally egalitarian lives.[23] This means that, setting aside possible gender differences, everyone was born with equal rights and standing in their community. From this egalitarian baseline, one's social status should accrue in direct proportion to one's accomplishments. The most successful adults received the most elaborate burials to commemorate the high status they achieved in life. Less successful people endured lower social status in life, which was reflected in the way they were buried (often being excluded from the high-status burial mounds). Because infants and juveniles had relatively little time to acquire such social status, they were rarely interred in the early mortuary mounds.

Landmark social, environmental, and ecological processes shook St. Catherines Island around AD 800. Burial practices shifted to include a very high proportion of infants and children, some singled out for special treatment. A few children were interred in large, pentagonal, log-lined tombs, with a burial mound constructed over the top (often with several burials added later). Because these individuals were far too young to have achieved high-level prestige during their lifetimes, archaeologists believe that family social status and political power must have ascribed them such status at birth—reflecting their genealogical affinity to a noble lineage. Twelve hundred years ago, hereditary inequality became the rule on St. Catherines Island, with power and social status accorded at birth within a structured and formalized hierarchy based on kin relations (rather than personal accomplishments or wealth accumulated in life).[24]

Around the world, similar rises of ranked, hierarchical societies are typically linked to the emergence of agriculture, but this did not happen on St. Catherines Island. The combined archaeological and biological evidence makes it abundantly clear that the transition to heritable social inequality took place entirely within the context of a stable shellfishing economy—predating maize farming on the island by several centuries.[25]

The Earliest Residents of the Georgia Coast

Scattered throughout the coastal southeastern United States are more than fifty "shell rings," massive circular piles of oysters, clams, mussels, and other aquatic bivalves that encircle broad, shell-free plazas. Dating back roughly five thousand years (more than two thousand years before agriculture), shell rings are not only some of the earliest large-scale architecture to be found in the United States, but, more importantly, they also mark a transformative point in the history of human habitation in North America. The people who created these structures—the "ring-builders"—organized their societies and their built environment in fundamentally different ways than did their predecessors who mostly lived in small, highly mobile groups in the interior of the Southeast. Shell rings are evidence that communities were becoming larger, more complex, and increasingly centered on the coastline.

Archaeologists and antiquarians have marveled at the size of shell rings for more than one hundred years—the largest rings are more than three hundred meters long, and some reach up to five meters in height—and have developed numerous theories to account for the shape of these remarkable deposits. Early on, some suggested that shell rings were defensive structures, fish traps, or even prehistoric torture chambers. More recently, archaeologists have largely come to the conclusion that these sites were villages as well as points where ring-builders held periodic festivals and gatherings. Some rings may have grown to such an extent that ring-builders no longer occupied them but instead used them as ceremonial gathering points.

Two shell rings are located on St. Catherines Island, both of which date to roughly forty-three hundred years ago and

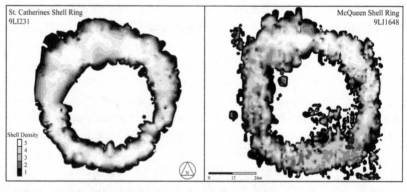

Ground-penetrating images of shell rings on St. Catherines Island. Image created by Matthew C. Sanger. Courtesy of the American Museum of Natural History and the St. Catherine's Island Foundation.

are the oldest evidence of human occupation of the island. Built up over several
hundred years, the rings on St. Catherines
Island are modest in size—seventy meters
across and roughly a meter in height—and
hold evidence that ring-builders lived on
the island year-round, perhaps in small
communities of a dozen or so people.
These local communities appear to have
held periodic gatherings in the winter,
during which they consumed massive
amounts of shellfish, the remains of which
now make up the shell piles that define
the rings.

The ring-builders of St. Catherines Island
were tied into larger trade networks and
peoples that spanned what is now the
eastern United States. Evidence of these
expansive relations includes the discovery
of a piece of copper at one of the shell
rings, copper that originated from the Great
Lakes more than fifteen hundred kilometers
away. These finds clearly show that the
ring-builders of St. Catherines Island were
part of a broad exchange network and
operated in a complex social landscape
that included village life and periodic ceremonial gatherings.

MATTHEW C. SANGER

The human population of St. Catherines Island increased exponentially after people first arrived on the island. During the Mississippian period (AD 800
to AD 1500), the population doubled and then dropped dramatically (if not
catastrophically) during the Spanish mission interval. Archaeology documents
two critical, interrelated dimensions of Late Mississippian environment-
human relationships: overharvesting the marsh and adopting maize-based agriculture.

With more people to feed, nearby shellfish beds inevitably experienced
greater harvesting pressure, forcing increased reliance on more distant, second-
tier resource patches. Late Mississippian foragers began harvesting eastern oysters, hard clams, and catfishes from a significantly greater number of intertidal
habitats or substrates (or both). Although people ate the same foods throughout the prehistoric era, there is evidence of considerable resource depletion in
the estuary, accompanied by higher transportation costs. Late Mississippian
middens show that hard clam populations were generally younger and smaller
than before, which is usually interpreted as a sign of heavy harvesting from
less-ideal substrates. Hard clams are scarce in some Mississippian sites, suggesting declining access to nearby healthy clam beds.[26] At the same time, fishing
strategies shifted toward more communal technologies such as massive fish

weirs. The more powerful matrilineages owned and defended from intruders the most productive fishing and shellfishing territories.[27] The St. Catherines Island marshland suffered as Mississippian populations expanded, with better habitats overharvested and less fortunate lineages forced to collect in secondary, less productive patches.

Terrestrial farming would seem to offer another way to provide more food for an expanding population, but slash-and-burn maize horticulture (of the kind feasible on St. Catherines Island) is remarkably inefficient, yielding about the same return on energy invested as collecting oysters and ribbed mussels, spearing small fish, hunting gray squirrels, and preparing acorn meal.[28] Hunting rabbits and ducks, collecting clams, and preparing hickory nut oil have a greater energetic return than maize cultivation, with only a few shellfish taxa and small-seed harvesting ranking lower. Depending on specific year-to-year conditions, slash-and-burn farming must have often generated lower caloric returns than most shellfishing and wild plant food collecting options on St. Catherines. This means that if a female grower cared only about energetic returns, she would do better by walking away from her cornfields and instead gathering hickory nuts and acorns (in the fall) or collecting hard clams (year-round).

But solid archaeological, bioarchaeological, and documentary evidence shows that significant maize cultivation and consumption did indeed take place two centuries before European arrival, which raises the following question: if growing corn is less energy-efficient than harvesting most marsh resources—and it certainly seems to be—why did late-precontact St. Catherines Islanders invest so heavily in maize cultivation?[29]

Why Did St. Catherines' Shellfishers Become Farmers?

According to undergraduate western civilization teachers, the Neolithic Revolution opened the doors to advanced civilization as we know it. We are all familiar with the scenario: some genius figured out how to domesticate animals and farm crops like wheat, corn, and rice—thereby precipitating a human population explosion. Because the others no longer had to hunt and gather acorns to feed themselves, they could think great thoughts and provide the world with monumental architecture, art, science, and literature. Farming was seen as the trigger for global civilization—reflecting the long-held belief that agriculture invariably yields a net increase in harvested food energy over that provided by foraging alone (conventionally viewed as less productive, less reliable, and certainly less desirable).

In his classic *Antiquities of the Southern Indians*, for instance, Charles C.

Jones Jr. in 1873 extolled the virtues of maize agriculture for Native people in Georgia:

> Maize, an American plant ... has received ready acknowledgment wherever introduced to the notice of civilized man. Regarded as a direct gift from the Author of Life to his red children, it was highly prized and held in peculiar esteem. ... Attached to the soil, often building considerable towns fortified by palisades and composed of huts and houses substantial after their kind ... they lifted themselves at least somewhat above that rude, beggarly, and precarious existence which so painfully characterized the condition of so many of the aborigines inhabiting other portions of this country, oppressed by greater penury and contending against the rigors of more tempestuous seasons.[30]

Jones's characterization of foraging as "rude, beggarly, and precarious" typifies a long-held attitude toward making a living as a hunter, a gatherer, or a fisher. More recently, in 1976, the eminent anthropologist Charles Hudson reflected on a Mississippian cultural tradition that uplifted hunter-gatherers in the Southeast—in almost bootstrap fashion—from their "bleak" foraging roots: "Agriculture did not replace food gathering in the [interior] Southeast, but existed side by side with it, making life more pleasant and secure."[31]

St. Catherines Island is one of the first places where archaeologists learned that this received wisdom is wrong. Farming did not tap a new energy source that alleviated the uncertainties of foraging.[32] Ethnohistorian and archaeologist John Worth has chided the conventional wisdom that sees a more intensive agricultural base as providing additional leisure time and an "inevitable florescence of elaborate cultural achievements such as art and public architecture. [The] emergence of an agriculture economy in the Southeast (and indeed around the world) was actually accompanied by a substantial increase in the need for collective human labor in order to effectively implement such a system."[33]

Prehistoric maize cultivation on St. Catherines Island must be situated within the overall Late Mississippian sociopolitical structure of Georgia.[34] The years AD 900 through 1450 saw a progressive buildup of major Mississippian occupations, with four significant chiefdoms dominating from modern-day Savannah all the way up through the Savannah River Valley. Dendrochronology (based on tree-ring sequences developed for bald cypress) recorded a remarkably severe drought around AD 1359–77, destroying maize crops and crippling the Mississippian populations living along the Savannah River. A combination of extreme environmental stress and shifting political landscapes led to the abandonment of the valley, which had become a "wilderness" by the time of Hernando de Soto's arrival in 1540.[35] Almost overnight, the complex foragers of St. Catherines Island were propelled into the intense regional political competition between rival chiefdoms of the Mississippian world of Georgia—and this is precisely when maize cultivation took hold. Although significant shellfishing continued, St. Catherines Island foragers began intensive maize farming by AD 1400 or so.[36]

Less than two centuries later, the earliest European explorers documented that Guale (pronounced "Wally") populations living on St. Catherines Island were engaged in highly productive maize farming. They were not only tending subsistence fields to feed their families, but farmers also sowed and cultivated designated cornfields for their elite—the caciques, healers, interpreters, and all others deemed worthy of tribute. They maintained large, communal fields to feed widows, orphans, and travelers; to finance public feasts; and to provide rations for those working on construction projects, long-distance trade, or military campaigns.[37] The most productive terrestrial and estuarine resource patches were owned by chiefly matrilineages, which required subordinates to pay tributary obligations for foraging rights.[38]

And therein lies our answer. Although expanding Mississippian populations had begun to degrade the marshland shellfishery, the local natural environment could still feed St. Catherines Islanders more efficiently than maize agriculture. Why would shellfishers become corn farmers? The simple answer is "tribute." When St. Catherines Islanders joined the larger Mississippian world of mainland Georgia, they discovered that the price of admission was maize, paid in the form of tribute. Easy to store, transport, and quantify, maize was the primary currency that fueled the Mississippian world, and the geopolitics of Georgia ultimately transferred this practice even to the shellfishers of St. Catherines Island. To be sure, growing corn was less efficient and more expensive than shellfishing, and there was heightened risk due to the droughts, torrential rains, and insect infestations that destroyed crops.

THE FIRST ATTEMPT AT SPANISH
UTOPIA IN NORTH AMERICA

The Mississippian world of the Guale was disrupted by the earliest European settlement in the United States.

This assertion may surprise some readers, but consider the larger question: when and where was this country's oldest European settlement? Conventional answers typically vary. Wasn't it Plymouth in 1620? No, Jamestown was earlier (in 1607). Roanoke, the earliest British settlement, dates back to 1585. Then, of course, there is St. Augustine, established by Pedro Menéndez de Avilés in 1565, right? While these answers recall single European moments in United States history, none is correct.

The earliest documented European settlement in the United States is the virtually forgotten colony of San Miguel de Gualdape, established by Lucas Vásquez de Ayllón in 1526. The exact location of San Miguel remains unknown. For quite a while, most scholars thought that San Miguel must be someplace in South Carolina. But compelling research by the distinguished historian Paul Hoffman of Louisiana State University strongly suggests that San Miguel was actually located in coastal Georgia, likely in McIntosh or Liberty County (and not far from St. Catherines Island). Several of us have looked, but so far we've come up empty.[39]

San Miguel was the first European settlement in North America after the Vikings settled in northern Newfoundland five centuries earlier.[40] The settlement of San Miguel predated Oglethorpe's Georgia enterprise by 207 years. This full-blown Spanish settlement, geared up for the long term, included Spaniards and Españolans (some married with families), a number of enslaved Africans, Indian interpreters, secular clergy, surgeons, and Dominican friars.[41]

Ayllón believed that, to achieve self-sufficiency, his new colony needed to rapidly establish a productive agricultural economy, and San Miguel's location was deliberately selected for its perceived farming potential. Steeped in the Ptolemaic geography of the time, Ayllón believed that lands situated at the same distance from the pole must share similar flora, fauna, and climate. It stood to reason that the Georgia Bight could potentially become a "new Andalusia" with the agricultural sylvan and mineral riches of his Hispanic homeland.[42]

Ayllón wanted to set up his colony next to a settled Native American population large enough to provide food, labor, and other necessities to the newcomers. Through peaceful trade rather than warfare and coercion, the Native locals would nurture the San Miguel settlers through the upcoming winter, when they could plant their own fields. So confident was his belief in the power of Hispanic culture, both material and spiritual, that Ayllón financed the San Miguel enterprise himself.[43]

Ayllón's plan unraveled almost at once. His largest ship was lost in transit, along with its cargo. Ayllón failed to find the anticipated Native American settlements, although search parties scouted inland in the hopes of finding populations with food supplies that could be acquired through barter, taken as tribute, or otherwise appropriated. Ayllón sometimes led these expeditions personally, and the process so exhausted him that he fell gravely ill. Supplies dwindled as winter set in, and many other settlers sickened too.

Ayllón died at San Miguel on October 18, 1526, and what happened next is unclear. Surviving documentary testimony suggests that an uprising broke out, with one faction trying to abandon the colony and another insisting on remaining.[44] Some colonists moved to an Indian village said to have been three leagues inland, but the coastal Native Georgians apparently failed to appreciate why they should support the Spanish freeloaders, whom they killed in three or four days.

A full-scale mutiny broke out at San Miguel. This confusion likely opened the door for the enslaved Africans to stage a rebellion of their own, and they torched at least part of San Miguel. The Spanish mutineers were overpowered, but the only surviving account does not spell out what happened to the African insurrectionists. Many of the Spanish survivors quit San Miguel sometime in late October or mid-November, but death due to exposure and disease followed them onboard their ship. Of the original 600 who sailed with Ayllón, only 150 made it home to Española. Maybe someday, when someone finds the actual site of San Miguel de Gualdape, archaeology can tell us more about this ill-fated enterprise.

The irony, of course, is that wherever San Miguel was set up, the starving Hispanic settlers must have been surrounded by an abundance of marine, estuarine, and terrestrial resources. But the newcomers were so steeped in Old World attitudes toward farming and agriculture that they were blinded to the coastal Georgia possibilities. St. Catherines Island foragers survived for millennia on readily available rich marshland and terrestrial resources of the island. Incapable of making the transition from starving farmers to fortunate beachcombers, many San Miguel settlers apparently sickened and starved in the midst of unrecognized bounty.

THE MISSISSIPPIAN SHATTER ZONE

Little more than a decade after Ayllón's failed attempt to colonize the Georgia coast, in 1540 Hernando de Soto probed interior Georgia for colonial possibilities. De Soto's party of 620 men and 220 horses, like most Hispanic explorations of the day, did not transport its own food supply, relying instead on plundering stored provisions from Native communities they met along the way.[45] Beginning in the swampy Gulf Coast, the Spaniards found much of the Tampa Bay landscape covered with standing water and ill-suited for Indian agriculture. Moving inland to the Mississippian heartland, the expedition moved across the piedmont, with its rich bottomlands along the courses of major rivers. De Soto saw that Indian farms prospered near Georgia's fall line, exploiting the light, well-drained, and nutrient-rich soils that were easily tilled with simple tools. The rivers flooded periodically, renewing the land and giving rise to an intensive type of agriculture, in which considerable quantities of maize, beans, and squash could be grown on small parcels of land.[46] De Soto traversed much of Mississippian America, and whenever he approached the margins of that world, he turned back to the farming towns of the interior. Although it failed to find gold and silver, the de Soto expedition had indeed located Native farming communities capable of supporting a Spanish colony.

Or so they thought. The next Europeans to pass through interior Georgia would find a social and environmental landscape vastly changed from what de Soto had experienced. While cutting this seventeenth-century exploratory swath through interior Georgia, de Soto's expedition had unwittingly destabilized the very chiefdoms he counted on to support the new Spanish enterprise.

These Mississippian chiefdoms were overseen and integrated by the personal power of a paramount chief (called "cacique" by the Spanish and "mico" by the Mississippians, Native ancestors of the Muskogean people). Anthropologists have long emphasized the relative instability of such Mississippian chiefdoms, which were typically overextended economically and rife with warfare, competition, and internal strife.[47] David Anderson's term "cycling" characterizes the sociopolitical change accompanying the conflict between and within such chiefdoms.[48]

Some savvy micos may have used de Soto's presence to bolster local power. But overall the fragile ties that bound together these interior Mississippian chiefdoms frayed in the presence of this new, more powerful Spanish force that upset the balance of indigenous leadership.[49] The direct military assaults certainly took a toll, made worse by the expedition's prolonged stay. De Soto's men ransacked stored food supplies and precipitated hardship for all and starvation for some. The failure of caciques to protect food stores weakened their hold over the fragile chiefdoms. Interior chiefdoms collapsed in rapid succession following de Soto's *entrada* (entry), creating a "Mississippian shatter zone" in his wake.[50]

BUILDING LA FLORIDA

An entirely different scenario played out along the Georgia-Florida coastline, where Pedro Menéndez de Avilés founded the colony of La Florida in 1565.[51] Establishing this strategic Spanish coastal foothold had become an imperial imperative to safeguard the treasure-laden fleets of the Indies passing through the Bahama Channel to sail back to Spain. The overarching strategic significance ensured a relatively stable source of royal funding but also required that Spanish colonists of La Florida rely heavily on coastal Native American populations to buffer against interruptions in external supply lines.

With rare exceptions, the soldiers and friars of St. Augustine stuck pretty close to the Atlantic coastline and Apalachee province to the southwest, home to Native people known as the Apalachee. In stark contrast to the "Mississippian shatter zone" of interior Georgia, Spanish Florida in the mid-seventeenth century would morph into a multiethnic colonial society based on unique political and economic relations between the Mississippian and Hispanic worlds.[52] Critical to this enterprise was the Spanish mission system that expanded from St. Augustine northward across coastal Georgia.

MISSIONIZING THE GEORGIA COAST

The contract of Pedro Menéndez de Avilés with the Spanish Crown required that he take with him to La Florida members from a newly formed religious community, the Society of Jesus—better known as the Jesuits. The La Florida enterprise represented the Jesuits' first missionary endeavor in the New World, but after a five-year missionary effort, the Jesuits decided that coastal Florida and Georgia lacked sufficient potential and withdrew wholesale.[53]

Following the Jesuit fiasco, Governor Menéndez turned to the Franciscans, who successfully missionized the Georgia coast. At its peak, approximately seventy Franciscan friars served La Florida at once, with approximately twenty-five thousand Indians in thirty-eight missions—considerably larger than their southwestern or California counterparts. The mission chain extending out of St. Augustine was eventually overrun by British slave raids that demolished missions along the Georgia coastline and across Apalachee by 1702.

Mission Santa Catalina de Guale

The missions of coastal Georgia are largely invisible today, but they had a lasting effect on the landscape and cultures of its Native peoples—and on the course of early colonial history. Mission Santa Catalina de Guale (on St. Cath-

FIGURE 2.1. Aerial photograph of the central compound at Mission Santa Catalina de Guale (St. Catherines Island, Georgia). True north is at the top, and the cleared area covers one hectare; the white plus-sign marks (+) are placed at twenty-meter intervals. The location of these sixteenth- and seventeenth-century mission structures was entirely unknown until discovery by the American Museum of Natural History in 1981. Photograph by Dennis O'Brien, courtesy of the American Museum of Natural History and the St. Catherine's Island Foundation.

erines Island) was an object lesson demonstrating what can be learned from significant scientific explorations of the Spanish period along the Georgia seacoast.

Franciscans established Mission Santa Catalina de Guale sometime in the 1570s, and it survived until 1680, when slavers from Charleston attacked the mission. The abandonment of Mission Santa Catalina signaled the waning of Spanish control in the Southeast and set the stage for British domination of the American colonies.

In 1680, Santa Catalina de Guale was a mission abandoned, and within a few decades it became a mission lost. For the next three hundred years, antiquarians, historians, and archaeologists speculated about the site of the mission, but the combined French, English, and Spanish historic documentation supplied little more than general geographic clues. In 1977, I led a team of archaeologists from the American Museum of Natural History to search for it. After five years of field reconnaissance—combining a probabilistic sampling survey with geophysical prospection (employing proton magnetometry, soil resistivity survey, and ground-penetrating radar analysis)—we found the long-lost Franciscan mission and have been excavating there ever since. The archaeology of Mission Santa Catalina de Guale has turned up multiple surprises and stimulated considerable conversation about the environmental-human relationships along the Georgia coastline.

Why Did the Franciscan Missions Succeed?

Early Jesuit missionary efforts in La Florida were a dismal failure. The priests, who lived for months on St. Catherines Island and elsewhere along the Georgia coast in 1569–70, left vivid accounts that long dominated scholarly thinking about coastal environmental history and the Guale Indians who lived there.[54] The Jesuit Antonio Sedeño, accustomed to the verdant farmlands of his Iberian upbringing, saw the St. Catherines Island landscape "as the most miserable thing ever discovered . . . even though they should wish to [farm,] the soil will not permit it, being thin and miserable and quickly worn out." Juan Rogel, another Jesuit stationed on the Georgia seacoast, complained that "for nine out of the twelve months [the Guale people] wander without any fixed abode . . . each goes his own way . . . they have been accustomed to live in this way for many thousands of years." The Jesuit order abandoned La Florida after only six years, blaming the "miserable" environment of the Georgia coastline, the lack of agricultural potential, and the endlessly wandering Guale Indians for their missionizing failures.[55]

Curiously, early Franciscan accounts had lauded the extraordinary agricultural productivity and potential of this same Georgia coastline. While visiting Franciscan missions along the nearby South Carolina coastline, British explorer William Hilton wrote in 1663 that "for a great space are severall fields of Maize of a very large growth. . . . They have plenty of corn, Pumpions, Water Mellons, Muskmellons. . . . They have two or three crops of Corn a year."[56] In 1597, after Governor Menéndez burned rebel Indian villages along the coast, he boasted, "Great was the harm I did their food stores, for I burned a great quantity of maize and other supplies."[57] That same year, Mission Santa Catalina de Guale and the other coastal Georgia missions shipped 360 *arrobas* of maize (nearly five tons) as annual tribute to the presidio at St. Augustine. Historian Amy Turner Bushnell calls the cornfields of St. Catherines Island "the breadbasket" of Spanish Florida.[58]

Why the conflicting accounts? How could the Jesuits term the St. Catherines Island environment "the most miserable thing ever discovered" and, just two decades later, Franciscan friars turn this same coast into the "breadbasket" of Spanish Florida? Multiple documentary accounts from St. Augustine verify the extraordinary agricultural productivity of the Georgia Sea Islands, prompting a question: did the Jesuits get it wrong?

Probably they did not. We now know that a prolonged drought struck the Georgia coast from 1562 through 1571, with the most severe conditions from 1565 to 1569.[59] The Jesuit missionaries living on the Georgia coast had no way of knowing that this was the driest interval of the sixteenth century. When Rogel and Sedeño wrote of extremely poor harvests, small stores of foodstuffs, rampant hunger, Native rebellions, and local unrest, they recorded exactly what they saw.

The Jesuits were impatient, and their local superior, Juan Baptista de Segura, declared Spanish Florida to be nothing more than a "long pile of sand . . . full of swamps and rivers. Florida," he concluded, "is not for the Society of Jesus."[60] In 1571, the Jesuit general Francisco de Borja pulled all Jesuits from La Florida, admitting, "One can count on the fingers of the hand the number of converts made."[61] Thus the first Jesuit attempt to missionize the New World had ended in utter failure.

Hybrid Town Planning at Mission Santa Catalina de Guale

Archaeological excavations on St. Catherines Island laid bare the earliest town plan in Georgia and reflected visionary principles that differ notably from those employed by James Edward Oglethorpe. The British Georgia colony was both a mercantile and philanthropic venture, initiated by private individuals operating with a Crown charter granting rights to trade and exploit resources. By contrast, institutional religion so thoroughly permeated everyday life in sixteenth-century Spain that all aspects of individual and collective life were, in one way or another, touched by it.

Spanish settlements in coastal Georgia (as elsewhere) were governed by formal policies designed both to apply Christian principles and to reap economic benefits. From the outset, Spanish policies reflected a sense of duty to change the Indians from heathen barbarians into good Christians. Natives were confronted by the priest, the soldier, and the bureaucrat—each of whom answered to a much higher authority.

"The Royal Ordinances Concerning the Laying Out of Towns" issued in 1573 by Philip II prescribed an idealized system for promoting colonization and laying out civil settlements throughout sixteenth-century Spanish America.[62] The royal ordinances compiled 148 regulations dictating the practical aspects of site selection, city planning, and political organization. The St. Catherines Island excavations demonstrate how these Hispanic templates were put in practice at Mission Santa Catalina de Guale. Native Americans at these missions lived a regimented life, and the Hispanic architecture of these settlements reflects the rigid organization of space, an idealized Spanish template upon which American forms were modeled.

But the Franciscan missions of the Georgia coast also embodied elements of local Mississippian architecture, including council houses capable of sheltering thousands.[63] Long the most important feature of Mississippian settlements, the council house functioned variously as the seat of chiefly government, community meeting place, place for ceremonialism, locus for interacting with Spanish authorities, and place to house enemy scalps. The council house at Mission San Luis fronted the main mission plaza, directly across from the mission church—the material consequence of a unique blending of Indigenous and Franciscan logic of place. Similarly, several missions in La Florida sported ball courts, where *pelota* games pitted traditional rivals in sometimes-violent combat.[64] These compromises in ritualized mission architecture constitute a hybrid blend of Franciscan ideals played out in the context of continuing Mississippian beliefs and motivations.[65]

Franciscans as "Amiable Anarchists"

The Guale cacique on St. Catherines Island pledged allegiance and obedience to Spanish officials, but some other Guale caciques refused to do so. Those paramounts siding with the Spanish not only annexed a powerful military ally, they also gained access to new tools and technologies.[66] John Worth compares the roles of Franciscan friars stationed along the Georgia coast to modern Peace Corps workers functioning among Indigenous communities as cultural brokers and agents of collaborative change.

Archaeological investigations reveal the nature of these hybrid Hispanic-Mississippian ideologies.[67] Whereas Franciscan practice called for burial without grave goods and embellishments, the Guale leaders felt differently. Virtually all of the 432 neophyte Guale Indians buried at Mission Santa Catalina were interred in characteristic Christian burial posture—in unmarked graves beneath the church floor, feet toward the altar, with arms crossed on chest. But for three millennia, native St. Catherines Islanders had believed specific grave goods were necessary to navigate the afterlife. Our excavations in dozens of pre-Columbian burial mounds on the island reflect the sacred and secular wishes of the now-dead. These long-standing Indigenous beliefs were clearly practiced at Mission Santa Catalina, where the church interments were accompanied by a truly astounding array of associated grave goods: complete majolica vessels, dozens of projectile points, a rattlesnake shell gorget, glass cruets, two dozen religious medallions (of bronze, gold, and silver), finger rings,

FIGURE 2.2. Bishop Gregory Hartmayer, a Franciscan, celebrating a Mass at the reconsecrated archaeological site of Mission Santa Catalina de Guale (St. Catherines Island, Georgia), the oldest church in Georgia. Each of the large cabbage palm trees has been planted on a major support beam of the seventeenth-century *iglesia*, creating a living, breathing church. Photograph by Nicholas Triozzi, courtesy of the American Museum of Natural History and the St. Catherine's Island Foundation.

and copper plaques. The cemetery also contained seventy thousand glass trade beads sewn onto clothing and sashes and made into jewelry and ornaments. Despite the Franciscan prohibition on grave goods, the cemetery at Mission Santa Catalina de Guale contained more Franciscan religious paraphernalia than is known from all the other sixteenth- and seventeenth-century missions in America put together.

Demise of Georgia's Coastal Missions

These Spanish colonial-Mississippian mission hybrids functioned to provide the external support necessary to maintain the authority of hereditary chiefs, who clung to timeworn vestiges of traditional rank and privilege. But the demographic and political realities of Spanish colonial existence doomed the missions of La Florida.[68] A near-total demographic collapse and English-sponsored slave raids would ultimately force surviving Franciscan missions southward into the shadow of St. Augustine. Spanish colonial officials, Franciscan friars, and Mississippian leaders in La Florida all complained, in effect,

The Guale People of Mission Santa Catalina

The Native people residing at Mission Santa Catalina de Guale on St. Catherines Island, Georgia, during the seventeenth century have generally been categorized as "the Guale people." Recent ethnohistoric and archaeological research, however, complicates this simplistic picture of a monolithic Guale identity. Documentary evidence suggests that the population at Mission Santa Catalina was actually an aggregation of numerous smaller Guale villages. While most of these were unnamed in the documentary record, the Mission Santa Catalina population also included the relocated Guale population of Mission San Diego de Satuache, which was located on the Georgia mainland until around 1663 to 1666, when it fled to St. Catherines for protection from British-allied slave raiders.

My own archaeological work at Mission Santa Catalina has indicated that these episodes of population aggregation are visible in the artifacts excavated at Mission Santa Catalina. Archaeological surveys and detailed subsurface mapping all indicate that the Santa Catalina residential area—rather than being evenly distributed across the site—was composed of at least five distinct and spatially segregated neighborhoods, likely corresponding to the multiple Guale villages assembling on St. Catherines Island.

Some researchers, studying food remains from Mission Santa Catalina, have identified differences in foodways between these mission neighborhoods. Analyses of remains of vertebrate fauna, such as deer and fish bones, indicate differences

Altamaha ceramic vessel recovered at Mission Santa Catalina de Guale, in the St. Catherine's Island Foundation and Edward John Noble Foundation Collection at Fernbank Museum of Natural History. Photo by Elliot H. Blair.

in the types of food being processed and consumed across the mission community, with some Guale groups consuming higher-quality cuts of venison and other Guale groups consuming more estuarine fishes. My own analyses of ceramics recovered from these neighborhoods also indicate differences among the aggregated Guale communities. While almost all of the ceramics found at the site are stylistically identical, fine-grained analyses of the technology used to manufacture these objects revealed significant differences in how the Guale potters within each neighborhood practiced their craft. These include differences in where potters were obtaining raw materials, the process of how the ceramics were being decorated, and how these materials were being fired. Though the pottery looks similar, detailed material analysis revealed distinct, spatially segregated groups of potters living at Mission Santa Catalina.

These recent data, suggesting variable patterns of daily activities and reflecting significant social differentiation within the aggregated community, highlight one of the most important aspects of the Mission Santa Catalina colonial experience: the central story of this colonial interaction is not about the relationship between the Spanish and the Guale, since only a handful of Spaniards were ever residing in the area at one time. Instead, the central story is about the pluralistic interaction of the diverse Guale communities, living together and maintaining distinct social identities even in the context of population aggregation. Rather than monolithically categorizing the Santa Catalina community as "the Guale people," this new research suggests "the Guale peoples" might be a better description.

ELLIOT H. BLAIR

that they were "running out of Indians."[69] The Franciscan missions of the Mississippian South survived for thirteen decades in a "functioning, though inherently flawed, colonial system," in the words of Worth.[70] By the late seventeenth century, Worth writes, "there were too many chiefs and nobles, and not enough subordinate Indians to support their existence. . . . In clinging to their traditional power by birthright, the mission chiefs ultimately ensured the persistence of a dysfunctional sociopolitical system that would not survive the trauma of the colonial era."[71] The diversity evident in such missionizing strategies is striking—perhaps reflecting to some degree a modern Franciscan self-perception as "amiable anarchists" willing to bend some rules to achieve the ultimate goal of salvation.[72] At a minimum, the colonial strategy of La Florida facilitated the survival of ancient chiefly lineages and Mississippian-

FIGURE 2.3. Gold and silver pietà from seventeenth-century
Mission Santa Catalina de Guale on St. Catherines Island, Georgia.
Photograph by Bill Ballenberg, courtesy of the American Museum
of Natural History and the St. Catherine's Island Foundation.

style social systems long after the total collapse of Indigenous interior polities
in the "Mississippian shatter zone."[73]

SOME ECHOES FROM DEEP HISTORY

This essay has tried to establish a baseline for understanding human-
environmental interactions in the millennia before 1733. That's a pretty tall order—one that I haven't entirely fulfilled—but some themes have emerged in
the process.

The barrier island environment of coastal Georgia is unique in the world, and so are some of the human adaptations to it. Barrier islands usually shape-shift in equilibrium with the tides and sea level, characteristically with arid and windswept landscapes dotted with sparse and depauperate vegetation. The Sea Islands are not typical barrier islands because, for more than one hundred thousand years, the underlying processes have driven sea level change, ocean sediment loads, and current patterns to craft a unique geomorphology—manifest in extraordinarily diverse tidal and dryland landscapes, the immediate juxtaposition of rich marine and terrestrial ecosystems, and a remarkable hydrological balance. But the downside of such uniqueness is that they are extraordinarily fragile and subject to short-term climatic fluctuations.

Half a century ago, archaeologist Joseph Caldwell pointed out that each of Georgia's Sea Islands probably has a unique human and environmental history.[74] With this caution in mind, St. Catherines Island is exemplary of the Sea Island chain—a place that can help foster a more complete understanding of the long-term human-environmental relationships that played out here.

The St. Catherines Island story—addressed from the perspective of deep history—is all about breaking up myths of human-environmental interactions. The first St. Catherines Islanders reacted to this unique landscape by re-writing the Indigenous rules of barrier island life. These first foragers defined a shellfishing economy that would persist, largely unchanged, for five thousand years. They settled down in year-round villages, built monumental shell-ring constructions, and manufactured the earliest pottery in North America.[75] A thousand years ago, the Mississippian people of St. Catherines Island evolved from their original egalitarian communities into complex chiefdoms, governed by powerful hereditary elites. Across most of the globe, transformations like this took place only within the framework of surging agricultural economies. St. Catherines Islanders engineered this evolutionary landmark entirely within the context of their long-term shellfishing lifeway.[76]

When these chiefdoms did eventually adopt maize agriculture, they did so with a characteristic St. Catherines Island twist—becoming farmers not because cornfields better fed their populace (which they did not), but rather to maximize their social, economic, political, and military leverage within the greater Mississippian society. In effect, the payment and collection of maize-based tribute, offerings, and taxes represented the social payment for the costs of performing rituals and conducting warfare for the polity as a whole—basically the cost of protecting the group within their culturally defined global world system, as they then knew it.

The earliest post-Viking European settlers to North America tried to colonize the Georgia coastline in 1526. But because the leaders of the San Miguel de Gualdape colony had so wholly embraced the Eurocentric myth of New Andalucia, they fully expected that European-style agricultural, sylvan, and mineral riches awaited their Georgian arrival. They completely misread the environmental and human landscape of coastal Georgia and paid the price.

Aware of Ayllón's failure, early Spanish conquistadores avoided the Georgia coastline altogether and marched into the interior Mississippian heartland. In their own way, the de Soto expedition's misunderstanding of the Mississippian landscape unwittingly undermined and destroyed the very Indigenous communities targeted for successful colonization. The result was the irreversible "Mississippian shatter zone" that came to characterize interior Georgia.

Ironically, when global strategic considerations required that the Florida peninsula be secured against British and French incursions, the Spanish Crown would establish La Florida to colonize coastal Florida and the Georgia coastline—returning to exactly the environmental setting prized by Ayllón and spurned by de Soto.

The history of Georgia's Spanish missions demonstrates the long-term evolution of fragile coastal landscapes. Jesuit missionaries would reprise Ayllón's misperceptions of the Sea Island landscape, arriving in a time of extreme drought and prematurely declaring coastal Georgia "the most miserable thing ever discovered" and "not Jesuit territory." Menéndez de Avilés would die within the decade (while commanding the Spanish Armada), unaware that the droughts had passed and that the Franciscan-Guale alliance had established St. Catherines Island as the "breadbasket" of Spanish Florida.

The same Echaw-Foxworth-Centenary soils that supported the Franciscan maize fields would underpin the antebellum Sea Island cotton plantations. But a century of intensive mission horticulture had worn out the soils to the extent that antebellum plantation farmers avoided the old mission fields altogether (leaving the mission ruins unplowed and undisturbed, creating a bonanza for the archaeologists to come later).

Coastal Georgia historiography has long been dominated by perspectives of informed (if occasionally heavy-handed) readings of textual evidence, thus skewed toward the Georgia colony at the expense of Indigenous and Hispanic populations already living there. Constructed centuries after the fact, this re-created colonial America mostly in terms of culture clash, encouraging investigators to dwell almost exclusively on themes of conquest, disease, assimilation, and loss—too often resulting in so-called terminal narratives.[77]

Although rarely addressed by environmental historians, the early days of La Florida dramatically highlight the productive yet brittle fabric of the coastal landscape—and particularly the islands' vulnerability to short-term climatic change. The historiography and archaeology clearly demonstrate that Oglethorpe and his colleagues did not inherit a blank slate upon which to impose their vision. Deeper historical perspectives reveal the uniqueness and fragility that have characterized the human-environmental relationships along the Georgia coast for millennia.

NOTES

I particularly thank the St. Catherine's Island Foundation and the Edward John Noble Foundation for supporting the long-term archaeological program on St. Catherines Island and gratefully acknowledge the assistance of Royce Hayes (former island superintendent and present program director) and Mike Halderson (current island superintendent) for helping to make it happen. I appreciate Paul Pressly's invitation to participate in the Coastal Nature, Coastal Culture symposium and am grateful for the guidance of Paul Sutter in crafting this volume. Diana Rosenthal and Lorann Pendleton Thomas helped prepare my manuscript.

1. Richard A. Davis and Duncan M. Fitzgerald, *Beaches and Coasts* (Malden, Mass.: Blackwell Publishing, 2004), 133; Orrin H. Pilkey, *A Celebration of the World's Barrier Islands* (New York: Columbia University Press, 2003), 29.

2. John M. Zeigler, "Origin of the Sea Islands of the Southeastern United States," *Geographical Review* 49 (1959): 222–37.

3. Pilkey, *Celebration of the World's Barrier*, 244–46, 253.

4. Zeigler, "Origin of the Sea Islands," 225–26.

5. Chester B. DePratter and James D. Howard, "History of Shoreline Changes Determined by Archaeological Dating: Georgia Coast, U.S.A.," *Transactions–Gulf Coast Association of Geological Societies* 27 (1977): 252–58; Chester B. DePratter and James D. Howard, "Indian Occupation and Geologic History of the Georgia Coast: A 5000 Year Summary," in *Excursions in Southeastern Geology: The Archaeology-Geology of the Georgia Coast*, Guidebook 20, Geological Society of America, ed. James D. Howard, Chester B. DePratter, and Robert W. Frey (Atlanta: Georgia Department of Natural Resources, 1980); George F. Oertel, "Post-Pleistocene Island and Inlet Adjustment along the Georgia Coast," *Journal of Sedimentary Petrology* 45 (1975): 150–59.

6. Gale A. Bishop, Harold B. Rollins, and David Hurst Thomas, eds., *Geoarchaeology of St. Catherines Island, Georgia*, Anthropological Papers of the American Museum of Natural History 94 (New York: American Museum of Natural History, 2011); David Hurst Thomas, *Native American Landscapes of St. Catherines Island, Georgia*, 3 vols., Anthropological Papers of the American Museum of Natural History 88 (New York: American Museum of Natural History, 2008).

7. A. Sydney Johnson, Hilburn O. Hillestad, Sheryl F. Shanholtzer, and G. Frederick Shanholtzer, *An Ecological Survey of the Coastal Region of Georgia,* National Park Service Scientific Monograph Series, No. 3 (Washington, D.C.: National Park Service, 1974).

8. Quoted in Virginia Steele Wood and Mary R. Bullard, introduction to Jonathan Bryan, *Journal of a Visit to the Georgia Islands of St. Catherines, Green, Ossabaw, Sapelo, St. Simons, Jekyll, and Cumberland, with Comments on the Florida Islands of Amelia, Talbot, and St. George, in 1753* (Macon: Mercer University Press, 1996), 19–20. Bryan was accompanied by William Gerard DeBrahm, a well-known cartographer and the most prolific southeastern mapmaker of his era. See also Royce H. Hayes and David Hurst Thomas, "The Hydrology of St. Catherines Island," in Thomas, *Native American Landscapes of St. Catherines Island,* vol. 1, 56–58.

9. See also William Hilton, "A Relation of a Discovery [1664]," in *Narratives of Early Carolina, 1650–1708,* ed. Alexander S. Salley Jr. (New York: Charles Scribner's Sons, 1911), 31–62; Robert Sanford, "A Relation of a Voyage on the Coast of the Province of Carolina, 1666," in *Narratives of Early Carolina, 1650–1708,* ed. Alexander S. Salley Jr. (New York: Charles Scribner's Sons, 1911), 75–108; Philipp Georg Friedrich von Reck and Kristian Hvidt, *Von Reck's Voyage: Drawings and Journal of Philip Georg Friedrich von Reck* (Savannah: Beehive Press, 1980).

10. James Miller, *An Environmental History of Northeast Florida* (Gainesville: University Press of Florida, 1998), 23.

11. William Boyd (chap. 8 of this book) provides a thorough discussion of the Floridan Aquifer, its geological structure, and its alarming susceptibility to saltwater intrusion.

12. Victor D. Thompson and John E. Worth, "Dwellers by the Sea: Native American Adaptations along the Southern Coasts of Eastern North America," *Journal of Archaeological Research* 19 (2011): 51–101.

13. Max Uhle, "The Emeryville Shellmound," *University of California Publications on American Archaeology and Ethnology* 7 (1907): 31.

14. Alan J. Osborn, "Strandloopers, Mermaids, and Other Fairy Tales: Ecological Determinants of Marine Resource Utilization—The Peruvian Case," in *For Theory Building in Archaeology,* ed. Lewis R. Binford (New York: Academic Press, 1977), 158, 172.

15. Betty Meehan, *Shell Bed to Shell Midden* (Canberra: Australian National University, 1982), 160.

16. Thomas, *Native American Landscapes of St. Catherines Island.*

17. Meehan, *Shell Bed to Shell Midden,* 160.

18. Sarah G. Bergh, "Subsistence, Settlement, and Land-use Changes during the Mississippian Period on St. Catherines Island, Georgia," PhD diss., Department of Anthropology, University of Georgia, 2012; Sarah G. Bergh, "Late Prehistoric Settlement Patterns: Zooarchaeological Evidence from Back Creek Village, St. Catherines Island," in *Seasonality and Human Mobility along the Georgia Bight,* Anthropological Papers of the American Museum of Natural History 97, ed. Elizabeth J. Reitz, Irvy

R. Quitmyer, and David Hurst Thomas (New York: American Museum of Natural History, 2012), 103–22; Nicole R. Cannarozzi, "Estimating the Season of Harvest of Eastern Oyster (*Crassostrea virginica*) from St. Catherines Shell Ring," in *Seasonality and Human Mobility along the Georgia Bight*, Anthropological Papers of the American Museum of Natural History 97, ed. Elizabeth J. Reitz, Irvy R. Quitmyer, and David Hurst Thomas (New York: American Museum of Natural History, 2012), 171–86; Carol E. Colaninno, "Zooarchaeological Analysis of Vertebrate Remains from Five Late Archaic Shell Rings on the Georgia Coast, USA," PhD diss., Department of Anthropology, University of Georgia, 2010; Elizabeth J. Reitz, "Nonhuman Vertebrate Remains," in Thomas, *Native American Landscapes of St. Catherines Island, vol. 2*, 615–65.

19. Harold B. Rollins and David Hurst Thomas, "Geomorphology, Sea Level, and Marine Resources," in *Geoarchaeology of St. Catherines Island, Georgia*, Anthropological Papers of the American Museum of Natural History 94, ed. Gale A. Bishop, Harold B. Rollins, and David Hurst Thomas (New York: American Museum of Natural History, 2011), 319–38.

20. David Hurst Thomas, "Terrestrial Foraging," in *Native American Landscapes of St. Catherines Island, Georgia*, Anthropological Papers of the American Museum of Natural History 88, pt. 1 (New York: American Museum of Natural History, 2008), 140–42.

21. David Hurst Thomas, "Diet Breadth," in *Native American Landscapes of St. Catherines Island, Georgia*, Anthropological Papers of the American Museum of Natural History 88, vol. 3 (New York: American Museum of Natural History, 2008), 961–63. The "island syndrome" is discussed in Gregory H. Adler and Richard Levins, "The Island Syndrome in Rodent Populations," *Quarterly Review of Biology* 69 (1994): 473–90.

22. All age estimates are expressed in calibrated radiocarbon years AD and BC, per conventions spelled out in Thomas, *Native American Landscapes of St. Catherines Island*.

23. David Hurst Thomas and Clark Spencer Larsen, *The Anthropology of St. Catherines Island*, vol. 2, *The Refuge-Deptford Mortuary Complex*, Anthropological Papers of the American Museum of Natural History 56, pt. 1 (New York: American Museum of Natural History, 1979); David Hurst Thomas, "Population Growth, Intensification, and the Emergence of Social Inequity on St. Catherines Island," in *Native American Landscapes of St. Catherines Island*, Anthropological Papers of the American Museum of Natural History 88, pt. 3 (New York: American Museum of Natural History, 2008), 1046–79.

24. Thomas, "Population Growth," 1046–79. See also Kent Flannery and Joyce Marcus, *The Creation of Inequality: How Our Prehistoric Ancestors Set the Stage for Monarchy, Slavery, and Empire* (Cambridge, Mass.: Harvard University Press, 2012).

25. Clark Spencer Larsen, Margaret J. Schoeninger, Nikolaas J. van der Merwe, Katherine M. Moore, and Julia A. Lee-Thorp, "Carbon and Nitrogen Stable Isotopic Signatures of Human Dietary Change in the Georgia Bight," *American Journal of*

Physical Anthropology 89 (1992): 197–214; Thomas, *Native American Landscapes of St. Catherines Island.*

26. See also Bergh, *Subsistence, Settlement, and Land-use Changes*; Irvy R. Quitmyer and Douglas S. Jones, "Annual Incremental Shell Growth Patterns in Hard Clams (*Mercenaria* spp.) from St. Catherines Island, Georgia: A Record of Seasonal and Anthropogenic Impact on Zooarchaeological Resources," in *Seasonality and Human Mobility along the Georgia Bight*, Anthropological Papers of the American Museum of Natural History 97, ed. Elizabeth J. Reitz, Irvy R. Quitmyer, and David Hurst Thomas (New York: American Museum of Natural History, 2012), 135–48; Rollins and Thomas, "Geomorphology, Sea Level, and Marine Resources," 319–38.

27. Bergh, *Subsistence, Settlement, and Land-use Changes*; John E. Worth, "Guale," in *Handbook of North American Indians*, vol. 14, *Southeast*, ed. Raymond D. Fogelson (Washington, D.C.: Smithsonian Institution Press, 2004), 238–44.

28. K. Renee Barlow, "A Formal Model for Predicting Agriculture among the Fremont," in *Foraging Theory and the Transition to Agriculture*, ed. Douglas J. Kennett and Bruce Winterhalder (Berkeley: University of California Press, 2006), 87–102. See also Thomas, *Native American Landscapes of St. Catherines Island.*

29. Larsen et al., "Carbon and Nitrogen Stable Isotopic Signatures"; Thomas, *Native American Landscapes of St. Catherines Island*; Worth, "Guale."

30. Charles Colcock Jones Jr., *Antiquities of the Southern Indians, Particularly of the Georgia Tribes* (New York: D. Appleton, 1873), 296–97.

31. Charles Hudson, *The Southeastern Indians* (Knoxville: University of Tennessee Press, 1976), 288–89.

32. There is also a pronounced downside to maize farming. Maize consumption causes high rates of tooth cavities—reasons behind this are varied and complex, but the chief factor is the presence of sucrose (a simple sugar) in maize, which is readily metabolized by oral bacteria. The specific results include infection (as periosteal reactions), dental caries, high rates of dental enamel defects, reduced levels of child growth and development, and reduced adult height. As with other agricultural practices, corn farming also tends to foster rapid population expansion, overcrowding, and poor nutrition. Health declined globally with the adoption of agriculture, with the focus on a limited number of often poor-quality foods. See Clark Spencer Larsen, *Bioarchaeology: Interpreting Behavior from the Human Skeleton*, 2nd ed., Cambridge Studies in Biological and Evolutionary Anthropology 21 (Cambridge: Cambridge University Press, 1999).

33. John E. Worth, *Timucuan Chiefdoms of Spanish Florida*, vol. 1, *Assimilation* (Gainesville: University of Florida Press, 1998), 6.

34. David G. Anderson, "Chiefly Cycling and Large-scale Abandonment Viewed from the Savannah River Basin," in *Political Structure and Change in the Prehistoric Southeastern United States*, ed. John F. Scarry (Gainesville: University Press of Florida, 1996), 150–91; John H. Blitz, "Mississippian Chiefdoms and the Fusion-Fission Process," *American Antiquity* 64 (1999): 577–92; Thomas, *Native American Landscapes of St. Catherines Island*; David Hurst Thomas, "The Shellfishers of St. Catherines Island:

Hardscrabble Foragers or Farming Beachcombers?," *Journal of Island and Coastal Archaeology* 9 (2014): 169–82.

35. David G. Anderson, *The Savannah River Chiefdoms: Political Change in the Late Prehistoric Southeast* (Tuscaloosa: University of Alabama Press, 1994), 327; Charles M. Hudson, *The Juan Pardo Expeditions: Exploration of the Carolinas and Tennessee, 1566–1568* (Washington, D.C.: Smithsonian Institution Press, 1990), 60–61; Charles M. Hudson, Marvin T. Smith, and Chester B. DePratter, "The Hernando de Soto Expedition: From Apalachee to Chiaha," *Southeastern Archaeology* 3 (1984): 71–72.

36. As amply documented by ethnohistoric and archaeological evidence summarized in David Hurst Thomas, "The 'Guale Problem' Revisited: Farming and Foraging on St. Catherines Island (cal ad 1300–1580)," in *Native American Landscapes of St. Catherines Island*, vol. 3, 1095–1115.

37. The Guale maintained at least two administrative levels, and a complex system of chiefly tribute was well ensconced along the Georgia Bight. Worth, "Guale." Lesser elites paid tribute to higher-ups—defining and formalizing the power relationship within and between chiefdoms "obsessed with status positions, alliances, and trade." Anderson, *Savannah River Chiefdoms*, 77.

38. Worth, *Timucuan Chiefdoms of Spanish Florida*.

39. See Louis De Vorsey and Jeannine Cook, *Columbus and the Land of Ayllón: The Exploration and Settlement of the Southeast* (Valona, Ga.: Lower Altamaha Historical Society—Ayllón, 1992).

40. Helge Ingstad and Anne Stine Ingstad, *The Viking Discovery of America: The Excavation of a Norse Settlement in L'Anse aux Meadows, Newfoundland* (St. John's, Newfoundland: Breakwater Books, 2000).

41. This sketch of San Miguel de Gualdape is grounded in the seminal account of Paul E. Hoffman, *A New Andalucia and a Way to the Orient: The American Southeast during the Sixteenth Century* (Baton Rouge: Louisiana State University Press, 1990), 38. See also Paul E. Hoffman, *Florida's Frontiers* (Bloomington: Indiana University Press, 2002), 24–29; and Douglas T. Peck, "Lucas Vásquez de Ayllón's Doomed Colony of San Miguel de Gualdape," *Georgia Historical Quarterly* 85 (2001): 183–98.

42. Hoffman, *New Andalucia*, 34–36.

43. Ibid., 60–61.

44. Ibid., 76–77.

45. Robbie Ethridge and Jeffrey M. Mitchem, "The Interior South at the Time of Spanish Exploration," in *Native and Spanish New Worlds: Sixteenth-Century Entradas in the American Southwest and Southeast*, ed. Clay Mathers, Jeffrey M. Mitchem, and Charles M. Haecker (Tucson: University of Arizona Press, 2014), 170–88.

46. Hudson, *Southeastern Indians*, 291–93.

47. Robin A. Beck, "Consolidation and Hierarchy: Chiefdom Variability in the Mississippian Southeast," *American Antiquity* 68 (2003): 641–62; J. H. Blitz, "Mississippian Chiefdoms and the Fission-Fusion Process," *American Antiquity* 64 (1999): 577–92.

48. David G. Anderson, "Factional Competition and the Political Evolution of Mississippian Chiefdoms in the Southeastern United States," in *Factional Competition and Political Development in the New World*, ed. Elizabeth M. Brumfiel and John W. Fox (Cambridge: Cambridge University Press, 1994), 61–75; Anderson, "Chiefly Cycling and Large-scale Abandonment."

49. Ethridge and Mitchem, "Interior South at the Time of Spanish Exploration," 182–84. European disease was previously thought to have precipitated the demise of the interior Mississippian chiefdoms, perhaps on the order of a 90 percent population loss. Current scholarship ranks disease as only one of many factors contributing to the demographic collapse.

50. Ethridge and Mitchem, "Interior South at the Time of Spanish Exploration," 170–88.

51. In this context, the terms "La Florida" and "Spanish Florida" include the entire Georgia coastline during the sixteenth and seventeenth centuries.

52. Worth, "Guale"; John E. Worth, "Catalysts of Assimilation: The Role of Franciscan Missionaries in the Colonial System of Spanish Florida," in *From La Florida to La California: Franciscan Evangelization in the Spanish Borderlands*, ed. Timothy J. Johnson and Gert Melville (Berkeley: Academy of American Franciscan History, 2013), 131–42.

53. J. Michael Francis and Kathleen M. Kole, *Murder and Martyrdom in Spanish Florida: Don Juan and the Guale Uprising of 1597*, Anthropological Papers of the American Museum of Natural History 95 (New York: American Museum of Natural History, 2011), 30–34.

54. Lewis Larson, "Aboriginal Subsistence Technology on the Southeastern Coastal Plain During the Late Prehistoric Period," PhD diss., University of Michigan, Department of Anthropology, 1969, 293–97. See also Lewis Larson, *Aboriginal Subsistence Technology on the Southeastern Coastal Plain during the Late Prehistoric Period* (Gainesville: University of Florida Press, 1980).

55. Nicholas P. Cushner, *Why Have You Come Here? The Jesuits and the First Evangelization of Native America* (Oxford: Oxford University Press, 2006), 47–48.

56. William Hilton, "A Relation of a Discovery by William Hilton [1664]," in *Original Narratives of Early American History*, vol. 15, ed. Alexander S. Salley (New York: Charles Scribner's Sons, 1911), 44.

57. Quoted in Grant D. Jones, "The Ethnohistory of the Guale Coast through 1684," in David Hurst Thomas, Grant D. Jones, Roger S. Durham, and Clark Spencer Larsen, *The Anthropology of St. Catherines Island*, vol. 1, *Natural and Cultural History*, Anthropological Papers of the American Museum of Natural History 55, pt. 2 (New York: American Museum of Natural History, 1978), 179–210.

58. Amy Turner Bushnell, *Situado and Sabana: Spain's Support System of the Presidio and Mission Provinces of Florida*, Anthropological Papers of the American Museum of Natural History 74 (New York: American Museum of Natural History, 1994), 147.

59. David W. Stahle, Malcolm K. Cleaveland, Dennis B. Blanton, Matthew D. Therrell, and David A. Gay, "The Lost Colony and Jamestown Droughts," *Science* 280 (5363): 564–67; Thomas, *Native American Landscapes of St. Catherines Island*, fig. 28.5.

60. As cited in Cushner, *Why Have You Come Here?*, 47.

61. Ibid., 47–48.

62. Dora P. Crouch, Daniel J. Garr, and Axel I. Mundigo, *Spanish City Planning in North America* (Cambridge, Mass.: MIT Press, 1982), 13–16; Guillermo de Zéndegui, "City Planning in the Spanish Colonies," *Américas*, special supplement 29 (1977): s1–s12.

63. John H. Hann, "1630 Memorial of Francisco Alonso de Jesús, on Spanish Florida's Missions and Natives," *Américas* 50 (1993): 85–105. See also Gary N. Shapiro and John H. Hann, "The Documentary Image of the Council Houses of Spanish Florida Tested by Excavations at the Mission of San Luis de Talimali," in *Columbian Consequences*, vol. 2, *Archaeological and Historical Perspectives on the Spanish Borderlands East*, ed. David Hurst Thomas (Washington, D.C.: Smithsonian Institution Press, 1990), 511–26; Bonnie G. McEwan, "The Historical Archaeology of Seventeenth-Century La Florida," *Florida Historical Quarterly* 92 (2014): 491–523; Bonnie G. McEwan, "Colonialism on the Spanish Florida Frontier: Mission San Luis, 1656–1704," *Florida Historical Quarterly* 92 (2014): 591–625.

64. Fray Jesús presented the ballgame in a favorable light. See Hann, "1630 Memorial of Francisco Alonso de Jesús"; Amy Turner Bushnell, "'That Demonic Game': The Campaign to Stop Indian Pelota Playing in Spanish Florida, 1675–1684," *Américas* 35 (1978): 1–19.

65. As Elliot Blair correctly notes in *The Guale Peoples of Mission Santa Catalina*, recent archaeological and documentary research demonstrates an unexpected social complexity within the Guale people attached to the Franciscan mission on St. Catherines Island. Beyond the founding Guale population, one or more additional Indian chiefdoms appear to have joined the mission complex in the mid-seventeenth century, at once becoming part of the greater community of Mission Santa Catalina de Guale but maintaining their long-term Mississippian leadership, allegiances, and governance.

66. David Hurst Thomas, "War and Peace on the Franciscan Frontier," in *From La Florida to La California: Franciscan Evangelization in the Spanish Borderlands*, ed. Timothy J. Johnson and Gert Melville (Berkeley: Academy of American Franciscan History, 2013), 105–30.

67. David Hurst Thomas, *St. Catherines: An Island in Time*, Georgia History and Culture Series (Atlanta: Georgia Endowment for the Humanities, 1988).

68. A Franciscan context for this argument is provided by David Hurst Thomas, "The Life and Times of Junípero Serra: A Pan-Borderlands Perspective," *Américas* 71, no. 2 (2014): 185–225.

69. David Hurst Thomas, "Honor and Hierarchies: Long-term Trajectory in the

Pueblo and Mississippian Worlds," in *Native and Spanish New Worlds: Sixteenth-Century Entradas in the American Southwest and Southeast*, ed. Clay Mathers, Jeffrey M. Mitchem, Charles M. Haecker (Tucson: University of Arizona Press, 2013), 251–73.

70. John E. Worth, "Spanish Missions and the Persistence of Chiefly Power," in *The Transformation of the Southeastern Indians, 1540–1760*, ed. Robbie Ethridge and Charles Hudson (Jackson: University Press of Mississippi, 2002), 55.

71. John E. Worth, "Inventing Florida: Constructing a Colonial Society in an Indigenous Landscape," in *Native and Spanish New Worlds: Sixteenth-Century Entradas in the American Southwest and Southeast*, ed. Clay Mathers, Jeffrey M. Mitchem, and Charles M. Haecker (Tucson: University of Arizona Press, 2013), 189–201.

72. I am grateful to Fr. Pat McCloskey for the phrase and for his insights on its larger implications.

73. Robbie Ethridge, "Creating the Shatter Zone: The Indian Slave Trader and the Collapse of the Mississippian World," in *Light on the Path: The Anthropology and History of the Southeastern Indians*, ed. Thomas J. Pluckhahn and Robbie Ethridge (Tuscaloosa: University of Alabama Press, 2006), 207–18.

74. Joseph R. Caldwell, "Chronology of the Georgia Coast," *Southeastern Archaeological Conference Bulletin* 13:89–91.

75. In "The Earliest Residents of the Georgia Coast," a sidebar to this chapter, Matthew Sanger emphasizes the ongoing puzzles of the enigmatic shell rings on St. Catherines Island and elsewhere along the Georgia Bight. At present, their cosmological, ritual, and/or social meanings remain an open question.

76. Albert Way (chap. 7 of this volume) has also appropriately highlighted the long-term use of fire as a land management strategy of indigenous coastal Georgians.

77. Michael V. Wilcox, *The Pueblo Revolt and the Mythology of Conquest: An Indigenous Archaeology of Contact* (Berkeley: University of California Press, 2009), 11–15.

CHAPTER 3

Visualizing the Southern Frontier

Cartography and Colonization in Eighteenth-Century Georgia

S. MAX EDELSON

James Oglethorpe and the other trustees formed Georgia to become a new-modeled colony, one designed from its inception to right the wrongs of unregulated colonization that had characterized North America's colonial history in the seventeenth century. This essay examines the cartographic record of Georgia's changing shape in the eighteenth century by focusing on the iconography of settler aspirations and imperial control as settlers and British officials—frequently at odds—ordered and reordered the colony's territory. It focuses on four moments in which officials attempted to impose a vision of spatial order on the Southeast in a bid to contain and direct the expansive energies of settler colonialism. First, two important published maps from the 1710s imagined mainland British America's southern frontier advancing as new settlers populated contested territories throughout the region. Second, the Yamasee War of 1715, in which southeastern Indians banded together to counter such expansive colonization by attacking South Carolina, shattered the presumption behind these images: that a natural and inevitable process of territorial expansion would plant British subjects within the broad boundaries of lands the Crown regarded as its chartered, sovereign space. In the wake of this war, British mapmakers produced a new body of maps that reflected an ethos of colonization made visible in the rectilinear boundaries of nucleated communities. Maps produced in the 1730s and 1740s illustrated the Georgia Plan as an extension of the idea of defensive expansion, organized around the idealized notion of model towns adapted from schemes of enlightened European social improvement. Third, this essay documents how planters worked to extend the Carolina Lowcountry's plantation landscape to the Georgia coast and thus reorient the colony's settlement pattern after the collapse of Trustee Georgia.

These maps of the 1730s and 1740s described territory in terms of rivers that could support plantation agriculture. Finally, I examine Britain's plan to expand Georgia's boundaries in 1763, following a negotiated end to French and Spanish occupation of eastern North America, and at the same time to restrict the expansion of plantation settlement through boundary diplomacy with Native Americans. Fear of more intensive imperial regulation of land granting drove colonial discontent throughout mainland British America, but this was a special concern in Georgia, where, after a half-century of British attempts to regulate occupation, ambitious settlers rejected the Crown's right to control the pace and extent of colonial expansion.

By taking note of the contrasting iconography drawn and etched onto eighteenth-century maps, we can see more clearly these two different visions of spatial order behind Georgia's changing forms. The image of controlled settlement, imposed by metropolitan authorities on the Georgia landscape, was represented by the rectilinear boundary; that of settler-driven colonization was represented by the sinuous shape of a river. As mapmakers traced the courses of the major waterways that flowed from the continental interior toward the Atlantic Ocean, they established potential vectors for new plantation settlement. Throughout the colony's history, the image of the bounded jurisdiction appeared on maps in tension with the image of the penetrating river, a contrast that marked ongoing conflicts over the development of the colony between those who wanted to limit Georgia's territorial growth and those who strove to expand its reach.

In the generation before Georgia's establishment, British writers, cartographers, and officials looked beyond South Carolina and saw American colonies in danger. Long before the first Georgia settlers arrived in 1733, imperial planners and commentators imagined the space it would occupy as the territorial solution to the problem of a vulnerable southern frontier. Herman Moll, one of Britain's most prolific mapmakers in the late seventeenth and early eighteenth centuries, produced *A New and Exact Map of the Dominions of the King of Great Britain on [the] Continent of North America* in 1715 to picture the mainland colonies, for the first time, as an integrated empire. The map gives a distinctly pro-British cartographic form to the terms of the Treaty of Utrecht, negotiated in 1713 with France, Spain, and other European states to end the War of the Spanish Succession, known in British America as Queen Anne's War. Moll's map, as historian John E. Crowley has argued, distorted sovereignty claims to make this territorial empire seem coherent. It "pushed New England up to the St. Lawrence, limited Louisiana to south of the Ohio River, appropriated Labrador as 'New Britain,' and expansively interpreted how the treaty had affected British claims to Hudson Bay, Newfoundland, and Acadia." Britain could lay claim to this large and integrated territorial empire, Moll's image contended, on the basis of its history of extensive occupation. Moll's map centers on the most settled part of this empire, the band of territory from Virginia to New England, home to some three hundred thousand settlers and slaves.[1]

But along the southern frontier of the empire, the case for the superiority of British numbers on the ground was hard to make. South of Virginia, British and African bodies were few and far between. Moll represents South Carolina's booming rice plantation economy in a large inset to emphasize how British settlers and their slaves were in the process of building rice plantations along the rivers that flowed into Charlestown's harbor. Another inset pictures the southeastern coast from Charlestown to the San Juan River, just north of St. Augustine, as a unified space for plantation enterprise. Moll drew a new boundary around Carolina that included the Savannah and "Allatamaha" Rivers, extending the scope of this rising coastal rice empire. In time, these images implied, such development would create a populous colonial society in the Southeast. In another inset map, Moll imagines the end product of this expansive settlement. For perhaps the very first time on any map, we can see an image of mainland British America labeled "Emp." (for "empire"), representing this array of individual colonies as a unified whole. This empire stretched, at least on paper, from Newfoundland in the north to Spanish Florida in the south. As Moll's map makes clear, taking possession of this imagined empire demanded intensive settlement south of South Carolina. If properly protected by British arms, British subjects might spread to the south as effectively as they had colonized the Chesapeake Bay, the Middle Colonies, and New England. Moll's *Map of the Dominions* illustrated how British sovereignty over a grand continental empire could be realized by populating the southern frontier.

Edward Crisp's 1711 *A Compleat Description of the Province of Carolina* reveals how British observers first conceptualized the geography of the southeastern coast. The map focuses on the surging plantation development that was extending the Carolina Lowcountry toward the southern Sea Islands. Like Moll, Crisp included insets that attempted to glimpse the future of such growth at a broader geographic scale. One of these, titled "A Map of South Carolina Shewing the Settlement of the English, French, & Indian Nations from Charles Town to the River Missisipi," reveals a wished-for network of Indian trading alliances capable of enlarging the Carolina colony until its boundaries extended to the banks of the Mississippi River. At the other corner of Crisp's map, his "New Chart of the Coast of Carolina and Florida" imagines a space prepared by nature for British occupation, picturing the territory from

North Carolina to Florida as a unified Atlantic coastal plain. Crisp understood the space that became the Georgia Lowcountry connected by common
geographic attributes: rivers flowing from the mountains to the shore; a rich,
arable zone for agriculture in the flat terrain behind the coast; and a complex
band of coastal islands that stood between the mainland and the ocean. Crisp's
map circulated, for the first time, the most common definition of the place
that would become Georgia as the territory formed by three of these defining
waterways: the Savannah, the Ogeechee, and the Altamaha Rivers.[2]

The confident expectation of an expanding southern empire made visible
on these maps collapsed after the cataclysmic Yamasee War. A series of devastating attacks by Native allies wiped away images of a greater Carolina and
encouraged an imperial policy of defensive occupation rather than unlimited
expansion. The ferocity of this Indian assault undermined Moll and Crisp's
presumption that ongoing plantation settlement could take command of this
promising coast and establish Britain's sovereignty over the contested Southeast. In the wake of this crisis, Carolina's Lords Proprietors granted Sir Robert
Montgomery the land between the Savannah and Altamaha Rivers to be developed as the "Margravate of Azilia." As its newly minted "margrave," Montgomery imagined himself as a military aristocrat like those who once bore
the title defending the borderlands of the Holy Roman Empire in the Middle Ages. He saw his prospective colony as a fortified bulwark "impregnable
against the Savages." His vision for Azilia, pictured in his 1717 tract promoting the venture, was a giant city protected by high walls from the dangers of
Indian attack. Azilia, although never settled, lived on in maps as a fantasy of
British control over the southern frontier. In 1720, Herman Moll redrew the
region to include this fictitious colony that spanned the territory between the
Savannah and Altamaha Rivers.[3] Although Azilia was little more than a cartographic fantasy, it established an idealized form of defensive colonization as
a sharply bounded domain, organized for defensive occupation, and settled
through planned colonization schemes.

In the wake of the political crisis caused by the Yamasee War, Britain displaced the Lords Proprietors and reestablished North and South Carolina
as royal colonies in 1719. Thereafter, the Lords Commissioners of Trade and
Plantations (the British committee that oversaw the colonies, more commonly
known as the Board of Trade) redoubled efforts to settle the empire's southern frontier, with the new priority of defensive settlement in mind. As the
Board of Trade assessed threats to British America in 1721, it saw Carolina "exposed in case of a rupture on the one side to the Spaniards, on the other to the
French, and surrounded by savages."[4] Imperial officials turned their attention

to new schemes to defend, settle, and define this vulnerable southern frontier. The first official images of the territory that would become Georgia were military plans for a fort on the Altamaha River, an effort led by British agent John Barnwell in 1721. His plans of Fort King George illustrated a concrete attempt by the Board of Trade to fortify the continental frontier against feared encroachments of the French and Spanish. Unlike the sweeping scale of the region depicted by Moll and Crisp for broad public consumption, these Fort King George plans were manuscript maps drawn up as working documents that focused on a small peninsula just north of the Altamaha and described the navigation to and from this remote, fortified position.[5] Beyond the area of the fort site, Barnwell's plans left the surrounding landscapes of rivers, wetlands, and pine barrens blank and undefined. Such fortification plans were utilitarian images that documented an attempt to reestablish a clear southern boundary within which Britain might reclaim its command over this disrupted and contested region.

After erecting Fort King George in the early 1720s, Britain's next major attempt to secure and settle the Southeast was South Carolina's interior township plan of 1730. The Board of Trade worked with Britain's newly appointed governor, Robert Johnson, to address the strategic liabilities of unregulated plantation settlement. Upriver from the settled rice plantation districts of the South Carolina Lowcountry, the board approved the creation of strategic townships whose lands were to be reserved for poor Protestant immigrants who would work as yeomen farmers, cultivating their own fields instead of importing large numbers of slaves like their coastal counterparts. Nine approved townships, each forming a square of ten thousand or twenty thousand acres, set aside large interior portions of the Carolina countryside for new white immigrants. This township scheme sought to establish a geographic perimeter around the black-majority rice-planting districts and populate a buffer zone with enough white men capable of bearing arms and serving in the provincial militia to ward off any future attacks from the interior.[6]

Georgia took form in the imaginations of its founders in the 1730s as part of this new ideal of defensive, planned settlement. This vision, promulgated in earlier forms in the idea of Azilia and the creation of the Carolina townships, was instilled at the highest levels of British officialdom by the shattering challenge of the Yamasee War. When the Board of Trade commissioners approved the Georgia Plan in 1732, authorizing the Trustees to create a buffer colony inhabited by yeoman farmers south of the Savannah River, they saw it as yet another way to occupy and stabilize the region. Georgia's leader, James Oglethorpe, articulated the defensive value of the new colony to the Board of Trade in this language of strategic concern: Georgia, he promised, would "render the Southern Frontier of the British Colonies on the Continent of America, safe from Indian and other Enemies." The first published map of the Georgia colony promoted such an image of the region. As an illustration for Oglethorpe and Benjamin Martyn's promotional pamphlet, *Reasons for Establishing the Colony of Georgia*, this map pictured a new southern frontier defended by Georgia as well as Carolina. Although this early promotional literature had virtually nothing concrete to say about the geography of the colony, it posited the well-worn notion of environmental determinism, by which Oglethorpe and Martyn asserted that the area possessed an ideal climate for producing lucrative commodities such as silk and wine. To this notion they joined the Trustees' social objectives of ennobling members of Great Britain's impoverished underclass by transplanting them to Georgia, where new opportunities for productive labor would permit them to make a positive contribution to the nation's power and balance of trade. Such a cartographic and promotional vision of the environment imagined it at a general scale and in abstract terms. It anticipated a lush and generative landscape as an inherent property of the province, but since the British surveyors had yet to examine and represent the land, water, and coastlines of the area, such images offered no specific details that illuminated the quality of any particular tracts of land.

As the first colonists arrived to establish the town of Savannah, Oglethorpe and his men explored the Lowcountry south of the Savannah River. He described the new maps he had produced from these exploratory journeys in letters to the Trustees in London. Although these manuscript images have not survived, they were used as source materials for the most important map of the British mainland colonies published before 1750. Henry Popple's 1733 *Map of the British Empire in America* redraws the watercourses of the new colony's three defining rivers based on firsthand information and locates evidence of the colony's early occupation, including Fort King George, Fort Argyle, Savannah Town, and Joseph's Town, the last a prospective settlement that aimed to attract Scottish Highlanders to Georgia.[7]

In 1732, Oglethorpe laid out his vision for Georgia's landscape in another published tract: *A New and Accurate Account of the Provinces of South Carolina and Georgia*. The central idea of his vision of improved colonization was that Britain's poorest people would change in America as they became landowners. After being provided with acres of wilderness, these migrants would clear and cultivate the land, producing valuable exports to Britain, and by improving the land they would also improve themselves. Through their industry, these former vagrants, debtors, and vagabonds, who had been liabilities to the nation, would become assets to the empire. The society they would form together would be one in which all inhabitants would become stakeholders in maintaining the colony's prosperity and security. This vision of "agrarian equality" meant that instead of subjugating incoming colonists as indentured servants or slaves, the Trustees enlisted only a portion of their labor to build the colony. From the beginning, they would be landowning settlers who would simultaneously support themselves and the new colony. Oglethorpe's idea of agrarian equality found expression in the maps that he and other early Georgia colonists produced to represent the new colony abroad. Just as the Georgia Plan foregrounded the idea of colonization as a shared social project, in which every individual had a role and an interest, these maps presented the plan's land policies in visual form, as a grid that divided the land into equal units for occupation, organized to promote the objective of nucleated settlement in discrete locations. An implicit environmental ideology adhered to this vision. Instead of releasing individual planters onto the landscape to disperse to particular sites that they evaluated and selected, the new colony's land policies viewed the land as a shared factor endowment in which particular tracts were considered to be interchangeable. Each inhabitant was entitled to a portion of a discrete settlement site that officials had defined as a communal space. This homogenizing idea of the land as a uniform resource undermined the vision of Oglethorpe and the Trustees because it failed to reckon with the enormous environmental complexity and variety of Georgia's coastal landscapes.

Before Oglethorpe and the first Georgia colonists fully explored the vast area between the Savannah and Altamaha Rivers, they sought to imprint its landscape with their vision for an improved agrarian society by settling and representing the town of Savannah and its environs. Colonist Peter Gordon recorded in his journal that the spirit of collective enterprise was present as the first settlers arrived on February 1, 1733. Some worked together to "digg trenches for fixing palisadoes 'round the place of our intended settlement as a fence in case we should be attacked by the Indians, while others of us were imployed in clearing of the lines, and cutting trees to the proper lengths for the palisades." A month after Gordon arrived, he noted with pride that the "first house in the square was framed and raised, Mr. Oglethorpe driving the first pinn."[8] Although he was the most exalted member of this nascent colonial society, James Oglethorpe was not above laboring to lay the foundation for a new dwelling within one of the town's new lots.

About a year after this first house was built, Gordon represented the progress of the colony by producing an image of the town. Perhaps no other picture of British colonization represents its fundamental ethos more clearly. His

FIGURE 3.1. This 1733 perspective of Savannah by colonist Peter Gordon imagined the settlement as a space of perfect order and civility carved out of an unruly American wilderness. Courtesy of Library of Congress.

"View of Savannah" opens a prospect of the town from an impossible vantage point high above Hutchinson's Island. It reveals the stark contrast between a dense and untrammeled forest wilderness and the open, measured, civil space that Gordon and others had created after a year's work. It is not technically a map but rather a chorographic view, a three-dimensional city drawing of a type common in European publications of the time. Such views typically allowed readers to take in the splendor of Europe's greatest cities from the comfort of their homes. No grand tour was complete without a view of Rome's churches, ruins, and hillsides to take home as a souvenir. This chorographic image of Savannah shares the same expectation of these more famous views: it invites the viewer to behold the town and appreciate it. It differs from most attempts to represent naturalistic cityscapes in its use of a grid of urban lots to blend the realism of urban chorography with the legal and instrumental figure of a property map.

An eighteenth-century viewer would have seen a strong imposition of civil order on unruly nature in Gordon's image. What looks realistic at first is clearly a fiction: the first colonists did not chop down all but six trees within the town limits, nor did they draw the precise boundaries of every town lot into a visible grid. Gordon presents this idealized view of the town—one that resembles the clarity of a map—in order to make the Georgia Plan visible. A 1735 image, "A Map of the County of Savannah," extends the orderly vision of Georgia's first town to the surrounding countryside. Beyond Savannah Town's grid of urban lots, it reveals the garden lots assigned to each colonist, and beyond them lies an expansive grid of farm lots. Town planning of this sort, far from being a distinctive part of the Trustees' vision, became a hallmark of colonial thought in the eighteenth century. As British imperial reformers sought to plant settlers in contested areas throughout North America and the Caribbean, they focused on perfected towns as centers of order around which new colonies could grow. Similar town plans guided the Board of Trade's settlement at Halifax, Nova Scotia, in 1748, and after 1763 they were featured in wide-ranging settlement schemes in places as diverse as the Caribbean island of Dominica, the Gulf Coast naval station of Pensacola, and new fishing villages earmarked for the rugged coasts of the Gulf of St. Lawrence. Everywhere British officials took a stronger hand in shaping colonies, they drew up plans that attempted to impose this kind of distinctive urban grid on new ports and outposts. Regardless of where these planned towns were situated, from the frigid maritime Northeast to the torrid tropics, their purpose was to thwart speculators who might appropriate valuable tracts, draw settlers together under the influence of religious and civil authorities, and ensure that residents could produce their own food rather than be vulnerable dependencies, easily besieged and cut off from sources of provisions.

These idealized visions for organizing colonial spaces masked a much messier reality on the ground, where Georgia's first settlers struggled to grow enough food to meet their basic needs. When confronted with vast spaces, British colonial planners and mapmakers focused on small areas and invested their careful organization with great importance. If Savannah could be well ordered from Georgia's inception, then perhaps the much larger territories between Georgia's three rivers could be settled with some degree of oversight and control. When the Board of Trade and the Georgia Trustees formulated this plan for organized settlement, they envisioned it as the mirror image of particularly unruly colonies like South Carolina and Jamaica, where local legislatures ignored the king's instructions and used their influence to deliver thousands of acres of land, much of it left undeveloped, into their own hands as well as those of their fellow settler elites. Not only did settlement in both colonies sprawl beyond any defensible perimeter, it also reproduced volatile black-majority populations that made them vulnerable to uprisings from within as well as attack from without. Georgia was to become, in the words of its promoters, a "regular colony," one that was to be "settled, structured, and governed in an orderly manner."[9]

This notion of colonial regularity was legal, administrative, and social in its expectations for orderly government and development, but it also carried with it an ideal form of colonization, one that sought to organize landownership beyond core outposts like Savannah. When Benjamin Martyn published *An Account Showing the Progress of the Colony Georgia in America* in 1741, this state-of-the-colony report included a newly engraved map by R. W. Searle that centered on another version of Savannah's distinctive grid and showed the regular expansion of farm lots surrounding it. It documented the established settlement of Salzburger emigrants from Germany at Ebenezer, whose community extended the line of upcountry townships across the Savannah River from Carolina into Georgia. Searle's map also made a bold departure from previous images in imagining the outer boundaries of the colony. Its toponym—that is, the printed name "Georgia" spread across geographic space—crossed the Altamaha River, previously considered the southernmost extent of the colony, to reach the outskirts of St. Augustine. The idea that Georgia encompassed the lands between the Savannah and Altamaha Rivers was basic to early eighteenth-century geographic understandings of the colony. It defined the boundaries of the imagined colony of Azilia in 1717 and prompted Britain to erect Fort King George along the banks of the Altamaha in 1721. Searle's bold claim of British sovereignty rested on the construction of new forts that defended Britain's southern frontier against Spanish and Indian attack. Published in the midst of the War of Jenkins' Ear, an American conflict pitting Britain against Spain for access to trade and territory throughout the Americas, the image reflected a newly aggressive posture by Britain that found expression in the idea of an expansive Georgia colony.

From 1730, South Carolina and then Georgia had recruited persecuted European Protestants to settle in strategic townships that formed a ring around the Lowcountry's plantation society. A number of skilled military engineers who had mastered surveying techniques in European armies joined this migration, contributing more than their agricultural labor to the tasks of colonization. Among these was Samuel Auspourger, who immigrated to South Carolina in 1734 with a party of Swiss Protestants who settled Purrysburg Township, located a dozen miles upriver from Savannah. To identify routes by which Spanish forces might threaten the province by sailing up the Altamaha River, Auspourger conducted rigorous surveys of St. Simons and Jekyll Islands. Appointed engineer and land surveyor by 1736, he drafted a meticulous sketch of the low-lying landscape of these southern Sea Islands.[10] In pencil and ink, he captured the watercourses of St. Simons's meandering streams and carefully denoted the island's small knolls of dry land, set within encircling marshes. His map identified locations where this high and dry land fronted navigable rivers and sounds and marked these locations for new fortifications.

Another military engineer, Captain John Thomas, drew up plans for Fort Frederica on one of these spots on the island's western side. He and others dreamed that the necessary work of fortifying Georgia's southern border against Spain would anchor new settlements beyond the cluster of existing communities along the Savannah River. Thomas's sketch drew an arc of town lots around Fort Frederica's outer embankments. Beyond them he placed a grid of garden lots to ensure these colonists would have the capacity to grow their own food, and beyond the garden lots he traced a grid of farm lots. The Georgia Trustees intended to replicate the Georgia Plan—and its landed vision of agrarian equality—throughout the province. Together these two manuscript maps suggested a modus operandi for colonial expansion in the Southeast. Through rigorous military surveys, army engineers would identify key sites for fortification to guard the entrances of river inlets. Around such strategic strongholds, the mapmakers etched the Georgia Plan's distinctive grids of lots intended to anchor new colonial communities in place and distribute land equitably.

The Georgia Trustees recruited a party of colonists to inhabit this strategic inlet to the Altamaha River in 1736. Spanish troops descended on Fort Frederica in a bid to seize St. Simons Island on July 7, 1742, and were defeated by British troops in the so-called Battle of Bloody Marsh. Although this victory enabled Britain to set the Altamaha River as Georgia's recognized southern boundary at the Treaty of Aix-la-Chapelle in 1748—thus retaining this contested location—the disruptions of the war depopulated the region. Rising settler grievances about the Georgia Plan's restrictions led to the lifting of the ban on African slavery in 1750 and the formal end of the Trustees' rule of the colony in 1752. The maps made under the auspices of the Trustees envisioned a militarized form for colonization that settled forts in strategic locations and organized societies of freeholders into civil jurisdictions. These images focused on particular parts of Georgia's coastal landscape to implant well-fortified and well-defended settlements across it. This vision collapsed with the Georgia Plan, opening the region to slavery and plantations in the 1750s and granting enterprising planters new authority to define how it would be settled.

Jonathan Bryan's account of his 1753 journey through the southern Sea Islands documented the colony's transition from a utopian reform project to an extension of South Carolina's plantation society. As a young man, Bryan had been an active leader in the settlement of Georgia. He had scouted the St. Johns River in Spanish Florida for Oglethorpe and took part in the failed siege of St. Augustine the general led in 1740. Spanish forces had, in reprisal, advanced on the Georgia coast, burning the scattered settlements that had taken root in the Sea Islands as part of Trusteeship Georgia's scheme of military colonization. When Bryan returned to the islands as a planter, slave owner, and land speculator in 1753, he sought to serve himself and his empire at the same time but on very different terms than had been imagined by Oglethorpe and the Trustees. By buying up promising plantation tracts in the Georgia wilds, he would extend British occupation and make himself rich. From 1753 to 1756, Bryan acquired more than eighteen thousand acres. In his eyes, the vast wilderness that lay unclaimed south of Savannah was an offense against the goal of an improving empire. "I Thought it a great pitty," he wrote, that "such fine Lands should be uncultivated, when fertility, fine Timber and pleasant Situation promise ample reward to its future possessors."[11]

After leaving his Savannah River plantation, Walnut Hill, and the sixty-six slaves he had imported to it from South Carolina the year before, Bryan joined traveling companions in Savannah. There the party boarded a small boat and sailed downstream into the open ocean, rounding Great Tybee Island and heading for the southern islands. No longer was he or any other prospective planter bound by the need to settle in predetermined lots close to established

towns and forts. Like Bryan, others among Georgia's new slave-owning colonists fanned out along the colony's islands and riversides in search of the best
land for rice, indigo, and other commodities. When Bryan and his party arrived at remote St. Catherines, they "took a Tour across the Island on foot
to view it," he wrote in his journal. "This Island is one of the most pleasant
and agreeable Place[s] in all Georgia," he pronounced, "[and] with a little Improvement would make one of the finest Seats for a Man of Fortune." Along
the banks of the Newport River, his traveling companion William Simmons
started a settlement with sixteen slaves. After camping on the site, Bryan
"could not help reflecting on the Special Providence of Almighty God, who
has cast out so many Thousands of the Heathen before us, who were but a few
years ago the numerous Inhabitants of these desolate Places so that it is now a
rare thing to see the Face of an Indian in any of these parts."[12] By seeing vacated
land opened by divine intention for settler occupation, Bryan echoed the common cant of New World colonization that regarded the clearing of forests and
the cultivation of riverside soils as an innate cultural and economic good, part
of a broader social project of "improvement" by which Britain ultimately justified its claims to North America and the West Indies.

Bryan and his traveling companions ventured up the Altamaha, where
wealthy South Carolina planters were already scheming to build vast new plantations. "This is a fine bold fresh River," Bryan declared, one that "runs up into
the Country several hundred Miles to the Indian Nations." It contained, he
wrote, an "abundance of fine Rice Land, where might be made great Quantities of Rice and very convenient for Exportation from Frederica."[13] Bryan pictured Frederica, laid out as a fortified community of soldiers-turned-farmers
under the Trustees, as an Atlantic port for the transshipment of slave-produced
rice. Before these planters arrived, Bryan could already imagine this place settled according to the geographic pattern of settler colonization that featured
dispersed plantations, each one engrossing large tracts of tidal river swamps,
the ideal land type for cultivating rice, the region's most important staple commodity.

At St. Simons Island, the party reached the site of Frederica, the forward
operating base of the British military against Spanish Florida in the 1740s.
More than a thousand soldiers had manned it during the war, but now, five
years after the peace and after its regiments were withdrawn in 1749, Frederica
had reverted to a barely defended garrison. Bryan wondered how a "place of
so great Importance [to] the Frontier of his Majestys Dominions on the Continent" had been left to molder. He found it "all in a ruinous Condition" and
noted that "the Melancholy Prospect of Houses without Inhabitants, Barracks

Rice, Georgia's First Staple Crop

After lifting the ban on slavery in 1750, Georgia saw a stream of planters from South Carolina cross the Savannah River in search of fresh rice lands, bringing with them both a workforce of slaves experienced in rice culture and the precious capital necessary for transforming the land. Plantation agriculture became the domain of a powerful and wealthy elite. Indeed, the coastal region became a striking repudiation of the efforts of the Georgia Trustees to create a colony of white men and women, the "worthy poor" of England, engaged in subsistence agriculture and free of the "Negro merchant" of South Carolina. Rice produced in swamps and along tidal rivers drove Georgia's early growth. Benefiting from an economic boom during the third quarter of the eighteenth century, the colony embraced a slave-powered plantation economy rooted in the harsh Caribbean model. The twenty-two thousand barrels of rice shipped in 1772 accounted for 57 percent of the £121,000 earned in the export trade and entailed a sophisticated industry in terms of port facilities, shipping, finance, and marketing.

The earliest plantations, located in swamps adjacent to rivers, typically followed older, less structured techniques of rice production. Planters cleared land near freshwater, constructed an impoundment pond above each rice field to supply water for the rice, and then built dikes around the field to hold that water. A floodgate between the pond and the field permitted a controlled flow during the growing season. The Medway and Newport Rivers in St. John's Parish, thirty-five miles south of Savannah, became the center of this early boom.

With the adoption of the tidal-flow method, the Savannah and Ogeechee Rivers emerged as the prime locations for rice plantations during the 1760s. As noted by Mart Stewart in chapter 1 of this volume, situating a new plantation at an appropriate "pitch" of the tide was essential. Tidal flow caused a layer of heavy saltwater to move beneath the freshwater, raising the river level sufficiently to inundate the rice. Clearing trees and vegetation from adjacent swamps, slaves constructed permanent embankments several feet high and many feet thick to separate river from land. Trunks and floodgates built into the exterior banks allowed water to flow in and out. During the growing season, successive flows provided nutrient-rich water that killed weeds and protected the young rice from birds.

Some historians speculate that much of the knowledge for building these huge hydraulic machines came from enslaved Africans brought into the ports of Savannah and Charleston. Rice growing was an important agricultural activity in West Africa, where planting took place on tidal floodplains in a complex system of production. Many parallels existed between rice cultivation in Africa and on Lowcountry Georgia plantations, including in land preparation, sowing, weeding, irrigating,

Rice culture on the Ogeechee River, 1867.
From Harper's Weekly, *January 5, 1867, p. 8.*
Courtesy of Library of Congress Prints and Photographs Division.

threshing, winnowing, and processing. Ultimately rice cultivation in the Lowcountry represented a fusion of African and European technologies.

At their peak, in 1859, rice plantations covered forty thousand acres and produced 51.7 million pounds of rice. The Civil War marked the end of rice as a major commodity in Georgia's economy as well as a basis for social and political power. The emancipation of slaves, destruction of property, and loss of capital, as well as a succession of hurricanes later in the century undermined the profitability of the industry. Equally corrosive was the emergence

of competing centers of rice production in Texas, Louisiana, and Arkansas, as well as Southeast Asia. By 1899, annual production had fallen to 8.9 million pounds.

Nevertheless, for 150 years rice cultivation transformed the Georgia coast from untamed swamps into a highly engineered landscape dominated by a tiny elite. Today only traces of the fields remain, most notably at the Savannah Wildlife Refuge, along the more remote portions of the lower Ogeechee River, and at the Hofwyl-Broadfield Plantation, a historic site maintained by the Georgia Department of Natural Resources.

PAUL M. PRESSLY

without Soldiers, Guns without Carriages and the Streets grown over with Weeds, appear to me with a very horrible Aspect, and so very different from what I once knew that I could scarce refrain from Tears." Without military protection, those who had migrated to the island had "mostly removed quite away, and left their Habitations, being afraid to expose themselves and Familys to the Insults of their troublesome Neighbours the Spaniards." Bryan arrived at St. Simons to view the remnants of the Trustees' abandoned colonization plan and to take advantage of these vulnerable, vacant lands at the vanguard of a new generation of independent, slave-owning colonists.

At nearby Jekyll Island, he visited the plantation of William Horton, the former commander at Frederica. When the Spanish attacked the island in 1742, they had burned his house to the ground. Since the peace, he had returned to the southern frontier and rebuilt this estate into a large indigo and cattle plantation. Although the nearly ruined condition of Frederica made Bryan fear that British efforts were faltering on this frontier, the industry of planters like Horton restored his confidence. General Oglethorpe had settled soldiers and their families on Cumberland Island in the 1730s, hoping the military presence would anchor a new settlement. But at the time of Bryan's visit in the early 1750s, he wrote, "[these] plantations are now all deserted and left desolate, so that there is not an Inhabitant on the Island, only a Corporal and Six Men that resides on the South End in Fort William." Nearby, Bryan spied good land for future plantations, "fine Swamps for Rice, and the High Lands very full of white oak for Staves."[14] Bryan witnessed the beginnings of the transformation of the Georgia Lowcountry after 1750. From the ruins of the Georgia Plan, a new landscape of slavery and plantations was beginning to take form.

After gaining experience as an officer and engineer during the War of Austrian Succession, William De Brahm immigrated to Georgia from Germany with the Salzburgers in 1751. His skills came to the attention of colonial authorities, who appointed him as South Carolina's chief surveyor and as one of Georgia's two provincial surveyors. De Brahm's 1752 manuscript map of the Savannah River pointed to a new understanding of the colony's geography, even as it recorded the signs that the Georgia Plan had left on the landscape. He reproduced some of the boxes and grids that emblematized the Georgia Plan's idea of ordered settlement. The town of Savannah occupied a red rectangle, as did the settlement of his fellow Salzburgers at Ebenezer. Along present-day Shipyard Creek, about ten miles south of the capital, the map locates the campus of the Bethesda Orphanage. Methodist evangelist George Whitefield founded the Bethesda Orphanage in 1740 to prepare the colony's parentless poor for a life of ennobling labor, a mission in keeping with Oglethorpe's vision of social improvement. But De Brahm's image of Georgia went beyond the boxes and grids that had once measured the orderly form of a society devoted to agrarian equality. As a whole he represented the colony as a dispersed patchwork of land types along the Savannah River. He color-coded the Georgia Lowcountry in preparation for plantation agriculture. Greenish brown forms inked across the map designated "River Swamp" suited for the most productive tidal rice agriculture; "Grass Green" denoted oak land good for growing provisions; yellow bands showed the "Pine Barrens" from which slaves could extract lumber, firewood, and tar. It was an ideal document for prospective planters to consult in London, Charlestown, or Savannah as they eyed choice unclaimed parcels of land along the riversides. De Brahm lay open the Savannah River for their scrutiny, dividing its lands to suggest how the bounds of individually granted tracts might be angled to gather together an assortment of productive lands. Gone were the fantasies of Georgia as a series of nucleated communities and as a bastion of order, regularity, and civility within an encroaching wilderness as celebrated by Peter Gordon's view of Savannah.[15]

During his fourteen-year tenure as a provincial official, De Brahm designed elaborate new defenses for Charlestown as well as Fort Loudoun in Cherokee country, and he pictured Georgia's three rivers in strategic terms as the Seven Years' War began in 1756. The Savannah River was already fortified at each end by Savannah and Fort Augusta. De Brahm imagined settling new forts along the Ogeechee and Altamaha to match, with a network of roadways to link all of these forts into a great trapezoid. This strategic plan for fort building was also a plan of colonial expansion that imagined plantation development proceeding up all three of Georgia's defining rivers. To achieve this, he drew up elaborate plans for the creation and improvement of fortifications along the colony's outer edges. This new "Map of the Inhabited Part of Georgia" presumed that, regardless of the legal status of negotiations with the neighboring Creek Indians, all of the territory between these rivers was part of a domain of settlement that was or would be granted and occupied by British subjects and their slaves.[16]

The bulk of De Brahm's work as provincial surveyor involved measuring out parcels of land so that they could be formally granted to colonists. De Brahm, his co-surveyor Henry Yonge, and their assistants traveled within the spaces that he had sketched and colored on his maps to measure out new claims as part of the legal process of creating tracts of real property in late-colonial Georgia.[17] His *Map of South Carolina and a Part of Georgia* (1757) codified this knowledge of the coastal Lowcountry, showing how European colonists

FIGURE 3.2. In his "Map of the Inhabited Part of Georgia," provincial surveyor William De Brahm designed a scheme of fortification for Georgia during the Seven Years' War. He imagined that Atlantic and interior forts, some of which lay deep within Creek Indian country, would secure the colony's three defining rivers: the Savannah, the Ogeechee, and the Altamaha. Courtesy of UK National Archives.

occupied land in the plantation districts and thus extending the boundaries of the southeastern frontier. As Mart Stewart has observed, the map "explains the process of colonization in coastal South Carolina and Georgia."[18]

De Brahm's 1757 map pictured the Georgia colony in the throes of ongoing territorial expansion. It charted the uneven spread of parish and township jurisdictions that organized the region's coastal riversides into settled places. It also acknowledged the previous work of the British Board of Trade in attempting to guide development in the region by marking the boundaries of South Carolina's and Georgia's interior townships. In one small portion of this territory, he traced the plat boundaries of individual properties in the rapidly settling plantation district between South Carolina's Combahee River and Georgia's Medway River. As no map had shown before, it took stock of the progress of settlement and pictured it comprehensively at a scale of roughly five miles to the inch. De Brahm's map differed from those produced to superimpose the Trustees' idealized settlement grid upon the landscape in that it incorporated the polygons from official plats, the firsthand surveys taken at ground level to facilitate the process of granting land. Environmental histories of commercial agriculture in the Southeast have described how plantation settlement, amplified by the labor of thousands of enslaved Africans, destabilized hydrographic systems, spread invasive weed species, and loosed grazing livestock that despoiled ecosystems well beyond sites of planting and habitation.[19] Although the impact of plantation development could disrupt and simplify complex ecosystems, De Brahm's maps show that the process of taking up planting land was also a means of acquiring detailed environmental knowledge that was highly responsive to its variety and attuned to the range of resources it offered.

By settling slaves and building plantations on islands and riversides at the reaches of the British Lowcountry, colonists claimed the land for Britain in ways that Oglethorpe's troops never could. De Brahm depicted a process of ongoing colonization that brought this contested space under British control, and his maps made a visual case that the Board of Trade's decision to deploy plantation settlement as a means of securing the southern frontier was a sound one. Indeed, he took care to dedicate *A Map of South Carolina and a Part of Georgia* to the board's powerful leader, the Earl of Halifax, and his fellow Lords of Trade, giving them credit for the robust expansion of plantation settlements that the map detailed. The agents behind this process were not visionary social reformers such as James Oglethorpe and George Whitefield but rather individual settlers whose tracts along the Combahee, Coosawahatchie, and Savannah Rivers formed a sprawling matrix of adjacent "Plantations, with proper Boundary Lines." This sampling of the holdings of the "Proprietors of Land" at the Lowcountry's southern edge lists them by name in a corresponding table, and, although it includes wealthy leaders like Oglethorpe, it features many more settlers whose only mark of public distinction was their appearance in provincial records as individuals owning land.

Why all of these landowners ventured to this frontier to claim their portions of British America is made clear by De Brahm's delineation of the land their boundaries encompassed, shaded to represent valuable river swampland for rice as well as hardwood and pine soils suited to the region's newest commodity, indigo. (The map's cartouche shows slaves agitating the steeping vats in which the dye was processed and cutting cured cakes of it for export.) De Brahm's map captured a view of the settled Lowcountry from the North Carolina border to the edge of Spanish Florida. But at this scale, it also exposed the process by which individual settlers claimed their acres, how these plantations formed neighborhoods clustered along rivers, and how these cleared and cultivated riversides combined to form British North America's southernmost edge.

Georgia's status as mainland British America's southern frontier ended officially in 1763. Once Spain ceded Florida to Britain, Georgia no longer served as the last defensive bastion in the Southeast. After the Crown negotiated the departures of France and Spain from the eastern continent in the Treaty of Paris, it tasked the Board of Trade with redrawing the boundaries of the colonies and producing a plan for integrating an enlarged American empire. Long conceived as a limited frontier buffer zone, Georgia expanded under this new order. No longer threatened by Spanish Florida—whose former territories appeared on the new map of American empire as the new colonies of British East and West Florida—Georgia's formal boundaries extended south beyond its formerly "too narrow Limits" so that the province could take on the proportions of a full-fledged colony.[20] The Board of Trade pictured Georgia's new stature along with the first representation of what would become the Proclamation Line on a published copy of Emanuel Bowen's *An Accurate Map of North America* (1763). To illustrate its proposals for settling and governing British America, the board annotated this map with new lines and colors and presented this image to the king and Privy Council. The guiding principle behind the board's new program of colonial development was to settle the "whole Coast of North America," populating the Atlantic coastal zone with colonists and reaping the various goods that settlers and slaves might produce for sale. Georgia's enlarged coastal plain, extending south to the St. Marys

River, was shaded blue like the rest of the coastal mainland and imagined as a zone for intensive settlement and commodity production.[21]

The problem with this vision for Georgia's expansion was that it conflicted with another imperial objective. Britain wanted to secure peace along the Indian frontier through diplomacy, and this meant recognizing Native claims to territory that would be off limits to new settlement. Although the Board of Trade at first imagined that the continent could be easily bisected along the spine of the Appalachian Mountains into colonial and indigenous zones of habitation, such a straightforward geographic rule made little sense in the Southeast. The extensive claims of the Creek Nation to lands within Georgia's territory blocked the legal settlement of much of the coastal plain beyond the tidewater. Southern Indian superintendent John Stuart convened the first major Indian congress after the Seven Years' War at Fort Augusta, Georgia, in early November 1763. Among the objectives for this formal diplomatic meeting that included the four southern governors and headmen speaking for the Choctaws, Chickasaws, Creeks, Catawbas, and Cherokees was to "ascertain and define the precise and exact boundary," beyond which "no settlement whatever shall be allowed."[22]

In preparation for the Creek-Georgia boundary negotiations, Georgia governor James Wright charged his two provincial surveyors, William De Brahm and Henry Yonge, to draw a map of Georgia's territory as defined by previous negotiations with the Indians. Although the surveyors wrote out the "Georgia" toponym boldly across the interior, their map revealed how little of this territory had been actually transferred by the Creeks to the colony. A yellow line stretching from the Altamaha River just above Fort Barrington to the Savannah River just above Ebenezer marked the original cession negotiated by James Oglethorpe in 1737. It revealed that Georgia's legally constituted domain for settlement was confined entirely to the tidelands. This "Map of the Sea Coast of Georgia" circulated among Indians and British negotiators as they debated where the new line should be located. When they reached an agreement, they traced it across this map.[23] This renegotiated boundary, colored in red, roughly tripled the acres that had been or could be legally granted under the terms of the king's 1763 proclamation. In addition to the tidelands between the St. Marys and Altamaha Rivers that Georgia now claimed by virtue of Spain's withdrawal from Florida, the Creeks relinquished a wedge of territory between the Altamaha and Ogeechee Rivers. Most dramatically, De Brahm and Yonge marked out a broad corridor for settlement between the Ogeechee and Savannah Rivers. No previous map described this detailed le-

Indigo and the Atlantic World

In the Southeast's semitropical environment, colonists attempted to grow exotic plants for which they possessed neither horticultural experience nor the workforce needed to cultivate and process them. As white planters faltered in the heat and from disease and as the supply of Native Americans for slave labor dwindled, enslaved Africans were tasked with wringing an export economy out of the coastal zone. The British textile industry's demand for indigo dye brought together an American plant and African people.

Indigo suffruticosa, native from the Caribbean region into the U.S desert Southwest, has been used for centuries as a textile dye and as a colorant in Mayan frescoes as far back as AD 800. This American species

came to dominate indigo production in the southeastern colonies. Across the Atlantic, Africans had an equally rich history of using African species of indigo in medicine and in tattooing. Indigo-dyed cloth signified wealth and power, and its blue color was tied to African spiritual beliefs.

What formerly had been an artisanal enterprise soon scaled up to an intense level of production. More arduous than field labor was dye processing. Freshly cut indigo branches steeping in water required precise fermentation. Once the plant liquor was drawn off, for hours it had to be agitated vigorously with huge paddles to incorporate oxygen and thereby precipitate the dye. The dyestuff then had to dry before being cut into briquettes for

Indigo plantation in St. Stephen's Parish, South Carolina.
Courtesy of the David M. Rubinstein Rare Book & Manuscript Library, Duke University.

shipment. The stench of the processing vats and the insects they attracted were so intolerable that vats were located far from housing, and the slaves who worked there reportedly had shorter life spans.

When the Revolutionary War halted the lucrative transatlantic indigo trade, Britain switched to imports from its newly established East India Company. In the postwar South, coastal plantations shifted to cotton and rice as indigo returned once more to small-scale production for local use. Emancipation and the advent of synthetic dyes in the 1880s further relegated indigo into the shadows. However, the Gullah Geechee, communities of emancipated slaves, kept their indigo heritage

alive. The Sapelo Island community continued to weave indigo-dyed cotton yarn into handmade blankets. All along the coastal corridor, the Gullah Geechee used dregs from indigo vats to paint window shutters, doorframes, and occasionally entire houses a signature "haint blue" to ward off evil spirits.

The discovery in 2005 of a wild population of *I. suffruticosa* on Ossabaw Island returned indigo to the spotlight. Without human assistance, these plants had self-seeded for 170 years since last reported in the island's agricultural accounts. Now, with the help of horticulturalists, dyers, and artists, Ossabaw indigo reminds us of the history held within its deep ocean blue.

DORINDA G. DALLMEYER

gal partitioning of the Georgia Lowcountry, and few British observers without direct experience negotiating these boundaries used them to conceptualize the shape of the colony. Since its inception, the idea that these three rivers defined Georgia had been fundamental in promoting, defending, and conceptualizing it. From Oglethorpe's first commissioned maps of the region, picturing these three rivers encouraged prospective settlers to imagine ample supplies of good planting land along their banks. Indian boundary lines disrupted these visions of development, imposing obstacles to their realization. De Brahm and Yonge's "Map of the Sea Coast of Georgia" adhered to a delimited understanding of frontier space—imposed by the superintendent of Indian affairs by instruction of the Board of Trade and proclamation of the king—that only land formally ceded by the Indians was open to settlement. White Georgians had imagined that, in the fullness of time, they would settle along the full lengths of these rivers. In fact, settlers had already occupied some of the land along rivers and creeks in this newly ceded area, and their quasi-legal presence had guided the negotiations. Both parties agreed to draw the new line around places where colonists had already settled, leaving an additional small buffer zone into which new settlers could expand. By cutting across the colony's three defining rivers, the new boundary set at Augusta, which was to be marked and blazed across the landscape by a joint Creek-Georgian surveying expedition to make it visible to all, threatened previous European expectations that this process of expansion would continue.

In the interior space that this newly negotiated boundary line defined, Creek Indians saw their own imperial and national aspirations validated. Like the Spanish before them, the Creeks had a conception of the Southeast that was almost entirely unrepresented on British maps. As partners with English military forces from South Carolina during Queen Anne's War, Creek warriors raided deep into Florida, killing and enslaving mission Indians and eroding Spanish claims to sovereignty in the region. They viewed Spain's departure from Florida as an acknowledgment of their territorial rights by conquest, and aside from those lands already settled and ceded by treaty, they believed that Britain could only rightfully claim those coastal lands affected by the ebb and flow of the ocean's tides. Southern superintendent John Stuart documented the results of the Augusta negotiations in a manuscript map that he drafted and dispatched to London. When the Board of Trade's commissioners unrolled it in Whitehall, they saw, perhaps for the first time, how the Creeks conceived of their national geography as a vast interior empire. At subsequent congresses convened in part to negotiate other sections of the boundary between the Creek Nation and British America, Creek spokesmen remained "tenacious of their hunting Ground" and maintained that British colonies should be confined to the "sea coast as far as the tide flows."[24]

Less than a decade after this boundary was marked across the landscape by surveying parties, groups of Europeans and Indians worked to erode the limits it imposed on colonization. In the early 1770s, Cherokees and Creeks sought to pay off their trading debts with British merchants by vying with one another to sell off a portion of land within Georgia's chartered boundaries but beyond the Augusta line. In 1773, surveyors defined a "New Purchase" that opened some 1.5 million acres along the Savannah, Ogeechee, and Altamaha Rivers and their tributaries to new settlement.[25] Deputy provincial surveyor Philip Yonge's "A Map of the Lands Ceded to His Majesty by the Creek and Cherokee Indians" pictured a topographically rich new picture of a riverine landscape laid out for planting throughout the New Purchase. Yonge's rivers and creeks were more than mere lines on paper. They represented waterways drawn to scale, some dotted with islands and rendered to emphasize the contours of their junctures with smaller creeks and streams that joined together in a hydrographic network. A lettered key parsed the lands between them into types: A for deep and rich oak and hickory hardwood soils, B for valleys with a light marl and clay mix, AB for fertile plains of tupelo and black walnut, D for rich, narrow veins of cane break soil, E for the "Mollato Lands" composed of sandy mixes of soil and clay, and F for wastelands of red clay and gravel. Yonge drew dotted circles with radial hash marks to signify "convenient places for mills" scattered across the New Purchase, a place that was in general "finely watered by abundance of Streams." Unadorned circles marked "Old Indian Town and Old Fields" conveniently cleared of their trees and tested for fertility by Native farmers. Such a map invited colonists to obtain warrants and survey grants as quickly as possible, and within a matter of months after the cession was approved in the summer of 1773 some fourteen hundred settlers arrived to take up tracts here, their labor augmented by the work of some three hundred slaves. The commissioners of the Board of Trade had imagined that the boundary so painstakingly negotiated and surveyed a decade earlier would serve as an enduring dividing line between Indian and European spaces. The New Purchase belied that expectation, and this map that described its bounds and lands hinted at new cessions to come. A small annotation at the edge of this map, by Governor Wright, marked a spot with tens of thousands of acres of "extraordinary fine land" that might yet be purchased in the future to expand this domain for planting. By using the process of treaty diplomacy to set lines of division intended to contain the expansion of Georgia's plantation landscape, the Board of Trade had hoped to avoid destabilizing settler incursions into Indian territory after the Seven Years' War. But after colonists and local officials realized that, with the right incentives proffered to the Creeks and Cherokees, they could use this process to renegotiate Georgia's boundaries to open new districts for settlement, such lines seemed fungible forms that could be resurveyed and remapped as settlers, speculators, and slaves followed the scent of good riverside land from the coast into the interior.[26]

British authorities targeted New Purchase lands for a new imperial project of regulation the year after its lands were added to Georgia's domain. As part of a larger legislative and administrative push to bring increasingly restive colonies into order, the king issued his "Additional Instructions . . . for the Disposal of His Majesty's Land" in 1774. This royal order dictated a procedure for granting new lands that was intended to organize settlement and generate revenue for the treasury. To prevent dispersed settlement along choice riverside lands, the "Additional Instructions" outlined a system by which surveyors should divide the land into tracts before the first colonist arrived and produce

FIGURE 3.3. In "A Map of the Lands Ceded to His Majesty by the Creek and Cherokee Indians," Georgia's deputy provincial surveyor Philip Yonge provided a detailed image of lands ceded by the Creeks and Cherokees in 1773 to promote their rapid acquisition by new planters. Courtesy UK National Archives.

a "Map of the district so Surveyed, with the several Lots marked and Number'd." This map was to be "hung up" at the provincial secretary's office for inspection, after which the tracts were to be auctioned to the highest bidder. Instead of encouraging settlers to fan out across the New Purchase's tantalizing riversides, claiming land where they thought best, such proposed maps were designed to shape a coherent pattern of settlement and keep officials in London informed of the qualities and ownership of "each particular Lot."[27] Surveyor Henry Yonge faced immediate resistance from aspiring New Purchase settlers when he attempted to carry out the king's instructions. The "people," he reported to his superiors in London, "were so fond of choosing (as they call it) for themselves."[28]

These new regulations for land selection became a special point of contention as Georgia colonists mobilized politically for the fight for independence. Georgia's revolutionary Darien Committee decried them, claiming that the ultimate intention behind them was to prevent colonists from expanding into the continent and thus artificially diminishing America's European population so that colonists could be more easily subdued and controlled. The committee cited the "shutting up" of the "land offices, with the intention of raising our quit-rents, and setting up our lands at publick sale" as a "principal part of the unjust system of politicks adopted by the present Ministry, to subject and enslave us."[29]

By focusing on the contrasting iconography of rivers and grids, we can read the cartography of colonial Georgia as a battle between two visions of colonization, one that followed from the independent acquisition of land by individual colonists and the other imposed by imperial officials as they attempted to remedy the strategic problems that unregulated colonization caused. Before 1730, imperial improvers imagined populating the southern frontier within the fortified walls of Azilia, distributing equal lots of land arrayed around town centers and promoting social equality through land grants. After 1763's Peace of Paris, they worked to set new boundaries with Native American nations to impose limits on the spread of plantation settlement into the Lowcountry interior and establish a centralized system for surveying and granting American land. At each attempt to inscribe lines and boxes around the region's natural landforms and watercourses, the forces of settler colonialism worked to undermine such limits. An incipient settler class challenged the Georgia Plan from within and worked to extend the South Carolina plantation system to the riversides and Sea Islands of the southeastern coast, speculating planters worked to erode the Georgia-Creek boundary set at Augusta, and white Georgians who joined the quest for independence cited land regulation as a grievance.

This intra-European conflict over the nature of colonization in Georgia was not the only tension that shaped the formation of the colony. Native Americans, particularly the Creeks, used the threat of war as well as avenues of diplomacy to draw a Native-European frontier line, rooted in visible and natural markers on the landscape. The maps served as legal documentation of diplomatic agreements but also as empirical documents that codified knowledge of river systems that could support the future growth of the colony's plantation economy. Indian boundaries were lines faintly inscribed on the landed consciousness of white Georgians as they imagined their plantation landscape advancing from the Lowcountry into the backcountry.

By reading coastal Georgia's eighteenth-century maps with these two sets of iconographic markers in mind—one that advanced the aspirations of expansive settlement and another that sought to mold and contain that settlement—we can understand, with new spatial precision, the animating tension at the heart of early Georgia's history between broad claims of territorial sovereignty and limited settlement. Before this contested space could be claimed, it had to be visualized. Years before any British settlers reached the shores of Georgia, mapmakers saw North America's edges and margins as places of danger. They dreamed up the territory that would become Georgia as a way of marking it as a space that demanded a secure design. These early maps dating from before 1730 set an agenda for colonization determined to expand the boundaries of British America southward. The British imagined Georgia a second time after its founding when the Trustees' Georgia Plan sought to create an egalitarian farming society emblematized by Savannah's town plan. The end of the Georgia Plan's land policies and restrictions on slavery opened the province to settlers and slaves from South Carolina, changing its form again.

As historian David Armitage has argued, Britain never fully reconciled the disjunction between *imperium*, or the sovereign right to rule, and *dominium*, the rights of property owners over their lands. The expansive sovereignty claims represented on maps that pictured the colony as a whole were powerfully suggestive of an expanding *dominium* by which more and more of Georgia's sovereign territory would in time be claimed by enterprising planters and improved for profit by their slaves. In colonial British America, broad claims of sovereignty over territory created entrenched expectations for ongoing settlement among those who inhabited these mapped spaces. In Georgia, conceived from the start as a new kind of colony, whose growth and development was to be regulated by the imperial state to mitigate the strategic and social problems of previously established colonies, this distance between outsized expectations and delimited possibilities was a defining feature of life. Historians have understood the contest between the Trustees' vision of planned social development and grievances of the settlers, sometimes known as the Malcontents, who worked to undermine the prohibitions against land speculation, African slavery, and expansive plantation settlement as a clash between unrealistic utopian visions and craven settler self-interest. Cartography allows us to set this moralizing interpretation aside in favor of a contrasting spatial understanding about how Britain implanted colonial societies in America. The rectilinear forms that imperial improvers attempted to impose on the landscape discounted the variegated qualities of the land they placed within adjacent lots in their settlement schemes. Colonists and the surveyors they employed to lay out tracts of riverside land were, by contrast, attuned to this variety, and they used their firsthand observations of land and water to create a plantation society that was as exploitative as it was productive. Expansive plantation settlement, by focusing on arable riversides, offered a settlement system that was far more adaptive to the resource endowment of the Georgia Lowcountry than were the more delimited imperial plans. Read with this analytical iconography in mind, these maps reveal the power of settler colonialism as a form of gathering and exploiting environmental knowledge. The key lesson they teach is that those who viewed America from London could map these distant shores and attempt to dictate the kind of societies that would take shape in the contested territories of the North American Southeast, but they did not see clearly the nature of these spaces or how they could be adapted to support a self-sustaining colonial society. Despite the best intentions of imperial officials, the forces of settler colonialism that determined settlement on the ground could not be easily restrained by lines, words, and colors on paper maps.

NOTES

For a digital atlas featuring images of the maps mentioned in this chapter, see http://www.mapscholar.org/georgia.

1. John E. Crowley, "'Taken on the Spot': The Visual Appropriation of New France for the Global British Landscape," *Canadian Historical Review* 86, no. 1 (2005): 9; Herman Moll, *A New and Exact Map of the Dominions of the King of Great Britain on [the] Continent of North America* (London, 1715).

2. Edward Crisp, *A Compleat Description of the Province of Carolina* (London, 1711).

3. Montgomery (1717) quoted in William P. Cumming, *The Southeast in Early Maps*, 3rd ed., revised by Louis De Vorsey Jr. (Chapel Hill: University of North Carolina Press, 1998), 210; "Plan Representing the Form of Settling the Districts, or County Divisions in the Margravate of Azilia," in *A Discourse Concerning the Design'd Establishment of a New Colony to the South of Carolina, In the Most Delightful Coun-*

try of the Universe (London, 1717); Herman Moll, *A New Map of the North Parts of America Claimed by France under ye Names of Louisiana, Mississipi, Canada, and New France* (London, 1720).

4. "State of Your Majesty's Plantations on the Continent of America," September 8, 1721, in *Documents Relative to the Colonial History of the State of New-York*, vol. 5, *New York Documents*, ed. F. B. O'Callaghan (Albany: Weed, Parsons, 1853), 591–630.

5. Journal, August 1720, *Journals of the Board of Trade and Plantations*, vol. 4, *November 1718–December 1722* (London, 1925), 191–204, British History Online, http://www.british-history.ac.uk/; John Barnwell, Southeastern North America (1721), CO 700/North American Colonies General 7, National Archives of the United Kingdom, Kew, Richmond, Surrey (hereafter cited as UKNA); Barnwell, "A Map or Plan of the Mouth of Alatamahaw River," 1721, CO 700/Georgia 1, UKNA; Barnwell, *The Northern B[ra]nch of Alatama River*, 1721, CO 700/Georgia 2, UKNA; Barnwell, *A Chart of St. Simon's Harbour*, 1721, CO 700/Georgia 3, UKNA; Barnwell, *A Plan of King George's Fort at Allatamaha, South Carolina*, 1722, UKNA, CO 700/Georgia 4, UKNA. See also Cumming, *Southeast in Early Maps*, 216–19; Verner W. Crane, *The Southern Frontier, 1670–1732* (Ann Arbor, Mich., 1964), 226–53.

6. Robert L. Meriwether, *The Expansion of South Carolina, 1729–1765* (Kingsport, Tenn.: Southern Publishers, 1940), chap. 2.

7. Louis de Vorsey Jr., "Maps in Colonial Promotion: James Edward Oglethorpe's Use of Maps in 'Selling' the Georgia Scheme," *Imago Mundi* 38 (1986): 35–45.

8. Peter Gordon, *The Journal of Peter Gordon, 1732–1735*, ed. E. Merton Coulter (Athens: University of Georgia Press, 1963), 37, 42.

9. Jack P. Greene, *Imperatives, Behaviors, and Identities: Essays in Early American Cultural History* (Charlottesville: University Press of Virginia, 1992), 117.

10. Farris W. Cadel, *Georgia Land Surveying History and Law* (Athens: University of Georgia Press, 1991), 20.

11. Jonathan Bryan, *Journal of a Visit to the Georgia Islands of St. Catherines, Green, Ossabaw, Sapelo, St. Simons, Jekyll, and Cumberland, with Comments on the Florida Islands of Amelia, Talbot, and St. George, in 1753*, ed. Virginia Steele Wood and Mary R. Bollard (Macon, Ga.: Mercer University Press, 1996), 7.

12. Ibid., 20.

13. Ibid., 20, 22.

14. Ibid., 28–29.

15. William De Brahm, "A Map of the Savannah River," [1752?], Geography and Map Division, Library of Congress, Washington, D.C., http://www.loc.gov/item /gm71000634.

16. William De Brahm, "A Map of the Inhabited Part of Georgia," 1756, CO 700 /Georgia 12, UKNA.

17. William De Brahm, *De Brahm's Report of the General Survey in the Southern District of North America*, ed. Louis De Vorsey Jr. (Columbia: University of South Carolina Press), 7–33.

18. William De Brahm, *A Map of South Carolina and a Part of Georgia* (London,

1757); Mart A. Stewart, "William Gerard de Brahm's 1757 Map of South Carolina and Georgia," *Environmental History* 16 (July 2011): 532.

19. See Timothy Silver, *A New Face on the Countryside: Indians, Colonists, and Slaves in South Atlantic Forests, 1500–1800* (New York: Cambridge University Press, 1990); Mart Stewart, *"What Nature Suffers to Groe": Life, Labor, and Landscape on the Georgia Coast, 1680–1920* (Athens: University of Georgia Press, 1996); Virginia De John Anderson, *Creatures of Empire: How Domestic Animals Transformed Early America* (New York: Oxford University Press, 2004).

20. Henry Ellis, "Hints Relative to the Division and Government of the Conquered and Newly Acquired Countries in America" [1763], CO 323/16, UKNA.

21. Representation of the Board of Trade, June 8, 1763, in Adam Shortt and Arthur G. Doughty, eds., *Documents Relating to the Constitutional History of Canada, 1759–1791* (Ottawa: S. E. Dawson, 1907), 100–101; Emanuel Bowen, *An Accurate Map of North America* (London, [ca. 1763]), MR 1/26, UKNA.

22. Louis De Vorsey Jr., *The Indian Boundary in the Southern Colonies, 1763–1775* (Chapel Hill: University of North Carolina Press, 1966), 41.

23. De Brahm, *De Brahm's Report of the General Survey*, 31. For a similar map, see Henry Yonge, "A Map of the Sea Coast of Georgia," 1763, Add MSS 14,036, fol g., British Library, London.

24. "Report of the Congress [Picolata]," in James W. Covington, *The British Meet the Seminoles: Negotiations between British Authorities in East Florida and the Indians: 1763–68*, Contributions of the Florida State Museum, Social Sciences, 7 (Gainesville: University of Florida Press, 1961), 37; John Stuart, "A Map of the Southern Indian District," 1764, Add. MSS 14,036, fol. d, British Library.

25. *Indian Documents*, vol. 12, *Georgia and Florida Treaties, 1763–1776*, ed. John T. Juricek (Bethesda, Md.: University Publications of America, 2002), 81–85; De Vorsey, *Indian Boundary in the Southern Colonies*, 161–72.

26. Yonge was the son of provincial surveyor Henry Yonge. [Philip Yonge], "A Map of the Lands Ceded to His Majesty by the Creek and Cherokee Indians at a Congress held in Augusta the 1st June 1773 . . . Containing 1616298 Acres," 1773, MPG 1/2, UKNA.

27. St. George L. Sioussat, "The Breakdown of the Royal Management of Lands in the Southern Provinces, 1773–1775," *Agricultural History* 3 (April 1929): 68–70; Clarence W. Alvord, *The Mississippi Valley in British Politics: A Study of the Trade, Land Speculation and Experiments in Imperialism Culminating in the American Revolution*, vol. 2 (Cleveland: 1917), 212; "Earl of Dartmouth to the Governor in America, February 5, 1774," in *Documents Relative to the Colonial History of the State of New-York*, vol. 8, ed. E. B. O'Callaghan (Albany, 1857), 409–13.

28. Sioussat, "Breakdown of Royal Management of Lands," 78–79; James Wright (1774) quoted in ibid., 79.

29. Preston (1775) quoted in ibid., 91; Resolution of the Darien Committee, January 12, 1775, quoted in ibid., 79.

CHAPTER 4

Lowcountry Creoles

*Coastal Georgia and South Carolina Environments
and the Making of the Gullah Geechee*

EDDA L. FIELDS-BLACK

GULLAH IN HERSKOVITS'S
SCALE OF AFRICANISMS

In a 1930 publication, Melville Herskovits, eminent anthropologist and founder of the first major interdisciplinary program in African studies at an American university, at Northwestern, called for the creation of a chart that would compare cultural data and indicate the extent to which blacks in different localities of the New World had retained "Africanisms" in their cultural behavior. Herskovits was most concerned with studying blacks' physical features and cultures, including languages, all of which he described as being of the "utmost scientific importance and far-reaching practical significance" in shedding light on humankind. Africanisms were the "aboriginal" African forms that proved "tenacious" among blacks in the New World despite their suppression by interaction with whites, particularly during the periods of enslavement. Herskovits's study was hampered in 1930 by a lack of data on the Western African origins of blacks in the New World. Nevertheless, he created a scale ranking "Bush Negroes of Suriname" as retaining the most Africanisms, followed by blacks on the coastal plains of Dutch Guiana, the peasants of Haiti and Santo Domingo, and then blacks on British, Dutch, and Danish islands in the Caribbean. Toward the bottom of the list he placed "isolated groups living in the United States as the Negroes of the "Savannahas [*sic*] of southern Georgia," or those of the "Gulla [*sic*] Islands off the Carolina coast." Though Herskovits hypothesized that Africanisms among these two populations were more "tenuous," he asserted that they were stronger than among the masses of blacks "of all degrees of racial mixture" living in the rest of the U.S. South.[1]

TABLE 4.1. Herskovits's "Scale of Intensity of New World Africanisms"

	Technology	Economic Life	Social Organization	Non-kinship Institutions	Religion	Magic	Art	Folklore	Music	Language
Guiana										
bush	b	b	a	a	a	a	b	a	a	b
Paramaribo	c	c	b	c	a	a	c	a	a	c
Haiti										
peasant	c	b	b	c	a	b	d	a	a	c
urban	e	d	c	c	b	b	e	a	a	c
Brazil										
Bahia	d	d	b	d	a	a	b	a	a	a
Porto Alegre	e	e	c	d	a	a	e	?	a	c
north-urban	e	d	c	e	a	b	e	d	a	b
north-rural	c	c	b	e	c	b	e	b	b	d
Jamaica										
Maroons	c	c	b	b	b	a	e	a	a	c
general	e	d	d	d	c	b	e	a	b	c
Trinidad										
Toco	e	d	c	c	c	b	e	b	b	d
Port-of-Spain	e	d	c	b	a	a	e	b	a	c
Cuba	?	?	?	c	a	a	?	?	b	?
Virgin Islands	e	d	c	d	e	c	?	b	?	d
Gulla Islands	c	c	c	d	c	b	e	a	b	d
United States										
rural South	d	e	c	d	c	c	e	c	b	e
rural North	e	e	c	d	c	c	e	d	b	e

The strength of the influence of African culture in each country is indicated using the following scale:
a) very African; b) quite African; c) somewhat African; d) a little African; e) trace of African custom, or no influence. Question marks indicate no report.

Source: Adapted from Melville Herskovits, "Scale of Intensity of New World Africanisms: The Persistence of Several Aspects of African Culture in the Americas," in "Problem, Method and Theory in Afroamerican Studies," Afroamerica 1 (1945): 14.

Published in 1945, Herskovits's "Scale of Intensity of New World African-isms" rated seventeen New World black societies on a scale from "a" ("a trace of African custom") to "e" ("very African"). The revised scale gives more insight into the categories Herskovits used in assigning rankings of intensity of Afri-canisms and the characteristics of each category. Each society on the scale was assigned a composite score of rankings in ten different African traits—entail-ing technology, economic life, social organization, non-kinship institutions, religion, magic, art, folklore, music, and language—that survived or were re-tained in the New World. The 1945 scale also disaggregated urban and rural black populations in Dutch Guiana, Haiti, Brazil, Jamaica, Trinidad, and the U.S. South. Cuba and the Virgin Islands were the exception, there not being enough data on them to disaggregate their rural and urban black populations. According to Herskovits's hypothesis, New World societies in which people of African descent constituted the majority of the population possessed little access to education, had limited interaction with European culture, and re-mained relatively disadvantaged would be more likely to retain elements of Af-rican culture than in societies where they were a minority, despite the histories of slavery and discrimination. Overall he ranked rural black societies as retain-ing more Africanisms than urban blacks.[2]

Although Herskovits did not rank the "Savannahs of southern Georgia" on the revised scale, he ranked the "Gulla Islands" in the middle of New World black societies that had retained Africanisms, lower than rural black popula-tions in the Guianas, Brazil, Haiti, and Jamaica, but higher than urban blacks in the same locales. Blacks in the rural U.S. South and North occupied the bot-tom of the scale, supposedly having the least intense Africanisms among black New World populations. Herskovits distinguished blacks inhabiting the Sea Islands of the Carolinas and Georgia from blacks elsewhere in the U.S. South in terms of their technology, economic life, magic, folklore, and language, all of which he found to retain more Africanisms.[3]

Herskovits was among the first scholars to investigate the creation of new cultures in the Atlantic world by people of African descent and to identify the inhabitants of the Carolina and Georgia Sea Islands, who are today called the Gullah Geechee, as exceptional in this regard. More than eighty years after Herskovits's work identifying Africanisms, scholars of many disciplines con-tinue to use his approach. And the concept of "Africanisms" has not only per-vaded academic literature but has also shaped how many African Americans inhabiting coastal South Carolina and Georgia identify their culture.

Today the Gullah Geechee are a prime example of coastal culture at the in-tersection of coastal nature. These African Americans inhabit, as their ancestors inhabited, the islands and coastal plain along the Atlantic shores thirty to forty miles into the interior, stretching from the Cape Fear River in North Carolina to the St. John's River in Florida. They are descendants of enslaved Africans who labored on indigo, rice, Sea Island cotton, and "naval stores" plantations. As a result of a surge in captives imported into the colony from West and West Central Africa, enslaved Africans constituted the majority of South Carolina's population by 1708. In the colonial period, the Lowcountry became a veritable Maroon community because of an environmental accident. In the mid-eighteenth century, the shift from inland to tidewater rice production created stagnant pools of water in the tidal swamps where mosquitoes bred. The spread of diseases such as malaria in the rural areas where rice was grown, and yellow fever in the urban areas, made absentee landlords of most white slaveholders and left tens of thousands of enslaved laborers with little supervision by whites for much of the year or even interaction with them. "Gullah" primarily refers to African Americans in coastal South Carolina, and "Geechee" refers specifically to the African American inhabitants of coastal Georgia. "Gullah" and "Geechee" are also the names given to the English-based Creole language spoken in these regions by the descendants of enslaved Africans.

The Gullah Geechee have proven an enigma for scholars. Early folklorists, such as Ambrose Gonzales, recorded fables in a made-up version of the language and wrote,

> Slovenly and careless of speech, these Gullahs seized upon the peasant English . . . , wrapped their clumsy tongues about it as well as they could, and enriched with certain expressive African words, it issued through their flat noses and thick lips as so workable a form of speech that it was gradually adopted by the other slaves and became in time the accepted Negro speech of the lower districts of South Carolina and Georgia.[4]

A contemporary of Herskovits, Lorenzo Dow Turner, conducted the first scientific study of the Gullah Geechee languages, tracing over three thousand words and hundreds of "basket names" from Gullah Geechee to West African and West Central African languages and recording texts in the Mende language, spoken in Sierra Leone, that were passed down by Gullah speakers. Turner pioneered the study of Western African substrate languages as important to the formation of Gullah and other African American vernacular English varieties.[5] He found that Western African languages were one of several influences on Gullah.[6] However, anthropologists and folklorists writing after Turner's watershed study have used it to continue Herskovits's search for

MAP 4.1. The Gullah Geechee Cultural Heritage Corridor

Note: Designated by Congress in 2006, the Gullah Geechee Cultural Corridor recognizes the home of a culture first shaped by captive Africans from West Africa and continued in later generations by their descendants.

"Africanisms" and African "survivals" and "retentions." They portray Gullah Geechee language and culture as fossilized bits of Africa frozen in time, rare examples of cultural resistance among African Americans in the U.S. South that have changed little since the importation of captives from West and West Central Africa and the Caribbean to the twentieth century.

Compared to the voluminous anthropological and folkloric literatures, the historical literature is much smaller. Whereas anthropologists and linguists have started from the premise of Gullah Geechee language, culture, and people, historians have had trouble defining Gullah Geechee. The earliest treatment of Gullah Geechee people in the historical literature incorporated them into larger treatment of the social, political, and economic evolution of enslaved communities on rice, indigo, and Sea Island cotton plantations in the South Carolina and Georgia Lowcountry.[7] None of these studies, however, use the terminology "Gullah" or "Geechee." They were examining the antebellum period, I argue, before a crystallized Gullah Geechee identity existed. Archaeologists are also attempting to define "Gullah" temporally (debating whether "Gullah" is a postbellum phenomenon) and spatially (limited to South Carolina).[8]

A much smaller body of work has examined Gullah communities in the antebellum period, of which Charles Joyner's *Down by the Riverside*, published first in 1984, is one example. Joyner's micro-study examined how an enslaved community on a rice plantation in the All Saints Parish near Georgetown, South Carolina, developed a cohesive Creole culture, Gullah. Focusing on language, proverbs, naming practices, and folklore, Joyner suggested that the Gullah shared similarities with diverse Western African cultures and that the Gullah language was related to West African languages and to English. But he classified Gullah as a new language and culture, not an African survival or retention. He credited enslaved Africans in South Carolina's Waccamaw Neck for creating a living culture, which he characterized as a bigger accomplishment than preserving an old one.[9]

Margaret Washington Creel's *A Peculiar People* (1989) examined how aspects of religion and community from Sierra Leone, Congo, and Angola regions of West and West Central Africa have survived among the Gullah Geechee in South Carolina and been reinterpreted by them.[10] A more recent collection of essays edited by Philip Morgan brings the Gullah Geechee into the Atlantic world. Its examination of African American history in coastal Georgia from the mid-eighteenth to the twentieth century is a rarity within the South Carolina–dominated literature.[11] A fresh historical perspective on the development of Gullah Geechee culture and communities, however, is long overdue. Before we can understand how Gullah Geechee people and culture changed and how their relationship to place evolved over time, historians must join archaeologists to resolve some questions: Who are the Gullah Geechee? When do Gullah Geechee people and culture first become evident in the historical record? What do geography and environment, the islands and coastal plain, have to do with it?

This chapter seeks to examine the nuances of how historians identify blacks inhabiting the Carolina, Georgia, and Florida Lowcountry. Looking at the diverse and fluid meanings of Gullah in the nineteenth century, I argue that contemporary notions of Gullah Geechee identity cannot be projected backward into the past. During the 1930s and 1940s, Scholars such as Herskovits, Lorenzo Dow Turner, and former plantation owners and slaveholders established the framework of Gullah Geechee identity as it is understood today. Herskovits and Turner both conducted research in the context of Jim Crow segregation when scientific theories were used to justify notions of African American inferiority.

As an aid in understanding the antebellum history of the enslaved inhabitants of the Lowcountry region, and to examine the evolution of Gullah Geechee people, language, and culture not only in time but also in space, I am coining a new phrase, "Lowcountry Creole." It simultaneously indicates the uniqueness of the Lowcountry microenvironments, vis-à-vis the adjacent uplands, and the complex processes of creolization that took place among people of African descent throughout the New World and in some portions of coastal Western Africa and East Africa, including (but not limited to) the people who became the Gullah Geechee.

FLUIDITY OF "GULLAH" IN THE NINETEENTH CENTURY

In the nineteenth century, when "Gullah" first appeared in print media, it conveyed fluid and multiple meanings, most of which are quite different from how the term is construed today. The best example comprises court proceedings from the trials of forty-six black men accused of involvement with Denmark Vesey's slave insurrection. In 1822, Denmark Vesey, a free and literate black man, skilled carpenter, and African Methodist Episcopal preacher, was tried (and would be executed along with others) for organizing a plot to kill white slaveholders in Charleston, burn down the city, liberate enslaved people, and sail to the Republic of Haiti. Had this plot transpired, it would have been the largest slave insurrection in U.S. history.[12]

Historians have questioned whether or not there was really a conspiracy—an actual plan that Vesey and coconspirators intended to carry out—or whether it was nothing more than rumors circulating among free and enslaved blacks in Charleston. Newspapers in the city imposed a blackout on reporting about the trial, confining their coverage to the sentences and subsequent executions. With few contemporary reports, much of the historical literature on Vesey and the 1822 conspiracy plot is based on a narrow set of primary sources, especially a pamphlet of the court's record of the trial, Lionel Kennedy and Thomas Parker's *An Official Report of the Trials of Sundry Negroes*. Published in October 1822, a few months after the court proceedings and six weeks after Vesey's execution, *Official Report* ended the media blackout in Charleston and presented the first substantial coverage of Vesey's plot and court proceedings to the masses of white Charlestonians.[13] Edited by the magistrates who conducted the trials, *Official Report* claimed to be "originally taken, without even changing the phraseology," from the court's proceedings and to represent testimony "generally in the very words and by the witnesses." There were dissenting voices among the public at large, namely William Johnson, a sitting U.S. Supreme Court justice, and South Carolina governor Thomas Bennett, Johnson's brother-in-law. But despite their positions of power and authority, neither was able to sway the minds of the majority and prevent Vesey and the others from being hanged.[14]

It is important to note that the court that handled the Denmark Vesey proceedings was not a court at all by American standards of today. After all, this was the antebellum South, and the accused were black men said to have been plotting to kill white people. Vesey and the enslaved men accused of organizing the insurrection were not considered innocent until proven guilty. They had already been convicted of treason in the minds of the slaveholders chosen as jury members, and all proceedings were conducted behind closed doors, away from public scrutiny. Vesey was not represented by counsel, and he did not make a statement in his own defense before his execution. In fact, none of the defendants who would be executed in June faced their accusers, made statements in their own defense, or were represented by counsel or even by the men who held them in bondage. Several "star witnesses" were never arrested and instead received immunity in exchange for identifying men supposedly involved in the conspiracy plot. Other cooperating witnesses received sentences of exile instead of death. As historian Michael Johnson has argued, one should not assume that coerced and tortured men would or could tell the truth. Most would have said whatever they thought might save their own lives.[15]

Relying heavily on *Official Report*, historians have accepted at face value the testimony of witnesses, many of whom had no doubt been tortured. Regardless, the testimony does provide us with something useful: a glimpse of a fluid and malleable "Gullah" identity known among blacks (enslaved and free) and whites in Charleston by the early nineteenth century. It shows how a select group of enslaved blacks born in Angola identified themselves as "Gullah"— and how slaveholders identified them thusly too. Playing to white Charlestonians' fears, some witnesses who testified in the Vesey trial also associated "Gullah" with "conjure," magic based in Western African spiritual practices and used for evil purposes. Although geographic association of Gullah with Angola would wane and perhaps be transmuted to African survivals and retentions in the mid-twentieth and late twentieth century, Gullah's association with conjure and magic would survive.

The term "Gullah" would come to take on other meanings in the Denmark Vesey trial court proceedings. It was assigned to people who had been enslaved in Charleston as well as in the surrounding rural Lowcountry on the outskirts of Charleston, on Sea Island cotton plantations, and on rice plantations in the coastal plain. The scope of the term is much broader and more fluid than Herskovits's narrow definition of Gullah people living on the "Gulla Islands" in his 1945 "Scale of Intensity of New World Africanisms."

Jack Pritchard was a defendant in the Vesey trial who brought "Gullah" identity and its association with magic to the forefront of Charlestonians' imaginations. This transpired via an 1828 treatise on slavery written by Zephaniah Kingsley, a Florida planter who held Pritchard in bondage. Kingsley described Pritchard as a conjurer or "priest in his own country, M'Choolay Morcema, where a dialect of the Angola tongue is spoken clear across Africa from sea to sea, a distance perhaps of three thousand miles." Kingsley had purchased Pritchard, then a prisoner of war, in "Zinguebar," a port in East Africa, and Pritchard sailed to Charleston aboard the slave ship *Gustavia* in 1805. According to Kingsley, Pritchard came prepared to practice his profession: "[He] had his conjuring implements with him in a bag which he brought on board the ship and always retained them."[16]

In the Vesey proceedings on June 21, 1822, "Witness Y" (Yorrick Cross) recounted that Jack Pritchard "was also called Gullah Jack [and] sometimes Cooter Jack." Cross was identified only as "Witness Y" in *Official Record* because the planter who held him in bondage required that the court protect his identity. During the June proceedings, the magistrates also granted Cross immunity despite his self-incriminating testimony, testimony that would be used to convict others, including Gullah Jack.[17]

Cross claimed that he had gone to visit Gullah Jack after he, Cross, had refused three times to join Denmark Vesey's insurrection plot. When the magistrates examined Cross, he testified that he had said that he would join the insurrection after it started if he found it "strong enough" to defeat the whites. Gullah Jack, he said, had attempted to prove to him the strength and invulnerability of the insurrectionary force by giving him "some dry food . . . parched corn and ground nuts." Cross testified that Gullah Jack had instructed him to eat only these foods on the morning the insurrection began. He was to "put in [his] mouth this crab claw" and "drop the large crab claw out of [his] mouth [and] then put in the small one" when he joined the forces. As if he was answering Cross's question of whether or not the insurgency was "strong enough," Gullah Jack had said, according to Cross, that he "[gives] the same to all the rest of [his] troops." Gullah Jack had designed these acts, Cross testified, eating only parched corn and groundnuts and holding a crab claw or "cullah" in their mouths, to prevent Cross and the other men from "being wounded" when whites in Charleston defended themselves against the insurgency. His charms had earned Gullah Jack the reputation as "the little man who [couldn't] be killed, shot, or taken."[18] Gullah Jack's charms, however, did "not protect him against the treachery of his own colour."[19] Cross's testimony under oath that he was reluctant to join the plot may have saved his life. After his examination there is no record in the court proceedings of his sentencing. Cross's testimony on Gullah Jack's role, however, may have cost Gullah Jack his life.

During July court proceedings, arrested witnesses continued to testify against Gullah Jack even after he had been pronounced guilty and executed. The court did not grant these witnesses immunity, so they provided the testimony they hoped would save their lives.[20]

On Wednesday, July 10, 1822, Harry Haig testified that Jack Pritchard (Gullah Jack) "[called] himself a Dr. negro," a "Conjurer."[21] Eight days after Denmark Vesey's execution, Harry testified that before Gullah Jack "was taken," he "felt as if [he] was bound up and had not the power to speak one word about it."[22] Testifying against another defendant, Julius Forrest, Haig accused Gullah Jack of charming him and Julius into consenting to join Vesey's slave insurrection and of having said that he would give Haig a "bottle with poison in it to put into my Master's pump, and into . . . pumps . . . about town."[23] Haig's statements about Gullah Jack's plans to poison wells in Charleston come from the official state senate copy of the court proceedings. They were blacked out of *Official Report*, partly a testament to white southerners' fear of being poisoned by enslaved blacks. White Charlestonians might have panicked, after all, had they known the extent and sophistication of the rebellion. However, the expunging no doubt was also done to limit the suggestion from reaching the wrong readers, ones who might follow Vesey's lead more successfully.

Testifying under oath that he had refused to poison may have saved Harry Haig from the gallows. In exchange for his cooperation, Haig and eighteen other arrested "star witnesses" were sentenced to "transportation beyond the limits of the United States by their masters."[24] On the same day, an arrested man and witness named Billy Bulkley gave evidence against Gullah Jack. Bulkley described a meeting in which Gullah Jack officiated over a ritual. He and two other enslaved men, Adam and Robert—the latter played a principal role in Vesey's plot—"roasted a fowl and ate it half raw as an evidence of union."[25] According to *Official Report*, another of the court's pet witnesses, "George," belonging to "Mr. Vanderhorst," testified against Jack but only with "considerable difficulty that the Court satisfied him that he need no longer fear Jacks [*sic*] *conjurations*." Vanderhorst reportedly begged the court to send George into exile if it spared his life, because he "[considered his] life in great danger from having given testimony" against Gullah Jack.[26] George got his wish. He was sentenced to banishment, possibly in exchange for his testimony against Gullah Jack. A section of Vanderhorst's testimony was not recorded in the original court record. It was added to *Official Report* to construct a "trial" for Gullah Jack that would justify his execution by dramatizing the depth of his mystical and magical powers and demonstrating the extent of his threat to whites in Charleston as well as members of the black community who had no desire to hurt white people.

Not in the original trial proceedings, Gullah Jack's sentence was added to the *Official Report* published months afterward. In it, the magistrates embellished the image of Gullah Jack, the "Negro doctor," as a "conjurer" and "Necromancer." For their audience of white Charlestonians, the magistrates described Gullah Jack's ritual and military leadership in Vesey's plot as "wicked designs" through which he enlisted "all the powers of darkness, and employed for that purpose, the most disgusting mummery and superstition." After his charms and rituals failed to make him and other members of his band invulnerable to the gallows, Gullah Jack, it was said, stood exposed.[27] On July 9, 1822, Gullah Jack was sentenced to death for his leadership role in the Denmark Vesey slave insurrection. He was hanged three days later. Margaret Washington Creel has argued that Gullah Jack's death was a significant blow to West African spiritual traditions and enslaved Africans in the Lowcountry who continued to practice them.[28] For white Charlestonians, his death also represented another rare appearance in print media of the word "Gullah." One cluster of meanings of "Gullah" in the Vesey court proceedings denotes the identity and culture (including language) that emerged among enslaved and freed Africans in the Lowcountry and its association with "conjure" in the minds of white Charlestonians. Throughout the nineteenth and early twentieth centuries, Gullah would take on additional meanings beyond origins in Liberia or Angola.

According to the testimony of several accused men, Gullah Jack was not only a conjurer and an integral part of Denmark Vesey's plot to liberate Africans enslaved in Charleston, he was also a leader in his own right. Gullah Jack reportedly organized African men from Angola whom he would mobilize at the appointed hour to take up arms against whites. Defendants described Jack as a "Gullah Negro," denoting his African origins in the Angola region of West Central Africa. They reported that he served as the "general" of the "Gullah Company" or "Gullah Jack's band," and leader of a "Gullah Society . . . which met once a month."[29] According to the defendants, Gullah Jack's company was one of several regiments in the Vesey rebellion plot composed of African-born members from the same Western African ethnic group or region (or both). For example, Monday Gell's band was said to be composed of men who were from the Ibo areas of present-day southeastern Nigeria, and men from the Senegambia were said to comprise Perault Strohecker's band.[30] Both Gell and Strohecker were witnesses who cooperated with the court. Gell was rewarded for his cooperation with exile, while Strohecker was hanged.[31]

The members of Gullah Jack's band reportedly spoke a language distinct from English. James Mall, a white blacksmith who worked with Tom Russell, an enslaved blacksmith who several defendants testified was Gullah Jack's apprentice, reported that Russell and Gullah Jack "frequently talked together in Gullah so that I should not understand them." Perault Strohecker testified that in his presence Jack and a man named Nero had sometimes conversed in "the Gullah language," after which Nero had translated for Strohecker.[32]

Gullah Jack and Russell, both born in Angola, spoke a language that seems to have been different than the language Billy Bulkley spoke when he testified against Gullah Jack. Bulkley was a member of Gullah Jack's company.[33] According to the trial transcript, the court postponed its proceedings until an agent of his owner could be present to translate, because Bulkley "spoke English very badly; It was with great difficulty that [he] could be understood." In all probability, he spoke an English-based Creole language, a nineteenth-century register of Gullah. Like Gullah Jack, he may have been born in Angola, or he may have been from the "rural lowcountry, where Gullah was widely spoken." If Bulkley had spoken an African language, it would probably have been unintelligible to his owner's agent as well. Bulkley's farm was said to have been a frequent meeting place of the "Gullah Society" or "Gullah band" that Gullah Jack led. There may have been other enslaved people at Bulkley's farm who understood Gullah Jack and Billy Bulkley's speech.[34] Both were different from the "creole French" Perault Strohecker and Louis Remoussin spoke when they discussed the "French band" that would assist the insurgents in fighting against whites and enslavement.[35] In this fluid nineteenth-century milieu, it is unclear exactly what languages the men spoke and just what "Gullah language" meant. Were Mall and Strohecker referring to Gullah Jack's natal language, spoken in Angola, which other members of Jack's band would probably have understood? Or did they refer to an English-based Creole language, Gullah, which was born in the Lowcountry and would have been a means of communication among witnesses who originated in different subregions of West Africa?

The original transcripts of the Vesey trials provide some answers to questions about the evolution of the Gullah language. Although the court clerk transcribed the proceedings in a relatively standard dialect of English, the transcript is peppered with Gullah words. Whether the men who testified in the court proceedings spoke these words or the court clerks who transcribed— and embellished—the court proceedings put the Gullah words into the witnesses' mouths, they are rare nineteenth-century written evidence of the Gullah language.

For example, according to Lorenzo Dow Turner's scientific study of the Gullah language, "Cooter" was used as a personal name in Gullah. It was derived from "kuta," "water turtle" in the Bambara language spoken in former French West African colonies and possibly "kuto," "saltwater turtle" and "totem of some of the noble clans of Gambia" in the Mandinka language spoken in present-day Gambia, in either case from the Senegambia subregion of West Africa.[36] There is no record of what "band" Yorrick Cross ("Witness Y") belonged to, though such knowledge would give historians a clue as to his natal language. Witness Y testified that Gullah Jack was also called "Cooter Jack." A second Gullah word recorded in the proceedings is derived from "bʌkrə," "white man," literally "he who surrounds or governs" in the Ibo and Efik languages spoken in present-day Nigeria.[37] Smart Anderson, who testified that Gullah Jack called him a "friend to the bukra," was part of Perault Strohecker's band and likely from the Senegambia, not from Iboland as one might expect from his use of a word derived from the Ibo language.

The Gullah words sprinkled into the trial proceedings originated in different West African languages and were spoken by African-born enslaved men.

The witnesses who spoke them were from altogether different West African subregions. Thus, they were attempting to communicate both with men who spoke their natal language and with men who did not. In their testimony, the men accused of being a part of Denmark Vesey's insurrection plot communicated in a Creole language, Gullah, which the trial proceedings recorded in its nascent stage.

In addition to conjure and Creole language, the Denmark Vesey trial proceedings provide a window into one more aspect of Gullah identity formation in the nineteenth century: geography or environment. This chapter has already discussed the importance of the African-born men who Vesey entrusted to recruit men in Charleston who would carry out his insurrection plot. According to star witnesses, enslaved Africans in the rural areas surrounding Charleston were also to take part in the insurrection. The Lowcountry's urban and rural environments played critical roles in the ways coerced witnesses constructed the Vesey conspiracy for the magistrates and simultaneously gave evidence of the construction of nineteenth-century Gullah identity.

In a confession less than two weeks before his execution for participation in the Vesey insurrection plot, Bacchus Hamet described another defendant, Charles Drayton, as having visited the "farm at the fork of the road." According to Hamet, Drayton had asked an enslaved woman on the farm to see the "old daddy" who was "marked on the both sides of his face or on his face." Drayton was one of the star witnesses who provided more than three-quarters of the testimony during the July proceedings. In exchange for this, his death sentence was commuted to exile.[38] Hamet recounted that he and Drayton had taken the old man into the stables and told him of the insurrection plan, particularly about enslaved people from the countryside joining the fight.[39]

According to some witnesses, several of Vesey's emissaries went from Charleston to the countryside to recruit men to join the insurrection. Gullah Jack was one of these who traveled into the country, sometimes by canoe, to "gather the people's mind on the subject [of insurrection]."[40] Gullah Jack's use of canoe transport is a reminder of the significance of water among the Gullah Geechee. Tiya Miles's contribution to this volume, chapter 5, reveals the recurring tropes of "wing," "water," metaphysical transformation, and resistance to the trauma and memory of enslavement in oral histories collected among Gullah Geechee descendants of the enslaved in the early twentieth century. J. Lorand Matory has argued that the Gullah Geechee were not isolated because of water, they were instead connected by it, and the region's black inhabitants traveled by water to and from the mainland even before the construction of bridges in the 1950s.[41]

Back to the Vesey case, Frank and Adam, enslaved men who belonged to "Mr. Ferguson," testified on June 16, 1822, that a local slave patrol had stopped Jesse Blackwood on his way to "the country" to enlist as many "country Negroes" as possible. According to the testimony, Vesey sent Blackwood on an important mission to be sure enslaved people in the rural areas outside of Charleston were "in readiness to come down and assist" in killing the whites in Charleston and throwing off the yoke of enslavement, intending to "bring the Country people down" before the revolution "broke out."[42] Like Vesey, Blackwood never testified in his own defense. His silence and plea of not guilty did not save him from the gallows. He was hanged on July 2, 1822, the same day Vesey was executed.

More of Vesey's emissaries testified about going into "the Country" on the outskirts of Charleston, along the Ashley River, to Dorchester and Goose Creek.[43] They reported traveling to the Sea Islands, where long-staple cotton plantations were located, particularly James and Johns Islands, the coastal plain where rice plantations predominated, along the Santee and Combahee Rivers, and to Georgetown and Christ Church Parish.[44] They reported traveling outside of South Carolina to Savannah and outside of the Lowcountry to Columbia.[45]

Vesey's emissaries are examples of ongoing communication networks between the free and enslaved men who were hired out in Charleston and Africans enslaved on rice, Sea Island cotton, and indigo plantations in the surrounding rural areas. The freedmen and slaves who were closest to Vesey were relatively autonomous compared to blacks enslaved on rural Lowcountry plantations, living on their own, running their own shops that even employed white artisans, and having freedom to move around and assemble as long as they paid their wages to their slaveholders. Jesse Blackwood's frequent recruiting trips interfered with his weekly obligation to slaveholder Thomas Blackwood. Bacchus Hamet testified that Vesey had asked those men who had attended a planning meeting to "throw in seven pence apiece . . . to make up for a friend to pay his wages to his Master" when Blackwood went to the country to recruit.[46] Some of the enslaved men involved in the rebellion visited their wives, children, and siblings in the country as well as reporting to slaveholders there. Men and women enslaved on country plantations came to Charleston on Saturdays to sell vegetables from their gardens.[47] Men accused of participating in the insurrection plot testified that they used these communication networks to spread information, gather support, and plan strategy.

Or did they? If Vesey's insurrection was not an actual plot, plans that the

Pin Point: A Traditional African American Community

In the last decade of the nineteenth century, a community of African Americans migrated from Ossabaw Island, where they had been forcibly located as slaves, to the mainland. They had been blown from their known world by the so-called Sea Islands Hurricane of 1893, an event that caused hundreds of deaths along the coast. When freedom had come at the end of the Civil War, and with it the promise of land, the community had expected that they would be more than tenant farmers on the twenty-six-thousand-acre island. They soon discovered, not for the last time, that promises made were not necessarily kept.

Rejecting tenancy on Ossabaw and retreating toward the mainland, the community sought land and the stability of ownership. Their opportunity for permanent settlement came in 1896 when Judge Henry McAlpin bought a nearby plantation, Beaulieu, to be marketed as property "on the Salts," as upper-class Savannahians termed the new summer retreats on the water. The backside of the plantation, a narrow bluff bordering a marsh with deepwater access at high tide, was divided into parcels and sold to several black families. The first purchase was made jointly by elders of the Hinder-Me-Not Baptist Church, the center of religious and cultural life on Ossabaw. On this spot, they re-created their island church and renamed it Sweetfields-of-Eden. With the church as a focal point, they re-created their older way of life built around the water, hard work, family, and a strong faith.

Relocation meant self-employment for many of the founding families. Some built rudimentary "factories" for processing local seafood, while others crafted sturdy, shallow draft bateaux for harvesting the waters, knitted seines, and made crab traps. Pin Point women disassembled the crabs, oysters, and shrimp that not only fed their families but also were shipped to the Savannah Market via trolley from neighboring Montgomery Heights.

The industrious community came to the attention of seafood dealer Algernon Varn, who moved into Pin Point in 1926. He first rented a "factory" site, and then in 1929 he built his own complex of processing buildings with labor-saving innovations. He bought the supplies for bateaux and traps and a motorized towboat to move the bateaux into working position on the early tide. Faced with this competition, the original "factories" of the first residents disappeared. The community benefited from a convenient workplace, and Varn was able to expand his business as far as Washington, D.C., on iced-down shipments via Greyhound bus. Varn took a paternal interest in Pin Point that was sometimes benevolent and at other times self-serving.

After World War II, the community faced challenges. The oystering industry faded due to overfishing, the younger generation began moving away, and white-

Baptism at Pin Point.
Courtesy of the Georgia Historical Society.

owned firms of a larger scale crowded out marginal producers. The Varn factory closed its doors in 1987, too small to compete with industrialization of the market. The last bateau maker is gone, and his last bateau rots, nearly unrecognized, as the trade symbol of a local fishmonger. The last waterman, very likely the best that Pin Point ever produced, knew the bottom of the local waters better than we know our own yards.

Now Pin Point has its feet firmly in the twenty-first century. The children and grandchildren have entered the mainstream of American life as dockworkers, teachers, soldiers, electricians, and professionals, including Supreme Court Justice Clarence Thomas. Its family histories are the substance of interpretation at a new museum in the Varn Factory Complex. Many of the present generation live contemporary lives in an urban landscape, returning for church on Sundays and for family events. While Pin Point still reflects a traditional African American community, its history joins the growing story of who we are as Americans.

BARBARA FERTIG

accused meant to carry out—if the men who testified to this lied and told the court what they hoped would save their lives, or if it was mostly or entirely based on rumors circulating among free and enslaved Africans who lived and worked in Charleston—would this change historians' ability to read the testimony as a valid historical source about the enslaved community? I think not. An Africanist would consider the accused men's testimony an example of "evidence in spite of itself." Other examples of "evidence in spite of itself" from precolonial African history include accounts by the first European explorers, traders, and missionaries to show up in any given locale on the continent, describing the place, its inhabitants, and their ways. In precolonial Western Africa, traders in the interior were sometimes Muslims from across the Sahara Desert, and traders on the coast were usually European or American slave traders who tortured African captives and trafficked in human flesh. All of these explorers, traders, missionaries, and, later, early colonial officials had in common biases, prejudices, and downright racist attitudes about Africans' bodies, mores, religious practices, methods of social and political organization, and more. They all described what they saw from their own biased points of view. Many Africanist historians have worked in societies that preserve oral traditions going back more than a few centuries about topics of interest to professionally trained Western historians. But even these oral traditions have their own inherent biases. And not all African societies, particularly not most stateless societies, possessed institutions that preserved and passed down history orally. In these cases, Africanists have made small interventions with interdisciplinary sources, studies of linguistics, archaeology, and biology (even pollen studies), but these are minuscule compared to the amount of precolonial African history that was never recorded in writing, or never passed down via oral narratives, and thus we may never know.[48]

From an Africanist's perspective, we do not have the luxury of throwing out the testimony of enslaved black men in the 1822 Denmark Vesey proceedings. It is exceedingly rare evidence of its kind, through which historians can hear enslaved Africans' voices in the early-nineteenth-century South Carolina Lowcountry, coerced and tortured though they were. While the testimony may not be conclusive evidence of a plot to kill white Charlestonians, burn the city, free the slaves, and remove them to a free black republic in the Caribbean, it does have value for historians. Would accused men who told the court what it wanted to hear paint a false picture of themselves and their communities that did not ring true to white Charlestonians?

Like the racist accounts by explorers, traders, missionaries, and colonial officials in Africa, the inherent biases in the Denmark Vesey trial must be interrogated and then the proceedings read "against the grain" as "evidence in spite of itself." I suggest that the testimony is evidence of identity formation and community-building among enslaved and free blacks in the early nineteenth century, when the identities of blacks in the Lowcountry were fluid and dynamic. African-born and American-born men still identified themselves as such, spoke different languages, and clung to their own kind. They had different experiences depending on whether they lived in the city, rural outskirts, or the islands and coastal plain, on indigo, rice, and Sea Island cotton plantations. But networks of commerce and family kept them bound together. In addition, the testimony in the Vesey proceedings is evidence that the diverse enslaved and free black populations came together over matters of mutual survival and potentially mutual liberation, drawing on common spiritual practices and communicating in an English-based Creole language. No one natal African language emerged as lingua franca. Instead the lingua franca was something entirely new, which I call Lowcountry Creole because it was born in the Lowcountry environment primarily among blacks who themselves were born there and were Creoles—people of blended cultures. The Lowcountry Creole language—and wider Lowcountry Creole culture—of the early nineteenth century would in the twentieth century become known as Gullah Geechee.

CONCLUSION

Understanding the "where," the place where the Gullah Geechee are rooted, is critical to broadening and deepening our understanding of *who* the Gullah Geechee are. The people today known as the Gullah Geechee and their culture evolved from Lowcountry Creoles in the colonial and antebellum periods to Gullah Geechee in the twentieth century. Although the Sea Islands are the locale most associated with them, the Denmark Vesey trial proceedings present evidence of a largely urban Gullah Geechee identity that reached out into the rural areas around Charleston. Within these rural areas lie a diversity of microenvironments, which are at the core of how historians should understand the Lowcountry Creoles, and in many respects these still resonate among the contemporary Gullah Geechee.

In comparing rice cultivation in precolonial West Africa and antebellum South Carolina, geographer Judith Carney found that soil types and water regimes, including but not limited to inches of annual precipitation, were defining characteristics in different rice cultivation systems and microenvironments. The landscape gradient in which West African farmers grew rice in the central Gambia ranged from well-drained uplands located a few hundred feet above sea level to along the banks of freshwater rivers, coastal estuaries all flooded by diurnal tides.[49] While Carney investigated the microenvironments in which Gambian farmers grew rice, the concept of microenvironments and the distinct soil types and water regimes therein can be broadened beyond the rice fields of West Africa to the South Carolina Lowcountry.

For example, Mart Stewart's contribution to this volume (chapter 1) discusses Quaker naturalist William Bartram's extensive tour of the southeastern United States, particularly coastal Georgia, North and South Carolina, and Florida in April 1773 (see map 4.1). In Georgia, Bartram described two subregions within the "Lower Coastal Plain" closest to the coast. First, on the barrier islands and in the coastal lands ("Coastal Strip and Tidewater"), Bartram found sandy soils and pine forests. Bartram also found pockets of sandy soils and "excellent hummocky land" as far south as Amelia Island, north of the St. Johns River in coastal Florida. Second, the "Flat Pine Lands," on the other hand, were riddled with swamplands, with rich, black earth supporting a wide variety of shrubs, trees, and canes.[50] North of the Savannah River in Two Sisters, South Carolina, Bartram described black oak and laurel trees growing in "dark, loose, fertile mould" topped with cinereous ash-colored clay. Along the Cape Fear River in North Carolina, "grand forests and expansive Cane meadows" grew on the riverbanks nearly seventy feet high and extending for two to three miles along the river. The soils and flora differed in microenvironments on the coast and in coastal plains. According to Bartram, so did the fauna. The "crying bird," "called by an Indian name (Ephouskyca)"—today known as limpkin—was found on riverbanks, in marshes and meadows, at the top of "tall dead Cypress trees," and on deserted rice plantations. "Crying birds" were not found in tidewater microenvironments on the salty coast, yet they were "never found a great distance from it."[51]

Bartram also described the people he observed in Lowcountry microenvironments. The enslaved blacks who inhabited the coastal lands stretching from Cape Fear, North Carolina, to Amelia Island, Florida, would not have identified themselves as Lowcountry Creoles or Gullah Geechee in the late eighteenth century, nor did Bartram identify them as such. But Bartram visited the Lowcountry microenvironments where enslaved Africans were in the process of creolization.

While the soils, flora, and fauna are paramount in Bartram's account, Bartram paid some attention to the crops growing in Lowcountry microenvironments and to enslaved Africans whose labor planters exploited to grow the region's commercial and staple crops: indigo and Sea Island cotton, thriving on the barrier islands of the coastal strip and tidewater, and "extensive plantations of rice."[52] As tidal rice production took hold of Georgia's coast, Bartram witnessed enslaved laborers felling cypress trees, a prelude to the establishment of tidal rice fields and the construction of irrigation systems. It was arduous work requiring "eight or ten negroes" to climb up on a stage raised high enough for them to reach the buttresses of majestic cypress trees "with their axes" and then fell giants with trunks measuring "eight, ten, and twelve feet in diameter."[53] Working in the swamps was also dangerous. "Miserable naked slaves" forced to labor in low-lying areas had to contend with the likes of water moccasins, "three to four and even five feet in length, and as thick as a man's leg," whose "crooked poisonous fangs" delivered potentially deadly venom.[54]

Africans enslaved on Sea Island cotton plantations experienced healthier working and living conditions than those enslaved on coastal plain rice plantations. Pierce Butler, proprietor of a rice plantation on Butler's Island and a Sea Island cotton plantation on St. Simons Island, Georgia, moved his family each summer from the rice plantation to the cotton plantation, where they "would suffer less from the heat." In her diary, Butler's wife, Fanny Kemble, wrote that her husband also "turned out to grass" his sickly, superannuated, and infirm enslaved laborers who could no longer work in the rice swamps. The healthier climate, better living and working conditions, and relatively lighter work regime on Sea Island cotton plantations did not diminish the high rates of miscarriage, stillbirth, and infant mortality. Although several enslaved women Fanny Kemble interviewed in 1838–39 had large families of surviving children, they had also buried approximately half of their offspring.[55] The realities of enslaved Africans' experiences on the Sea Islands defy the old notions of them as "utopian places . . . of reserve and retreat," which Stewart questions in his contribution to this volume.

Coastal Georgia's rice plantations, particularly along the Savannah River, had some of the highest death rates in the Americas, second only to sugar plantations in the Caribbean and the U.S. South. Historian William Dusinberre estimates that two out of three children born on rice plantations in the nineteenth century died before the age of fifteen. Historians do not have the tools or the sources to count stillbirths and miscarriages among enslaved women; doing so would make these already ghastly death rates even higher. More complete plantation records for the eighteenth century would probably reveal even higher death rates during the early years of commercial rice production. According to Dusinberre, approximately 61 percent of children enslaved on Butler's Island died before age sixteen of gastro-intestinal diseases, malaria and other summer fevers, and what was referred to as "puniness." On Gowrie Plantation, enslaved laborers were made to live on swampy islands in the vicinity of rice fields flooded with stagnant, mosquito-infested water, and they were dependent on polluted water supplies so that the slaveholder could maintain plantation discipline. Ninety percent of infants born to these laborers died between 1833 and 1861, many from malaria and gastro-intestinal diseases.[56] The diversity of Lowcountry microenvironments contributed to the diversity of enslaved people's experiences on indigo, rice, and Sea Island cotton plantations, important factors in Lowcountry creolization in the colonial and antebellum periods.

Focusing on an examination of place allows historians to interrogate change over time in the making of the Gullah Geechee. As early as the seventeenth century, African captives from diverse subregions of West and West Central Africa were imported into Carolina ports. I have argued elsewhere that these captives originated primarily in two distinct Western African subregions, the Upper Guinea Coast and Kongo/Angola, where centuries of warfare, transatlantic trade, Catholic conversion, and interaction with European traders led to creolization that would influence the formation of Lowcountry Creole culture, including language, in the seventeenth through nineteenth centuries.[57] Place mattered in the Lowcountry, and Creole culture developed among enslaved and freed blacks not only on the Sea Islands but also in cities and in coastal plains. In diverse coastal microenvironments, enslaved Africans' labor and ingenuity produced staple crops—indigo, rice, and Sea Island cotton. Historians should next examine how enslaved Africans' diverse experiences in these places—Lowcountry cities and microenvironments where the commercial crops were grown—contributed to the diversity of Lowcountry Creole culture through the nineteenth century and what became the Gullah Geechee in the twentieth century. Lowcountry Creoles, the microenvironments they inhabited, their experiences of enslavement, and the Creole culture they developed in the coastal region make more nuanced and enrich the environmental history of Georgia's coast and the sense of why this unique place remains important to their Gullah Geechee descendants.

NOTES

I would like to express my sincere thanks to Paul Pressly, Paul Sutter, and the Ossabaw Island Foundation for organizing and executing the Coastal Nature, Coastal Culture Symposium and edited volume and inviting me to participate, and to Terry Weik for his feedback.

1. Melville J. Herskovits, "The Negro in the New World: The Statement of a Problem," *American Anthropologist* 32, no. 1 (1930): 145, 146, 148, 149–50.

2. Herskovits, "Problem, Method and Theory in Afroamerican Studies," *Afroamerica* 1 (1945): 5–24.

3. Ibid., 14, 13.

4. Ambrose Elliott Gonzales, *The Black Border: Gullah Stories of the Carolina Coast (with a Glossary)* (1922; repr., Gretna, La.: Pelican, 1998), 2.

5. Lorenzo Dow Turner, *Africanisms in the Gullah Dialect* (Columbia: University of South Carolina Press, 2002 [1949]).

6. Salikoko Mufwene, *The Ecology of Language Evolution* (Cambridge: Cambridge University Press, 2001), 95.

7. Julia Floyd Smith, *Slavery and Rice Culture in Low Country Georgia, 1750–1860* (Knoxville: University of Tennessee Press, 1985); Daniel C. Littlefield, *Rice and Slaves: Ethnicity and the Slave Trade in Colonial South Carolina* (Baton Rouge: Louisiana State University Press, 1981); Betty Wood, *Slavery in Colonial Georgia, 1730–1775* (Athens: University of Georgia Press, 1984); William Dusinberre, *Them Dark Days: Slavery in the American Rice Swamps* (Oxford: Oxford University Press, 1996); Leslie Ann Schwalm, *"A Hard Fight for We": Women's Transition from Slavery to Freedom in South Carolina* (Urbana: University of Illinois Press, 1997); Leslie Ann Schwalm, "'Sweet Dreams of Freedom': Freedwomen's Reconstruction of Life and Labor in Lowcountry South Carolina," *Journal of Women's History* 9, no. 1 (1997); Brian Kelly, "Black Laborers, the Republican Party, and the Crisis of Reconstruction in Lowcountry South Carolina," *International Review of Social History* 51, no. 3 (2006); Daina Ramey Berry, *"Swing the Sickle for the Harvest Is Ripe": Gender and Slavery in Antebellum Georgia* (Urbana: University of Illinois Press, 2007); Brian Kelly, "Labor and Place: The Contours of Freedpeoples' Mobilization in Reconstruction South Carolina," *Journal of Peasant Studies* 35, no. 4 (2008): 653–87; Ras Michael Brown, *African-American Cultures in the South Carolina Lowcountry* (New York: Cambridge University Press, 2012); Akiko Ochiai, *Harvesting Freedom: African American Agrarianism in Civil War Era South Carolina* (Westport, Conn.: Praeger, 2004); Frederick C. Knight, *Working the Diaspora: The Impact of African Labor on the Anglo-American World, 1650–1850* (New York: New York University Press, 2010).

8. Jodi A. Barnes and Carl Steen, "Archaeology of the Gullah Past: A Community Scale Analysis," *South Carolina Antiquities* 44 (2012): 85–95; Christopher T. Espenshade, "A Few Words on Gullah Archaeology," http://www.academia.edu/; Theresa A. Singleton, "Reclaiming the Gullah-Geechee Past: Archaeology of Slavery in Coastal Georgia," in *African American Life in the Georgia Lowcountry: The Atlantic World and the Gullah Geechee*, ed. Philip Morgan (Athens: University of Georgia Press, 2010), 151–87.

9. Charles Joyner, *Down by the Riverside: A South Carolina Slave Community* (Urbana: University of Illinois Press, 1984).

10. Margaret Washington Creel, *"A Peculiar People": Slave Religion and Community-Culture among the Gullahs* (New York: New York University Press, 1989).

11. Philip Morgan, ed., *African American Life in the Georgia Lowcountry: The Atlantic World and the Gullah Geechee* (Athens: University of Georgia Press, 2010).

12. Michael P. Johnson, "Denmark Vesey and His Co-Conspirators," *William and Mary Quarterly*, 3rd series 58, no. 4 (2001): 940.

13. Lionel Kennedy and Thomas Parker, *An Official Report of the Trials of Sundry Negroes Charged with an Attempt to Raise an Insurrection in the State of South-Carolina Preceded by an Introduction and Narrative and, in an Appendix, a Report of the Trials of Four White Persons on Indictments for Attempting to Excite the Slaves to Insurrection* (Charleston: Printed by J. R. Schenck, 1822), 107; Edward A. Pearson, ed., *Designs against Charleston: The Trial Record of the Denmark Vesey Slave Conspiracy of 1822* (Chapel Hill: University of North Carolina Press, 1999), 13, 196. For a thorough critique on how *Official Report* falsified and sanitized "evidence" (the original court proceedings), see Michael P. Johnson, "Denmark Vesey and His Co-Conspirators," 941, 926, 928, 933–35, 941–42, 944, 946, 950–52, 958, 961.

14. Richard C. Wade, "The Vesey Plot: A Reconsideration," *Journal of Southern History* 30, no. 2 (1964): 150, 149, 144–46, 151–52. In her letters, Anna Hayes Johnson, William Johnson's daughter and Thomas Bennett's niece, expressed panic and fear over the reported brutality that insurgents plotted to commit, particularly against white women, then skepticism that the plot was real. See Johnson, "Denmark Vesey and His Co-Conspirators," 915–16, 919.

15. Johnson, "Denmark Vesey and His Co-Conspirators," 916, 919, 924–25, 933–35, 942–44, 946–48, 950–53, 967, 971.

16. Zephaniah Kingsley, *A Treatise on the Patriarchal, or Co-Operative System of Society as It Exists in Some Governments and Colonies in America, and in the United States, under the Name of Slavery, with Its Necessity and Advantages* (Freeport, N.Y.: Books for Libraries Press, 1970), 13.

17. Johnson, "Denmark Vesey and His Co-Conspirators," 944–45.

18. "Enclosure B, Court Proceedings and Testimony Regarding the Denmark Vesey Rebellion, Senate Copy," in *Legislative Papers, 1782–1866*, in collection of South Carolina Department of Archives and History, 145, 149, 152, 153, 161, 167, 184, 241.

19. Ibid., 146.

20. Johnson, "Denmark Vesey and His Co-Conspirators," 945–47.

21. "Enclosure B, Court Proceedings and Testimony Regarding the Denmark Vesey Rebellion, Senate Copy," 183, 146.

22. Ibid., 183–84.

23. Ibid., 184, 183; "John Potter to Langdon Cheves 16 July 1822," Langdon Cheves, "Langdon Cheves Family Papers, 1807–1932," South Carolina Historical Society, Charleston; Lois A. Walker and Susan R. Silverman, *A Documented History of Gullah Jack Pritchard and the Denmark Vesey Slave Insurrection of 1822* (Lewiston: E. Mellen Press, 2000), 270n.

24. "Enclosure B, Court Proceedings and Testimony Regarding the Denmark Vesey Rebellion, Senate Copy," 146.

25. Ibid., 191.

26. Ibid., 149–50; Kennedy and Parker, *An Official Report of the Trials of Sundry Negroes*, 105–6.

27. "Enclosure B, Court Proceedings and Testimony Regarding the Denmark Vesey Rebellion, Senate Copy," 179.

28. Creel, *Peculiar People*, 157.

29. "Enclosure B, Court Proceedings and Testimony Regarding the Denmark Vesey Rebellion, Senate Copy," 145, 148, 149, 152, 205, 208–9, 153, 167, 201.

30. Ibid., 146–47, 211, 212, 214, 222, 197, 148, 191, 192.

31. Johnson, "Denmark Vesey and His Co-Conspirators," 944–47.

32. "Enclosure B, Court Proceedings and Testimony Regarding the Denmark Vesey Rebellion, Senate Copy," 184, 194, 253.

33. Johnson, "Denmark Vesey and His Co-Conspirators," 944–47.

34. "Enclosure B, Court Proceedings and Testimony Regarding the Denmark Vesey Rebellion, Senate Copy," 191, 201.

35. Ibid., 185, 194.

36. Turner, *Africanisms in the Gullah Dialect*, 118–19, 197.

37. Ibid., 191; "Enclosure B, Court Proceedings and Testimony Regarding the Denmark Vesey Rebellion, Senate Copy," 177; Pearson, *Designs against Charleston*, 297; Johnson, "Denmark Vesey and His Co-Conspirators," 944–45.

38. Johnson, "Denmark Vesey and His Co-Conspirators," 944–47.

39. Pearson, *Designs against Charleston*, 307.

40. "Enclosure B, Court Proceedings and Testimony Regarding the Denmark Vesey Rebellion, Senate Copy," 208, 253, 143, 179, 203, 190.

41. J. Lorand Matory, "The Illusion of Isolation: The Gullah/Geechees and the Political Economy of African-American Cultures in the Americas," *Comparative Studies in Society and History* 50, no. 4 (2008): 959, 949, 951, 956–58, 961, 966, 972–73, 975–76.

42. "Enclosure B, Court Proceedings and Testimony Regarding the Denmark Vesey Rebellion, Senate Copy," 165, 199, 167, 223, 154, 168, 171, 207, 208, 209, 211, 166, 158, 161, 172, 174, 179, 187, 196, 204, 201, 214, 219, 221, 231; Johnson, "Denmark Vesey and His Co-Conspirators," 921.

43. "Enclosure B, Court Proceedings and Testimony Regarding the Denmark Vesey Rebellion, Senate Copy.", 210, 177, 143, 147, 211.

44. Ibid., 153, 154, 158, 163, 160, [210], 209.

45. Ibid., 189, 211, 221, 250.

46. Ibid., 174.

47. Loren Schweninger, "Slave Independence and Enterprise in South Carolina, 1780–1865," *South Carolina Historical Magazine* 93, no. 2 (1992): 101–25; Ellen Hartigan-O'Connor, "'She Said She Did Not Know Money': Urban Women and Atlantic Markets in the Revolutionary Era," *Early American Studies* 4, no. 2 (2006): 322–52.

48. Jan Vansina, *Paths in the Rainforests: Toward a History of Political Tradition in Equatorial Africa* (Madison: University of Wisconsin Press, 1990); David Lee Schoenbrun, *"A Green Place, a Good Place": Agrarian Change, Gender, and Social Identity in the Great Lakes Region to the 15th Century* (Portsmouth, N.H.: Heinemann, 1998); Edda L. Fields-Black, *Deep Roots: Rice Farmers in West Africa and the African Diaspora* (Bloomington: Indiana University Press, 2008).

49. Judith Ann Carney, *Black Rice: The African Origins of Rice Cultivation in the Americas* (Cambridge, Mass.: Harvard University Press, 2001), 28–29, 57–60.

50. Mart A. Stewart, *"What Nature Suffers to Groe": Life, Labor, and Landscape on the Georgia Coast, 1680–1920* (Athens: University of Georgia Press, 2002), 14.

51. William Bartram, *The Travels of William Bartram*, naturalist's ed., ed. Francis Harper (1958; repr., Athens: University of Georgia Press, 1998), 42, 19–21, 5, 195–96, 381, 430, 11–13, 14, 21, 298–302, 420, 476, 437–38, 93–95, 31–32; Stewart, *What Nature Suffers to Groe*, 14.

52. Bartram described indigo plantations on Winyaw Bay, South Carolina, St. Marys River and barrier islands in Georgia, and Amelia Island and St. Johns River in Florida. Bartram, *Travels of William Bartram*, 298, 16, 42–43, 50, 64–65, 91, 160. He recorded Sea Island cotton being grown on plantations on the St. Marys River and on barrier islands off the coast of Georgia. Ibid., 16, 43. Lastly, he toured rice plantations more extensively on Georgia's Savannah, Altamaha, Ogeechee, and St. Marys Rivers. Ibid., 6, 43, 196, 237, 6–7, 11, 43, 43, 16.

53. Ibid., 59, 197–98.

54. Ibid., 171.

55. Frances Anne Kemble, *Journal of a Residence on a Georgian Plantation in 1838–1839*, ed. John A. Scott (1863; repr., Athens: University of Georgia, 1984), 161, 207–8, 227, 223, 229–31, 241, 245, 255.

56. Dusinberre, *Them Dark Days*, 80, 103, 237, 240, 238, 48–83, 445–51, 410–16; Kemble, *Journal of a Residence on a Georgian Plantation in 1838–1839*, 55.

57. Edda L. Fields-Black, "Creolization in Pre-Modern West Africa and the African Diaspora: 'Lowcountry Creoles' and the Making of the Gullah Geecchee," in *General History of Africa*, vol. 9, *Global Africa*, ed. Carol Boyce-Davies, Mamadou Diouf, Paul Lovejoy, Vanicleia Silva Santos, and Sheila Walker (Berkeley: University of California Press, forthcoming).

CHAPTER 5

Haunted Waters

*Stories of Slavery, Coastal Ghosts, and
Environmental Consciousness*

TIYA MILES

The great African American intellectual W. E. B. Du Bois opens the first chapter of his classic work *The Souls of Black Folk* with haunting words about water. Borrowing from the poetic writings of British author Arthur Symons, Du Bois begins: "Oh water, voice of my heart, crying in the sand, / All night long crying with a mournful cry. . . . / All life long crying without avail. / As the water all night long is crying to me." In doing so he frames his meditation on black consciousness in America with an image of water, the coast, and loss. Du Bois's decision to launch this philosophical treatise with a reference to coastal waters, and to focus later in the book on "the crimson soil of Georgia" as "a spot which is to-day the centre of the Negro problem," indicates the centrality of Georgia to African American cultural memory and to the history of American slavery and race relations.

Indeed, as anthropologist Paulla Ebron has explained in her analysis of slavery and public memory, the "southeastern coast of the United States where Gullah Geechee communities reside . . . has particular significance to US American history, for it is the region where much of the early accumulation of capitalist wealth of the United States happened."[1] Du Bois calls this critically important region "the Cotton Kingdom,—the shadow of a marvelous dream," where "a resistless feeling of depression falls slowly upon us despite the gaudy sunshine." Water is a predominant natural feature of this "marvelous" and "depressing" place, reflecting fluid borders between beauty and pain, realism and supernaturalism. The tears of the poet are echoed by the wet terrain of Georgia, a landscape of emotional resonance and psychic mourning that captures a contradictory cultural history.

The weight of water in the African American experience of Georgia ripples into wider domains of black southern life, including recurring religious references to the River Jordan as a locus of spiritual crossing in African American spirituals, which W. E. B. Du Bois called "the sorrow songs" born of slavery, as well as a long tradition of communal baptism in rivers and creeks.[2] Historian Michael Gomez writes that the reverence for water in African American religious traditions may echo "Yoruba, Fon, and Akan affinities for water" and the Bakongo spiritual belief that ancestors dwelled in a world underneath the waters.[3] As silent witness to black oppression and resistance, and as a place of transformation and final rest, water has played a consequential regional and diasporic role.

Contests over oppression and the refusal to be dehumanized were waged through the medium of water. Euro-American slaveholders constructed an entrenched system of bondage along the fertile coasts and soggy rice fields of Georgia, imprinting memories of trauma onto the lives of the enslaved against backdrops of water-rich landscapes. Among many other strategies of noncompliance to their objectification, African Americans created an imaginative story-world that enlisted water as an enabler of their survival. This story-world, structured by recurring tropes of winged flight and water-borne magic, traveled across the generations with those held as slaves, preserved through memory as well as revision into our own time. Originating on the coast of Georgia among the population often described as Gullah Geechee and redefined by historian Edda Fields-Black in this collection as "Lowcountry Creoles" who fashioned dynamic cultural practices, this place-based wing-and-water corpus of stories has become essential to trans-regional African American culture, which embraces it as a rich source of collective identity, meaning, and strength.

This essay explores African American oral tradition in coastal Georgia with a focus on stories and the cultural work they perform. The chapter steers through two distinct narrative shoals in order to trace the developmental contexts and cultural meanings of this oral tradition and its imprint on contemporary publics. The first shoal is the capacious genre of interconnected "flying African" and Ebo Landing lore first articulated by formerly enslaved residents of Georgia. The second shoal is a sampling of "ghost tour" narratives in the Lowcountry South that repackage and retell these traditional stories for travelers and consumers. Ultimately this chapter asks whether an African American oral tradition that is still capturing the imagination of diverse storytellers and listeners today can be channeled into an eco-cultural consciousness that

motivates habits of preservation along the Georgia coastline. This consciousness would recognize the integral links between environmental awareness and
cultural memory, as illustrated by the theme of water in stories of the enslaved,
and would also, I hope, lead to the protection of coastal waterways as well as
historic sites of slavery marked by them.

No folklore in the African American cultural canon possesses greater resonance than the story of enslaved men and women who "flew" back to Africa from the coast of Georgia during the period of chattel slavery. This lore,
sometimes referred to as "the myth of the flying Africans," was handed down
across generations of enslaved black people and recorded by local employees of
the Federal Writers' Project in the 1930s. Twenty-three reports of flying Africans appear in the interviews of the Georgia Writers' Project in a problematic
but revealing 1940 volume titled *Drums and Shadows: Survival Studies among
the Georgia Coastal Negroes*.[4] As Drew Swanson further discusses in chapter
6 in this volume, *Drums and Shadows* poses difficulties for scholars and interpreters today. Savannah-based project managers framed and compiled the
book amid unequal power relations between mostly white interviewers and
formerly enslaved African American interviewees. State interviewers, seeking
to salvage the remnants of an "exotic" African past on the relatively secluded
Georgia coast where Gullah Geechee cultural formations remained strong,
shaped these exchanges with leading and limiting questions meant to elicit information about racialized folk practices (such as drumming and the fashion-
ing of charms) and superstitious beliefs (such as visions of ghosts and witches).
The narrow and indeed racist tenor of these interview scripts shaped a skewed
picture of black memories of coastal slavery. We will never know what these
elder women and men would have said had they been asked open-ended questions by members of their own families or communities who respected their
agency and knowledge. Nevertheless, the existing interviews offer a window—
clouded though it is—into the deep oral tradition of black Georgians in particular and African Americans in general. For the story of the flying Africans,
found primarily in these Georgia records, is claimed for African American
culture writ large and has yielded masterworks of African American letters,
cinema, and photography, including Toni Morrison's epic novel of black identity *Song of Solomon* (1977), Paule Marshall's moving portrayal of a woman's
spiritual rebirth *Praisesong for the Widow* (1983), Virginia Hamilton's beautiful children's book *The People Who Could Fly* (1985), Julie Dash's poetic film
Daughters of the Dust (1991), and the award-winning visual artist Carrie Mae
Weems's photographs in the Sea Island Series (1991–92).[5]

The flying African accounts as retold by former slaves in Georgia offer testimony—two to three generations removed—about the ability of an oppressed black people who had been seized from their homelands to resist the physical and psychological brutality of bondage.[6] By accessing forms of magic hidden to their slaveholder-captors, the protagonists of these stories flew like birds over the Atlantic Ocean back to the places of their births. One formerly enslaved man, Thomas Smith, credited the original homeland as the source of this secret power, citing events from the book of Exodus in the Bible as evidence that "Africa was a land of magic power since the beginning of history" and asserting that this power was transportable across the Middle Passage. "Well, then," he continued, "the descendants of Africans have the same gift to do unnatural things. I've heard the story of the flying Africans and I sure believe it happened."[7] As religious studies scholar Timothy Powell has explained, these flight tales are narratives of transformation that reshape "the hardships of slavery into the magical powers of freedom."[8] Across the many retellings of this tale, speakers indicate that they themselves had been told the story at an earlier point in their lives, often from an eyewitness born in Africa and thus able to engage in cultural translation for the American-born listener. "All their lives," an unnamed shopkeeper in the community of Springfield reported in her Georgia Writers' Project interview, "they hear about them [magical things] from the old folks."[9] The flying African tales are therefore evidence not only of a collective resistant spirit that relies on spirituality as well as creativity for its enactment, but also of a living oral tradition in which the great themes of black life in America—bondage, freedom, dual identity, and an insistence on human dignity—are expressed.

Among these magical flight tales—actually a suite of related stories—are subtle differences indicating a textured oral tradition that took on varying emphases in the voices of multiple tellers to reflect the changing moments and circumstances of slavery. In their most basic form, just one or two sentences long, these stories attribute enslaved people born on African soil with a special ability sourced through spiritual power and strength of conviction, as characterized in this statement by former slave Jack Wilson: "Some had magic power which came to them from way back in Africa. . . . If they believed in this magic, they could escape and fly back to Africa."[10] Many of these brief articulations of the tales include an addendum stressing the truth of what can only be described as incredible reportage, such as former slave James Moore's comment: "They say that people brought from Africa in slavery times could disappear and fly right back to Africa. From the things I see myself I believe that they could do this." Moore, like many others, attested that he believed. This belief

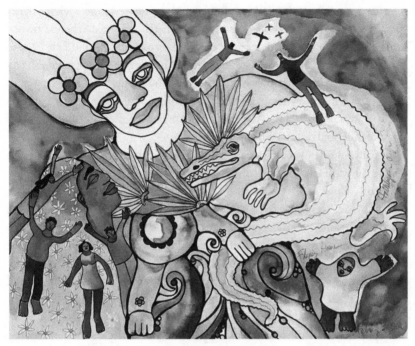

FIGURE 5.1. *Flying Home*, by Ruth Showalter. In this watercolor created in response to the author's public presentation at the symposium that preceded this book, Georgia artist Showalter imagines black spiritual flights to freedom as both past and present happenings.

in the reality of human flight stressed by the interviewees is crucially important for both these storytellers and the generations that came before them. Possessing the clandestine ability to do wondrous things through the power of faith in a people's inner strength posed a fundamental threat to the psychological aspect of slavery that constantly assaulted black subjectivities.

Several of the flying African stories are more elaborate and emphasize an individual's levitation in direct response to overwork, physical abuse, or psychological strain. In one example, Mose Brown reported: "My gran used to tell me about folks flying back to Africa. A man and his wife were brought from Africa. When they found out they were slaves and got treated so hard, they just fretted and fretted. One day they were standing with some other slaves and all of a sudden they said, 'We're going back to Africa. So goodie bye, goodie bye.' Then they flew right out of sight."[11] Rosa Grant recounted a detailed story passed down to her by her mother about her grandmother, Ryna, who was originally from Africa. Grant said: "Her mother, Theresa, was caught too and they were brought to this country. After they [had] been here a while, the mother got to where she couldn't stand it and she wanted to go back to Africa. One day my grand Ryna was standing with her in the field. Theresa turned round so.... She stretched her arms out so and rose right up and flew back to Africa. My gran said she was standing right there when it happened. She always wished that her mother had taught her how to fly."[12] Grant's version of the story includes key recurring themes (conflict, flight from slavery, an eyewitness account passed down) as well as a longing on the part of descendants to have inherited or retained this special ability.

Finally, in one of the most detailed versions of the flying African tales on record, Shadd Hall described an act of flight in response to a threatened punishment. "Those folks could fly too," Hall told the Writers' Project interviewer. "Their master was fixing to tie them up to whip them. They said, 'Master, you ain't going to lick me,' and with that they ran down to the river. The overseer he sure thought he'd catch them when they got to the river. But before he could get to them, they rose up in the air and flew away. They flew right back to Africa."[13] Hall's telling suggests that the river was a destination, a liquid launchpad that needed to be reached before one could take flight. Hall's version of the tale introduces water as an essential element in black resistance and metaphysical transformation that reappears in another flying African account to be treated later in this chapter.

Scholars of slavery have sometimes tied the genesis of the magical flight stories to a specific historical event in Georgia, an Ibo uprising on St. Simons Island, suggesting that these tales originated from enslaved people's interpretations of that event.[14] Although there is no clear evidence that a single incident marks the origins of these tales in the Southeast, it *is* apparent that formerly enslaved people's understandings of magical flight stories and the uprising in question sometimes overlapped, leading to a merger of the tales in African American collective consciousness. (And there may be a greater interpolation of these flying African and Ibo uprising stories than the written record accounts for, as the flying African tales, according to literary studies scholar Olivia Storey, are "more vast and less knowable in oral genres, such as narratives, songs, and jokes."[15]) The historical slave uprising that is now attached to magical flight tales unfolded in May 1803. A slave ship had docked outside of Savannah on Skidaway Island after having collected souls from the West Coast of Africa. Captives of this ship included members of the Ibo (also spelled "Igbo" or "Ebo") tribe of present-day Nigeria (in West Central Africa). Brokers working on behalf of planters John Couper and Thomas Spalding purchased a group of these newly arrived slaves and put them on another ship en route to St. Simons Island. On the banks of an interior waterway now called

Dunbar Creek, the captured Ibos rebelled, capsizing the craft. A terrified overseer along with two sailors died while trying to swim away.[16] The Ibos leapt off
the ship, sinking into the waters at a place that is now called Ebo Landing.

The assessment of this event put forward by a white witness at the time was
that the Ibos could not bear their immediate situation and so took their own
lives. In the view of this witness, theirs was a desperate impulse born of claus-
trophobic distress rather than an act of political resistance. Local slave trader
William Mein penned a letter to plantation owner Pierce Butler recounting the moment: "Spalding and Couper [bought] a whole cargo of Ibos . . .
the Negroes rose by being confined in a small vessel. . . . The Negroes took to
the Marsh." Mein's letter sympathetically details the death of the overseer on
board when describing how the "poor fellow," startled by the sudden action of
the captives, had been "frightened & when swimming ashore he with two sailors were drowned." When turning to a report of the loss of African lives, however, Mein's words take on a pecuniary cast. The investors in this "cargo" had,
in Mein's words, "lost at least ten or twelve recovering them besides being subject to an expense of ten dollars a head for salvage." In this slave trader's view,
formed within a cultural context that valued black bodies only as commodities, the salient point to be reckoned with was the financial cost of retriev-
ing cadavers from the water. This expensive outcome could have been avoided,
Mein implies in his missive, if not for the "mismanagement of Mr. Couper's
overseer," a tragic character with the fatal flaw of weak managerial skills.[17]

In contrast to the perspective of a man in the slaving industry who put forward blind panic as the motivating force behind the Ibos' collective action, the
interpretation of this event passed down by the enslaved community and expressed in the ex-slave interviews of the Georgia Writers' Project is ambiguous
and linked to the flying African stories. Two interviewees described the revolt
in detail. Paul Singleton, a man born into the caste of slave on a plantation
near Darien, Georgia, gave this, the lengthiest existing account:

> My daddy used to tell me all the time about folks what could fly back to
> Africa. They could take wing and just fly off. Lots of times he told me an-
> other story about a slave ship about to be caught by revenue boat. The slave
> ship slipped through back river into creek. There were about fifty slaves on
> board. The slave runners tied rocks around the slaves' necks and threw them
> overboard to drown. They say you can hear moaning and groaning in the
> creek if you go near there today.[18]

In Singleton's story, the Ibos do not enter the water of their own volition but
are instead thrown overboard by the slave ship's crew. Former slave Floyd

White also narrated the Ebo Landing event but with a different interpretation, saying: "Heard about the Ibo's Landing? That's the place where they brought the Ibos over in a slave ship and when they got there, they didn't like it and so they all started singing and they marched right down in the river to march back to Africa, but they [weren't] able to get there. They drowned."[19] White's account emphasizes purposeful collective action and conscious resistance even though the ending is tragic, as in Singleton's version.

Neither Floyd White nor Paul Singleton deny the historically accurate conclusion that black deaths resulted from the docking of this slave ship at Dunbar Creek in 1803. Perhaps in keeping with the historicity of their reports, these men do not state that the captive Ibos could fly. Nevertheless, the imprint of the magical flight lore is present and discernible in their words. White includes elements that regularly occur in other flying African stories, connecting his tale thematically to this oral tradition. Those elements include rhythmic movement accompanied by singing or chanting as the Ibos moved toward the water with the intention of fleeing (other accounts would say flying) to Africa. The marching that White describes, as historian Michael Gomez has pointed out in his examination of a South Carolina flying African account, has similarities to the ring shout, a religious ritual among enslaved blacks that was believed to open communication with the ancestors.[20] Similarly to White's tale, which echoes the flying African stories, Singleton's version holds the flying African lore close. While admitting that the Ibos did drown, Singleton frames his tale with a reference to flying Africans as told to him by his father. In so doing, he infuses the sad story that follows with an alternative possibility: even though the Ibos on this particular ship did not fly, others might have.

African diaspora studies scholars have seized on this ambiguity in black accounts of the Ebo Landing uprising, reading into it an alternative consciousness about the strength of black slaves and the meaning of resistance. According to this scholarly view, the Ibos consciously resisted their enslavement, viewing suicide as preferable to lives of bondage. Embedded in this action was the West African–based cultural belief that by drowning they could transport themselves spiritually, thereby "flying" back to their African homeland. Gomez has explained this interpretation, noting as a matter of context that South Carolina planters tended to avoid Ibo slaves, stereotyping them as suicidal. In an analysis of Ibo cultural beliefs about death, burial, and suicide in Africa, Gomez concludes: "For the Igbo, then, suicide was perhaps the ultimate form of resistance, as it contained within it the seed for regeneration and renewal.

The story of Ebo Landing is an attempt to convey this message, that something more profound than simple suicide had taken place."[21] Timothy Powell writes in a similar vein that "when the Ibo enter the water and cross beneath the kalunga line [in the Kongo cosmogram used by Powell as a tool of analysis], they do not perish but are transformed into ancestors who continue to take part in the flying Africans' story for centuries to come."[22] Taken as a whole, the suite of flying African stories told by former slaves on the Georgia coast leave open an interpretation of the Ebo Landing event and other conflicts between master and slave as moments that defied reason—moments during which the oppressed could resist and through resistance be transported. Rather than ending their lives in vain, the Ibo captives took wing and flew away in a metaphorical and psychological sense, enacting a symbolic flight redolent with the power of spiritual beliefs carried across the Middle Passage.

This oral tradition recounting the feats of rebel Africans has become a recognizable feature of black folklore within and beyond the Georgia and Carolina Lowcountry. These David-and-Goliath stories shimmer with bold defiance against inhumane treatment and serve as inspiration for the descendants of African American slaves. But the storied events at Dunbar Creek are currently being reformulated in a very different context than as expressed by African American writers and artists. Proprietors of southern ghost tours and authors of popular books on southern hauntings have discovered the tale of Ebo Landing and are selling it to a modern, mostly white audience seeking all things supernatural.

The quest for paranormal experience that has surged in American popular culture for decades has led to a plethora of ghost tours across the country, offered by large companies, independent entrepreneurs, and owners of private historic homes. As participation in organized religion declines and individuals contend with the anxieties of a new century fraught with the massive threats of climate change, global political instability, and economic collapse, people seem to be turning toward a more amorphous form of spiritual engagement embedded in the notion of ghosts returned from the other side. Hearing stories about and even "witnessing" spirits of the dead can satisfy the widely shared human desire to peer into the haze of the afterlife, a desire spurred by fear of our corporeal demise and the need to find transcendent meaning in our time on earth. A fascination with ghosts and the supernatural is, according to American studies and cultural studies scholars, tied to our present moment in not only a new century but also a new millennium. The rise of what I have called "ghost fancy" is linked, in their view, to a widely experienced contemporary worry about societal transformation at the start of the twenty-first century.[23]

Tourism professionals have taken advantage of this popular turn toward the supernatural, launching hundreds of packaged, for-profit death-and-disaster experiences. This sector of the commercial tourism industry has been deemed "dark tourism" due to its emphasis on macabre themes of torture, death, and hauntings. A form of travel-oriented entertainment in line with the supernatural zeitgeist, dark tourism highlights sinister and somber historic sites and museums augmented by tour narratives and published accounts. Glenn Gentry, a geographer who has scrutinized Savannah ghost tourism, succinctly defines dark tourism as "the transformation of death and disaster into saleable tourism-based commodities."[24]

It was professors of tourism studies in the United Kingdom, John Lennon and Malcolm Foley, who coined the term "dark tourism" in their book *Dark Tourism: The Attraction of Death and Disaster*, first published in 2000. The two had visited tourism sites around the world to assess the state of the field in the 1990s and during their travels had noted this growing branch of the industry. They conclude: "It is clear from a number of sources that tourist interest in recent death, disaster and atrocity is a growing phenomenon in the late twentieth and early twenty-first centuries."[25] Increased tourist travel to battlefields, cemeteries, and museums that commemorate atrocities such as the Jewish Holocaust evidences this trend. Based on this finding, Lennon and Foley posit, similarly to American studies and cultural studies scholars who had noted "millennial anxiety" as a cause for interest in hauntings in the same period, that these gloomy "tourism products" tap into a fascination with death that springs from concerns about features of postmodern life: "late capitalism," cultural decentralization, spatial disorientation, disassociation from traditional institutions, and the rise of rational inquiry and technological innovation. Dark tourism, Lennon and Foley explain, is an indirect means for the expression of collective public doubt about a shared subjectivity at the turn of the twenty-first century.[26]

As more people demonstrated their interest in visiting disturbing sites in the 1990s and early 2000s, the number of entrepreneurs willing to provide dark tourism experiences steadily increased. British tourism studies scholar Richard Sharpley explained in a coedited book, *The Darker Side of Travel*, that "over the last half century and commensurate with the remarkable growth in general tourism, dark tourism has become more widespread and diverse. . . . There appears to be an increasing number of people keen to promote and or profit from 'dark' events as tourist attractions."[27] In a recent investigative study

of "big tourism," journalist Elizabeth Becker calls tourism the "stealth industry of the twenty-first century," based on her finding that tourism skyrocketed
between the 1960s and 2000s and was in 2007 the "biggest employer" in the
world economy. In order to achieve this growth, Becker argues, the travel and
tourism industry needed to attract new, untapped markets. Dark tourism was
a result of diversification in a booming field, becoming a "lucrative niche market" in the 1990s. Visitors are drawn by the opportunity to hear what Becker
calls stories of "sadism and pain."[28] By maintaining the traditional attractions
of tourism—pleasure and escape—and by adding in transgressive dimensions
of violence, suffering, and mortality, dark tourism entrepreneurs satisfied an
increasingly mainstream public desire to explore disturbing themes during leisure time. The "dark" sector of the tourism industry combines contrasting positive and negative elements that come together to produce a unique effect of
attraction and repulsion that is proving irresistible to hardcore ghost hunters,
casual vacationers, and history buffs alike.

Tourism studies scholars have categorized ghost tourism as a lighter manifestation in the broad spectrum of "dark tourism" offerings.[29] While ghost
tours lead paying consumers on guided experiences of the supernatural
through some of America's oldest cities, recounting stories of terrible deaths
and eerie hauntings, they do so with an air of lighthearted fun and frivolity.
Ghost tours can take many forms, including walking tours, hearse tours, bus
tours, and haunted house tours, all of which have proliferated in the coastal
Southeast. The draw of tourists to colonial cities like Charleston and Savannah has made these chief locations for ghost tour companies to set up shop
over the last two decades. The most popular of these attractions tend to include stories about black slaves from the nineteenth century who reappear as
ghosts.

Between 2012 and 2014, I endeavored to identify ghost tours in the South
that centered on stories of enslaved African American specters. Across seven
trips to Savannah, Charleston, New Orleans, rural Louisiana, and St. Simons
Island, during which I took seventeen ghost tours, I discovered not only that
ghost tours are the primary arena within mainstream tourist offerings where
the history of black slavery is broached, but also that Savannah has been called
the most haunted city in America. There are two major reasons why Savannah
has received special notice for possessing a supernatural aura. In the decade
following the publication of journalist John Berendt's best-selling book *Midnight in the Garden of Good and Evil*, Savannah became an epicenter of the
ghost-touring zeitgeist.[30] And then in 2002 the American Institute of Para-
psychology, a Florida-based research center dedicated to supernatural studies,

cemented this reputation by awarding Savannah the title of America's Most Haunted City. The institute's director, Dr. Andrew Nichols, explained:

> We based our award (and the selection of this site for our conference) on the fact that we had received more reports of haunting-type activity from Savannah during the previous five years than from any other American city. Other contenders for the title were New Orleans, Charleston SC, and St. Augustine FL. All the old colonial cities have a higher probability factor for hauntings due to the abundance of ancient structures, which have remained relatively unchanged since early times.[31]

In addition to the "ancient structures" noted by Nichols, I have argued elsewhere that the stain of black chattel slavery contributes significantly to the sense of a "dark" and haunted Savannah. Added to this are the layered histories of Native American dispossession, Revolutionary and Civil War battles, and deadly waves of yellow fever.[32] What is more, the subtropical natural environment of the southeastern coastal region—the marshy waterways, eerie fogs, moss-draped oaks, and hissing waves—enhance the sense of a shrouded netherworld reality on which the ghost tour depends. It follows then, that African American lore rooted in the landscape just beyond Savannah presents alluring primary material for the ghost tour industry. These stories that emerge from the horrors of slavery are intimately tied to the atmospheric coastal environment and overflow with the dark torment of whippings, drownings, and death.

Just as African American writers and artists have reproduced the stories of flying Africans and Ebo Landing, the ghost tour industry, dominated by white historic site owners and tour guides, has taken up those tales. I was caught off guard the first time I heard the story of Ebo Landing during my observation of southern ghost tours. It was September 2012, and I had traveled to St. Simons Island, the most populous of the fourteen tidal islands on Georgia's Atlantic coastline known as the Golden Isles, to take what is billed as the island's "original" ghost tour. I strolled to the pier at St. Simons Village at nine in the evening to purchase tickets for the St. Simons Island Ghost Walking Tour. Promotional materials described the tour as an experience of "strange tales of local folklore, murder, mystery, and fright," for which participants were warned, "Bring your camera and your courage."[33] The owner, a longtime local businesswoman, had told me by phone that the tour was "great fun and great history" and that the price of a ticket was an affordable thirteen dollars. That evening the tour was led by an older man who had donned period dress, carried an old-fashioned lantern, and told our group of approximately twenty that he had performed in shows for the History Channel. Our guide's acting experience showed. He started off at a steady pace, following a route that wove the group along the windswept shoreline, past historic buildings and an "Indian burial ground" among the shadowy oaks. When asked if he had ever seen a ghost, our guide replied that he had seen several. Others in the tour group enthusiastically echoed this claim. An able storyteller who drew energy from his engaged audience, our guide launched into a string of tales made more dramatic by the cover of night and the hypnotic sound of lapping waves. He told us about a man who haunts the Jekyll Island Hotel; about Mary the Wanderer, a lovelorn young immigrant woman lost at sea in a storm; about ghosts that haunt the historic lighthouse, a "monstrous boy" of the antebellum period, and the mystical origins of Spanish moss. Our guide's second story of the evening was about a landmark that he called a "deepwater creek." He surprised me then, and perhaps others, by launching into a detailed explanation of the hydrological characteristics of the waterways around St. Simons. Some of these waters were salty, some fresh, and some brackish. Some flowed around the edge of the island, some within the landmass, and some, he said, were deep enough to convey ocean-faring vessels far into the interior of the island. His story sailed off from there. He described a ship carrying slave "contraband," illegally acquired slaves, by way of a deep channel known today as Dunbar Creek. He painted a vivid scene. Twelve enslaved African warriors chained together on the deck of that ship rose up in rebellion and killed most of the crew. The warriors chanted in their own tongue—"It is the waters that brought us and the waters that will take us away"—as they jumped from the vessel, drowning themselves in Dunbar Creek. To conclude his tale, our guide described the fancy, high-end houses that now surround the area where the slaves sank into the depths of the waters. Residents of the neighborhood do not dare venture out at night, he told us. For in the darkness, Dunbar Creek goes preternaturally still, a strange buzzing begins, and the eerie chant of the Africans sounds faintly in the air. After telling this tale, the tour guide proclaimed that St. Simons' slaveholders had been "dumb," and then he casually disclosed the unmarked intersection where we might locate the haunted creek.

Although I would offer impetus other than stupidity for slavers' actions in the Ebo Landing tragedy, I appreciated the analysis embedded within this tour guide's framing of the story. I had found elsewhere in my travels that ghost tours featuring stories about slavery tended to romanticize master-slave relationships and diminish the brutal realities of the system, and I had therefore written that "ghost tourism at historic sites of slavery appropriates African American history" in damaging ways.[34] But this guide had incorporated

FIGURE 5.2. Contemporary Dunbar Creek bathed in light and shadow
conjures a sense of the transforming and transformative place where the
Ebo Landing slave uprising occurred in 1803. Photo by Ben Galland.

Ebo Landing not only to tell a hair-raising tale that would satisfy the desires of
tourists but also to highlight an abuse of human rights in that place. His conclusion to the story transformed it into a cautionary tale. Although the captive
Ibos had sacrificed their own lives, they had taken the ship's crew down with
them. The guide's narrative implicitly equated slaveholders of the past with
wealthy Dunbar Creek residents of the present and included what could be
read as a class critique of the wealth gap and the cordoning off of coastal areas
for private estates. The residents of Dunbar Creek could not enjoy the natural
surroundings for which they had paid a premium for fear of being haunted by
the spirits of the deceased. They stood under constant rebuke by the past, witnessed and chastised by the ghosts of slaves.

   In addition to this surprising tour on St. Simons Island, I heard and read
the Ebo Landing story during a Charleston tour linked to a local book about
haunted places and in two popular books on ghosts in Georgia. Two versions
of the story were told by the same person, Geordie Buxton, co-owner of Walks
in History tours in Charleston and author of the book *Haunted Plantations*.[35]
A man perhaps in his early thirties, Buxton led me on an extended, private
version of his company's ghost tour in the winter of 2013. He said that when
his company began lacing traditional local history narratives about the Civil

War with stories of "haints" and ghosts in 1995–96, the ghost story element captured the interest of the tourists. The company then developed the first Charleston ghost tour, which became their most popular offering. Now, he said, "everyone [in the local tourism industry] wants to end their tour with a bang, [with] a ghost story." As we walked among the preserved antebellum manor homes, Buxton shared his views on the nature of ghosts and hauntings. He then told a series of stories, describing a slave woman who haunts a brick kiln at Boone Hall Plantation, a drunken plantation owner's son who haunts Drayton Hall, and the demise of what he called the "Lost Tribe of Israel." This lost tribe, he said, evolved into the Ibo tribe, which ended up on a slave ship headed for Savannah or Charleston around the year 1803. During a ferocious storm that hit the ship, the crew made for St. Simons Island. The chief of the tribe was shackled together with all the others. When he realized that they were fated to be slaves, he began a chant to the West African goddess "Mami Wata," meaning "the Waters." The chief jumped in, taking others with him due to the shackles. His chant, the guide concluded, can still be heard today.[36]

Buxton tells a similar, extended story in *Haunted Plantations*. This published version does not mention Israel but instead attends more closely to the details of the Ibos' actions. During the "gale winds and torrential rain" of the storm, the "chieftain sang an ancestral song" that "called on the great water spirit, Mami Wata, to take the tribe back across the ocean to their loved ones." In Buxton's rendering, the storm responded to the song, finding its silent eye as the captives sang. Before the captives jumped into the waters beneath a full moon revealed by the quieted storm, "the chieftain looked back directly into the captain's eyes." In the written account of Ebo Landing, Buxton emphasizes both the defiant attitude of the captives and the role of water, concluding that "water and the spirit world have always held special significance to many Africans . . . it is water that acts as the passage to the next life."[37]

The final appearance of the Ebo Landing story comes from a book titled *Georgia Ghosts* (1997), fifty-four tales from across the state collected and retold by the prolific North Carolina author Nancy Roberts.[38] I have included this text in my discussion because volumes like it often serve as gateways and guidebooks for ghost tourists. In this modern-day story, a multiracial group of white and black young men have returned home to St. Simons from college during summer vacation. Seeking a thrill, they decide on an evening outing to Dunbar Creek, where one of the white men claims: "Folks say that you can sometimes hear a chanting if you sit out there late at night." As the evening grows deeper and darker by the shoreline and midnight approaches, only two of the young men remain: Jeff, a white student, and Jerry, a black student. With mosquitoes buzzing in his ear, Jeff begins to "feel a strange sense of expectancy." He stares at the creek, noticing that the waterway has grown wider. Sounds of the water lapping against the bank echo in the moonlit night. The breeze picks up, carrying a "sickening stench." As the young men watch, a ghost ship approaches, "beautiful" and "savage," with "every foot of her deck swarm[ing] with cargo—black men, women, and children." The men on board, "chained together," begin to chant and then plunge into the water. "One head after another disappeared below the surface, and the weight of the chains was so great that none could be saved." The black student, Jerry, tells Jeff "the story about how the captured Africans brought here were Eboes" who "couldn't understand what was happening to them" and "chose death instead," chanting "'[t]he water brought us and the water will take us away." Upon hearing this story, Jeff expresses his guilt that his "race" participated in "that." Jerry tells Jeff he need not feel guilty, as the Africans who sold each other into slavery were just as culpable as the whites. After this cathartic exchange, the ghost ship disappears, and the young men promise never to speak of the incident to anyone. While Roberts's rendition of this story includes sympathy for the slaves and a representation of racial reconciliation between the boys, it does so while using regrettably dehumanizing language ("swarming" as a verb to describe the Ibos) and by sidestepping a critical issue. In the end, the black character absolves the white character (and one can presume, white readers) of an uncomfortable guilt and absolves slave traders and slaveholders of moral responsibility for slavery.

All of these three contemporary storytellers—the St. Simons tour guide, Buxton, and Roberts—elaborate on the centuries-old Ebo Landing lore in ways that are particular to their own interpretations and political viewpoints. The Georgia ghost story author describes the Ibos' action as a desperate and almost accidental group suicide. The Charleston tour guide and author describes it as a conscious and tactical act of resistance. The St. Simons tour guide emphasizes violent resistance on the part of the captives. All of the storytellers, it must be noted, use this awful historical event as fodder for a moneymaking enterprise, and to differing degrees they play on the notion of the naturalized African "exotic." None of these storytellers includes the memory of flying Africans who attempt to escape their state of bondage, a key aspect of the stories as handed down among former slaves. But while the omission of the possibility of flight in the ghost tourism stories diminishes the metaphor of the power of the oppressed to effect transformation, it also stops short of full appropriation of a precious black coastal narrative tradition. These ghost tour guides and authors take up a traditional black story in order to fill out and enhance their dark tourism menu, but they seem to do so with a sense of reserve and with an intention of reproducing aspects of the story as previously documented. The tellers of these modern tales seem to have read the Georgia Writers' Project interviews with former slaves (or secondary literature about the interviews), which clearly serve as a basis for their elaborations. They exercise restraint in their versions, avoiding the kind of rampant sensationalism and exaggeration evident in other ghost tourism contexts (such as the Sorrel-Weed story in Savannah and the Madame LaLaurie story in New Orleans). For instance, they do not zoom in on the captives' suffering for the titillation of tourists or readers; they do not add gratuitous details featuring punishment, torture, or black bodies in pain; and they do not describe the immediate sights or sounds of death. This holding back and resisting the urge to caricature or sensationalize slavery is something that I did not see elsewhere in my observation of southern ghost tours. The majority of tour narratives and stories in books targeted toward tourists that I reviewed emphasized illicit sex between masters and slaves, tortured and mutilated black bodies, the dangerous taint of voodoo or Gullah Geechee spirituality, and the passivity of slaves who return as ghosts and are content to rock on the master's porch or turn down the big house bedsheets. Gratuitous sexuality, gruesome violence, and dangerous pagan rituals were central features in most of the tours I took during my two-year study of ghost tourism. But these Ebo Landing stories, even in the hands of white tourism professionals, seemed to contain a difference. That difference may stem from respect for the long tradition of a body of narratives embedded in the local landscape and the view that those narratives are closed stories that outsiders should not misrepresent.

In his essay on the spiritual meaning of the flying African tales on the Georgia coast, Timothy Powell describes "the curative powers of storytelling." By this he means that stories help to heal the psychic wounds of slavery by conveying the message to all black people that the generations who suffered through bondage always had within them deep reserves of strength. I agree with this assessment and add to it that tales of Ebo Landing resonate with such a broad narrative power that they seem to discourage the gruesome and hyperbolic tendencies often indulged by the ghost tour industry. The Ebo Landing stories capture serious and compelling themes that translate across cultural groups as well as generations. After I presented this material at the Coastal Nature, Coastal Culture symposium, several audience members shared their personal stories with me. Miriam Lancaster said that her great grandparents had lived on Dunbar Creek and had always taught their children to have respect for the Ibos' story as history. Donna Bassett, a St. Simons homeowner, said she has herself heard a "beautiful chanting on the waters." Pat Gunn, vice president of the Coastal Nonprofit Resource Center and founder of the Geechee Institute, said about the African slaves who could fly: "I personally believe it happened. . . . Just as I believe Moses parted the Red Sea and the people went through."[39] Interlaced within this multivalent narrative tradition that gathers within it the Ebo Landing and magical flight stories is a revelation of the trauma produced by enslavement, a testament to the resilience of people of African descent, a record of the transformative powers of spirituality, and a conceptual mapping of the water as a place where salvation in the form of escape can occur.

These tales of transcendence through flight and escape emerged from a fluid landscape and might only have been imaginable in such a setting. Water represented power and possibility, motion and magic, to the enslaved and their descendants. Flying African and Ebo Landing stories told by former slaves in Georgia evoke the water as a place of spiritual power that serves as a fluid runway for flight or rebellion. As Shadd Hall put it: "They ran down to the river. The overseer he sure thought he'd catch them when they got to the river. But before he could get to them, they rose up in the air and flew away." And it is in the account of a former slave that the first sign of haunted waters at Dunbar Creek appears. Paul Singleton said about the place where the Ibos sank into the depths, "You can hear moaning and groaning in the creek if you go near there today." Contemporary ghost tour narratives have highlighted this aspect of the oral tradition, emphasizing the enabling role of the water. In the St. Simons Island tour, the guide opened his tale by detailing the hydrology of Dunbar Creek. In Charleston, the tour guide personified water as a living spirit. The author Nancy Roberts tells a story in which the waters move in synergy with the return of the Ibo spirits, rising and opening as the ghost ship appears and receding when it disappears. Tales from the Georgia Writers' Project interviews as well as present-day ghost stories show water as a natural entity that exists in special relationship to the enslaved, is called upon by them for aid, and projects their voices of protest into our time by marking the places where they resisted and echoing their sounds of struggle.

It is disturbing, in light of this meaning that flows within the waters, to recognize the civic neglect visited upon Dunbar Creek, the site of the legendary revolt. I first encountered the waterway in 2012, at the surreptitious suggestion of the St. Simons Island ghost tour guide. Following his clues, I took Frederica Road and turned into a manicured neighborhood where houses flanked the street and faced the marsh, blocking off views of the water from all but the homeowners and their guests. I pressed on past the "private road" signs, barely glimpsing the closeted creek, hoping I would not be spotted by a resident and tagged as an interloper. After a series of turns and a wash of worry that I was merely driving in circles and sticking out all the more, I reached Atlantic Street, the dead end intersection that our historically minded ghost tour guide had pointed us to. Here, in this rear corner of the neighborhood, the line of sprawling modern homes abruptly ceased, and the road gave way to unwieldy weeds and thin-hipped trees grasping for soil in which to sink their roots. I got out and walked past a patch of overgrown grasses, toward the spot where terra firma melted into marsh in the distance, where sea oats fanned like a muted array of feather pens, and the grassy banks of a broad, meandering, river-like creek carried a society of water birds—brown pelicans, spotted sandpipers, and dozens more. But as I drew closer to the edge of the marsh, my hopes were disappointed. There was no intimate water access even in this forgotten corner, nor was there any human-made cue connecting this site to the story of a slave uprising. The creek side looked like an abandoned privately owned lot with a red-and-white-striped physical barrier warning all away. There is no need, the blockade implied, for anyone to proceed here, for anyone to probe, to see, and to remember. Yet the Georgia coastal lands such as these were long places of deep importance for thousands of Africans who came here by way of these waters, against their will.

It was not until four years later that I understood why that off-the-beaten-track road near the creek looked so forlorn and learned of the present-day controversy surrounding the waterway. Currently used by Glynn County as a human wastewater disposal site for St. Simons Island and its smaller sister isle, Sea Island, Dunbar Creek has become an aquatic dumping ground. Near the intersection of Frederica and Sea Island Roads, the Water Pollution Control Facility (WPCF) waste treatment center screens incoming sewage and then "surface water discharge[s]" the "effluent" directly into Dunbar Creek. (Lanier Island, another sister isle to St. Simons, manages its sewage privately.) Dependence on the creek for waste disposal is increasing as the population of St. Simons grows at the rate of 1 percent per year, according to a 2006 county study of the sewer master plan. An onrush of development, most of it in private home and luxury condominium construction, is threatening the protective yet fragile wetlands between the thirty-six-square-mile island's slightly elevated interior and low-lying coastline, and it is taxing the sewer system that relies on the creek as a liquid trash receptacle.[40]

The environmental cost of such a system has not escaped the vigilant notice of St. Simons residents or Georgia environmentalists, who have made vociferous objections to the county's approval of new development projects and decried the damage to Dunbar Creek. In a 2014 memo to the county planning commission, the Center for a Sustainable Coast pointed out that a proposed private development would discharge waste at the Dunbar Creek plant, "which is at or very near capacity at peak use, causing periodic contamination in surrounding waters." Individuals are also tracking water contamination. A local blogger keeps a running record of her exchanges with the Glynn County Joint Water and Sewer Commission (JWSC), the state Environmental Protection Division, and the Water Pollution Control Center under the heading: "Toward the elimination of the cesspool in the dunes," in which she has reprinted her comment to a county official that the very name of the "Water Pollution Control Permit" assigned to developers "signals that 'control' rather than prevention is the name of the game." Local activists and outspoken residents make clear in their protests that they support human enjoyment of remaining open island land when that land is undeveloped or lightly developed and remains accessible to the public. The Glynn County Environmental Coalition, for instance, is fighting for the maintenance of a public park on donated acreage but challenges officials to forestall large-scale private development for profit that poses a threat to the island's intricate ecosystem.[41]

County officials are aware of the issues wrought by St. Simons Island's combination of high popularity and inadequate infrastructure, but they avoid acknowledging pollution in the creek as an immediate problem to be solved. Instead government representatives focus on technological fixes that can insure the carriage of increasing loads of sewage more securely to the creek without incident. In 2015 JWSC executive director Steve Swan was quoted as saying that "the line that transports raw sewage to the Dunbar Creek wastewater treatment facility needs to be replaced." Time-consuming and costly repairs to the sewage pipes "to stave off a line rupture" in the winter of 2016 disrupted traffic flows and delayed school buses, leading to still more public consternation. Though the issues seem worlds apart and have vastly different consequences for human life in past time and present time, the crisis of overdevelopment on St. Simons Island today shares an ethos of capitalist exploitation with the plantation culture that proliferated there centuries ago when Sea Island cotton brought slaveholders a heady compensation. In both cases, development of land for private gain led to human costs for the many and high rewards for the few. In the nineteenth century, enslaved people of African descent suffered most as a consequence of this ethos. Today the land and waterways to which they turned for succor suffer in silence. It is perhaps not ironic, then, that the same deep body of water subjected now to the effluvia of overflowing human waste was at one time, in 1803, the receptacle of resistant African bodies, viewed as nothing more than waste by a local slave trader.[42] While

FIGURE 5.3. Dunbar Creek today, showing the sinuous shape of the waterway, bringing to mind nonlinear senses of time that characterize both enslaved people's ideas of "flying" home to Africa and widely shared cultural understandings of hauntings in the present. Photo by Ben Galland.

natural areas that preserve the "romantic" ruins of the planter elite are currently seeing environmental "regeneration," as Drew Swanson details in this volume, a site that holds the memory of slave resistance as well as the intertwined fates of blacks and whites, nature and culture, stagnates.

Dunbar Creek stands victim to rampant development and the population pressures of a wastewater treatment plant, and the site where the Ibos struggled remains unmarked by the State of Georgia. But the strength of the stories rooted here suggests that another future is possible for this waterway and the many others to which it connects. The symbolic presence of water in early accounts of flying Africans and Ebo Landing resisters as well as in contemporary ghost tour stories points to the possibility of new uses of this oral tradition for our present, when environmental crisis looms in the form of climate change, damaged oceans, and pillaged natural resources. From the deep waters of Dunbar Creek emerge a deep well of stories, not only about slavery but also about the natural world. These stories tell us that the waterways that meandered through the lives of the marginalized helped them access powers of transformation for fighting the system of chattel bondage. And today these same "haunted" waters preserve the memory of black people's creative struggle for freedom. These old Georgia tales might therefore be repurposed to further a motivating sense of eco-cultural consciousness, not only among the descendants of slaves but also among residents and visitors to this rare place where the waters hold secrets and the people had wings.

NOTES

I would like to extend my sincere thanks to those who offered feedback that improved this chapter, including coeditors Paul Pressly and Paul Sutter, copyeditor Chris Dodge, the anonymous reviewers, and fellow speakers and audience members, named and unnamed, who contributed rich insights and stories at the Coastal Nature, Coastal Culture symposium. I also appreciate symposium attendees who offered remembrances of the Civil War atrocity at Ebenezer Creek, a tributary of the Savannah River. In December 1862, thousands of African American survivors from slavery were following Union troops to what they hoped was safety, but many of them drowned when soldiers followed orders to dismantle the bridge after the troops had safely crossed.

1. Paulla A. Ebron, "Slavery and Transnational Memory: The Making of New Publics," in *Transatlantic Memories of Slavery: Reimagining the Past, Changing the Future,* ed. Elisa Bordin and Anna Scacchi (Amherst, N.Y.: Cambria Press, 2015), 149.

2. W. E. B. Du Bois, *The Souls of Black Folk,* in *Three Negro Classics* (New York: Avon Books, 1965), 213.

3. Michael A. Gomez, *Exchanging Our Country Marks: The Transformation of African Identities in the Colonial and Antebellum South* (Chapel Hill: University of North Carolina Press, 1998), 273, 274.

4. My count of references to flying Africans in *Drums and Shadows* yielded twenty-four mentions distributed across at least twenty coastal communities. One of these twenty-four states that the people did *not* fly; hence twenty-three stories are noted in the text as being affirmatively about flying. Georgia Writers' Project, *Drums and Shadows: Survival Studies among the Georgia Coastal Negroes* (1940; repr., Los Angeles: Indo-European Publishing, 2010). University of Michigan undergraduate researcher Alexandra Passarelli helped to confirm this number while working with me on the Georgia Writers' Project narratives. For a detailed discussion of the behind-the-scenes production of *Drums and Shadows,* see Melissa L. Cooper, *Making Gullah: A History of Sapelo Islanders, Race, and the American Imagination* (Chapel Hill: University of North Carolina Press, 2017), 112–50.

5. Toni Morrison, *Song of Solomon* (New York: Plume, 1977); Paule Marshall, *Praisesong for the Widow* (New York: Putnam, 1983); Virginia Hamilton, *The People Who Could Fly* (New York: Knopf, 1985); Julie Dash, director, *Daughters of the Dust* (Kino International, 1991). Historian Melissa Cooper offers an illuminating analysis of black women writers' discovery and imaginings of this "mythic group of Ibos" as a means of highlighting connection to ancestors, meaning-making, and survival in the 1970s–90s. See Cooper, *Making Gullah,* 175–77.

6. Olivia Smith Storey details the generational and cultural differences between

"Creole" narrators and "African" protagonists of the flying African "trope." Olivia Smith Storey, "Flying Words: Contests of Orality and Literacy in the Trope of the Flying Africans," *Journal of Colonialism and History* 5, no. 3 (2004): 1–46.

7. Georgia Writers' Project, *Drums and Shadows*, 25–26.

8. Timothy B. Powell, "Ebos Landing," *New Georgia Encyclopedia*, www.georgiaencyclopedia.org/articles/history-archaeology/ebos-landing.

9. Georgia Writers' Project, *Drums and Shadows*, 39.

10. Ibid., 8. I have rendered these quotations from *Drums and Shadows* in Standard English although the recorded speech in the book consists of a heavy "black" dialect. This dialect is overdetermined and unreliable, reflecting an approximation of black southern speech that was informed by prejudicial views of the time. I therefore think the risk to accuracy of standardizing it is less than the risk to accuracy of reproducing it word for word. I have corrected spelling as well as subject-verb tense agreement. Words that I have added while making changes to verb tense are placed within brackets. I have left in words that seem to be substitutions that the interviewees may have made, such as "what" for "that."

11. Ibid., 19, 17.

12. Ibid., 120.

13. Ibid., 139.

14. Timothy Powell, "Summoning the Ancestors: The Flying Africans' Story and Its Enduring Legacy," in *African American Life in the Georgia Lowcountry: The Atlantic World and the Gullah Geechee*, ed. Philip Morgan (Athens: University of Georgia Press, 2010): 253–80; Gomez, *Exchanging Our Country Marks*, 118.

15. Storey, "Flying Words," 3.

16. Timothy Powell narrates this event in detail in an essay that analyzes spiritual beliefs and the Kongo cosmogram revelation of time as a conceptual underpinning of the flight stories: Powell, "Summoning the Ancestors," 253–54, 257.

17. William Mein to Pierce Butler, May 24, 1803, box 6, folder 27, Misc correspondence 1802–1803, Butler Family Papers Collection 1447 Historical Society of Pennsylvania, Philadelphia; quoted in Powell, "Summoning the Ancestors," 257. Powell cites overseer Roswell King as another commentator on the tragedy who said the Ibos "took to the swamp" and as a result drowned. Powell, "Ebos Landing." I was not able to identify this exact passage in Roswell's letter, although I did note his mention of slave ships meeting high winds and bad weather, of captives "rejoicing when they found they could drink the water out of the river," and of wanting to get a price from Mr. Couper. Roswell King to Pierce Butler, May 13, 1803, Roswell King May–Sept. 1803, box 2, folder 10, Butler Family Papers, Collection 1447 Historical Society of Pennsylvania, Philadelphia. A review of several boxes of the Butler Family Papers and Letterbooks for 1803 and several surrounding years, including "Lists of Slaves," "Transactions in Slaves," "Miscellaneous-Slaves," revealed no further records about the uprising. I am grateful to Dana Dorman of the Historical Society of Pennsylvania for her careful research assistance with the Butler and Wister Families papers.

18. Georgia Writers' Project, *Drums and Shadows*, 17.

19. Ibid., 152. While some scholars include Wallace Quarterman's account of slaves flying away from the fields to prevent a whipping by an overseer named Mr. Blue as one that refers to the event at Ebo Landing, I would categorize Quarterman's tale as one of the more generalized flying African stories. When asked by the interviewer if he was talking about "the Ibos on St. Simons who walked into the water?" Quarterman responded that he did not mean them. Ibid., 125–26; Gomez, *Exchanging Our Country Marks*, 118.

20. Gomez, *Exchanging Our Country Marks*, 118.

21. Ibid., 115, 120.

22. Powell, "Summoning the Ancestors," 268.

23. Maria del Pilar Blanco and Esther Peeren, introduction to *Popular Ghosts: The Haunted Spaces of Everyday Culture*, ed. Maria del Pilar Blanco and Esther Peeren (New York: Continuum, 2010), ix; Catherine Spooner, *Contemporary Gothic* (London: Reaktion Books, 2006), 8; Jeffrey Andrew Weinstock, "Introduction: The Spectral Turn," in *Spectral America: Phantoms and the National Imagination*, ed. Jeffrey Andrew Weinstock (Madison: University of Wisconsin Press / Popular Press, 2004): 3–17; Tiya Miles, *Tales from the Haunted South: Dark Tourism and Memories of Slavery from the Civil War Era* (Chapel Hill: University of North Carolina Press, 2010), 2.

24. Glenn W. Gentry, "Walking with the Dead: The Place of Ghost Walk Tourism in Savannah, Georgia," *Southeastern Geographer* 47, no. 2 (November 2007): 223.

25. John Lennon and Malcolm Foley, *Dark Tourism: The Attraction of Death and Disaster*, new ed. (Andover, UK: Cengage Learning, 2010), 3.

26. Spooner, *Contemporary Gothic*, 8; Weinstock, "Introduction: The Spectral Turn," 5; Lennon and Foley, *Dark Tourism*, 3, 11.

27. Richard Sharpley, "Shedding Light on Dark Tourism: An Introduction," in *The Darker Side of Travel: The Theory and Practice of Dark Tourism*, ed. Richard Sharpley and Philip R. Stone (Bristol, UK: Channel View Publications, 2009), 5.

28. Elizabeth Becker, *Overbooked: The Exploding Business of Travel and Tourism* (New York: Simon and Schuster, 2013), 92, 17, 16, 37.

29. Philip R. Stone, "'It's a Bloody Guide': Fun, Fear and a Lighter Side of Dark Tourism at the Dungeon Visitor Attractions, UK," in *The Darker Side of Travel: The Theory and Practice of Dark Tourism*, ed. Richard Sharpley and Philip R. Stone (Bristol, UK: Channel View Publications, 2009), 167–85; Miles, *Tales from the Haunted South*, 10.

30. John Berendt, *Midnight in the Garden of Good and Evil* (New York: Vintage, 1994).

31. Andrew Nichols, e-mail to Tiya Miles, February 2, 2013.

32. Miles, *Tales from the Haunted South*, 17, 119.

33. St. Simons Original Ghost Walk, http://www.ghostwalkofstsimons.com/.

34. Miles, *Tales from the Haunted South*, 123.

35. Geordie Buxton, *Haunted Plantations: Ghosts of Slavery and Legends of the Cotton Kingdom* (Charleston, S.C.: Arcadia, 2007).

36. Walks in History Tour with Geordie Buxton, January 30, 2013; Walks in History, http://walksinhistory.com.

37. Buxton, *Haunted Plantations*, 59–60.

38. Nancy Roberts, *Georgia Ghosts* (1997; repr., Winston-Salem, N.C.: John F. Blair, 2008).

39. Mary Landers, "Symposium Tells the Hidden Stories of Georgia's Coast," Savannahnow.com, February 20, 2016.

40. *Glynn County, Georgia, St. Simons Island Sewer Master Plan Volume 1— Report* (Jacksonville Beach, Fla.: Applied Technoilogy & Management Inc., 2006), https://www.glynncounty.org/DocumentCenter/Home/View/759, pp 2.10, 2.5, 2.1.

41. "Re: PP 2713 Cloister Residences East," Center for a Sustainable Coast, January 17, 2014, http://www.sustainablecoast.org/site/cloisterletter.pdf; "Towards the Elimination of the Cesspool in the Dunes," *Hannah Blog*, March 6, 2014, http://hannah .smith-family.com/?p=9181; Mike Morrison, "Environmentalists Sue to Preserve St. Simons Island Park," *Florida Times-Union*, January 25, 2016.

42. Mike Morrison, "Sewage System Deficiency Obstructing Development on St. Simons Island Growing South End," *Florida Times-Union*, February 20, 2015; Mike Morrison, "Detour for Sewer Work Snarls Traffic on St. Simons Island," *Florida Times-Union*, February 4, 2016; Mike Morrison, "Environmentalists Ask Glynn County Commissioners to Halt Development of Land Off Sea Island's Southern Tip," *Florida Times-Union*, May 2, 2014.

CHAPTER 6

A Rhetoric of Ruin

Imagining and Reimagining the Georgia Coast

DREW A. SWANSON

Look east, a Georgia Writers' Project guidebook advised boaters plying Georgia's Fancy Bluff Creek past St. Simons Island. Across the marsh grass flats they might catch a glimpse of the historic South sleepily moldering. The 1937 guidebook described the ruins of Retreat Plantation, a brushy tangle of regrowing forest and briar patches sprinkled with ghostly foundations and chimneys. Once the King family home, Retreat housed gardens that prompted visitor John James Audubon to call it "a fairyland." Another guest described the island as a place "where not only all of the valuable crops of the south are cultivated in rotation, but where they are also prepared for market on the place, and where every arrangement exhibits both science and skill."[1] Alas, the guidebook continued, things had changed. This fairyland was gone, for "the Civil War put an end to the gay plantation life of St. Simons Island, many of the homes being burned, the church used for stabling horses, and the fields laid waste. Few of the old families returned later to the scene of their former affluence."[2] To use the title of the Pulitzer Prize–winning novel from the same year, which entailed Georgia ruins of a sort, Retreat's heyday was "gone with the wind."

The Writers' Project guidebook's description of St. Simons played on several themes of a well-established narrative of Lowcountry history in place by the 1930s. It was a story of decline, of a grand society that had experienced tragedy and slowly faded into picturesque ruin. But the guidebook also put forth an increasingly common set of ideas about regional nature. It brought together outdoor recreation—viewing the expansive marshes and tangled hammocks from boat deck—with memory of historic uses of the Lowcountry environment, tangible in the ruins of a once-grand "big house." It was a nature

FIGURE 6.1. The ruins of Retreat Plantation on St. Simons Island in the late 1930s.
Historic American Buildings Survey, ca. 1936. Courtesy of the Library of Congress.

where plantation agriculture had failed and landscapes had reverted to wilder
states. This renewed nature could be gloomy, wrapped as it was in Spanish
moss and the trappings of the Lost Cause, but it also held tourist attractions.
The old cotton and rice coast became a landscape of recreation, hunting, sight-
seeing, and public history, a place of inseparable nature and culture. Thus this
essay explores one of this volume's central themes: preserving Georgia's coastal
environment cannot focus on nature alone since that environment is as much
a cultural as a natural construction.

   Despite the facade and talk of ruin, the early-twentieth-century Georgia
coast was a region with a diversified economy centered on varied uses of nature that had evolved after the Civil War. Farming of watermelons, potatoes,
green beans, and other truck for urban and northern markets provided agricultural diversity. The lumber industry and paper manufacturing had renewed
the profitability of coastal pineland that had previously produced ship timbers and naval stores. (For a time Darien was one of the world's busiest timber ports, and Union Bag and Paper Company's massive kraft pulp and paper
mill in Savannah opened in 1936, with Mead and Scott paper companies cooperating to open another in Brunswick in 1938.)[3] And, gaining steam from
the 1880s into the early twentieth century, tourism had become the region's

driving economic engine. St. Simons itself was hardly suffering from the disappearance of planters' "former affluence" when the guidebook appeared. By the 1930s it was awash in new money. A decade earlier, two Detroit businessmen, Howard Coffin and Eugene Lewis, had established a lavish golf community on the island.[4]

But for all the real economic and ecological variety of the coast, public portrayals of its past and present relied heavily on a language of decay and imagery that privileged antebellum agricultural history over recent economic developments and that linked local environments to the legacy of the Civil War. A number of historians have noted the prominence of an emphasis on ruin during the war itself. Union officials sought to remake productive southern landscapes into ruined "wildernesses" in an effort to shorten the conflict, most intentionally in Philip Sheridan's Shenandoah Valley campaign and William Tecumseh Sherman's march through Georgia and the Carolinas.[5] As their body politic seemed to dissolve, Americans noted the symbolism of charred cities, stump forests, and "the ruins of men" who had lost life and limb in service.[6] Some found these ruins more romantic than gloomy: a substantial body of literature on the Lost Cause entails paeans to the ruins of a lustrous "Old South."[7] Less well documented is the persistence of this portrayal of the physically ruined landscape and its connections to memory, myth-making, and tourism.

A growing body of recent literature has explored the selling of Dixie as a tourist destination in the years after the Civil War, a practice that accelerated around the turn of the twentieth century. These scholars emphasize how southern history (romanticized and tragic) and southern nature (usually portrayed as idyllically balmy) were almost always part of the tourist industry's pitch.[8] But what, if anything, linked the two? I argue that in certain times and places the concept of ruin furnished the linkage. Crumbling plantation homes and rice fields regrowing in brush and saplings became rhetorical as well as ecological spaces, holding meaning for those who reinterpret history and promote tourism. Descriptions of coastal nature came to rely on what I label a "rhetoric of ruin," an intentional discourse, replete with reference to decay, that portrayed relics of past society and economy as intertwined with a regenerating natural environment. It simultaneously lamented an imagined history and suggested the possibility of pleasure and recreation in the new nature formed at the nexus of ruin and renewal. This rhetoric of ruin defined the nature of the languid, sleepy South as a product of its past, and descriptions of the Georgia coast epitomized this narrative. As ideas about outdoor recreation and environmental preservation evolved in the twentieth century, these ruined yet regenerating landscapes became one basis of modern Lowcountry tourism and regional conservation efforts.

The following historic portrayals of the coast were largely white visions. White southern landowners and northern tourists—for reasons elucidated below—wrote and spoke of their understandings of an orderly antebellum landscape devastated by the physical and economic impacts of the Civil War, and of "ruins" that carried a specific set of meanings. Their uses and definitions of Lowcountry landscapes were no more legitimate than those of enslaved people, free African Americans, or poor whites, but as cultural elites their takes dominated national understandings of the coast and over time shaped regional tourist landscapes in important ways. Only in recent years have coastal tourist sites started to interrogate African American history, albeit, as Tiya Miles reveals in this volume, in a sometimes problematic way.[9]

Georgia's modern tourist coast is built upon these evolving conceptions of the intersections of history and environment, combining as it does historic ruin and natural amenities. Savannah has defined itself as a destination providing both history and outdoor recreation, and similar sales pitches appear from Tybee Island to the Saint Marys River. St. Simons's official website, for example, advertises "pristine, natural beaches and marshlands, abundant wildlife, historic sites and monuments, parks and outdoor recreation" and provides links to golf, fishing, and canoeing options next to those for historic plantations.[10] Likewise, Sapelo Island's tourist literature describes its rich antebellum history while portraying the modern island as a wonderful nature reserve where visitors can see the descendants of former slaves who live at Hog Hammock and enjoy "the gentle island sun trickl[ing] down through trees whispering in the wind."[11] And Broadfield, a fifty-eight-hundred-acre hunting resort in Camden County, advertises its lineage as a club like those that catered to northern tourists after the Civil War. It offers falconry, "continental pheasant shoots," and hunting of deer, quail, and wild boar. For the full planter-redux experience, guests enjoy "farm-to-table" meals in the gracious lodge.[12] These and other sites offer for consumption fragments of history (real or imagined) and the natural environments that have emerged in what were once plantation landscapes. They sell a rhetoric of historic ruin and environmental regeneration.

Georgia's antebellum Lowcountry was a landscape of extremes, a mosaic of spaces that seemed either completely wild or firmly tamed. On the one hand it was a place of dark swamps, vast salt marshes, braided watercourses that filled and drained with the tides, and thick hammocks of pines, live oaks, and saw palmettos. It was a landscape of oyster beds, Spanish moss, and cryptic bitterns stalking the marsh grass. On the other hand it contained substantial plantations producing rice and Sea Island cotton for world markets and served as the seasonal home of some of America's richest slaveholders. It was a land of rice mills, drainage ditches, white columns, and overseers' shouts. It was an environment owned and administered by people whose economic outlook was Caribbean and whose estates were deeply enmeshed in the commerce and intellectual ideas of the Atlantic world.[13]

Lowcountry planters never achieved the complete mastery of the world around them that they desired. They struggled to impose their will on labor, but enslaved people resisted in myriad ways, and the soil had limits, especially on Sea Island cotton plantations exhausted by decades of cultivation. Nonetheless planters believed that the defining characteristic of the Lowcountry built environment was order, and they took great pride in its creation. The tendency that Mart Stewart emphasizes in this volume's first chapter, to view the coast as a set of islands, found its ultimate expression on coastal plantations, where masters conceptualized their estates as "islands," discretely bounded land where they were free to manipulate nature's forces.[14] This mastered landscape, they assured themselves, was both necessary and beautiful. It was the fullest expression of the potential of nature, and this vision became a template for later public memorialization of the antebellum coast.

Planters continually stressed that rice and Sea Island cotton cultivation required intensive agriculture. They wrote tracts dedicated to fieldwork, from preparing the land to laying off arrow-straight rows, debating even the best way to hoe weeds, and the built environment drew special attention. Accounts of grand mansions, new barns, cotton gins, and sugar mills swelled plantation narratives, and neat slave houses, complete with "small gardens and hen houses," symbolized the extension of mastery from land to people in planters' eyes.[15] This work of environmental conquest was continual, and planters praised ongoing efforts to bring wilder spaces under the plow. On the Altamaha River, a Generals Island planter took typical pride in slaves' work shaping the swampy island into a rice plantation, timbering, banking, ditching, and draining eight hundred acres. It was an unceasing struggle, thanks in part to endemic malaria and "gales which do at times not only sweep off entire crops, but a large portion of the negroes." Nonetheless, he seemed cheered that "there is much fine land yet to be brought under culture."[16] Likewise, George Wymberley Jones of Wormsloe Plantation (the subject of this chapter's sidebar) filled his journal with accounts of carefully managing crops, animals, forests, tidal flows, and people, his spirits rising and falling with his successes and failures.[17] Even the ostensibly wild plantation margins could be mastered, such as

Noble Jones's Wormsloe

Located on the coast a few miles south of Savannah, Wormsloe is one of the most significant historical, cultural, and natural sites in the southeastern United States. In 1733, Noble Jones, a surveyor and carpenter, was one of the original colonists to come over on the ship *Ann* to settle the new colony of Georgia. With his wife Sarah he established a five-hundred-acre estate on the Isle of Hope that has remained largely intact to the present day. For over nine generations, their descendants—the Jones, De Renne, and Barrow families—retained ownership, making it the oldest continuously owned family estate in Georgia. Wormsloe has served as a military outpost, plantation, dairy farm, country residence, repository for Georgia history, and tourist attraction,

serving the needs of the succession of landowners spanning almost three centuries.

In 1972 the State of Georgia acquired ownership of Wormsloe, except for the plantation house, where the descendants of Jones still reside, sixty-five acres surrounding the house, eighteen acres owned by descendants, and a sixteen-acre tract owned by the Wormsloe Foundation. Today Wormsloe is a state historic site of 822 acres visited by tens of thousands of people annually. The grand allée of live oak trees created in 1893 is arguably the image most frequently used in literature marketing Savannah as a tourist destination. The ruins of the original family home, a tabby-fortified house from the 1730s, provide a visible reminder of the earliest days of the colony.

Allée of live oak trees at Wormsloe Historic Site. Courtesy of Jeri Nokes.

The hundreds of acres of maritime forest, freshwater sloughs, and pine-dominated forest along the salt marsh suggest a timeless ecology, but tension undergirds the story of Wormsloe. How should a site that has undergone such radically different transformations over the centuries be interpreted? That story includes colonial Wormsloe, antebellum Wormsloe, postbellum Wormsloe, Wormsloe Gardens, and a state-owned Wormsloe with a pine forest unrepresentative of the trees that Jones found there. For most of the eighteenth century, the family farmed a small acreage with a handful of enslaved African Americans. In the early nineteenth century, the family expanded activities and developed a plantation to grow Sea Island cotton. After the Civil War, the family created extensive gardens, rented land to tenant farmers, and opened a dairy farm. A recurring pattern of clear-cutting, ditching, draining, and plow-

ing left a rich history of altered landscapes, cultural artifacts, and, fortuitously, a legacy of record-keeping.

In 2012 the Wormsloe Foundation donated a sixteen-acre parcel to the University of Georgia to establish an innovative research facility for the study of environmental history, with a focus on the Georgia coast. The Center for Research and Education at Wormsloe (CREW) supports research in ecology, geography, archaeology, engineering, forestry, and history as well as landscape architecture, environmental planning, and historic preservation. This transdisciplinary approach delivers an emerging body of knowledge about Wormsloe and its environmental history and provides a revealing case study of regional land use and development, from the thousands of years of Native American habitation to the arrival of the first colonists in Georgia and subsequent transformations.

SARAH ROSS

---

through the reservation of coastal live oaks for naval construction and planters' use of unpopulated tracts for hunting and other recreation.[18] Seen through planters' eyes, efforts to ornament and beautify agricultural landscapes symbolized the completion of their dominance of the coast. Neat kitchen gardens were utilitarian, but they also symbolized well-ordered nature. Experimental tracts of new sugarcane varieties, arrowroot, or black pepper plants could be attractive and useful. Orchards and vineyards promising perennial fruit were the perfect expressions of this desire to combine beauty, permanence, and productivity. No "beautiful" plantation was complete without one or both.[19] Planters seemed convinced that beauty, profit, and order marched hand in hand on the coast.

In these portrayals of the orderly, beautiful coast, certain planters became symbolic, with Thomas Spalding at the fore. Spalding's vision of well-groomed nature began at his estate on Sapelo Island, where he attempted to sell his fellow Lowcountry planters on the merits of Sea Island cotton as a staple crop. An inveterate experimenter, like many antebellum agricultural reformers he often wrote how-to tracts for agricultural journals. Much of Spalding's writing focused on cotton, but he found opportunity to cover almost every crop imaginable, including sugarcane, indigo, Bermuda grass, oranges, and tea.[20] Profitability was a hallmark of well-run plantations, and to that end he also wrote on the structured management of enslaved laborers.[21] But practical landscapes could be beautiful too, according to Spalding. The very order created to maximize profit was aesthetically pleasing, at least to the master's trained eye. He wrote of satisfaction in gazing over the sweating backs of slaves "labour[ing] in reclaiming a considerable body of salt marsh" on Sapelo, and he favorably compared Georgia's coastal plantations to the farms of Flanders, a center of European agricultural innovation.[22] He took the greatest enjoyment in endeavors that combined the ornamental and practical, marveling at the beauty of Bermuda grass, orange trees, and fat cattle.[23]

John Couper's Hopeton Plantation, on the Altamaha, was another estate that drew admiration. During an 1830s tour of the Georgia coast, *Southern Agriculturalist* editor J. D. Legare found Hopeton the epitome of a well-managed landscape, telling readers that it "formed a sight truly pleasing."[24] Legare was clear that it was human enterprise that made for beauty on a coast where so many acres remained "wild." He wrote of canals and drainage ditches, careful crop rotation, weed-free fields, and an orderly plantation records office, and he carefully quantified Couper's work, informing readers that more than 900 of Hopeton's 1,261 swampland acres were drained, with embankments surrounding approximately 730 of those acres. Even the uplands served a purpose, supplying cordwood for steam-powered machinery.[25] Hopeton grew all three of the Deep South's major commodity crops: cotton, sugar, and rice, and these staples required disciplined workers, Legare noted. Couper's slave management, a complex blending of the task and gang labor systems, mirrored the landscape's orderly lines. Couper quantified people, labeling each slave first as "rateable" (a working hand) or "unrateable," then as a field hand or specialist. Next he assigned the individual to a gender-specific gang, and finally he gave one of four efficiency ratings that governed the daily task. In Couper's accounting, a slave might appear as a rateable female field hand in the second gang, with a rating of ¾ (assigned three-fourths of a "prime" male field hand's task). Couper expressed satisfaction that "disobedience, running away, and riotous conduct are scarcely known on the plantation, and the necessity for punishment is very small, and almost confined to very slight inflictions for neglect of work."[26] He seemed to say that mastering people and mastering nature marched in lockstep.

This mastery was always partial. Despite planters' emphasis on the self-sufficiency and beauty of these real and imagined "islands," Lowcountry plantations were always the products of slaves as much as masters. Enslaved people did most clearing, draining, cultivating, weeding, and harvesting of the land, but their shaping extended beyond brute toil. For example, historians have made convincing arguments that the technology of tidal rice culture came largely from West Africa, brought to the Lowcountry by slaves.[27] And, despite a Georgia law requiring that absentee planters employ white overseers, many planters—Spalding and Couper included—entrusted daily management and decision-making to enslaved "drivers."[28] The beautiful landscapes that planters celebrated were in large part the products of black labor, administration, and intellect.

On and beyond plantation margins existed different landscapes that planters imagined less orderly and slaves found more liberating. Woods, marshes, and creeks—even hedgerows—offered opportunities for enslaved people to hunt, fish, or just escape overseers' eyes. On Couper's St. Simons plantation, Cannon's Point, slaves used woods and marshes for food and recreation. Archaeological excavations of fish and game bones at the slave cabins there document widespread hunting and fishing, as does evidence of slave firearm ownership. Game included opossums, raccoons, and terrapins, and of greatest importance were marine resources like oysters, catfish, and red drum. Most slave cabins held fishing gear, and slaves on nearby Butler's Point Plantation owned and sold wooden canoes that could navigate the countless Lowcountry waterways.[29] Enslaved and free black watermen had taken fish and shellfish for themselves and for sale in Savannah since the colonial era, and generally "Savannah's urban slave population was inextricably linked to the rural areas surrounding it" through the movement of the products of wild as well as cultivated spaces.[30] In the plantation margins slaves "created their own social and cultural world."[31]

These margins remained largely hidden from white eyes, however. Contemporary print sources consistently emphasized "orderly" nature. Even slavery's critics could find the Lowcountry's regimented landscapes impressive. Frederick Law Olmsted went to great lengths in his 1850s travel narrative of the South to equate ramshackle vistas with societal failures. Olmsted would eventually become the architect of some of the nation's most famous orderly

landscapes—from the winding drive of George Vanderbilt II's Biltmore Estate
to New York's Central Park—and throughout his southern journey he seemed
personally affronted by what he saw as shifting and shiftless cultivation.[32] But
the Georgia Lowcountry challenged his interpretation of the South as a region
of immediate profit at the expense of future returns. In describing the coast he
was careful to differentiate between elites' model plantations and the poorer
homesteads in their interstices, but even he could be captivated by the orderly
environs through which he rode. Traveling past "a continued succession of very
large fields, of rich dark soil—evidently reclaimed swamp-land—which had
been cultivated the previous year, in Sea Island cotton," he recorded that "beyond them, a flat surface of still lower land, with a silver thread of water curling
through it, extended, Holland-like, to the horizon." There is irony in Olmsted's
favorable comparison of a cradle of slave culture to agricultural scenes of one
of the birthplaces of the Protestant work ethic and an epicenter of agricultural
reform. (As if to shrug off this impression, he speculated that the many connections of Sea Island planters to New England families might explain their inge-
nious environmental management.)[33]

By the Civil War, then, Lowcountry planters had come to believe that
beauty was firmly tied to displays of mastery: of people, of capital, and of
nature. According to this view, in the most challenging of environments—a
marshy, pestilential landscape of muck and swamp—a handful of planters
had carved out agricultural empires, and to some, in a nation characterized by
rapid expansion and extractive farming, the neat, orderly, and profitable plantations seemed fairylands. Moreover, to planters themselves these landscapes
suggested the "rightness" of their system, both profitable and permanent. For
outsiders like Olmsted, the Georgia Lowcountry smoothed over slavery's
rough edges so apparent in the society and landscapes of the rougher frontier of slaveholding capitalism, the booming Southwest. Coastal plantations
seemed a sort of literal and figurative middle ground between the idealized
and orderly farms of the Northeast and the rough labor camps of the Deep
South.

But these peaceful landscapes were more illusory than real. They rested on
a knife's edge between ocean and land, between quiescence and rebellion, between profit and debt. Slavery was a fragile framework, one that had to be constantly defended and that depended on regional and national structures. The
Civil War would shatter the illusion, eliminating forever the notion that plantations were islands and planters sovereign over people and nature. Union naval supremacy made Lowcountry plantation work uncertain soon after hos-
tilities commenced, encouraging planters to move slaves inland and to halt

growing rice and cotton. It was a war that evolved to attack the very foundations of Lowcountry plantation society and agriculture, as the Union eventually made emancipation a central goal. By 1865 not only had planters' authority crumbled, prospective distribution of the landscape itself into the hands of
former slaves seemed to upend their world.

The war remade coastal landscapes and, just as importantly, recast the
ways in which many observers imagined these landscapes. After Appomattox,
northern journalists headed south, intent on reporting conditions in the defeated region. Their accounts continued the "outsider" readings of the coastal
plantation district that had begun before the war with Olmsted and others.
These postwar travel narratives often read like disaster tourism, as they were
enamored with visible signs of destruction and despoliation.[34] They also intimately connected right and might, with the crumbled glory of the Lowcountry certifying the completeness of Union victory. Here in the seat of the
slave power's wealth, where order had once seemed to reign supreme, journalists could not help but revel a bit in the North's triumph. These observations
also marked a shift in the center of interpretive power regarding the Georgia
coast. Prior to the war, white planters' visions dominated print interpretations
of Lowcountry rural landscapes, even as tourist narratives augmented them.
During Reconstruction, northern perceptions of the Lowcountry became increasingly influential, as Union victory unraveled the slave South's social and
economic skein. In the months following the war's end, these interpretations
remained fluid, though they would eventually settle on a particular narrative
that celebrated antebellum order, emphasized the destructive power of the
Civil War, and tried to make sense of the resulting environments that combined ruin and natural regeneration.

Ohioan Whitelaw Reid, who wrote for the *New York Tribune*, was typical
of early postwar tourists. Shortly after Appomattox he found Savannah's environs a virtual wilderness, the rice swamps overrun by "lush vegetation" in the
midst of a generally "squalid country."[35] Abolitionist writer John Trowbridge
made a similar report. Traveling across eastern Georgia toward Savannah, he
noted with some satisfaction the ruin wrought by war. Sherman's soldiers had
"got used to their wild business by the time they arrived there, and the General
[had], I suspect, slipped one glove off." He crowed a bit that the city's margins
clearly showed the hard hand of war.[36]

Even John Muir, quick to praise wild landscapes, proved critical of the
Lowcountry when traipsing through the South in the autumn of 1867. Muir,
who had opposed the Civil War, fleeing to Canada to avoid being caught up
in the conflict, walked south prepared to witness scenes of destruction.[37] East

of the city he complained that "the ragged desolate fields, on both sides of the road, are overrun with coarse rank weeds, and show scarce a trace of cultivation." This ruin carried over to the people themselves, Muir claimed, for "the traces of war are not only apparent on the broken fields, burnt fences, mills, and woods ruthlessly slaughtered, but also on the countenances of the people."[38] Muir's take on disturbed landscapes was different than that of the hawkish Reid and Trowbridge, who saw such change as evidence of Union might and southern failings, but Muir's inclination to see in abandoned plantations the hideous effects of all war also highlighted the transformative power of the Civil War on Georgia's coastal environments.

This ruin could also be quite scenic, however, and no place was more so than the historic Bonaventure Cemetery located a few miles east of Savannah. Here, seemingly, neglect was salutary, or at least intellectually and emotionally stimulating. Reid found Bonaventure enchanting in its beautiful gloom. He praised the live oaks draped with Spanish moss and noted decaying human improvements. "This very barbarism, with the absence of the rows of carefully-tended graves, and the headstones with affectionate inscriptions that mark all other cemeteries, increases the impressive gloom of the lonely place." He dwelt on nature's power to erode artifice, symbolically displayed by the "deathly festoons of the Spanish Moss, slowly stealing sap and vigor—fit funeral work—from these giant oaks, and fattening on their decay." Then Reid seemed to shake off Bonaventure's morbid attraction, penning a few cheerier lines. "Some day, when Georgia has fully recovered, this spot too, will feel the returning tide of her generous, healthy blood. The rank undergrowth will be cleared away, walks will be laid out among the tombs where now are only tangled and serpent-infested paths; [and] shafts will rise up to the green arches to commemorate the names of those most deserving in the State."[39] In short, culture would undo the erosive, if artistic hand of nature. In the meantime, said Reid, the ruined South was worth seeing.

Muir also found Bonaventure enchanting, though in his eyes the burial ground was more reborn than ruined. Camping in Bonaventure as he awaited funds to continue his travels (and perhaps contracting malaria in the meantime), Muir was at first despondent, but the cemetery soon cheered him.[40] It was a "grand old forest graveyard, so beautiful that almost any sensible person would choose to dwell here with the dead rather than with the lazy, disorderly living." And Muir was clear that it was nature overtaking human work that made Bonaventure so beautiful: "Those spots which are disordered by art, Nature is ever at work to reclaim, and to make them look as if the foot of man had never known them." Perhaps war could produce beauty, if only through the power of redirecting human energy. Most eloquent were his musings on the graves themselves: "It is interesting to observe how assiduously Nature seeks to remedy these labored art blunders. She corrodes the iron and marble, and gradually levels the hill which is always heaped up, as if a sufficiently heavy quantity of clods could not be laid on the dead. . . . strong evergreen arms laden with ferns and tillandsia [Spanish moss] drapery are spread over all—Life at work everywhere, obliterating all memory of the confusion of man."[41] In gazing across Bonaventure's burial plots, both Reid and Muir dwelt on the newfound prominence of death and destruction in the American experience, and they recognized the exoticism and interest of affected landscapes. They carried away very different interpretations of the place, however. Reid saw the cemetery's solemn corruption as scenic but fleeting, to be erased if and when Georgians embraced northern ways. Muir found the creeping nature itself the beautiful goal, an attraction for future generations. For the region as a whole Muir more accurately predicted the future than Reid, as portrayals of declining built environments and expanding natural ones would become central to coastal tourism in the twentieth century.

Southerners often echoed elements of travelers' sketches of a decaying landscape in the following years. The South's most famous mid-nineteenth-century novelist, South Carolina's William Gilmore Simms, who before the war praised Lowcountry landscapes and criticized the wild and disorderly nature of the Old Southwest in much of his writing, saw the Civil War as an environmental as well as social disruption. In postwar writing he lamented Sherman's march across the coastal plain and the destruction left in its wake (which included the ruins of Simms's own plantation house).[42] Likewise, Savannahian Charles Colcock Jones Jr. worried about what seemed to be disappearing. The son of a planter, he published *The Dead Towns of Georgia* in 1878, and though the book focused on the historic and physical traces of the state's colonial settlements, the shadow of the Civil War, which had so disrupted his family's fortunes, hung over the text. Jones, Savannah's mayor at the start of the war, introduced the book with an apology replete with echoes of defeat: "Surely it will not be deemed inappropriate to gather up the fragmentary memories of towns once vital and influential within our borders, but now covered with the mantle of decay, without succession, and wholly silent amid the voices of the present."[43] He closed on a similar note, gloomily asserting, "We cannot hope to arrest the potent influence of inherent decay, or to stay that unseen hand which remorselessly worketh change and destruction among human habitations."[44] This was a recurring theme in Jones's work. In 1888 he would publish a Gullah folktales anthology, tapping into the popularity of Joel Chandler Harris's

Georgia dialect stories. A scholar of Jones's work identifies his driving motivation as a fear "that such tales were about to vanish along with the plantations and slaves of his youth."[45] His Lowcountry was a land of lost opportunities and neglected histories, overrun by a new political order and overgrown with forest and swamp.

More than a few people sensed opportunity in the ruins. Southern boosters like tour book writer Adelaide Wilson were keen to tout rather than damn the decay if it promised visitors. In an 1889 pitch, she enticed European tourists by promising the scenic in Savannah's crumbling walls, declaring, "Come to America, we will show you plenty of ruins."[46] Northern sportsmen in particular saw recreational opportunities in the successional landscapes of old cotton and rice fields, and they often wrote as if the crumbling vestiges of the old plantation economy added allure to the hunting grounds. Where saplings sprouted, weeds choked drainage ditches, and brambles eroded field edges, the ecological processes of succession began reverting agricultural landscapes into wilder habitat. What was "ruin" to some perspectives was also a sort of "rebirth," providing cover and food for deer, quail, and other wildlife. Feral hogs, an increasingly popular quarry for northern sportsmen, seemed the epitome of an agricultural landscape gone to seed through neglect.[47]

The subtropical nature of the coastal environment contributed to the impression that ruin appeared almost overnight. Varied soils and abundant rains promoted luxuriant vine and moss growth, and the salt marsh, one of the world's most productive ecosystems, supported rapidly rebounding wildlife populations. Without regular maintenance of embankments, spring floods broke them down and transformed rice fields back into swamps (if regularly shaped ones), and vegetation choked drainage ditches, spilling storm waters onto surrounding land. Mildred and John Teal, two popular science writers with close ties to Sapelo Island and mid-twentieth-century ecological research, famously defined Georgia's coast as a landscape that simply looked wild. When cultivation ended, slash and longleaf pines quickly colonized old fields. Where fire was suppressed, a thick understory of hardwood saplings grew, and where it burned, fire-tolerant saw palmettos carpeted the ground. Live oak forest grew with similar speed and "looks old almost from the moment it begins to grow," with gnarled branches on older trees sprouting lichen, resurrection fern on their upper surfaces, and trailing Spanish moss below. Where old drainage works failed, cattails and cypress proliferated, home to hordes of spiders, frogs, and insects.[48]

Fecundity could transform cultivated landscapes into wilds, but other coastal environmental processes changed vistas even more rapidly. Hurricanes periodically swept the southeastern bight, and their wind and water altered all before them. Coastal ecological communities were adapted to these periodic upheavals, but they destroyed built environments. Twenty hurricanes made landfall in the Lowcountry or passed close offshore between the Civil War and 1928, including a monstrous storm in August 1893 that claimed an estimated two to three thousand human lives along the Atlantic coast. These storms could instantly transform order into chaos. In Darien after an 1896 storm passed through, one witness said, "Everywhere destruction and ruin were visible."[49]

Even as hurricanes and abandonment "ruined" plantations, correspondents to *Forest and Stream*, perhaps the era's most popular outdoor sports magazine, praised the regrowing tangle of life in the region and saw it as a sporting paradise for northerners in search of a mild climate and abundant game.[50] One writer captured the connection between the disappearing Old South and the emerging hunter's playground: "The plantations are abandoned, most of them, and countless bevies of quail forage in the old fields. Herds of deer and droves of turkeys and coons come out of the hammocks into the overgrown garden patches to feed on the succulent plants that have come up spontaneously year after year from self-sown seed. Here and there is an old concrete chimney, made of cemented oyster shells, where an overseer's house once stood; or the decaying remnants of some negro quarter hidden in a tangle of orange trees, cat briars, sprawling fig trees, vines, and palmetto scrub."[51] Like the romantic ruins of European castles and abbeys, signs of the old regime ornamented rather detracted from the landscape; they impressed nature with the gravity of the hoary past.[52]

Massachusetts writer Frederick Ober stressed the role of the Civil War in creating this recreation paradise. Ober hunted across Georgia, Florida, and the Caribbean during the 1870s, and in an 1880 *Lippincott's Magazine* article he turned his attention to Cumberland Island. Cumberland was a cornucopia of fish, game, and forests, but he also characterized it as "a waste," for it was in some ways a shadow of its former state. He began the article with a rather romantic account of the island's history, writing of African-born slaves, the region's early settlement, the once-important live oak timber industry, and the semitropical crops made possible by the island's microclimate. In particular he focused on Mulberry Grove, the plantation of Revolutionary War hero Nathaniel Greene and his descendants. If antebellum Cumberland had been a well-managed Elysium of cotton fields, orange groves, and ornamental gardens, the Civil War brought ruin: "Cumberland to-day is nearly depopulated, the fertile cotton- and corn-fields run to waste, and wild hogs and half-wild horses roam over the pasture and scrub that cover once-cultivated fields." Within the old borders of Mulberry Grove, "ruin everywhere stares you in the face: on every side are deserted fields and gardens—fields that employed the labor of four hundred negroes; fields that were fertile and yielded large crops of the famous 'Sea-Island cotton.'" Dungeness, the family mansion, had burned during the war, and "its ruins alone testify to the wealth of former years which is now departed, and the broad acreage of untilled fields and the ruined negro cabins cry out loudly for those who will never return to bless them." Ober found some consolation in the plantation's skeleton, however: the hunting was excellent. Here as elsewhere along the coast, thickets, patches of brambles, and regenerating forest created an ecologically varied landscape, and coupled with fewer people living on the island this led to booming game populations. Ober relished describing the wildlife that swarmed the island and described creeks full of fish and fat oysters.[53] The planters' loss became the sportsman's gain.

The coast was not a monotonous vista of decay and rubble, nor was it a vast thicket full of unwary game. New economic networks emerged and grew in the decades following Reconstruction, with their fair share of boosters. Truck farming for northern markets became increasingly important, as regular steamship lines could move watermelons, strawberries, and cantaloupes from Chatham County to Philadelphia, Boston, and New York. Coastal forests, long an economic resource, became even more important as industrialists worked in concert with Georgia railroads to transform pines into lumber to satisfy northern and European demand. As a consequence, formerly sleepy ports like Darien boomed.[54] Publications like the daily *Savannah Press*, founded in 1891, relentlessly championed the region's growth and business opportunities. The *Press* celebrated the coast's combination of historic charm and natural beauty, though even it occasionally commented on the silting river channel, dirty streets, and the ominous nature of the plantations-turned-swamps on the city's outskirts.[55] But acreage reclaimed by nature offered other opportunities, the *Press* was quick to note. There was usually a way to spin coastal re-wilding as a vibrant new recreational landscape, much as *Forest and Stream* writers claimed, as the paper did when it published stories of gun clubs' wild-game suppers and cottage beach societies enrolling members on Tybee Island.[56]

As the coastal economy changed, reimagining and redeveloping old plantations took multiple forms around the turn of the century. Some families opened their historic estates as public tourist attractions. South Carolina's Magnolia Plantation and Wormsloe, a few miles southeast of Savannah, were prominent examples. These sites drew visitors by touting a combination of old homes (or their ruins) and natural amenities, but they rarely highlighted historic agricultural practices and especially avoided discussion of slavery.[57] For historic plantations, there seemed more potential in cultivating tourists than in identifying new commodity crops. As a consequence, many former plantations would begin touting a combination of natural and historic tourism.

Northerners played a significant part in these developments. Across the Lowcountry, industrialists like Howard Coffin and Andrew Carnegie bought former plantations and turned them into personal playgrounds and resorts. Like the sportsmen who contributed to *Forest and Stream*, many turned to the wilder corners of the outdoors for pleasure. These activities could "re-create" an imagined Old South, as in the case of formal hunts that took place across Sea Island estates, in which African American guides shepherded newcomers in pursuit of game. These hunts at once drew on African Americans' real environmental knowledge and presented a tableau with white northerners as the new masters of landscape and a black servant class.[58] Or they could draw on newer fads. For those attracted to the open water, the Isle of Hope was home to a sailing club that regularly hosted races, the Savannah Yacht Club headquartered at Thunderbolt maintained a round-trip course to Cabbage Island, and there were motor yacht races along the inland waterways.[59]

These northerners also found pleasure in rehabilitating old estates. Although new mansions dotted the coast, many "snowbirds" took pride in their work restoring the "ruins" of old plantations, decrying the derelict condition of historic homes, raising money to rehabilitate antebellum structures, and working to cultivate scenic landscapes. There was a romance to these ruins and their restoration, although "virtually to a rule, northerners allowed elements of former working landscapes and, by implication, their association with slavery, to remain glossed over by the patina of time." These impulses often seemed contradictory. Some northerners saw neglected old plantations as a clean slate where they might fashion new recreational playgrounds, such as the Jekyll Island Club. Others took great pleasure in selectively restoring portions of the "Old South," perhaps envisioning a gentler sort of paternalism that preserved noteworthy architecture and landscapes while minimizing the historic social structures that had made the planters' world possible.[60] These tensions live on in regional tourism largely focused on plantation mansions, ecologically diverse marshlands, and outdoor recreation, with comparatively little emphasis given to historic racial or labor relationships. Or, as Tiya Miles shows in this volume, if black history is present, it is often in the form of exotic, "dark" tourism, cloaked in mystery, voyeurism, and the supernatural rather than holding slavery up to a light, more recreation than remembrance.[61]

Statistics bore out perceptions of a landscape of declining agricultural productivity, with farms yielding to the encroaching wild. Although an imperfect source, census records reveal the Civil War as a watershed for coastal land use. In 1860, Georgia's six coastal counties (Bryan, Camden, Chatham, Glynn, Liberty, and McIntosh) contained 152,502 acres of improved farmland. By 1880, this acreage had shrunk by more than a third, to 99,403 acres. The old economic kings—rice and Sea Island cotton—were mere shadows of their former selves in the Lowcountry by 1900, as that year Chatham County produced a total of just ten bales of cotton. Even as late as 1920, in the wake of the agricultural prosperity accompanying World War I, improved land in the six counties covered thirty thousand fewer acres than at the Civil War's start. And the decline continued through the Depression and World War II. Census takers no longer recorded "improved acres" after 1920, but the 1950 census listed just 23,593 "acres of cropland harvested" in the six counties. The Civil War really had proven a death knell of sorts for coastal commodity plantations.[62]

These views of ruin were not universal, however. The changing landscape in the wake of emancipation offered freedpeople opportunities. In both actions and words African Americans testified to the freedom that could come with the disintegration of plantation order and the ensuing successional landscapes. Freedpeople eagerly seized upon government promises of land, most notably through General Sherman's Special Field Order No. 15, and indeed took up thousands of acres on the Sea Islands. When the promise of acreage for each family of freedpeople fell apart, African Americans still found ways to own or rent land they could farm.[63] On Sapelo by 1880, for example, sixteen freedmen owned small farms, and twenty-two more rented land.[64] The most common evidence of black efforts to control landscapes were the gardens dotting every community, a continuation of antebellum practices. Coastal travelers noted the ubiquity of neat African American vegetable and herb plots, tidy spaces carved from old plantations growing up in brush and briars.[65] They also fished and hunted marshes and forests, another continuity of land use from enslavement to freedom. Fishermen like Frank Tyler, Quirus Frazier, and Julius Williams frequented the marshes southeast of Savannah, even if they sometimes faced poaching charges for their efforts.[66] Residents of tiny communities like White Bluff and Thunderbolt relied on crabbing, fishing, and oystering—expanding the importance black watermen had long held in the Lowcountry—especially after seafood canneries opened near Savannah in the 1890s. Other African Americans foraged for wild produce such as palmetto "cabbage" (*Sabal palmetto*).[67]

Wild spaces retained cultural power as well as served as a source of sustenance and profit. "Root doctors" harvested medicinal plants like mayapple

and palmetto roots from field and forest. The drums that were an important part of Lowcountry black worship might be made from raccoon hide
stretched tight across a hollowed-out cypress or cedar log. Coastal African
Americans had many stories demonstrating connection to plantation margins,
woods, swamps, and waters. In these tales, anthropomorphized rabbits, alligators, and terrapins used wilder Lowcountry corners in ways much like enslaved
and later freedpeople. Throughout the late nineteenth and early twentieth
centuries, the coast's wilder spaces continued to offer economic, recreational,
and spiritual opportunities for African Americans.[68]

White observers noted African Americans enjoying a coast where plantations were much less important. Ober wrote that freedpeople remained on
Cumberland in substantial numbers, enjoying the island's hunting and fishing,
although he equated former slaves with feral livestock. In Ober's eyes, African Americans had become naturalized, falling into a leisurely life of hunting,
gathering, and gardening following emancipation.[69] Another observer in 1876
noted the avid pursuit of game by Lowcountry blacks but chastised them for
their unsporting hunting practices.[70] And a white critic wrote of Sapelo that
former slaves and their descendants led an "easy, carefree life which consists
chiefly of fishing, crabbing, and cultivating a small patch of garden."[71] The
swampy, wilder portions of the coast had once sheltered African Americans
escaping the boundaries of the plantation. Some whites found similar postwar
activities quaint or primitive but also seemed discomfited that the changing
nature of plantations, not just their boundaries, offered succor to freedpeople.
In these peopled landscapes they drew parallels between nature gone feral and
labor and race relations grown askew.

As was the case in the antebellum era, these landscapes shaped and used
by African Americans remained largely hidden in published accounts. White
narratives of a coast devastated by the Civil War yet made scenic dominated
the collective national imagination. The New Deal cemented this paradigm,
labeling the region as an important historical tourism and recreation destination. The period's expansion of federal government is most remembered
for economic planning and infrastructural endeavors, some of which, like
the Santee-Cooper Project, reshaped Lowcountry environments in dramatic
ways.[72] Several agencies, most notably the Works Progress Administration
(WPA), gave federal funding to public history projects, seeking "evidence of
distinctive local aesthetics" through documenting the past.[73] The WPA's Federal Writers' Project, designed to provide work for unemployed intellectuals,
was particularly influential, and its subsidiary Georgia Writers' Project's Savannah Unit, supervised by Mary Granger, was exceptionally productive. The

Savannah office conducted interviews with former slaves as part of a national oral history project and published work on the city's and adjoining countryside's history and tourism opportunities. In all work its writers celebrated the region's antebellum past, described the postwar period in terms of romantic decay, and promoted the recreational opportunities of a Lowcountry characterized by re-wilding.

The Savannah Unit managed to turn even ex-slave narratives into paeans for the Old South. The writers published selected interviews combined with pseudo-ethnographic sketches and folklore as *Drums and Shadows: Survival Studies among the Georgia Coastal Negroes* in 1940. The book portrayed coastal African Americans as an exotic remnant people of West African culture who, if not entirely admirable, were distinct and thus interesting. It drew on the now-familiar story of a wealthy plantation region upset by war and emancipation, which led to ruin and stagnation. In this case, the lethargy of defeat offered the benefit of preserving a novel set of customs and beliefs. The book's publication connected to the period's scholarly interpretations of coastal black culture. During the 1930s anthropologist Melville Herskovits was popularizing the notion that Lowcountry African Americans were culturally distinctive, more "African" than other black Americans, and, as Edda Fields-Black argues in chapter 4 of this volume, solidifying the "Gullah Geechee" label. Seeming to channel Herskovits, in a chapter on Sapelo, the authors of *Drums and Shadows* described the plantation glory days of Thomas Spalding and saw in their wake a landscape populated largely by African Americans who were "descendants of the slaves of the plantation era," many leading lives seemingly frozen in time by an "isolated island existence." As this example suggests, like Herskovits's work the entire collection touted the power of deterioration-as-preservation, presenting the contemporary Georgia coast as an antebellum relic preserved through salutary neglect rather than as a landscape and culture that had changed over time like any other.[74]

Other projects of the Georgia Writers' Project's Savannah Unit even more explicitly celebrated the juxtaposition of "orderly" and "ruined" nature. *Savannah* (1937), a book on the city and its surroundings, in the popular American Guide Series, neatly summarized the narrative that had coalesced by the 1930s. The antebellum Georgia Lowcountry was a place where, thanks to "prosperity under the agrarian system . . . plantations grew to be almost like small kingdoms sufficient unto themselves. The master in his palatial mansion was the king and his white tenants and Negro slaves were his subjects. Almost everything the family needed could be grown or manufactured on the efficiently run plantation." But "the War Between the States completely obliterated this picture of the southern plantation. After the war families returned to desolate, charred fields to find in the ashes of their proud homes the symbol of a dead prosperity, and many left the scene of their misfortunes never to return. Brambles and trees reclaimed the land as a wilderness, and today the spectator drives for miles past acres of untenanted woods and weedy fields."[75] In this simplified retelling of the nineteenth century, paradise had been lost.

Here too the ruin was portrayed as scenic. The meat of the guidebook lay in its tours, complete with annotations on the suggested stops. Some were walking tours of the city's historic squares, others motor tours of the coast dominated by waypoints at historic antebellum plantations or their ruins. These Depression-era tours drew on a white understanding of coastal history that minimized or hid the physical and emotional costs of slavery, relegating African American interpretations of the Lowcountry to folklore collections like *Drums and Shadows*. Only in the late twentieth century would slavery begin to be more thoroughly incorporated into historical tours like those sold in *Savannah*. The creeping wild also brought with it environmental amenities, according to the authors. Savannah's environs had become a sportsman's paradise, where tourists could enjoy hunting, horse riding, golf, and "surf bathing."[76]

The Savannah Unit's most sprawling effort at commemorating the plantation world came in a series of plantation studies published serially in the *Georgia Historical Quarterly*. In an introductory piece, the agency framed the articles as a tribute to an old system, once industrious and orderly, noting that "those deserted plantations in inaccessible areas are being slowly transformed into an impassable wilderness."[77] What followed were twenty articles spanning five years, seventeen journal issues, and 483 pages, examining twelve plantations along the Savannah River in Chatham County. The individual articles, rooted in archives and family papers, amounted to an impressive if hagiographic memorial to the region's most prominent slaveholders.[78] The proximity of the selected sites to Savannah dovetailed nicely with WPA efforts to create a historic driving tours network in the countryside surrounding the city, akin to the one connecting Virginia's colonial James River plantations. Intentionally or not, the articles collectively accepted antebellum planters' portrayals of the world they had built, an orderly and attractive landscape brought low by the Civil War, and they largely ignored any other challenges to this order—whether from enslaved peoples or external forces.

Representative of the collection's interpretations was the second article of two on Mulberry Grove (a different plantation than the one on Cumberland Island). The author or authors presented the familiar dichotomy of "golden days of prosperity" followed by the war and "desolation and ruin." A sketch from the war illuminated this scene, in which "the outbuilding where young [Eli] Whitney first experienced the thrill of watching his tiny 'cotton engine' separate the lint from the seed, [and] the mansion house honored with the presence of President Washington in 1791, were destroyed by foraging soldiers of General Sherman's Army. With one of his own slaves set to guard him, Zachariah Winkler stood and watched his home go up in smoke."[79] Unlike *Savannah*, the *Georgia Historical Quarterly* series failed to present the contemporary appeal of ruin, although there was much that was romantic in its histories.

The Historic American Buildings Survey (HABS), a New Deal program under the aegis of the National Park Service, also built upon the romance of Lowcountry memory and ruin. HABS officials documented the nation's built environment through photographs, field notes, and architectural renderings of antebellum structures (like many New Deal endeavors, providing temporary work for unemployed professionals). Historian Mike Wallace labels HABS's work as fundamentally populist, noting its documentation of vernacular architecture—from barns to slave cabins—but such was hardly the case in the agency's coastal Georgia studies.[80] There HABS architects focused almost exclusively on plantation landscapes and the ruins of the distant past, celebrating the grandeur and charm of an imagined colonial and Old South. As professionals justifying their work, coastal HABS employees had a vested interest in interpreting plantation structures as once grand, now neglected, and worthy of celebration and conservation.

A quick survey of New Deal HABS studies in the state's six coastal counties illustrates an overwhelming focus on two categories of sites: plantation homes (or their ruins) and vestiges of colonial Spanish structures. Omitting Savannah's numerous city homes (many of which were connected to planters), ten of the eighteen sites were historic plantations, and four were ruins of Spanish missions.[81] Some of the surveys highlighted well-preserved grand architecture, with artistic shots of staircases and mantelpieces, but others juxtaposed opulence and ruin in both buildings and landscapes, implying what might have been had history followed a different course. Of McIntosh County's Ashantilly, surrounded by thick forest, one HABS author wrote that it was in "poor" condition, having been "shelled during the war."[82] The file for Chatham County's Hermitage contained a similar terse note: the estate had "not been occupied by a resident since it was sacked by Sherman's soldiers."[83]

The study of the remnants of Retreat Plantation made the implications more obvious. The Library of Congress HABS files on Retreat entail two

FIGURE 6.2. Ashantilly Plantation, McIntosh County. This photograph of a plantation's big house framed by an encroaching forest of live oaks, saw palmetto, and Spanish moss epitomizes HABS portrayals of the crumbling coastal built environment. Historic American Buildings Survey, 1936. Courtesy of the Library of Congress.

parts. The first documents the big house on St. Simons, once home of the Page family and then the King family, left in "ruins" by the war and its aftermath. The second examines the plantation's old tabby greenhouse, which served a dual purpose as a slave hospital. The text accompanying the photographs and architectural renderings conveys a particularly paternalistic view of the antebellum Lowcountry. In highlighting the combined greenhouse and slave hospital, HABS workers focused on a site that emphasized the intersection of planter control over land and human beings. One half of the structure had been a modern room for slave medicine, and the other had been a place to experiment with crop varieties and start plants. Through the operations of this building, the HABS text and images suggest, planters had once improved landscapes and repaired enslaved bodies. But those days were gone; the destruction of war and economic crisis of emancipation had destroyed the old order as thoroughly as they had ruined this structure. Paired with the ruins of the plantation house, the message about the war and its consequences for

Lowcountry nature and society could hardly be clearer. They laid to waste a beautiful, orderly landscape. That ruin was regrettable, but it was also scenic and memorable, worthy of preservation.[84]

The Civil War shifted perceptions of the Georgia coast in dramatic and lasting ways. Supporting historians' twenty-first-century arguments about the thoroughly capitalist nature of the slave South, many antebellum planters and tourists admired landscapes that combined profit and order.[85] Yet at the same time coastal planters stressed the beauty of stewardship. They seemed to truly believe that the most aesthetically pleasing forms of nature demonstrated permanent as well as profitable agriculture, and these vistas justified paternalistic control over nature and people.[86] It was no accident that these portrayals of plantation environments made an argument for the perpetuation of slavery. The Civil War transformed the value and meaning of coastal environments; new narratives emphasized ruin when interpreting plantation environments, and found it grimly beautiful. Some big houses had been destroyed, the gins and mills had fallen into disrepair, and the ditches were choked with weeds. For some white southerners these landscapes were reminders that northern victory meant a loss of their way of life. Lonely chimneys and brushy cotton fields were emblems of the Lost Cause, starkly beautiful in a funereal way. Placing the onus of these changes on the war and the North allowed white southerners to ignore African American contestation of enslavement and the challenges of increasing global commodity competition.[87] Visiting northerners likely found pleasure in seeing evidence of the power of the Union war machine. Abandoned plantations, once powered by human bondage, demonstrated the might of a right cause.

The crumbling plantation kingdom offered new opportunities, however, and sportsmen found outdoor recreation in the tattered agricultural landscapes of the late nineteenth century. The thickets and marshes were places to pursue deer and quail, to collect oysters, and to sail in a regatta past crumbling plantation docks. And the old plantations themselves held attraction for northerners, who in some cases came to imagine themselves as the new lords of the Lowcountry. The public historians of the New Deal would firmly cement these two conceptions of coastal nature through work that celebrated the antebellum era, identified the Civil War and emancipation as its downfall, and emphasized the tourist potential of memory, ruin, and decay. If boaters could catch a glimpse of Retreat Plantation in 1937, led there by Georgia Writers' Project guidebook *The Intracoastal Waterway*, what they saw likely reflected a century of imagination as surely as it bore evidence of the coast's environment and history.

In this history of a century of portrayals of coastal Georgia, it is tempting to reduce interpretations to either defensiveness (on the part of Lowcountry whites) or a sort of disaster tourism (on the part of northern travelers). Something else appeared at work, however, certainly as the years passed after the Civil War. For all the rhetorical wilds of the coast, many people—southern and northern, white and black—came to find genuine pleasure in real Lowcountry landscapes. Oystering, fishing, and hunting provided recreation and sustenance. Crumbling mansions and tabby forts were scenic, especially in a nation that emphasized newness. Ruins in the midst of nature captured a growing regional and national sense of nostalgia, and an expanded forest proved as much an attraction as a chastising historical lesson. The combination of ruin and regeneration, then, offered different things to different people. It promised historical lessons to those inclined to see them, and it offered pleasant diversions to those more focused on the present.

By the mid-twentieth century, ideas about the coast brought together the historic and environmental elements that still characterize Lowcountry tourism and conservation. This fusion today pervades the literature of hunting clubs, housing developments, Savannah's tours, golf courses, and beach retreats. Tourists' dinner plates also reflect this history. The romanticized plantation landscapes, made more exotic by their near-disappearance, help fuel the revival of "heritage foods" in hip coastal restaurants, foods like the Carolina Gold rice, benne (sesame), and Sea Island "petite rouge" peas that were once integral to the Lowcountry plantation system.[88] Even John Berendt's bestselling book about Savannah, *Midnight in the Garden of Good and Evil* (1994), tapped into this intersection of history and nature by featuring Bonaventure Cemetery's decaying charm, which so captivated Reid and Muir more than a century earlier, in the text and on the cover of the first edition.[89]

Ideas about coastal nature may have sprung in part from efforts to imagine what landscapes had to say about the Civil War, but in the physical environments themselves people fashioned a new, re-wilded recreational coast. Modern coastal living expresses concern for preserving nature and history, but preservation cannot hold either environment or culture in stasis. Instead, today's recreational coast can draw on a potent cultural and environmental blend. Modern coastal narratives celebrate and interpret the wealth and beauty of plantation landscapes once powered by bondage; they convey a sense of loss stemming from the social, economic, and physical outcomes of the Civil War;

and they have come to see regenerative nature as an opportunity as much as evidence of decline. In true southern fashion these stories define the past as tragedy, a tragedy that imparts distinctiveness and hence value. There have long been dissenting visions of the meanings of coastal landscapes, but this narrative of near perfection eclipsed by ruin, followed by a long period of environmental regeneration, has become a dominant portrayal of the Georgia coast. We would do well to remember that it is itself a historical artifact.

NOTES

1. Federal Writers' Project, *The Intracoastal Waterway: Norfolk to Key West* (Washington D.C.: Government Printing Office, 1937), 50; J. D. Legare, "Account of an Agricultural Excursion Made into the South of Georgia in the Winter of 1832," *Southern Agriculturalist and Register of Rural Affairs* 6, no. 7 (July 1833): 359.

2. Federal Writers' Project, *Intracoastal Waterway*, 53.

3. See Albert Way, "Longleaf Pine, from Forest to Fiber: Production, Consumption, and the Cutover on Georgia's Coastal Plain, 1865–1900," chap. 7 in this volume; William Boyd, "Water Is for Fighting Over: Papermaking and the Struggle over Groundwater in Coastal Georgia, 1930s–2000s," chap. 8 in this volume.

4. Barbara Hull, *St. Simons, Enchanted Island: A History of the Most Historic of Georgia's Fabled Golden Isles* (Atlanta: Cherokee, 1980), 99–102.

5. Lisa M. Brady, *War upon the Land: Military Strategy and the Transformation of Southern Landscapes during the American Civil War* (Athens: University of Georgia Press, 2012).

6. Megan Kate Nelson, *Ruin Nation: Destruction and the American Civil War* (Athens: University of Georgia Press, 2012), chap. 4; Aaron Sachs, "Stumps in the Wilderness," in *The Blue, the Gray, and the Green: Toward an Environmental History of the Civil War*, ed. Brian Allen Drake (Athens: University of Georgia Press, 2015), 96–112.

7. Caroline Janney, *Burying the Dead but Not the Past: Ladies Memorial Associations and the Lost Cause* (Chapel Hill: University of North Carolina Press, 2008); Gaines Foster, *Ghosts of the Confederacy: Defeat, the Lost Cause, and the Emergence of the New South* (New York: Oxford University Press, 1988); Charles Reagan Wilson, *Baptized in Blood: The Religion of the Lost Cause, 1865–1920* (Athens: University of Georgia Press, 1980).

8. Good places to start on this literature include Reiko Hillyer, *Designing Dixie: Tourism, Memory, and Urban Space in the New South* (Charlottesville: University of Virginia Press, 2014); Karen L. Cox, *Dreaming of Dixie: How the South Was Created in American Popular Culture* (Chapel Hill: University of North Carolina Press, 2011); Anthony Stanonis, *Creating the Big Easy: New Orleans and the Emergence of Modern Tourism, 1918–1945* (Athens: University of Georgia Press, 2006).

9. For the ambiguity of regional tourist sites' slave stories, see Tiya Miles,

"Haunted Waters: Stories of Slavery, Coastal Ghosts, and Environmental Consciousness," chap. 5 in this volume, and Miles, *Tales from the Haunted South: Dark Tourism and Memories of Slavery from the Civil War Era* (Chapel Hill: University of North Carolina Press, 2015), chap. 1.

10. ExploreStSimonsIsland.com ("The official website of St. Simons Island"), http://www.explorestsimonsisland.com.

11. Sandy Jones, "Sapelo Sojourn," Golden Isles Navigator, http://www.gacoast .com/navigator/sapelo.html.

12. "Broadfield," Sea Island Company, http://www.seaisland.com/broadfield -brochure.

13. Matthew Mulcahy, *Hubs of Empire: The Southeastern Lowcountry and British Caribbean* (Baltimore: Johns Hopkins University Press, 2014); Paul Pressly, *On the Rim of the Caribbean: Colonial Georgia and the British Atlantic World* (Athens: University of Georgia Press, 2013); Timothy Lockley, *Lines in the Sand: Race and Class in Lowcountry Georgia, 1750–1860* (Athens: University of Georgia Press, 2004).

14. Mart Stewart, "Islands, Edges, and Globe: The Environmental History of the Georgia Coast," chap. 1 in this volume.

15. Thomas Spalding, "On the Cotton Gin and the Introduction of Cotton," *Southern Cultivator* 2, no. 11 (May 29, 1844): 83–84; J. D. Legare, "Account of an Agricultural Excursion Made into the South of Georgia in the Winter of 1832," *Southern Agriculturalist and Register of Rural Affairs* 6, no. 3 (March 1833): 140–47; Legare, "Account of an Agricultural Excursion Made into the South of Georgia in the Winter of 1832," *Southern Agriculturalist and Register of Rural Affairs* 6, no. 5 (May 1833): 252; Legare, "Account of an Agricultural Excursion Made into the South of Georgia in the Winter of 1832," *Southern Agriculturalist and Register of Rural Affairs* 6, no. 4 (April 1833): 165–67, 173.

16. "Culture of Rice on the Embanked Marshes in Georgia," *Farmer's Register* 1, no. 4 (September 1833): 235, 237.

17. Farm Diary of George Wymberley Jones, 1854–1861, George Wymberley Jones De Renne Family Papers, box 12, folder 26, Hargrett Rare Books and Special Collections Library, University of Georgia, Athens.

18. Alatamaha, "Deer Hunting on the Seaboard of Georgia," *American Turf Register and Sporting Magazine* 3, no. 1 (September 1831): 28–30.

19. J. D. Legare, "Account of an Agricultural Excursion Made into the South of Georgia in the Winter of 1832," *Southern Agriculturalist and Register of Rural Affairs* 6, no. 5 (May 1833): 249, 251, 252; Legare, "Account of an Agricultural Excursion," *Southern Agriculturalist and Register of Rural Affairs* 6, no. 4 (April 1833): 170–73.

20. Thomas Spalding, "Observations on Bordering Our River Banks with Orange Trees, and Protecting the Embankments with Bermuda Grass," *Southern Agriculturalist and Register of Rural Affairs* 4, no. 1 (February 1830): 71–75; Spalding, "On the Introduction of Tea into the Southern States, with a Few Observations on the Silk Worm," *Southern Agriculturalist and Register of Rural Affairs* 3, no. 7 (July 1830): 359–63; Spalding, "On the Culture, Harvesting and Threshing of Rice, and on the Rust in

Cotton," *Southern Agriculturalist and Register of Rural Affairs* 8, 4 (April 1835): 169–74; Spalding, "Culture of the Sugar-Cane—No. I," *American Agriculturalist* 3, no. 6 (June 1844): 165–67; Spalding, "Gama and Bermuda Grass," *American Agriculturalist* 3, no. 11 (November 1, 1844): 335; Spalding, "Culture of Indigo," *American Agriculturalist* 5, no. 2 (February 1846): 54–55.

21. Spalding, "On the Cotton Gin," 83–84.

22. Ibid., 83; Spalding, "On the Culture, Harvesting and Threshing of Rice," 174.

23. Spalding, "Gama and Bermuda Grass," 335; Spalding, "Observations on Bordering Our River Banks," 73–74.

24. J. D. Legare, "Account of an Agricultural Excursion Made into the South of Georgia in the Winter of 1832," *Southern Agriculturalist and Register of Rural Affairs* 6, no. 7 (July 1833): 362.

25. Ibid., 358–63; J. D. Legare, "Account of an Agricultural Excursion Made into the South of Georgia in the Winter of 1832," *Southern Agriculturalist and Register of Rural Affairs* 6, no. 8 (August 1833): 410–16.

26. J. D. Legare, "Account of an Agricultural Excursion Made into the South of Georgia in the Winter of 1832," *Southern Agriculturalist and Register of Rural Affairs* 6, no. 11 (November 1833): 571–77, quote on 576.

27. Edda Fields-Black, *Deep Roots: Rice Farmers in West Africa and the African Diaspora* (Bloomington: Indiana University Press, 2008); Judith Carney, *Black Rice: The African Origins of Rice Cultivation in the Americas* (Cambridge, Mass.: Harvard University Press, 2002); Daniel C. Littlefield, *Rice and Slaves: Ethnicity and the Slave Trade in Colonial South Carolina* (Champaign: University of Illinois Press, 1991).

28. Charles Joyner, *Remember Me: Slave Life in Coastal Georgia* (Athens: University of Georgia Press, 2011), 22–26; Jacqueline Jones, *Saving Savannah: The City and the Civil War* (New York: Alfred A. Knopf, 2008), 61, 93.

29. John Solomon Otto, *Cannon's Point Plantation, 1794–1860: Living Conditions and Status Patterns in the Old South* (Orlando: Academic Press, 1984), 45–58.

30. Walter J. Fraser Jr., *Savannah in the Old South* (Athens: University of Georgia Press, 2003), 95; Jacqueline Jones, *Saving Savannah*, 154; Leslie M. Harris and Daina Ramey Berry, "Slave Life in Savannah: Geographies of Autonomy and Control," in *Slavery and Freedom in Savannah* (Athens: University of Georgia Press, 2014), 104–5.

31. Otto, *Cannon's Point Plantation*, 6.

32. Witold Rybczynski, *A Clearing in the Distance: Frederick Law Olmsted and America in the 19th Century* (New York: Charles Scribner's Sons, 2000).

33. Frederick Law Olmsted, *The Cotton Kingdom: A Traveller's Observations on Cotton and Slavery in the American Slave States*, ed. Arthur M. Schlesinger (New York: Knopf, 1966), 179–183, quote on 181.

34. John Lennon and Malcolm Foley, *Dark Tourism: The Attraction of Death and Disaster* (Boston: Cengage, 2000); Brigitte Sion, ed., *Death Tourism: Disaster Sites as Recreational Landscape* (New York: Seagull Books, 2014).

35. Whitelaw Reid, *After the War: A Southern Tour, May 1, 1865, to May 1, 1866* (London: Sampson Low, Son, & Marston, 1866), 134, 138.

36. John Townsend Trowbridge, *The South: A Tour of Its Battlefields and Ruined Cities, a Journey through the Desolated States, and Talks with the People, 1867*, ed. J. H. Segars (Macon, Ga.: Mercer University Press, 2006), 502, 508.

37. Donald Worster, *A Passion for Nature: The Life of John Muir* (New York: Oxford University Press, 2008), 85–93.

38. John Muir, *A Thousand-Mile Walk to the Gulf* (Boston: Houghton Mifflin, 1916), 66, 84.

39. Reid, *After the War*, 140–41.

40. Worster, *A Passion for Nature*, 130–33, 140.

41. Muir, *Thousand-Mile Walk to the Gulf*, 67, 71–72.

42. Jeffrey J. Rogers, *A Southern Writer and the Civil War: The Confederate Imagination of William Gilmore Simms* (Lanham, Md.: Lexington, 2015), 175–85; Ehren Foley, "Isaac Nimmons and the Burning of Woodlands: Power, Paternalism, and the Performance of Manhood in William Gilmore Simms's Civil War South," in *William Gilmore Simms's Unfinished Civil War: Consequences for a Southern Man of Letters*, ed. David Moltke-Hansen (Columbia: University of South Carolina Press, 2013), 90; William Gilmore Simms, *A City Laid Waste: The Capture, Sack, and Destruction of the City of Columbia*, ed. David Aiken (Columbia: University of South Carolina Press, 2005); David Moltke-Hansen, "Between Plantation and Frontier: The South of William Gilmore Simms," in *William Gilmore Simms and the American Frontier*, ed. John Caldwell Guilds and Caroline Collins (Athens: University of Georgia Press, 1997), 3–26. On Simms as historian, see Sean R. Busick, *A Sober Desire for History: William Gilmore Simms as Historian* (Columbia: University of South Carolina Press, 2005).

43. Charles Colcock Jones Jr., *The Dead Towns of Georgia* (Savannah: Morning News Steam Printing House, 1878), 5; Jacqueline Jones, *Saving Savannah*, 34–35, 121.

44. Jones, *Dead Towns of Georgia*, 255.

45. Susan Millar Williams, foreword to Charles Colcock Jones Jr., *Gullah Folktales from the Georgia Coast* (Athens: Brown Thrasher Books/University of Georgia Press, 2000), xi.

46. Quoted in Hillyer, *Designing Dixie*, 176.

47. Abraham H. Gibson, *Feral Animals in the American South: An Evolutionary History* (Cambridge: Cambridge University Press, 2016), 90–91.

48. Mildred Teal and John Teal, *Portrait of an Island* (New York: Atheneum, 1964), esp. 29–37, 50–74, quote from 31.

49. Walter J. Fraser Jr., *Lowcountry Hurricanes: Three Centuries of Storms at Sea and Ashore* (Athens: University of Georgia Press, 2006), 260–65, quote from 188–89.

50. N. H. Bishop, "Bishop's Canoe Voyage," *Forest and Stream* 4, no. 6 (March 18, 1875): 92; T. C. Rice, "Getting Lost," *Forest and Stream* 16, no. 11 (April 14, 1881): 204–5; Henry C. Kittles, "Field Notes from Georgia," *Forest and Stream* 25, no. 15 (May 6, 1886): 285.

51. "Editorial Notes of Southern Travels," *Forest and Stream* 6, no. 7 (March 23, 1876): 105.

52. Aaron Sachs, *Arcadian America: The Death and Life of an Environmental Tradition* (New Haven: Yale University Press, 2013), 120–36; Roderick Nash, *Wilderness and the American Mind*, 4th ed. (New Haven: Yale University Press, 2001), 67–81.

53. Frederick A. Ober, "Dungeness, General Greene's Sea-Island Plantation," *Lippincott's Magazine of Popular Literature and Science* 26 (August 1880): 241–49.

54. Mart Stewart, *"What Nature Suffers to Groe": Life, Labor, and Landscape on the Georgia Coast, 1680–1920* (Athens: University of Georgia Press, 1996), 225–29; Mark Finlay, "The Postbellum Transition from Agriculture to Industry," in *Slavery and Freedom in Savannah*, ed. Leslie M. Harris and Daina Ramey Berry (Athens: University of Georgia Press, 2014), 188–89.

55. "Savannah, She Is All Right," *Savannah Press*, November 26, 1891; "Too Much Sand," *Savannah Press*, November 21, 1891; "Is He a Murderer?" *Savannah Press*, January 16, 1892.

56. "Sportsmen at Dinner," *Savannah Press*, November 27, 1891; "The Cottage Club," *Savannah Press*, January 11, 1892.

57. Charles Snell, "Middleton Place Gardens," National Register of Historic Places Inventory—Nomination Form, June 14, 1971, http://focus.nps.gov/pdfhost/docs /NHLS/Text/71000770.pdf; Drew Swanson, "Tending the New Old South: Cultivating a Plantation Image in the Lowcountry," in *Leisure, Plantations, and the Making of a New South: The Sporting Plantations of the South Carolina Lowcountry and Red Hills Region, 1900–1940*, ed. Julia Brock and Daniel Vivian (Lanham, Md.: Lexington/Rowman & Littlefield, 2015), 83–103.

58. Scott Giltner, *Hunting and Fishing in the New South: Black Labor and White Leisure after the Civil War* (Baltimore: Johns Hopkins University Press, 2008), 110–12; Mary Bullard, *Cumberland Island: A History* (Athens: University of Georgia Press, 2003), 228–33.

59. "Savannah Y. C., Annual Regatta," *Forest and Stream*, June 11, 1885, 398; "Motor Boatmen Ready for Race," *Savannah Morning News*, July 3, 1910; Drew Swanson, *Remaking Wormsloe Plantation: The Environmental History of a Lowcountry Landscape* (Athens: University of Georgia Press, 2012), 137.

60. Jennifer Betsworth, "Reviving and Restoring Southern Ruins: Reshaping Plantation Architecture and Landscapes in Georgetown County, South Carolina," in Brock and Vivian eds., *Leisure, Plantations and the Making of a New South*, 58.

61. Miles, "Haunted Waters," chap. 5 in this volume.

62. University of Virginia Library's Historical Census Browser, http://mapserver .lib.virginia.edu (site discontinued; last accessed April 29, 2016); Finlay, "Postbellum Transition from Agriculture to Industry," 191.

63. Stewart, *What Nature Suffers to Groe*, chap. 5; Jacqueline Jones, *Saving Savannah*, chaps. 10 and 11.

64. William S. McFeely, *Sapelo's People: A Long Walk into Freedom* (New York: W. W. Norton, 1994), 143.

65. Georgia Writers' Project, *Drums and Shadows: Survival Studies among the Georgia Coastal Negroes* (Athens: University of Georgia Press, 1940), 12–13, 138, 159.

66. Swanson, *Remaking Wormsloe Plantation*, 119–20.

67. Georgia Writers' Project, *Drums and Shadows*, 73, 103, 110; Finlay, "Postbellum Transition from Agriculture to Industry," 188.

68. Joyner, *Remember Me*, 45–59; Georgia Writers' Project, *Drums and Shadows*, 75, 148.

69. Ober, "Dungeness," 243.

70. "Editorial Notes of Southern Travels," 105.

71. Georgia Writers' Project, *Drums and Shadows*, 159.

72. T. Robert Hart, "The Lowcountry Landscape: Politics, Preservation, and the Santee-Cooper Project," *Environmental History* 18, no. 1 (January 2013): 127–56.

73. Denise D. Meringolo, *Museums, Monuments, and National Parks: Toward a New Genealogy of Public History* (Amherst: University of Massachusetts Press, 2012), 121.

74. Georgia Writers' Project, *Drums and Shadows*, 159. On the importance of coastal Georgia and *Drums and Shadows* in popularizing the Gullah and Geechee labels, see Melissa L. Cooper, *Making Gullah: A History of Sapelo Islanders, Race, and the American Imagination* (Chapel Hill: University of North Carolina Press, 2017), chap. 4.

75. Georgia Writers' Project, Savannah Unit, *Savannah* (Savannah: Review Print, 1937), 44–46.

76. Ibid., 11.

77. Georgia Writers' Project, Savannah Unit, "Plantation Development in Chatham County," *Georgia Historical Quarterly* (hereafter *GHQ*) 22, no. 4 (December 1938): 305.

78. All by the Georgia Writers' Project, Savannah Unit: "Causton's Bluff, Deptford, Brewton Hill, Three Allied Plantations, Part I," *GHQ* 23, no. 1 (March 1939): 28–54; "Causton's Bluff, Deptford, Brewton Hill, Three Allied Plantations, Part II," *GHQ* 23, no. 2 (June 1939): 122–47; "Mulberry Grove in Colonial Times," *GHQ* 23, no. 3 (September 1939): 236–52; "Mulberry Grove from the Revolution to the Present Time," *GHQ* 23, no. 4 (December 1939): 315–36; "Richmond Oakgrove Plantation, Part I," *GHQ* 24, no. 1 (March 1940): 22–42; "Richmond Oakgrove Plantation, Part II," *GHQ* 24, no. 2 (June 1940): 124–44; "Drakies Plantation," *GHQ* 24, no. 3 (September 1940): 207–35; "Colerain Plantation, Part I," *GHQ* 24, no. 4 (December 1940): 342–73; "Colerain Plantation, Part II," *GHQ* 25, no. 1 (March 1941): 39–66; "Colerain Plantation, Part III," *GHQ* 25, no. 2 (June 1941): 120–40; "Colerain Plantation, Part IV," *GHQ* 25, no. 3 (September 1941): 225–43; "Whitehall Plantation, Part I," *GHQ* 25, no. 4 (December 1941): 340–63; "Whitehall Plantation, Part II," *GHQ* 26, no. 1 (March 1942): 40–64; "Whitehall Plantation, Part III," *GHQ* 26, no. 2 (June 1942): 129–55; "Rae's Hall Plantation, Part I," *GHQ* 26 nos. 3–4 (September/December 1942): 225–48; "Rae's Hall Plantation, Part II," *GHQ* 27, no. 1 (March 1943): 1–27; "Brampton Plantation," *GHQ* 27, no. 1 (March 1943): 28–55; "The Hermitage Plantation," *GHQ* 27, no. 1 (March 1943): 56–87; "The Plantation of the Royal Vale," *GHQ*

27, no. 1 (March 1943): 88–110. These were compiled and published later as *Savannah River Plantations* (Savannah: Georgia Historical Society, 1947).

79. Georgia Writers' Project, Savannah Unit, "Mulberry Grove from the Revolution," 331.

80. Mike Wallace, *Mickey Mouse History and Other Essays on American Memory* (Philadelphia: Temple University Press, 1996), 16–17, 184–85. See also Patrick H. Butler III, "Past, Present, and Future: The Place of the House Museum in the Museum Community," in *Interpreting Historic House Museums*, ed. Jessica Foy Donnelly (Walnut Creek, CA: Alta Mira, 2002), 26–27.

81. The surveys included Camden County's Orange Hall (HABS GA-14–16), Refuge Plantation (GA-248), and ruins of the Spanish Santa Maria Mission (GA-14–18); Glynn County's Hamilton Plantation (GA-219), Altama Plantation (GA-235), ruins of Retreat Plantation (GA-220 and GA-21), ruins of Fort Frederica (GA-2162), ruins of Santo Domino Mission (GA-2118), and ruins of the Couper's Point lighthouse rest house (GA-255); McIntosh County's Ashantilly Plantation (GA-282), a slave cabin near Darien (GA-283), the Epping House (GA-234), ruins of the Tolomato Mission (GA-271), and ruins of a Spanish fort on Sapelo (GA-2129); Liberty County's Midway Congregational Church (GA-14–44); and Chatham County's Hermitage Plantation (GA-225), Wormsloe Plantation (GA-2126), and Wild Heron Plantation (GA-253). All can be found by searching the above file identifiers at the Library of Congress's "Collections with Photos, Prints, Drawings," http://www.loc.gov/photos /collections/.

82. "Ashantilly Plantation," Library of Congress, http://www.loc.gov/item /ga0390.

83. "Hermitage Plantation," Library of Congress, http://www.loc.gov/item /ga0004.

84. "Ruins of Retreat Plantation," Library of Congress, http://www.loc.gov/item /ga0233; "Slave Hospital and Greenhouse, Retreat Plantation," Library of Congress, http://www.loc.gov/item/ga0544.

85. Calvin Schermerhorn, *The Business of Slavery and the Rise of American Capitalism, 1815–1860* (New Haven: Yale University Press, 2015); Edward E. Baptist, *The Half Has Never Been Told: Slavery and the Making of American Capitalism* (New York: Basic Books, 2014); Sven Beckert, *Empire of Cotton: A Global History* (New York: Knopf, 2014); Walter Johnson, *River of Dark Dreams: Slavery and Empire in the Cotton Kingdom* (Cambridge, Mass.: Belknap Press, 2013); Joshua D. Rothman, *Flush Times and Fever Dreams: A Story of Capitalism and Slavery in the Age of Jackson* (Athens: University of Georgia Press, 2012).

86. On planters' stewardship, see Steven Stoll, *Larding the Lean Earth: Soil and Society in Nineteenth-Century America* (New York: Hill and Wang, 2002); Edmund Ruffin, *Nature's Management: Writings on Landscape and Reform, 1822–1859*, ed. Jack Temple Kirby (Athens: University of Georgia Press, 2000).

87. Peter A. Coclanis, "The Road to Commodity Hell: The Rise and Fall of the First American Rice Industry," in *Plantation Kingdom: The American South and Its*

Global Commodities, ed. Richard Follett, Sven Beckert, Peter A. Coclanis, and Barbara Hahn (Baltimore: Johns Hopkins University Press, 2016), 30–38.

88. David S. Shields, *Southern Provisions: The Creation and Revival of a Cuisine* (Chicago: University of Chicago Press, 2015).

89. John Berendt, *Midnight in the Garden of Good and Evil* (New York: Random House, 1994).

CHAPTER 7

Longleaf Pine, from Forest to Fiber

Production, Consumption, and the Cutover
on Georgia's Coastal Plain, 1865–1900

ALBERT G. WAY

On the Brooklyn side of the East River, March 19, 1870, the first caisson for the Brooklyn Bridge awaited launch. This fortress of wood and iron weighed three thousand tons, covered the area of a city block, and contained 111,000 cubic feet of longleaf pine timber, all "bound together into one solid unyielding platform," according to chief engineer Washington Roebling.[1] The caisson first served as a diving bell for those workers who excavated the river bottom until they reached bedrock, and then it became the foundation of the bridge itself, that symbol of American ingenuity, determination, and strength at the dawn of the industrial age. Most of the longleaf pine timbers were cut from Georgia's coastal plain and milled on St. Simons Island. Before he fell ill with caisson's disease, or the bends, Roebling said that "the yellow pine timber was selected especially for the purpose . . . and much of it was so pitchy that the sticks would not float."[2] In other words, it was dense, with the density and strength that made it most desirable to one looking to construct a pressurized underwater chamber that would double as the foundation for three-hundred-foot granite towers. It is appropriate that longleaf pine is the foundational material of the Brooklyn Bridge. The bridge is one of the primary symbols of America's industrial age, a utilitarian structure cum monument, as its creator John Roebling predicted: "[It] will not only be the greatest Bridge in existence, but it will be the greatest engineering work of this continent, and of the age. . . . As a great work of art, and as a successful specimen of advanced Bridge engineering, this structure will forever testify to the energy, enterprise and wealth of that community which shall secure its erection."[3] No species of wood would be more important than longleaf during this period of growth. Much like its

FIGURE 7.1. The Brooklyn-side caisson for the Brooklyn Bridge, a solid
block of 111,000 cubic feet of longleaf pine. Photograph by S. A. (Silas
A.) Holmes, courtesy of Museum of the City of New York.

more celebrated peers, steel and oil, longleaf pine was a foundational material
of the industrial age.

If the Brooklyn Bridge was a charismatic symbol of industrial energy, the
factories, office buildings, and residential buildings erected throughout the
industrializing world were the mundane drivers of demand for structural materials. The longleaf pine region's importance in the industrial age was largely
a result of timing. While builders and engineers already knew longleaf as one
of the best structural timbers in the world, other wood could also have performed its work. But in the late nineteenth century, longleaf was abundant
and accessible. Extensive logging had already diminished vast stores of northeastern and midwestern lumber at this time of greatest demand, and the forests of the Pacific Northwest were remote and in the early days of exploitation. The South and its forests, on the other hand, were in a prime position.
The region's residents, and perhaps more importantly its leaders, were open
for business after years of wartime devastation, and its forests were still substantial. This timely convergence of supply with unprecedented demand cat-
alyzed the movement of capital into the South's coastal plain at extraordinary
levels.

And thus forest resources moved out of the region. New York, Boston,
Philadelphia, Baltimore, Chicago, London, Buenos Aires, São Paulo, and
other cosmopolitan centers were growing up and out, and longleaf lumber

became an essential part of their structural framework. Today's markets in reclaimed longleaf tell us something about this history. The "country's largest repository of the lumber that formed the spine of the Industrial Revolution," according to one recent report, "is the five-borough safe deposit box" of New York City.[4] There is in all probability a higher volume of longleaf heart pine in New York City today than in its native range, on the stump or finished. What do we make of such a rural dweller as urban denizen? Are the timbers out of place, unmoored, alienated from their home? Did these living things become lifeless objects of exchange and use, no longer related to the assemblage of life in the forest? Are they simply part of new assemblages that together represent "a trophy of triumph over an original obstacle of Nature," as one contemporary observed of the Brooklyn Bridge?[5] Or do they connect two worlds, one made up of plants, animals, soils, fire, farmers, and herders, and another comprising sawyers, graders, buyers, shippers, wholesalers, retailers, carpenters, engineers, and fanciers? I would argue for connection. Materials such as longleaf pine, whether in the forest or floating through markets or fixed as floor joists, have a life with meaning, a life that begins in the woods and continues even after the final nail is driven. We add new meanings to the old. The trees are ecological beings, fire-dependent keystones in a web of life, but their timbers are economic beings, structural pillars in a web of granite and steel that come to mean something else altogether.[6]

Longleaf pines, then, along with other extractive natural resources, do not reside only in the forest. Forest historians have a tendency to separate the history of the forest from the history of the timber industry, but as Joachim Radkau has recently argued, "the history of the forest cannot be understood if one looks only at the forest."[7] As much as many of us may want longleaf pines to remain in the forest, to continue to supply fuel for the perpetuation of such tremendous ecological bounty, they haven't done so. We have cut them down and moved them, and here I want to take seriously the motivations and mechanisms that made longleaf pines mobile in Georgia's coastal plain region. Environmental historians and others have rightfully lamented the decimation of the longleaf range during the South's industrial timber era, but we have not paid much attention to where all of this wood went and to how and why people moved it. Doing so helps us to see Georgia's coastal plain as a more dynamic space with intimate connections to the world and to understand its natural resources as organic objects with a life beyond death.[8]

The matter of spatial scale is important. As does Mart Stewart's "Islands, Edges, and Globe" (chapter 1 of this volume), this essay encounters "meaningful historical space [as] a palimpsest of different spaces at different scales." It has an interior and exterior orientation from the coast proper. The forest itself during this period resided mostly in Georgia's coastal plain interior, miles away from coastal shores, but there has always been a fluid movement of people and natural resources between the coast and its coastal plain hinterlands.[9] In some ways, we can think of the coastal plain and the coast as one space, indistinguishable from one another. The region has also looked outward into the Atlantic, with the interior and coastal waterways acting as portals through which longleaf pine and other commodities entered the world. Coastal towns were the arbiters of passage and the most important distribution nodes along the wood's journey, and the arrival of the post–Civil War timber industry was as transformative for these coastal communities as it was for the interior. Indeed, coastal Georgia is the geographical fulcrum of this story. It had long been the place where Georgia's natural resources entered the broader world as valuable commodities, and it continued to fulfill that role during my period of interest, the decades after the Civil War, roughly 1870–1900, when the heaviest cutting of longleaf pine occurred in Georgia. Beginning with a broad view of the longleaf region and the emergence of the postwar timber industry, I scale down to a case study of one of the largest companies operating in the state, the Georgia Land and Lumber Company. An examination of this globally connected company exemplifies the larger story of longleaf pine cutting and provides an intimate view of how longleaf pine knit the industrializing world together in a particular geography of first and second nature.

The longleaf pine's economic strengths reside in its nature. Indeed, one of the central arguments of this chapter is that the economic and cultural value of the longleaf pine largely resulted from the historical and evolutionary ecology of the longleaf forest. We cannot hope to fully understand one without the other. As a number of recent historians have argued, evolutionary history and the resulting biological traits of particular species have been important influences on human history.[10] The natural history of longleaf pine makes that point abundantly clear. The wood is strong and durable, and it was desirable to people because of its ecosystem's evolutionary history and the unique circumstances under which it had grown. Georgia's longleaf pine region was part of a ninety-million-acre ecoregion that included the entirety of the southern coastal plain and some piedmont areas, from southern Virginia to East Texas. The region shares a number of characteristics of soils, climate, and terrain, but perhaps its most important shared trait is the frequent occurrence of fire. This was, as one twentieth-century observer remarked, "the forest that fire made."[11] Lightning-caused fires began to sweep through the region soon after the last

ice age about ten thousand years ago, and coastal plain plant communities developed adaptive strategies to survive. These natural communities not only developed resistance to fire, their very survival came to depend on it. More than
that, plants, animals, and fire became locked in a cycle of mutual dependence.
Fire needed the resinous longleaf needles and flammable grasses of the longleaf system as much as the system needed fire.

Around the same time that the system was taking shape as we know it, Native Americans also applied fire as a tool to shape the woods for their own purposes, a form of land use that worked rather well with the ecology of the woods.
Whether natural or anthropogenic fire shaped the longleaf system is beyond
the scope of this essay, but it is clear that Native Americans played a significant
role in its development.[12] They set fire to the woods to gather the edible plants
and fruits that follow a burn; they set it to clear agricultural fields; they set it
to create habitat attractive to game animals; and they set it to generally make
the woods a more livable space. Without fire, coastal plain woodlands grow
into dense forests dominated by scrubby hardwoods, a unique ecosystem in
its own right but not one highly valued by Native Americans or subsequent
settlers. Such a forest provided less ecological and nutritional bounty and was
a more difficult space to live in and navigate. By the time European explorers,
colonists, and African slaves arrived, the frequent fires of the coastal plain had
resulted in what has come to be a classic southern scene: open woodland with
a grassy understory lightly shaded by a canopy of hundred-foot-tall longleaf
pines.[13]

Georgia's early colonists recognized the significance of longleaf pine,
both for its economic value and as a cautionary sign to farmers. As in other
pine-dominant regions of the country, longleaf land quickly became known
as the "pine barrens," and settlers avoided it if they could. Pine-barren soils
were and are geologically young, being mostly under water until the end of the
Pleistocene about twelve thousand years ago, when the oceans retreated. They
are coarse, sandy, and fast-draining, which means that they hold little organic
matter and water. These soils caused a great deal of anxiety for colonial Georgians. One official reported in 1737 of "the great Hardships which those People labour under who have only Pine Lands to employ their Industry upon.…
The Crop they produce is so very small that it discourages the most Pains taking People amongst us."[14] Those with the misfortune of drawing pine-barren
lots hoped to quickly move elsewhere. In Ebenezer, for instance, Colonial Secretary William Stephens was impressed with the orderly Salzburger settlement
but not with the land itself. He witnessed cropland "lying … almost wholly on
the Pine-Barren, where they apprehended it would be lost Labour, and there-

Georgia's Naval Stores Industry

While many colonies, including Georgia, experimented with the production of naval stores over the course of the eighteenth century, North Carolina developed into the largest colonial producer and Britain's principal supplier of tar, pitch, spirits of turpentine, and rosin. North Carolina achieved this distinction not solely because it possessed expansive longleaf pine forest, as did other colonies, but because North Carolinians lacked any other staple they could produce profitably. Georgia's colonial settlers found rice and indigo cultivation to be more lucrative than naval stores. Thus, North Carolina, not Georgia, was poised to take first advantage of an early nineteenth-century demand surge for turpentine, which became widely used as a solvent and an ingredient in a popular lamp oil.

Within a few decades, the naval stores industry's destructive harvesting practices threatened the North Carolina producers' essential supply of longleaf pines, and production began a gradual migration southward to areas with virgin longleaf pine stands. Before the Civil War, some North Carolina producers began buying virgin pine forests in states to their south and relocating their enslaved laborers there. Turpentining in Georgia began with such men along the Savannah and Altamaha Rivers during the 1840s and expanded during the 1850s as newly constructed rail lines connected the vast pine forests of

Barrels of rosin ready for shipment, Savannah, circa 1895. Courtesy of Georgia Archives, Vanishing Georgia Collection, ctm 280.

the Georgia coastal plain to coastal port facilities.

After the Civil War, as the destruction of North Carolina's pine forests continued and the pace of rail construction across Georgia's pine-covered Wiregrass Region quickened, the industry's migration pattern resumed, with North Carolinians controlling more than 73 percent of Georgia's naval stores industry by 1880. The majority of the black labor force in postbellum Georgia's naval stores industry was also from North Carolina. Once relocated to Georgia, naval stores laborers found their freedom curtailed by vagrancy laws, which forced blacks to sign labor contracts, and enticement acts, which outlawed one employer hiring a laborer away from another. Most notorious was debt peonage, whereby an employer forced a worker who owed a commissary debt, as many

turpentine workers did, to stay until the debt was paid.

By 1900, all thirty-nine Georgia counties with naval stores operations had rail service, and the industry was growing rapidly, having doubled in the 1890s. At the turn of the twentieth century, 524 producers employed nineteen thousand workers who produced a product valued at over $8 million. The industry's southward movement was great enough to affect port activity, channeling naval stores traffic away from Wilmington, North Carolina, and toward Savannah, where handling of naval stores surpassed Wilmington in 1882. As regulators of the world's largest naval stores port, Savannah's Board of Trade established industry-wide quality standards and set world naval stores prices. Georgia's dominance over the naval stores industry continued well into the early twentieth century.

ROBERT B. OUTLAND III

---

fore would wait in Hopes of better Land being assigned them farther down the River."[15] The pine barrens was so hopeless for early agricultural settlers that Georgia's Common Council passed a resolution in 1741 allowing any land grantee with pine-barren land to exchange it for "a Quantity of Good Land" elsewhere of equal acreage.[16]

While settlers could not grow their favored crops in the pine barrens, throughout the colonial and antebellum periods they did come to appreciate and make use of what grew there. The native grasses formed one important part of the forest economy. Like other southerners, Georgians developed an open-range system of livestock husbandry that wholly depended on the abundance and biological diversity of the longleaf understory. Herders both exploited the region's diverse plant life and helped to perpetuate it. Wiregrass

and other fire-adapted plants grow tough and fibrous as they mature, so herders burned the range every winter or early spring to refresh the fodder of their
wooded pastures.[17] The trees and their resin were the other major forest products during the colonial and antebellum periods. Merchants, planters, herders,
government officials, speculators, and a growing slave force all participated in
the lumber and naval stores industries in one way or another. By the time of
the Revolution, Georgia was shipping more lumber to the West Indies than
any other colony in the South Atlantic, and the state's forests continued producing longleaf pine timber for domestic and international markets throughout the first half of the nineteenth century. Naval stores were less integral to
Georgia's colonial and antebellum economy, but by the 1850s many North
Carolina producers began buying large tracts of the state's untapped longleaf
forests, setting the stage for a steep increase in production after the Civil War.[18]

The persistent cutting after the colonial era was such that very little mature
longleaf pine remained standing along the Georgia coast by the time of the
Civil War. The South's preeminent postwar botanist, Charles Mohr, reported
to the U.S. Department of Agriculture (USDA) in the 1880s that Georgia's
ten-to-thirty-mile-wide strip of coastline had already endured a transformation that would soon happen farther inland: "The Longleaf Pine once prevailed [here], but almost everywhere ... the original timber has been removed
by man and replaced by the Loblolly Pine and the Cuban Pine." Thus, "the flatwoods and savannas" of the Georgia coast had been "almost entirely stripped
of the Longleaf Pine."[19] Nonetheless, longleaf cutting had rarely encroached
farther inland than what was easily accessible along the immediate coastal strip
and larger rivers like the Savannah, Altamaha, and Ogeechee. With a few exceptions, most of the antebellum sawmills were small and had little control
over supply, with the labor force in the woods being seasonal and loosely organized, made up mostly of planters, slaves, and small farmers interested in
supplementing farm income during the offseason.[20] Mohr found that the interior coastal plain continued to be "covered exclusively with the forest of this
tree for many hundreds of square miles without interruption. Here it reigns
supreme."[21] When the Civil War came, then, most of Georgia's coastal plain
longleaf continued to shelter droves of livestock and occasional farmsteads but
few timber cutters.

That changed after the war. As Reconstruction ground to a halt in the
1870s, former Confederates and new civic leaders began to embrace the rhetoric of reconciliation through loud and lengthy appeals for capital investment
in industrial growth. Many with capital to invest, from both North and South,

saw tremendous opportunity in the region, and thus the Georgia coastal plain embarked on a new epoch in its economic and environmental history. The region's growing extractive economy after the war complemented its continued reliance on agriculture, and as capital flooded the region to build the necessary infrastructure, the forest products industry became the largest sector of Georgia's industrial economy.[22]

The new activity along Georgia's coast caught the attention of the nation's commercial trade press. Even before the war, Freeman Hunt's *Merchants' Magazine and Commercial Review* claimed that "the crop of yellow pine forests . . . gives cargoes to more ships from the southern ports than cotton or any other article of commerce." It predicted that Georgia's woodlands would soon feed an unprecedented timber boom, estimating that "Georgia possesses *more of this pine forest, perhaps, than all the other States put together.*"[23] The war delayed the boom, but it came soon after. *Debow's Review* announced in 1866 that the lumber business was "deserving of the gravest consideration by capitalists who desire to invest in Southern lands." One correspondent wrote to *Debow's* from Brunswick that the lumber trade in south Georgia and north Florida was "assuming proportions almost incredible," a fit enticement to an investor looking for a business with "so little risk and so certain a remuneration."[24]

The industrial exploitation of the longleaf pine belt meant tremendous change for towns along Georgia's coast. Docks and sawmills in Savannah, Darien, and Brunswick were the centers of the state's forest economy during and after Reconstruction. Turpentine and its various distillates formed a major part of this economy, while world-class mill complexes finished and shipped lumber, especially structural timbers, for a variety of construction markets. Like other port towns along the coast, Georgia's were cosmopolitan. While maintaining their regional identities and inland connections, coastal communities hosted sailors and traders from across the Atlantic world. International demand for longleaf pine was so strong that little Darien, for example, had consulates from Great Britain, Holland, Norway, Sweden, Italy, Germany, Portugal, and Brazil by the 1880s.[25]

More so than Savannah or Brunswick, the fortunes of Darien were almost wholly dependent on the lumber trade during the postwar boom. Its location at the mouth of the Altamaha River had everything to do with Darien's boom and eventual bust. The character of coastal plain waterways like the Altamaha was critical to the region's longleaf trade. The Altamaha is an alluvial river that is slow and wide, ideal for floating large rafts of logs, and its watershed covers more than fourteen thousand square miles of what was mostly longleaf land,

FIGURE 7.2. Loading schooner with lumber, Darien, Georgia,
1908, at the Hilton-Dodge sawmill in Darien. Hilton-Dodge
resulted after the Dodge family sold its interest in the
St. Simons mill in 1888. Photo by Huron H. Smith, courtesy
of Field Museum of Natural History, CC-BY-NC, CSB29528.

ideal for accessing many logs. According to *Debow's Review*, the Altamaha was
one of "the innumerable streams which make almost a network of the map."
These "accessible avenues to forests interminable" connected coastal plain people and forests to the world.[26] As had long been the practice, upstream operators, large and small, cut and skidded logs to the riverside, where they were tied
together into rafts to be floated down river. Sometimes the logs were squared
by broadax or portable sawmill before rafting, and sometimes they were not,
depending on the size of the operation and the capacity of the destination
mill. But all of them drifted into Darien.[27]

The town's public log boom was the first stop for most log rafts. City-appointed inspectors measured and graded the logs at the boom, and buyers from several of the area's sawmills gathered to make bids. Once sold, company crews transported the logs through a decentralized network of company-owned booms and docks positioned throughout the Altamaha delta's labyrinth of creeks, rivers, and sounds. Larger, oceangoing vessels could not consistently navigate the shifting channels and shallow water leading to the Darien waterfront, so companies constructed larger facilities on small islands miles out in the deep waters of the Doboy and Sapelo Sounds as well as down the coast at St. Simons Island and Brunswick. Darien's waters were also connected to Savannah's port infrastructure, and much of the Altamaha's commerce passed through there as well. Such a sprawling infrastructure created a large local economy for inshore transportation, with commercial and company-owned steamers moving people and logs up and down the coast. The volume of timber shipped out of Darien grew from 20 million board feet in 1868 to a peak of more than 112 million in 1900, and it was second in the world only to Pensacola, Florida, in volume of pine timber shipments. For three decades after the war, the lumber industry connected the Georgia coast into an interlocking series of nodes that all made further connections into the Atlantic world.[28]

Understanding the qualities of longleaf wood fiber is critical to understanding this story of forest transformation. Trees possess what we might call an interior life; their fibers act in particular ways and help shape the way we value them. In its chemical essence, wood fiber's strength comes from its combination of cellulose, hemicellulose, and lignin. Cellulose, formed by long chains of sugar molecules, is chiefly responsible for wood strength, while the latter two polymers act to bond the fibrous structure together. Endless combinations of these internal components give trees their relative use value. Some wood fiber reacts well to woodworking and takes stain easily, for instance, while others may be too dense for furniture but perfect for structural support. Still others have little economic use but might possess properties that make them appealing for cultural or ritual use. The possibilities are many.[29]

The longleaf pine's internal components bond in such a way that make it strong and dense and to some eyes beautiful. Here we see the longleaf pine's evolutionary history intertwine with its economic history. Longleaf was born of difficult conditions. Fire, disease, and drought made perennial appearances in the coastal plain, and the region's plants and animals had to adapt. Many of the longleaf pine's adaptations and the resulting characteristics of its growth helped to account for its eventual economic utility. First, it evolved to grow very slowly, especially in a tree's early years.[30] Soils, water, and fire largely account for this slow growth. Soil of the coastal plain was generally poor not only for agriculture but also for large, water-loving trees. To compensate for a lack of surface water, longleaf pines spend their first five to seven years growing a long taproot—sometimes as deep as fifteen feet—to reach a steady groundwater supply. It remains in the so-called grass stage aboveground while the taproot descends below, with its needles appearing as one of many bunch grasses in the understory. As the tree's name suggests, those needles are long, and they form a protective barrier around the terminal bud so that ground fire does no damage. After the taproot completes its development, the tree is ready to grow aboveground, and a growth spurt begins that lasts for several decades. Longleaf pines mature into canopy dominance over the course of several centuries.

A number of characteristics make identification of longleaf pines relatively easy in the forest. In one of the best descriptions of the tree during the years of the industrial cut, USDA Forestry Division chief Bernard Fernow took special care to distinguish longleaf pines from other southern pines in his 1891 annual report. In addition to noting its very long needles, Fernow described the bark as reddish brown and surprisingly thin and flaky for a fire-resistant tree. As a longleaf matures, its buds grow long and silvery white, "its most striking character," according to Fernow. It drops its lower limbs quickly due to its evolutionary adaptation to fire—which also makes for knotless logs, well-liked by buyers on the docks—and its upper limbs develop into "candelabra-like naked branches with brush-like tufts of foliage at the end," a singular trait among southern pines. Its mature crown resembles a misshapen umbrella, with "massive but twisted gnarled limbs."[31]

The task of identification gets trickier after cutting. It takes a trained eye to distinguish longleaf timber from that of other common southern pines such as slash and loblolly. As Fernow admitted, "No more difficult task could be set than to describe on paper the wood of these pines, or to give the distinctive features so that the kinds can be distinguished and recognized by the uninitiated."[32] A cross section of a mature longleaf log, though, is instructive of the link between ecology and economy. The size of annual rings is probably the best visual indicator of longleaf. Fernow reported that because of its slow growth, "annual rings [were] uniformly narrow throughout . . . [with] mostly about 25 rings to the inch," compared to anywhere from 3 to 12 rings per inch in the other, faster-growing southern pines.[33] A cross section also reveals two different ratios of fiber type important to overall strength: earlywood to latewood, and sapwood to heartwood. The lighter section of an annual growth ring is earlywood, spring growth that is responsible for moving water up the tree when it needs it most. Latewood is the darker portion that grows through the summer and has a tightly packed, thick-walled cellular structure. In other words, latewood is stronger and denser. The other ratio is even more distinctive to the eye. Sapwood is the narrow outer portion of the tree that does all the work of moving water and sap to carry on the business of living. The heartwood is the core of the tree and is perhaps longleaf's most legendary quality after trees have been removed from the forest. It is old, dark, and dead, even in the living tree, and it dominates the cross section of a mature longleaf. It is the most widely sought part of the tree primarily because of its structural strength but also historically because its reddish-brown hue increasingly resonated with consumers' aesthetic sense of what makes a pretty piece of wood. Because longleaf pines cannot always rely on an easy water supply, they convert to both latewood and heartwood earlier than other southern pines, thus making it denser, stronger, and, it is thought, more beautiful.[34]

Just as its flammable dry needles and its fire resistance made longleaf an ecological centerpiece in the forest, its fiber made it an economic centerpiece in the marketplace. And its place in both worlds was intimately connected. Its evolutionary adaptations and the tree's resulting interior life directly accounted for the market demand that drove longleaf exploitation at the turn of the twentieth century. Engineers, tradesmen, and government officials all marveled at longleaf pine's capabilities as structural material.

Government agencies began to take note of longleaf as it became more important in the marketplace and government capacity to study forest resources developed after the war. In what became the first major report on the nation's forest resources in 1884, Harvard biologist Charles S. Sargent reported for the Interior Department and echoed what locals and industry veterans had said for years, that longleaf was "a tree of first economic value . . . heavy, exceedingly hard, very strong, tough, coarse-grained, compact, durable."[35] Within a few years, as the federal government devoted more attention to forest resources, longleaf pine became the focal point of considerable study for its economic uses, but government study of its ecology would have to wait a few decades. Many liked to compare longleaf to commonly used metals. Fernow reported for his Division of Forestry in 1891 that it "is superior wherever strength and durability are required. In tensile strength it approaches, and may surpass, cast iron." Its hardness made it difficult to work for furniture or decorative purposes, so its best uses at the time were structural: "It is best adapted for princi-

Live Oaking

Given its role in the history of coastal Georgia, the indigenous live oak (*Quercus virginiana*) is eminently worthy of being the official state tree. From the early colonial period, Georgia's live oaks were prized for shipbuilding and became the most expensive domestic timber for that purpose. Renowned for its great tensile strength, hardness, durability, and resistance to rot, the wood of the live oak tree—particularly its massive, curved branches—were perfect for "compass pieces" such as knees and the futtocks that make up the frames of ships.

Prior to the American Revolution, shipyards in Philadelphia were using live oak, and by 1774 Ossabaw Island resident John Morel of Bewlie Plantation and his master shipbuilder Daniel Giroud were involved in ship construction. Soon Morel was offering for sale in the *Georgia Gazette* custom-cut live oak "lower, upper and middle futtocks" as well as "a Quantity of sterns, stern posts, transoms, bow timbers . . . aprons, knees, &."

Following the Revolution, tens of thousands of cubic feet of live oak timber were required for building U.S. naval vessels, including the USS *Constitution*, and for constructing merchantmen and whaleships by those who could bear the expense. For decades, numerous skilled workmen agreed to go "live oaking" in the South during winter months. Choppers, hewers, teamsters,

Live oak on Cumberland Island. Photograph by Diane Kirkland.

cooks, blacksmiths, and flatboatmen—all were called "live oakers."

The timber often grew near swamps in dense, semitropical forests requiring crude roads cut through for hauling. At nearly seventy-five pounds per cubic foot, a massive branch of green live oak could weigh tons. Too heavy to float, live oak timber was hauled out by oxen and huge two-wheeled timber carts. Hewers dulled their broad-axes shaping each piece of the hard wood. These ship timbers, loaded into flatboats, were then stowed into schooners bound for northern shipyards.

VIRGINIA STEELE WOOD

All this activity denuded the great live oak forests of prime trees until the age of sail gave way to ironclads and steel ships. Live oaking became a thing of the past and was nearly forgotten. These days, live oak forests are found mostly in areas designated for conservation, and some long driveways lined with the trees lead to historic antebellum plantations. But majestic live oaks, with Spanish moss (*Tillandsia usneoides*) trailing from their branches, still survive as prized specimens on public and private property in the South.

---

pal members of heavy construction, for naval architecture, for bridges, trestles, viaducts, and house-building."[36] These were the types of uses most in demand in the new industrial economy.

New capital brought industrial-scaled organization to the woods after the war. Riverside sawmills became more plentiful, as did mills along major new rail lines, fed by spur tracks, company tram roads, droves of draft animals, and armies of wage laborers and their supervisors. William Pitt Eastman and William E. Dodge were among the earliest northeasterners to send capital into Georgia. Eastman, a New Hampshire–born manufacturer, ventured into the region in 1866 to scout potential land for purchase and two years later secured more than three hundred thousand acres between the Oconee and Ocmulgee Rivers above their confluence that forms the Altamaha. The huge tract included portions of Laurens, Montgomery, Telfair, and Pulaski Counties and had been cobbled together into single ownership in the early nineteenth century after most of it went unclaimed following one of Georgia's land lotteries. The tract passed through several hands during the antebellum years, including the short-lived Georgia Lumber Company in the 1830s and then, oddly enough, the State of Indiana. After Eastman purchased title in 1868, he briefly joined with William E. Dodge and his sons to form the Georgia Land and Lumber Company before selling his stock to focus on developing real estate in the eponymous town of Eastman, Georgia. The Dodge family took over and began to develop the infrastructure to move longleaf fiber from the forest to finished product.[37]

William E. Dodge's biography provides critical context for the postwar cutover. A New Yorker with a background in the import of metals and other goods, as well as the buying and cutting of extensive timber holdings in the Northeast, Midwest, and Canada, Dodge was experienced at entering undeveloped forests and bringing timber to market. He was also connected politically and economically. He had served as a U.S. congressman and a three-time president of the New York Chamber of Commerce, and his business interests extended across the Atlantic to England and throughout Europe. Dodge's Georgia company was just one piece of his overall portfolio, but it was a substantial investment for both Dodge and Georgia. He amassed an initial capital investment of $1.5 million, and his son Anson G. P. Dodge soon moved south from their timber stronghold in Ontario to oversee the operation.

State and local leaders were thrilled with the organization of the Georgia Land and Lumber Company. This was just the sort of capital investment they hoped would pull the state out of the economic doldrums of Reconstruction and propel it toward an industrial future. Someone of William E. Dodge's prominence was especially notable. The state legislature, being "mindful . . . of the interest taken by yourself and friends in the commercial prosperity of our State," carved a new county from the heart of Dodge's lands in 1870 and named it Dodge County in his honor.[38] As a prominent Republican and former member of the House of Representatives, Dodge's appearance in Georgia appealed to the then–Republican state senate and governor, but he was also sympathetic to southern Democrats. While in Congress from 1865 to 1867 he had opposed new taxes on cotton and was one of the most vocal Republican opponents of the Reconstruction Acts.[39]

Despite Republican Party membership and being a wartime supporter and supplier of munitions to the Union, Dodge had long watched out for the interests of the southern planter class because his interests were largely the same. His primary commercial interest, Phelps, Dodge & Company, was one of the pillars of the New York merchant community, with forty years of experience importing tinplate, copper, lead, and other metals, and exporting cotton and lumber. Phelps, Dodge & Company eventually became the Phelps Dodge Corporation, one of the largest copper mining firms in the world as well as one of the most notorious strikebreakers and environmental villains of the twentieth century.[40] But the basis for that later activity was in the nineteenth-century mercantile trade.

Like other Atlantic-scale merchants, Dodge's entire import business relied on having access to a ready commodity for export, and cotton was still king in that regard. Whatever threatened the production and export of cotton not only threatened Dodge's livelihood, it also threatened the nation's livelihood. As Dodge said from the floor of Congress in 1867, "Cotton is the basis upon which our chief importations are to be made in the future. . . . We cannot have large importations unless we have some large article to export. There is nothing to my mind more important than that our country should gain as soon as possible the position we held in European markets previous to the war."[41] He thus supported lenient plans for Reconstruction while in Congress and was eager for the political and social stability necessary to continue his and the nation's lucrative cotton-based trade. As Reconstruction continued into 1875, Dodge reiterated in the *New York Times*, "How can we at the North expect to prosper, when a large part of the Union is suffering? . . . Many of us feel that the General Government has made a mistake in trying to secure the peace and quiet of the South by appointing many Northern men to places of trust in the South. . . . As merchants, we want to see the South gain her normal position in the commerce of the country."[42] Regaining that normal position required the successful transition from slave to free labor as well as reestablishing the plantation system on which the nation's commerce had thrived.

With this bigger picture in mind, Dodge pitched his southern timber business as being about something more than reaping an immediate bonanza. It was also about stabilizing the region for national economic growth, which would mean stable growth for merchants and industrialists such as Dodge as well. With the future of American cotton production uncertain during the tumultuous period of Reconstruction, it might appear at first glance that Dodge aimed to substitute timber for cotton as an exchange commodity in Atlantic markets. But timber was not yet a fungible commodity. That is, there was no universally accepted identification and grading standard that would allow one quantity of timber to be freely replaced by another, a necessity for exchange in large commodities markets. Timber was instead a liquid asset, an excellent source of one-off cash returns but not a reliable contract commodity. And, importantly, no one yet thought of timber as a renewable resource that could maintain a stable position in the market economy. Very few large operators entered the timber market to stay, and those who did experienced incredible market volatility due to competition and overcutting.[43]

Dodge's timber operation was certainly a hedge against unsure cotton production, but it was not a replacement for it. As a short-term, industrial-scaled operation, Dodge's timber business would in theory lay the infrastructural groundwork for stable production of commodity crops, which would then fuel the national economy. It would open new land for agricultural expansion, provide an immediate source of freight to support a fledgling rail network, and create a waged job market to aid in the transition from slave to free labor. Once the timber was gone, the region could make an easy transition into more stable markets, primarily cotton. The prospectus of the Georgia Land and Lumber Company stressed the local familiarity with cotton, explaining that although cotton agriculture "has been rude and without fertilizers, this district has largely depended on its cotton in times past for its ready money." Importantly, the timber operation would encourage industrious habits in the local population and catalyze emigration, so that "at least two-thirds of the land of the Company can be sold as the timber is removed for good average cotton land."[44]

Rather than a profiteering endgame, then, Dodge saw timbering as an embryonic stage in the long-term process of infrastructural development and national economic growth. He predicted as much on a public tour of his Georgia holdings, reassuring the state that "the next decade would be signalized by extraordinary progress, and that the growing intercourse between the people of both sections would establish the best mutual understanding, and the capital from abroad would be increasingly attracted to the South, and especially to Georgia."[45] It is easy to dismiss such talk as hollow boosterism or as high-minded justification for rapacious exploitation, but that diminishes the classical economic thinking behind it. This was the normative capitalist worldview, and it was highly influential: invest in infrastructure, cultivate a comparative advantage in choice commodities such as cotton, expand access to new markets of supply and demand, and prosperity will follow.

Railroads were the linchpin for such plans. Most of the antebellum South had relied primarily on wagon and river transport, which had worked well for those communities near rivers. However, the lack of rail transport had left those in the backcountry isolated from markets. The few rail lines that did penetrate the backcountry could hardly find enough freight to cover costs. Southern railroad boosters faced a dilemma. They needed freight-paying producers to live along the lines to make a venture profitable, but producers would not move to isolated areas in large numbers without an established transportation network to haul their goods to market. The postwar solution was twofold: first court timber interests to clear the countryside and provide freight, and then promote settlement schemes with the promise of cheap land and cheap shipping costs.[46]

Just such a plan accounts for the Dodge Company's discovery of Georgia's coastal plain. The Macon & Brunswick Railroad had languished since its charter in 1856, its completion seemingly always on the horizon. That changed when its president, George Hazlehurst, met William Eastman and introduced him to the large and well-timbered tract of land between the Ocmulgee and Oconee. To sweeten the deal, Hazlehurst offered to name a rail stop after Eastman, which would grow into the town of Eastman. Eastman and Dodge's commitment to develop and extract timber gave Hazlehurst the impetus to finish the road at last in 1870, two years after the Dodge Company formally organized. The M&B ran "for fifty miles across the territory of the Company, furnishing, with the rivers, great facilities for conveying the product of the soil to market," according to the company prospectus. It was "destined to be one of the most important and prosperous railways in the South."[47] While that didn't happen—the M&B floundered after the region was cut over—the simultaneous development of these lumber and rail companies was mutually beneficial in the short term and clearly not coincidental.

While boosters and investors never thought timber would sustain the national economy in the same way as commodity agriculture, it was lucrative nonetheless, especially in the first two decades after the Civil War. William E. Dodge found reassurance in his experience in antebellum lumber markets. Timber had always been a reliable source of income, even in the roughest of downturns. As the chief agent of his Pennsylvania holdings had advised earlier, "This lumber business is what you can depend on, not like cotton or tin plate—changing every new moon."[48] Importantly, Phelps, Dodge & Company had extensive commercial networks already in place, so the Georgia Land and Lumber Company was uniquely positioned to capitalize on the postwar boom. The company prospectus made as much of Dodge's position in the Atlantic marketplace as it did the land and lumber it owned. With Dodge agents and offices spread throughout the Americas and Europe, the company had "unusual opportunities for organizing a successful [southern lumber] industry" and sought "at an early day to control the shipments to England, France, the West Indies and South America, while organizations already in New York, Philadelphia, and Baltimore [meant] a large share of home business."[49] Dodge may not have sought to replace cotton with timber in global trade, but he would certainly take advantage of previously established cotton networks.

Dodge's agents in Liverpool were especially important. As it was in the cotton trade, Liverpool was the center of England's lumber business. Phelps, Dodge & Co. had a subsidiary firm already located in Liverpool, providing Dodge's Georgia interests a ready outlet in English and European markets.[50] English and European builders had long known of longleaf pine—known there usually as "pitch pine"—and during Dodge's years of operation it became one of their favored construction materials. One English lumber trade manual summed up its status in the 1890s: "Of far more importance [than white pine] is the pitch pine. . . . It is the timber or material of construction of the hour." In its strength and rate of decay, some English builders were said to "rank it almost with the oak," and "next to the oak the pitch pine is the wood that most enters into church, school, and house fittings, [and] it also finds a place in ship building and in coal mining, the frame work at the pit mouths being mostly of this wood."[51] By 1891, Bernard Fernow estimated that, of the southern pines, "probably nothing but longleaf pine is handled" in England.[52]

Closer to the land, the company was rightly proud of its newly acquired acreage because its timber and infrastructure placed it at a competitive advantage over other timber interests. It was a "land covered with long leaf yellow pine timber of a superior quality," which "outranks all others in the New York and Liverpool markets." Unlike the wet, low-lying lands nearer the coast, this tract was "level or slightly undulating, resembling in appearance the rolling prairie land of Illinois, is well drained and perfectly healthy, and is the nearest land of this description to the coast."[53] The company estimated "an almost immediate production" of thirty million board feet per year, with the "safest estimates" of up to ten dollars per one thousand feet in net profit. In other words, they had a lot of timber, a lot of capacity, and both the timber and its markets were easily accessible. All told, the company's prospectus stated, "The present and future value of this extensive forest can hardly be exaggerated."[54] In addition to the long-range motivations for economic expansion, then, Dodge and his associates had short-term motivations as well: to make substantial immediate profit.

The company found confidence in what would become one of the driving ideas of the early conservation movement: an impending timber famine. Disappearing timber resources had concerned Europeans since at least the eighteenth century, but similar concerns only arrived in the United States during the rapidly industrializing decades after the Civil War. The USDA began issuing statements of warning soon after the war ended in 1865, and the fears only grew, culminating in Teddy Roosevelt and Forest Service chief Gifford Pinchot making extraordinary claims about diminishing timber supplies at the turn of the century and the need for conservation-based remedies.[55] These

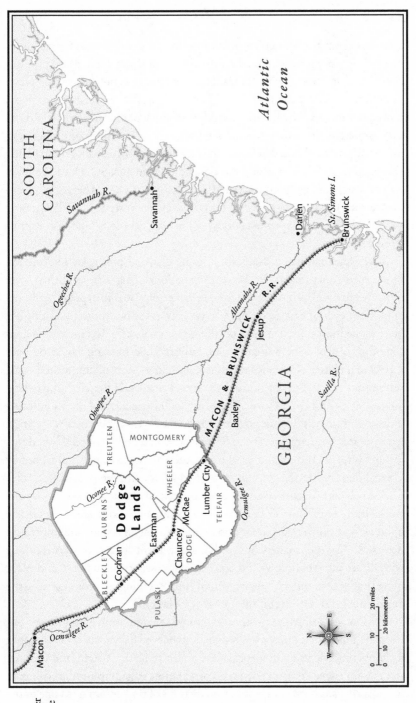

MAP 7.1.
Central
Georgia Timber
Holdings of the
Dodge Land
and Lumber
Company

concerns about timber famine didn't just drive the early conservation movement, they also motivated much of the timber industry. Dodge and his associates were clear about what it meant for their business prospects in Georgia: assured success. In making the case that their forest was valuable, they cited most prominently "the famine in timber so lately predicted" in the USDA's 1865 annual report, which was among the earliest discussions of timber famine in the postwar United States.[56] The report, titled "American Forests, Their Destruction and Preservation," was penned by Frederick Starr Jr., a Presbyterian minister who grew so concerned with deforestation that he gained an audience with Congress to advocate for government conservation. The recently formed USDA was impressed enough by his presentation to publish it in its annual report.

Starr's jeremiad was a thorough critique of wood profligacy in America. He warned Americans of "an impending national danger, beyond the power of figures to estimate, and beyond the province of words to express." After detailing "the evils of past destruction," especially in the Northeast and Midwest, Starr looked to future demands on the nation's forests.[57] The increasing consumption of wood for railroads, fuel, industry, and housing would outpace supply in a matter of decades without a conscious effort of conservation and restoration. It was a national problem, Starr argued, and therefore the federal government's problem to solve. The efforts of individuals and the wood-using industries were helpful, but government research and application was critical because "it is not remunerative to those who would do it privately."[58] In drawing up his report and engaging in his advocacy, Starr was heavily influenced by George Perkins Marsh's recently published *Man and Nature* (1864), a landmark in American conservation. Starr quoted liberally from Marsh, whose work "bears testimony on every page to the existing wants and evils already upon us, and which make the action of government an instant and imperative necessity."[59] Starr ultimately hoped that government-sponsored science, along with direct intervention, would convince landowners to conserve and plant more timber than they cut, which would "be something towards offsetting the destruction, and warding off the coming desolation."[60]

The Dodge Company's prospectus quoted at length from Starr's report, but it stopped short of his proposals for government-led forest conservation. Since its lumbering operation in Georgia was meant to be short-term, and its long-term vision called for expanded crop production, it had no need to conserve forestland. Instead it stressed Starr's predictions of timber famine as one of the central economic justifications for the company's existence. Timber famine signaled a market opportunity. The company's prospectus cited the exhaustion of white pine in the North as an incentive to move south, and, unlike many others on the front end of the southern timber boom, it also predicted that the longleaf forest, "which has but a limited extent," would run out within fifteen years.[61] They were not far off, and if the world was running out of timber, then those in its possession would surely be in a prime position to capitalize on the resulting demand.

With title ostensibly settled and capital raised, the Dodge Company began the business of timber extraction in 1872. The company's actual operation on the ground was short but eventful. It established an inland headquarters at the new town of Normandale, named for Dodge's son, Norman, who joined his brother Anson to manage the Georgia operation. By the mid-1870s, the company employed thousands in the woods and mills and spread its operation quickly and efficiently. The company constructed a sawmill in Normandale and built a rail network extending into its landholdings that connected with the Oconee River to the east, the Ocmulgee River to the west, and the Macon & Brunswick Railroad in the middle. Numerous observers used "immense" and "grand scale" to describe the business. In one section alone, it was reported, "about two hundred and twenty-five mules are used in hauling the timber from the woods to the little railroad."[62] One sympathetic correspondent wrote that the region "looks as if a magician's wand had touched it, and change (for the better) is visible on every hand."[63] The company rail network gave it access to the three major arteries out of the area, and timber soon began arriving in Darien via the Altamaha River and in Brunswick via the M&B. From both of these locations, company steamers towed it all to St. Simons Island, where the company had erected a sprawling sawmill complex. A large labor force of mostly African American workers then milled the timber to order into a variety of structural and trim materials and loaded it onto ocean-going vessels for voyage to ports to the north, south, or across the Atlantic.

Even though the company's major landholdings were inland, St. Simons Island became the real home of the Dodge Company. St. Simons offered better deepwater access to the Atlantic than Darien, and as one of the more populated islands of the Georgia coast it held a ready labor force for the mill complex. A dozen or so large plantations made it a major antebellum producer of cotton and rice, and like most other centers of plantation slavery it had struggled to find its economic footing after the war. Former slaves had maintained their livelihoods through a mix of sharecropping, market gardening, and subsistence hunting and fishing, and the mill's arrival offered one of the few opportunities for wage-paying work. Indeed, it was likely a familiar setting for many mill workers, at least in terms of location if not workplace. The mill sat on Gascoigne Bluff, the former site of one of several plantations owned by planter-agriculturalist James Hamilton Couper.

Like Couper's own experiments in agriculture and plantation management, the Dodge mill unified the latest technology with capital to maximize production and profit. At its height in the early 1880s, it had two large steam-powered sawmills for cutting pine timber and a third that specialized in a smaller volume of cypress logs. In all, these mills could handle over one hundred thousand board feet of lumber daily, an amount unheard of at the time of construction but that would become increasingly common up and down the coast. Below on the Frederica River was a series of docks with a capacity to hold at least twenty of the largest oceangoing barks and schooners at once. Mills such as this one quickly changed the identity of the Georgia coast. A region that was once centered on the distribution of plantation crops throughout the world become one temporarily fixated on forest products.[64]

St. Simons was also appealing to the Dodges for another reason. They arrived at a time when others from the urban North began to take notice of the pleasures of the Georgia coast. Just across the St. Simons sound, Jekyll Island would soon become home to the Jekyll Island Club, a group of vacationing sportsmen and women that included J. P. Morgan, William Rockefeller, and William K. Vanderbilt. South of Jekyll, the Carnegie family purchased much of Cumberland Island and turned it into their winter retreat. St. Simons was already carved up into too many landholdings for such a transformation to take place, but the Dodges took a liking to it nonetheless and became firmly entrenched in local society through a number of business and religious activities.[65]

The Dodge Company had all the parts in place for the easy transformation of forest into fiber—the capital, the competence, the infrastructure, the markets, and the personal touch. But they did not plan for a fierce strain of resistance from inland locals. The complex details of what came to be known as "the Dodge land wars" are really beyond the scope of this chapter, but it demands a short discussion at least. It was a southern Georgia saga nonpareil, involving so-called carpetbaggers and scalawags, murderous conspiracies, hundreds of court cases and disputed judicial jurisdiction, fraudulent land deeds, and even an eye-patch-wearing local lawyer eager for either justice or personal power, depending on narrative perspective. As sagas go, this was a complicated one, but it boiled down to land ownership. Title disputes began almost immediately after the Dodges announced their purchase. Some claimants were squatters with years of actual possession, and many others appeared with at least some color of title to the land. At one point during the antebellum years, much of the Dodge land was held by the State of Indiana, which failed to pay taxes in 1844. Local county clerks took the opportunity to issue a writ of fieri facias and sold hundreds of land lots. The details of what happened next are murky, but another owner emerged with Indiana's title to the entire landholding, which was passed to the Dodge Company and later judged valid in federal courts. Regardless, many locals felt entitled to their lands, and a long series of court battles ensued, the last of which was only resolved in 1923.[66]

Most participants in the drama saw it through the lens of sectionalism, going so far as to call Dodge a "red-mouthed Radical," which was patently untrue.[67] Nonetheless, the coming of the Dodge Company meant real hardship for many residents who thought they had purchased legal title to their land. Those with some color of title kept a small portion of their land, but others had to give it all up or be faced with eviction notices, "for these poor men well knew that they did not have the money to contest their suits against this monied monopoly," according to one correspondent to the *Hawkinsville Dispatch*.[68] As the heated rhetoric began appearing in local papers, William Pitt Eastman felt compelled to defend his friend, William Dodge, in print. He told local readers, "Mr. Dodge has always been a good friend of the South . . . he is soon coming among us and will use his money here in removing the timber and developing the property." Eastman went on to explain the benefits of such good work and was sanguine about the future, explaining, "The plan is to strip off the timber from ten to twenty thousand acres per year, and then the land will be for sale, or to lease to those who are unable to purchase. Mr. Dodge does not intend to carry away the land."[69] Condescension did not play well to the audience, and the fight continued for years, culminating with the murder of the company's superintendent at Normandale in 1890.

None of this stopped the company from doing what it was there to do. This dramatic contest over land and resources unfolded under the rapidly diminishing canopy of Georgia's longleaf pine forest. The botanist Charles Mohr could have been referring directly to the Dodges' quick work when he addressed the 1888 meeting of the American Forest Congress in Atlanta about the South's depleted forests. As one of a growing number of concerned observers who acknowledged how the logic of capital was sweeping through the southern coastal plain, Mohr reported on what he characterized as timber "production under the high pressure of capital." He spoke of sprawling company rail infrastructures "penetrating the forests to the very divides which separate the basin of one river from another." Such efforts, Mohr suggested, "require the outlay of vast sums of money and are costly to maintain. Temporary as they are, to render them profitable they must be kept working to their fullest capacity and without loss of time." Anyone familiar with the Dodge operations would have recognized such an assessment, but they were but one of many. Mohr concluded that wherever such expenditures "have been introduced the depletion of the timber lands within reach is effected at a rate never existing before."[70] Indeed, the Dodges' timber was beginning to run out by the late 1880s, just as they had anticipated it would. They sold their interest in the St. Simons mill to a large Darien firm in 1888, and from there the interior cutting began to wane until the inland mill at Normandale burned in 1892. The land continued to be a source for courtroom adjudication but not for timber. The latter was now spread throughout the Atlantic world, serving as structural support for the industrial age.

In the Dodge lands we see two seemingly contradictory explanations of the postwar cutover and of much New South industry writ large. One built on the long-term and one might say idealistic purpose of expanding national prosperity, and the other built on the short-term and one might say cynical motivations for immediate profits. But they were not contradictory, at least not in the eyes of a turn-of-the-century industrialist like William E. Dodge. The short-term profiteering served the purpose of long-term prosperity. Historians and others have often characterized turn-of-the-century timber companies such as Dodge's as myopic forces hell-bent on extracting the resource and then fleeing the scene of the crime. That characterization is hard to dispute, but many had a more expansive and even progressive view of what they were doing. Dodge and his partners saw their Georgia timber investment as part of the process of reintegrating the South into the national economy and thus expanding the national economy by using southern resources to engage international trade. Dodge, like many others, never meant for his southern timber business to last, because he saw forests as a barrier to permanent economic growth. Only by removing the forest could one see the potential in the land.[71]

But such explanations still leave us with a cutover forest, a reality with long-term economic, social, and ecological consequences unforeseen by the likes of Dodge. The cotton economy of the South did expand as Dodge had hoped, and while that may have benefited many in the Atlantic economy, the outcomes on the ground fell infamously short of prosperous. In the region of the Dodge lands, cotton replaced what had been a relatively prosperous agricultural economy based on extensive open-range grazing and small-scale cultivation. After the company depleted the forests, rural dwellers had little choice but to expand cultivation. Longleaf ecology fell apart without the trees, and so too did the rangeland economy that depended on that ecology. As one of the few cash crops that residents knew, cotton was the logical replacement, and it helped that thousands of black and white laborers had migrated to the region for work in the forests. Most of them stayed after the Dodge Company left, and while some became landowners, most ended up burdened by the same sharecropper's debt as so many others throughout the South.[72]

Exploring the many geographies of nature offers a fuller story of environmental and social change. Natural organisms with economic value like the longleaf pine have not remained in their place, but they also have not simply disappeared. People have moved them around from place to place, and it is important to understand where resources came from, where they went, and how they got there. In Georgia's coastal plain after the Civil War, the movement of no natural resource was more important than that of longleaf pine. The international demand for timber materials during the second Industrial Revolution, along with the growing ability to supply them, transformed the ecology, economy, and society of the coastal plain in ways inconceivable at the beginning of the period. But the movement of the resource not only transformed its native ground, it also influenced every place it encountered. Whether the waterfront of a coastal community, the bottom of the East River, or a factory site in London's West Ham, materials such as longleaf pine were part of the ongoing international dissemination of nature throughout the world. In this case, people throughout the Atlantic world who needed structural timber looked to the South's coastal plain for a few decades after the Civil War, and the coastal plain provided.

Finally, my overall goal here has been to think about longleaf pine as both ecological and economic keystone, to somehow integrate our understanding of its ecological and economic history. Simply put, the evolutionary ecology of longleaf pine had a lot to do with its economic value. Fire, drought, and poor soils led to adaptations in longleaf pine that created wood fiber ideal for structural purposes and thus valuable in the marketplace. The same traits, in other words, that made it a keystone species in the forest made it a keystone product in the market. A central paradox in much historical writing about forests is that we lament the forest's destruction while simultaneously celebrating the raw material and its finished products. Heart pine is revered for its strength and beauty, and the Brooklyn Bridge is a cultural, technological, and economic symbol of greatness. But the stumps remaining in Georgia's coastal plain are ruins, symbolic of the destruction we have inflicted in producing those cultural gems. Both of these stories, though, are of a piece, interconnected in a web of nature, people, institutions, and ideas that transforms ecological actors into economic actors, both with considerable value in their own right.

NOTES

1. W. A. Roebling and W. C. Kingsley, *First Annual Reports of the Chief Engineer and General Superintendent of the East River Bridge, June 12, 1870* (Brooklyn, N.Y.: Eagle Book and Job Printing Dept., 1870), 15.

2. Ibid., 7–8. On the dimensions and material of the caisson, see ibid., 5–10; and *Report of the Committee Appointed by the Board of Trustees, Consisting of the Mayors of the Cities of New York and Brooklyn, Together with the Report of the Accountants to Said Committee in the Matter of an Examination of the Financial Affairs of the New York and Brooklyn Bridge, December 31, 1883* (Brooklyn, N.Y.: Eagle Book and Job Printing Dept., 1884), 121.

3. John A. Roebling, *Report of John A. Roebling, C.E., to the President and Directors of the New York Bridge Company on the Proposed East River Bridge* (Brooklyn, N.Y.: Eagle Book and Job Printing Dept., 1870), 3. On the Brooklyn Bridge, see Alan Trachtenberg, *Brooklyn Bridge: Fact and Symbol* (Chicago: University of Chicago Press, 1965); David McCullough, *The Great Bridge: The Epic Story of the Building of the Brooklyn Bridge* (New York: Simon and Schuster, 1972).

4. Vivian Yee, "Salvaging a Long-Lasting Wood, and New York City's Past," *New York Times*, July 21, 2015.

5. "Oration of Richard S. Storrs," in *Opening Ceremonies of the New York and Brooklyn Bridge, May 24, 1883* (Brooklyn, N.Y.: Brooklyn Eagle Job Printing Dept.), 96.

6. Anna Lowenhaupt Tsing, *The Mushroom at the End of the World: On the Possibility of Life in Capitalist Ruins* (Princeton: Princeton University Press, 2015); Arjun Appadurai, *The Social Life of Things: Commodities in Cultural Perspective* (Cambridge: Cambridge University Press, 1986); Jennifer L. Anderson, *Mahogany: The Costs of Luxury in Early America* (Cambridge, Mass.: Harvard University Press, 2013); and Gregory T. Cushman, *Guano and the Opening of the Pacific World: A Global Ecological History* (Cambridge: Cambridge University Press, 2013).

7. Joachim Radkau, *Wood: A History* (Malden, Mass.: Polity, 2012), 3. This historiographical problem may result from a similar historical problem—that the timber industry itself has become a separate concern from forest conservation. See Brett Bennett, *Plantations and Protected Areas: A Global History of Forest Management* (Cambridge, Mass.: MIT Press, 2015).

8. On the turn-of-the-century cutover in the South, see Michael Williams, *Americans and Their Forests: A Historical Geography* (Cambridge: Cambridge University Press, 1989), 238–88; Thomas R. Cox, *The Lumberman's Frontier: Three Centuries of Land Use, Society, and Change in America's Forests* (Corvalis: Oregon State University Press, 2010); Lawrence S. Earley, *Looking for Longleaf: The Fall and Rise of an American Forest* (Chapel Hill: University of North Carolina Press, 2004).

9. A now classic account of "hinterland" geography is William Cronon, *Nature's Metropolis: Chicago and the Great West* (New York: W. W. Norton, 1991).

10. Edmund P. Russell, *Evolutionary History* (Cambridge: Cambridge University

Press, 2011); Susan R. Schrepfer and Philip Scranton, eds. *Industrializing Organisms: Introducing Evolutionary History* (New York: Routledge, 2004); Alan L. Olmstead and Paul W. Rhode, *Creating Abundance: Biological Innovation and American Agricultural Development* (Cambridge: Cambridge University Press, 2008); Albert G. Way, "'A Cosmopolitan Weed of the World': Following Bermudagrass," *Agricultural History* 88, no. 3 (Summer 2014): 354–67.

11. S. W. Greene, "The Forest that Fire Made," *American Forests*, October 1931, 583–84. Most of my discussion of longleaf ecology comes from Jose Shibu, Eric J. Jokela, and Deborah L. Miller, eds., *The Longleaf Pine Ecosystem: Ecology, Silviculture, and Restoration* (New York: Springer, 2006).

12. Most historical ecologists argue that fire appeared in the coastal plain well before Native Americans. Their evidence is strong, but others—myself included— have argued that regardless of the timing, the cultural and economic uses of fire were equally important in shaping and maintaining what we understand as a healthy longleaf system. See Reed F. Noss, *Forgotten Grasslands of the South: Natural History and Conservation* (Washington, D.C.: Island Press, 2013), 203–7; Cecil Frost, "History and Future of the Longleaf Pine Ecosystem," in Shibu, Jokela, and Miller, eds., *The Longleaf Pine Ecosystem*, 9–42; Williams, *Americans and Their Forests*; Albert G. Way, *Conserving Southern Longleaf: Herbert Stoddard and Rise of Ecological Land Management* (Athens: University of Georgia Press, 2011).

13. On Native American uses of fire, see Timothy Silver, *A New Face on the Countryside: Indians, Colonists, and Slaves in the South Atlantic Forests* (Cambridge: Cambridge University Press, 1990), 59–63; Williams, *Americans and Their Forests*, 22–49.

14. John Brownfield to the Trustees, June 19, 1737, in *Colonial Records of Georgia, 1735–1737*, vol. 21, ed. Allen D. Candler (Atlanta: Chas. P. Byrd, 1910), 482.

15. William Stephens, June 22, 1738, in *Colonial Records of Georgia*, vol. 4, *Stephens' Journal, 1737–1740* (Atlanta: Franklin Printing and Publishing, 1904), 160.

16. Allen D. Candler, *Colonial Records of Georgia*, vol. 1 (Atlanta: Franklin Printing and Publishing, 1904), 389.

17. Mart Stewart, "'Whether Wast, Deodand, or Stray': Cattle, Culture, and the Environment of Early Georgia," *Agricultural History* 65 (Summer 1991): 1–28; John Solomon Otto, "Open-Range Cattle-Herding in Southern Florida," *Florida Historical Quarterly* 65 (January 1987): 317–34. The open range has been subject to much study and lively debate, especially its origins and closing. See Forest MacDonald and Grady McWhiney, "The South from Self-Sufficiency to Peonage: An Interpretation," *American Historical Review* 85 (December 1980): 1095–1118; Shawn Kantor and J. Morgan Kousser, "Common-Sense of Commonwealth? The Fence Law and Institutional Change in the Postbellum South," *Journal of Southern History* 59 (May 1993): 201–42; Steven Hahn, "A Response: Common Cents or Historical Sense?," *Journal of Southern History* 59 (May 1993): 243–58.

18. On the colonial and antebellum trade in lumber and naval stores, see Silver, *New Face on the Countryside*; Paul M. Pressly, *On the Rim of the Caribbean: Colonial Georgia and the British Atlantic World* (Athens: University of Georgia Press, 2013);

Robert B. Outland III, *Tapping the Pines: The Naval Stores Industry in the American South* (Baton Rouge: Louisiana State University Press, 2004); Mart A. Stewart, *"What Nature Suffers to Groe": Life, Labor, and Landscape on the Georgia Coast, 1680–1920* (Athens: University of Georgia Press, 1996); Lawrence Earley, *Looking for Longleaf: The Fall and Rise of an American Forest* (Chapel Hill: University of North Carolina Press, 2004).

19. Charles Mohr, *The Timber Pines of the Southern United States*, USDA Bulletin 13 (Washington, D.C.: Government Printing Office, 1896), 31, 34. "Cuban pine" was the common name for what we now call slash pine.

20. Mark V. Wetherington, *New South Comes to Wiregrass Georgia, 1860–1910* (Knoxville: University of Tennessee Press, 1994); Ann Patton Malone, "Piney Woods Farmers of South Georgia, 1850–1900: Jeffersonian Yeomen in an Age of Expanding Commercialism," *Agricultural History* 60, no. 4 (Fall 1986): 51–84; Carlton Morrison, *Running the River: Poleboats, Steamboats and Timber Rafts on the Altamaha, Ocmulgee, Oconee and Ohoopee* (St. Simons Island, GA: Saltmarsh Press, 2003).

21. Mohr, *Timber Pines of the Southern United States*, 31.

22. The literature on the New South economy is large. For overviews of the timber industry's role in it, see Edward Ayers, *The Promise of the New South: Life after Reconstruction* (New York: Oxford University Press, 1992), 123–31; Gavin Wright, *Old South, New South: Revolutions in the Southern Economy since the Civil War* (New York: Basic Books, 1986), 159–65; Michael Williams, *Americans and Their Forests: A Historical Geography* (Cambridge: Cambridge University Press, 1992), 238–88. For two recent environmental histories of New South industrialization, see William Boyd, *The Slain Wood: Papermaking and Its Environmental Consequences in the American South* (Baltimore: Johns Hopkins Press, 2015); and William D. Bryan, "'Constructive and not Destructive Development': Permanent Uses of Resources in the American South," in *Green Capitalism? Business and Environment in the Twentieth Century*, ed. Hartmut Berghoff and Adam Rome (Philadelphia: University of Pennsylvania Press, 2017).

23. "Pine Forests of Georgia," *Merchants' Magazine and Commercial Review*, October 1, 1860, 445, italics in original.

24. "The Lumber Business of the South," *Debow's Review*, August 1866, 201.

25. Morrison, *Running the River*, 112.

26. "Lumber Business of the South," 202.

27. The evocative language of "drifting into Darien" comes from Janisse Ray, *Drifting into Darien: A Personal and Natural History of the Altamaha River* (Athens: University of Georgia Press, 2013).

28. The best source on Darien as a timber port is Buddy Sullivan, *Early Days on the Georgia Tidewater: The Story of McIntosh County and Sapelo* (Darien, Ga.: McIntosh County Board, 1990); Buddy Sullivan, *High Water on the Bar: An Operational Perspective of a Tidewater Timber Port, with the Memoir of Thomas Hilton and the Minutes of the Darien Pilot Commissioners, 1874–1930* (Darien, Ga.: Darien Development Authority, 2009). On timber rafting, see Morrison, *Running the River*.

29. Jerrold E. Winandy and Roger M. Rowell, "Chemistry of Wood Strength,"

in *Handbook of Wood Chemistry and Wood Composites*, ed. Roger M. Rowell (Boca Raton: CRC Press, 2012), 413–56.

30. There remains considerable debate about the relationship between growth rate and density, but the rate of growth certainly helps to define wood's economic characteristics. See John Barnett and George Jeronimidis, eds., *Wood Quality and Its Biological Basis* (New York: John Wiley and Sons, 2009), 102–4.

31. "Report of the Chief of the Division of Forestry," in *Report of the Secretary of Agriculture, 1891* (Washington, D.C.: Government Printing Office, 1892), 213–14. This report was based on the ongoing work of Charles Mohr.

32. Ibid., 218.

33. Ibid.

34. W. G. Wahlenberg, *Longleaf Pine: Its Use, Ecology, Regeneration, Protection, Growth, and Management* (Washington, D.C.: Charles Lathrop Pack Forestry Foundation, with US Department of Agriculture, 1946), 25–34.

35. Charles S. Sargent, *Report of the Forests of North America*, Department of Interior, Census Office (Washington, D.C.: Government Printing Office, 1884), 202.

36. "Report of the Chief of the Division of Forestry," in *Report of the Secretary of Agriculture, 1891* (Washington, D.C.: Government Printing Office, 1892), 219.

37. On the Dodge company in Georgia and the resulting "land wars," see Jane Walker and Chris Trowell, *The Dodge Land Troubles, 1868–1923* (Fernandina Beach, FL: Wolfe, 2004); J. N. Talley, "The Dodge Lands and Litigation," in *Report of the Forty-Second Annual Session of the Georgia Bar Association*, ed. Harry S. Strozier (Macon, Ga.: J. W. Burke Co., 1925), 236–73; Mary Ellen Tripp, "Longleaf Lumber Manufacturing in the Altamaha River Basin, 1865–1918," PhD diss. (Florida State University, 1983); Carlton Morrison, *Running the River*. For a study that places the Dodges within the broader context of the New South, see Wetherington, *New South Comes to Wiregrass Georgia*.

38. D. Stuart Dodge, ed., *Memorials of William E. Dodge* (New York: Anson D. F. Randolph and Company, 1887), 39.

39. The best sources on William E. Dodge are Richard Lowitt, *A Merchant Prince of the Nineteenth Century: William E. Dodge* (New York: Columbia University Press, 1954); and Sven Beckert, *The Monied Metropolis: New York City and the Consolidation of the American Bourgeoisie, 1850–1896* (Cambridge: Cambridge University Press, 2001).

40. See Katherine Benton-Cohen, *Borderline Americans: Racial Division and Labor War in the Arizona Borderlands* (Cambridge, Mass.: Harvard University Press, 2009); Linda Gordon, *The Great Arizona Orphan Abduction* (Cambridge, Mass.: Harvard University Press, 1999); and Timothy J. LeCain, *Mass Destruction: The Men and Giant Mines That Wired America and Scarred the Planet* (New Brunswick, NJ: Rutgers University Press, 2009).

41. *Memorials of William E. Dodge*, 122.

42. *New York Times*, January 12, 1875. There has been a recent boom in scholarship stressing the importance of cotton and slavery in the global economy. See especially Sven Beckert, *Empire of Cotton: A Global History* (New York: Alfred A. Knopf,

2014); and Edward E. Baptist, *The Half Has Never Been Told: Slavery and the Making of American Capitalism* (New York: Basic Books, 2014).

43. On the creation of standard grades in the cotton trade, see Bruce E. Baker and Barbara Hahn, *The Cotton Kings: Capitalism and Corruption in Turn-of-the-Century New York and New Orleans* (Oxford: Oxford University Press, 2015), 3–8; Beckert, *Empire of Cotton*, 208–12; Harold D. Woodman, *King Cotton and His Retainers: Financing and Marketing the Cotton Crop of the South, 1800–1925* (Lexington: University of Kentucky Press, 1968). Enforceable standardized grading did not reach the timber trade until World War I. On timber grading, regulation, and market competition, see William G. Robbins, *Lumberjacks and Legislators: Political Economy of the U.S. Lumber Industry, 1890–1941* (College Station: Texas A&M Press, 1982); James E. Fickle, *The New South and the "New Competition": Trade Association Development in the Southern Pine Industry* (Champaign: University of Illinois Press, 1980).

44. *The Georgia Land and Lumber Company* (New York: Major & Knapp Engraving, Manufacturing, and Lithographic Company, 1870), 8–9.

45. Dodge, *Memorials of William E. Dodge*, 40.

46. For general discussion on railroads, see Ayers, *Promise of the New South*, 3–33.

47. *Georgia Land and Lumber Company*, 6. On the relationship between Hazlehurst and Dodge, see Wetherington, *New South Comes to Wiregrass Georgia*, 243; and Wilbur W. Caldwell, *The Courthouse and the Depot: The Architecture of Hope in an Age of Despair* (Macon, GA: Mercer University Press, 2001), 250.

48. Quoted in Lowitt, *Merchant Prince*, 113.

49. *Georgia Land and Lumber Company*, 13.

50. Lowitt, *Merchant Prince*, 61–81.

51. William Stevenson, *Wood: Its Use as a Constructive Material* (London: B. T. Batsford, 1894), 149, 152–53.

52. *Report of the Secretary of Agriculture, 1891* (Washington, D.C.: Government Printing Office, 1892), 222.

53. *Georgia Land and Lumber Company*, 6.

54. Ibid., 7–8.

55. On timber famine, see Williams, *Americans and Their Forests*, 393–446; and David A. Clary, *Timber and the Forest Service* (Lawrence: University Press of Kansas, 1986).

56. *Georgia Land and Lumber Company*, 7.

57. Frederick Starr Jr., "American Forests, Their Destruction and Preservation," in *Report of the Commissioner of Agriculture for the Year 1865* (Washington, D.C.: GPO, 1866), 210.

58. Ibid., 222.

59. Ibid., 227. George Perkins Marsh, *Man and Nature, or, Physical Geography as Modified by Human Action* (New York: Charles Scribner, 1864).

60. Ibid., 210.

61. *Georgia Land and Lumber Company*, 7–8.

62. *Hawkinsville (Ga.) Dispatch*, April 29, 1880, quoted in Walker and Trowell, *Dodge Land Troubles*, 160.

63. *Brunswick Advertiser*, March 12, 1879, quoted in Morrison, *Running the River*, 114.

64. On the mill complex, see Abbie Fuller Graham, *Old Mill Days: St. Simons Island* (St. Simons: St. Simons Public Library, 1976); Stewart, *What Nature Suffers to Groe*, 209–10.

65. The Dodges became part of local lore through the popular romantic novels of Eugenia Price. See Price, *The Beloved Invader* (Philadelphia: J. B. Lippincott, 1965).

66. See note 38 above.

67. *Savannah Morning News*, November 1, 1873, quoted in Walker and Trowell, *Dodge Land Troubles*, 64.

68. "Alpha," *Hawkinsville (Ga.) Dispatch*, April 24, 1873, quoted in Walker and Trowell, *Dodge Land Troubles*, 45.

69. *Hawkinsville (Ga.) Dispatch*, May, 18, 1873. Quoted in Walker and Trowell, *Dodge Land Troubles*, 49.

70. Charles Mohr, "The Interest of the Individual in Forestry in View of the Present Condition of the Lumber Interest," in *Proceedings of the American Forest Congress at Its Meeting Held in Atlanta, Georgia, December 1888* (Washington, D.C.: Gibson Bros., 1889), 36.

71. On the idea of permanence in the New South economy, see Bryan, "Constructive and Not Destructive Development."

72. Wetherington, *New South Comes to Wiregrass Georgia*; Malone, "Piney Woods Farmers of South Georgia, 1850–1900."

CHAPTER 8

Water Is for Fighting Over

*Papermaking and the Struggle over Groundwater
in Coastal Georgia, 1930s–2000s*

WILLIAM BOYD

When it rains on the coastal plain of Georgia, much of the water runs off into various creeks and rivers, swamps and bays, ponds and lakes. Some of this water eventually ends up in the Atlantic Ocean. Most of the rest evaporates to begin the cycle anew, but a small amount (less than 10 percent of the total, about five inches of rain per year) percolates down below the surface.[1] This water eventually reaches the underground aquifer that lies deep beneath the coastal plain of Georgia, adding to the billions of gallons of freshwater in an aquifer system that is one of the most prolific in the world.[2] Spread over one hundred thousand square miles, the Floridan Aquifer acts as a huge limestone sponge capturing and storing freshwater underneath parts of Georgia, South Carolina, Alabama, Mississippi, and Florida.[3] Prior to its tapping by means of deep wells, water flowed through the aquifer from areas of recharge along the fall line and upper coastal plain south and east toward the coast until it was discharged into the Atlantic. Much of this water was thousands of years old by the time it reached the ocean.[4]

The aquifer's productivity has long been the stuff of legend. Discharges into the ocean off the coast of Georgia and Florida provided freshwater for passing ships. Reports from early settlers spoke of plentiful, free-flowing natural springs in the area.[5] Archaeological evidence suggests that some of the shell rings built by precontact peoples may have functioned to maintain access to dependable supplies of groundwater during times of drought.[6]

During the late nineteenth century, municipal leaders in Savannah and other cities in the region dug the first deep wells to tap the aquifer.[7] Up until this time, Savannah had been drawing water from the Savannah River and from shallow wells and cisterns.[8] The new, deeper wells that reached the

MAP 8.1. The Floridan Aquifer

Note: The Floridan Aquifer extends over an area of a hundred thousand square miles underneath Florida and parts of Alabama, Georgia, Mississippi, and South Carolina.

Source: Adapted from Marella and Berndt, *Water Withdrawals and Trends from the Floridan Aquifer System in the Southeastern United States, 1950–2000*, 1.

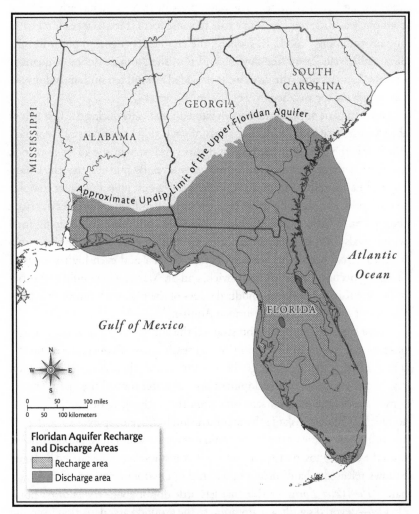

MAP 8.2. Discharge from and Recharge into the Floridan Aquifer prior to Development
Source: Adapted from Peter W. Bush and Richard H. Johnston, *Ground-Water Hydraulics, Regional Flow, and Ground-Water Development of the Floridan Aquifer System in Florida and in parts of Georgia, South Carolina, and Alabama*, U.S. Geological Survey Professional Paper 1403-C (Washington, D.C.: GPO, 1988), plate 11.

aquifer, some of which were hundreds of feet deep, produced high-quality, free-flowing "artesian" water.[9] The water pressure in Savannah's early wells, for example, was such that the water rose to some forty feet *above* sea level without any pumping.[10] As E. R. Conant, the city's chief engineer, put it in 1918, Savannah's wells "were free-flowing and furnished a most desirable quantity of water." At the time, the city's wells provided around ten million gallons per day, supplying the vast majority of Savannah's water.[11]

Development of the aquifer accelerated dramatically during the first half of the twentieth century, with thousands of wells dug across coastal Georgia.[12] But it was the arrival of the pulp and paper industry in the 1930s that took groundwater withdrawals to an entirely new level. By mid-century, the Union Bag and Paper mill at Savannah, which was the largest pulp and paper complex in the world, was pumping more than twenty-five million gallons per day from the aquifer. When combined with the city's own pumping, this brought total withdrawals for the Savannah area to sixty million gallons per day, five times what they had been a half-century before. Similar and even higher levels of pumping occurred at Jesup, Brunswick, and St. Marys, where pulp and paper mills established during the middle decades of the twentieth century took advantage of the bounty of the Floridan Aquifer.[13]

These large withdrawals soon strained the aquifer, creating what hydrogeologists call "cones of depression" underneath areas of concentrated pumping. By altering the hydraulic gradient in the aquifer, these cones of depression reversed the natural, predevelopment flow of water toward the ocean and, in some cases, began to draw saltwater from the outlying coastal areas into the aquifer.[14] While the risk of saltwater intrusion had been apparent to geologists and others since at least the 1940s, it did not arouse widespread public concern until the early 1970s, particularly after a Ralph Nader study group led by James Fallows released a hard-hitting book on the "environmental crisis" in Savannah.[15] *The Water Lords*—a title that left little doubt about the author's point of view—devoted significant attention to the groundwater depletion issue and painted a damning portrait of Union Camp's environmental record.

Although the State of Georgia responded to rising concerns about overpumping with a new Groundwater Management Act in 1972, the legislation did little more than establish a permit system for large withdrawals and placed no restrictions on pumping.[16] By the late 1980s, with pumping rates in Savannah close to ninety million gallons per day, concerns grew about the long-term health of the aquifer. The State of South Carolina actually threatened to sue the State of Georgia several times during the early 1990s for failing to control pumping rates and causing saltwater intrusion underneath Hilton Head Island.[17]

As the politics intensified, Georgia regulators took some tentative steps toward a management strategy for the aquifer. Over the next two decades, groundwater was prominent on the public agenda, and by the middle of the first decade of the new millennium, Savannah and its major industries, notably the Union Camp mill (now owned by International Paper), had significantly reduced pumping. But problems with saltwater intrusion in outlying areas worsened, leading to yet more talk of a lawsuit by South Carolina and a 2015 decision by Georgia's Environmental Protection Division to require further reductions in groundwater pumping in Savannah and Chatham County.[18] Whether these reductions, which clearly signal a new era in the region's approach to groundwater, will be sufficient to repair the aquifer and halt saltwater intrusion, particularly in the face of emerging threats such as climate change, remains to be seen.

This chapter chronicles these struggles over groundwater in coastal Georgia during the last century. It focuses on the pulp and paper industry and specifically on the handful of mills that were established in coastal Georgia starting in the 1930s, with particular attention to the Savannah area. This chapter draws on and complements a recently published history of the pulp and paper industry in the post–New Deal South.[19] Few industries have had more of an impact on the southern environment—its land, air, and water—and few have made more demands on the region's prolific groundwater resources than pulp and paper. Nowhere has this been more apparent than in Savannah and coastal Georgia.

The chapter begins with a short discussion of the industry's dramatic relocation to the South starting in the 1930s. It then describes the basic process of papermaking and the associated water demands, emphasizing the scale and speed of pulp and paper production at the new southern mills, which were among the largest in the world. The perspective then shifts to focus on groundwater science and how aquifers were understood and made visible over the last century. This provides an important backdrop for a discussion of groundwater development and depletion in the Savannah area and coastal Georgia and the ensuing struggles over groundwater regulation and management. The final section of the chapter discusses the changing legal status of groundwater and the recent trend toward a regulatory framework that, at least in theory, is oriented toward the long-term sustainability of the resource.

In many respects, the history of groundwater use in southern Georgia during the twentieth century is part of a broader story about industrialization and environmental change in the post–New Deal South. As such, it is a story about a relentless logic of extraction applied to a part of the environment that, while largely invisible, has long played a vital role in supporting economic development across the region.

Water has often been hailed as one of the South's great advantages—a natural endowment that opened up worlds of possibilities. As the famous southern regionalist Howard W. Odum put it in 1936: "Here is natural wealth of the first order, the most potent of all geographical influences—life-giving waters from abundant clouds and from swift moving streams from mountain to shore, nature's endowment for land and crops, for power and commerce, for man and beast, a regional keynote to health and happiness, inspiration and wealth, beauty and utility, work and play."[20] But the vast majority of attention (past and present) has been directed at the South's bountiful supplies of *surface* water. Far too little thought has been given to the region's aquifers and the role they have played in southern economic and environmental history.[21] This chapter seeks to begin filling that gap, focusing on the role of groundwater in underwriting one of the region's most impressive industrial success stories—the pulp and paper industry.

THE GRAND MARCH SOUTH

The 1930s proved to be an auspicious time for pulp and paper firms to establish operations in the South. Although there were already a dozen or so mills operating in the region, lingering concerns over the destruction of the southern timber resource and the appropriateness of immature southern pine for papermaking continued to raise questions in the board rooms of major northern paper manufacturers into the 1920s. By the 1930s, however, technical barriers to making pulp and paper out of southern pine had been overcome, and the preliminary results of the first regional forest surveys indicated that the southern forest, which had been under virtually continuous assault since the collapse of Reconstruction, was capable of rapid regeneration.[22] Despite a series of government reports and hearings as well as rising public concern over the possibility of a national timber famine during the 1920s, the so-called second forest that was growing up in the wake of the destruction of the South's old-growth forest testified both to the resilience of the timber resource and, more importantly, to the rapid growth rate of loblolly and other short-leaf varieties of southern pine.[23] At the same time, southern states and towns, still reeling from the Depression, were eager for any sort of industrial development and provided generous incentives to pulp and paper mills to entice them to locate in their areas.[24] Key raw materials—wood, water, and energy—abounded. Land and labor were plentiful and cheap. Unions were virtually nonexistent, and the big eastern markets lay close at hand. By the end of the decade, the South had radically reshaped the industry's competitive landscape.[25] Without a southern mill, as Alexander Calder, president of Union Bag and Paper, put it in 1936, his company "would make about as much progress on the road to fame and success as Colonel Lindbergh would have made without an aeroplane."[26]

Thus began the "grand march South."[27] Between 1935 and 1940, fifteen new kraft mills were established in the region, and pulping capacity more than doubled.[28] After a brief interruption due to war, the procession resumed at an even faster pace. By 1950, the South accounted for 55 percent of total wood pulp production capacity, up from 15 percent in 1929. Two decades later, the South had emerged as the undisputed leader in the production of pulp and paper, accounting for almost two-thirds of domestic wood pulp production and half of paper and paperboard production.[29]

If there were a signal event in this dramatic process of industrial relocation, it would surely be the 1936 decision by Union Bag and Paper to build in Savannah what would become the world's largest pulp and paper complex. With this move, the race was on to find and develop the most suitable sites for pulp and paper mills in the South. Because the new mills were massive by the standards of the day, reflecting the huge economies of scale available in kraft pulp and paper manufacture, their investments in fixed capital dwarfed anything previously seen in the forest products sector.[30] Unlike the small "peckerwood" sawmills that could be moved in search of new timber supplies, these new pulp and paper mills weren't going anywhere. Operating under an imperative to keep their fixed capital in motion, many of these mills ran twenty-four hours a day, seven days a week. Their appetites for water, energy, and timber were almost inconceivable.[31]

As the pulp and paper industry expanded in the South, industrial advocates throughout the region heralded the dawn of a new age. Echoing the boosterism of Henry Grady and other pro-business advocates, the *Savannah Morning News* proclaimed that the Union Bag plant signaled a "New Industrial Epoch" for southeastern Georgia, noting that the "lowly pine tree . . . has taken on a new aura of grandeur and significance as a symbol of vast potential wealth."[32] Speaking at a banquet celebrating the formal opening of the plant, Savannah mayor Thomas Gamble exulted: "No one can safely limit the possibilities which center in the pine tree and its various possible products. . . . We appar-

FIGURE 8.1. The new Union Bag and Paper Mill at Savannah in 1937. Photo by
Margaret Bourke-White. Courtesy of LIFE Picture Collection, Getty Images.

ently are on the threshold of discoveries which will incalculably broaden the
use of products common to our section. The South, especially our own immediate territory, is recognized as a coming industrial empire. A new world seems
to be opening before us. Savannah must be prepared to enter and possess it."[33]
Savannah's Charles Holmes Herty, who played an important role in promoting the virtues of southern pine during the 1920s and 1930s, declared in 1933
that "some day, in the not far distant future, King Cotton is going to be replaced by King Pulp."[34]

   And so it came to be. By the end of 1947, slightly more than a decade after Union Bag opened its mill, Savannah's last cotton compress had been dis-
mantled. King Cotton, which had shaped the fortunes of the city for so long,
had been replaced by the pine tree as the new staple of regional economic development. As a *New York Times* reporter put it: "The industrializing of the
New South is being dramatically illustrated in Savannah, as cotton is no longer
brought here and the old river and wharves support a new business that still
draws upon the countryside and the farmer. The cotton farmer has been suc-
ceeded by the tree farmer in a large section of the South. The pine tree has become the new cash crop."[35]

THE BIG COOK

Turning these pine trees into paper on an industrial scale was no small task. As noted, the cost advantages of the new southern mills were driven largely by economies of speed and scale. These were some of the biggest and fastest pulp and papermaking complexes in the world, with huge appetites for water and raw materials. Given the very large investments in fixed capital they embodied, they operated under an imperative to maintain velocity of throughput. This created strong incentives for vertical integration. Most southern pulp and paper mills thus owned or had access to large areas of timberlands, and most of them combined pulp and paper production into a single industrial complex: raw logs entered at one end of the mill via truck, rail, or barge, and finished paper products left at the other.[36] In between, the logs were processed into wood chips, cooked in huge "digesters," and turned into pulp. The pulp was then washed and sometimes bleached before being made into paper.

For these new mills, speed was everything. Like their counterparts throughout the South, managers and technicians at Union Bag's new Savannah mill worked continually to reduce the time it took to transform timber into paper bags. On the basis of various process refinements and a vertically integrated production structure, the company soon achieved one of the fastest rates of throughput in the industry. According to a *Fortune* magazine profile written shortly after the Savannah mill opened, "Union's superior speed means that at top tempo a log leaving the storage yard is converted into finished paper within twelve hours. The process goes on for twenty-four hours of the day. The paper is then taken to the bag factories. Every second of the working day, Union makes 480 bags—28,000,000 bags per day."[37]

At the center of this process was a voracious industrial metabolism working constantly to turn trees into paper. And of all the raw materials used in this process, none was more important than water. Huge volumes of high-quality water mixed with chemicals were needed to cook and digest the wood chips in order to separate the cellulose from the lignins or natural glues that give wood its strength.[38] The resulting pulp was then washed, often multiple times, and sometimes bleached before being spread out over the thin wire net of the Fourdrinier paper machines and run through a series of rollers and dryers in order to press the fibers together into uniform sheets of paper.[39] Unlike the other materials used in papermaking, there was no substitute for water. While a modern pulp and paper complex could use various sources of fiber, energy, and chemicals, it could not survive without access to plentiful clean water.

Charles Herty and the Savannah Pulp and Paper Laboratory

Over a long career, Charles Herty (1867–1938), an internationally recognized chemist, revolutionized the southern forest products industry not once but twice. In the early years of the twentieth century he left teaching chemistry at the University of Georgia (where he had also organized the school's first football team) and accepted a position with the U.S. Bureau of Forestry. In an effort to preserve the rapidly dying turpentine industry of his native region, he devised and patented a workable and inexpensive cup-and-gutter system of gum collection. Besides producing better-quality turpentine in greater quantities, Herty's method extended the productive life of the trees and made them usable at maturity as saw timber. By the late 1920s, some form of his cup-and-gutter system was employed throughout the turpentine region of the South.

Herty subsequently taught chemistry at the University of North Carolina, served as president of the American Chemical Association, and acted as a chemical consultant to universities, trade associations, municipalities, and private firms. He became an advisor to the City of Savannah's Industrial Committee, a body charged with developing new industry based on raw materials available in Georgia, and it was in this role that Herty envisioned the development in the South of a white paper and newsprint industry, something then restricted to the northern states and to Canada. The northern industry used spruce, not pine, for pulpwood, insisting that its high resin content rendered pine unusable for technical and economic reasons. Herty disagreed, convinced that money, research, and determination could remove whatever obstacles pine pulp might present. With the plantation South in decline, Herty hoped to convert the region's rapidly regenerating "second forest" into raw materials for a modern pulp and paper industry.

Herty secured funding for an experimental pulp and paper laboratory where he could test his theories regarding the substitution of cheap, fast-growing southern pine for expensive, slow-growing northern spruce in the manufacture of newsprint. By the late summer of 1931, he managed to secure an appropriation from the Georgia legislature, a matching grant from the Chemical Foundation, and a facility and free power from the City of Savannah to house what was dubbed the Savannah Pulp and Paper Laboratory. There Herty spent the next few years answering the technical questions that had to be answered before any manufacturer would consider investing the $4 million to $5 million necessary to build the South's first newsprint mill. In this jointly funded research facility, Herty perfected a new process for making pine into the pulp that would become paper, using acidic sulfite solutions to digest the wood, remove impurities, and increase the effectiveness of bleaching agents.

Charles Herty (seated, fourth from left) and laboratory staff.
Courtesy of Georgia Archives, Vanishing Georgia Collection, ctm033.

Shortly after Herty's death in 1938, Southland Mills Inc., the first southern newsprint mill, broke ground in Herty, Texas. By 1940, fifteen pulp and paper mills had appeared in the southern United States—including the Union Bag and Paper mill in Savannah, for a long time the largest pulp and paper complex in the world—simultaneously pumping badly needed dollars into the South's economy while creating a new set of environmental problems associated with water extraction and pollution. Across the twentieth century, the pulp and paper industry that Herty's innovations made possible transformed coastal Georgia and its timber hinterland.

Adapted from "Charles Herty," *New Georgia Encyclopedia*, and *Crusading for Chemistry: The Professional Career of Charles Holmes Herty*, both by Germaine Reed.

FIGURE 8.2. Diffusers at Union Bag's Savannah mill were used to wash the
pulp before making it into paper. Photo by Margaret Bourke-White.
Courtesy of LIFE Picture Collection, Getty Images.

Not surprisingly, the availability of high-quality groundwater was one of
the reasons why coastal Georgia was so attractive to pulp and paper firms.
Other than the cost of pumping, groundwater from the Floridan Aquifer was
essentially free.[40] There was no need to pay for the water or for any sort of pre-
treatment, and there was plenty of it.

As these new southern mills expanded, their water demands soared.
Groundwater withdrawals at Union Bag's Savannah mill increased by almost
700 percent during its first twenty years of operation.[41] Throughout the second half of the twentieth century, this mill was the largest pulp and paper complex in the world, producing roughly a fifth of all the brown paper bags used
in the United States.[42] Few consumers, of course, likely ever stopped to think
about the water used to make those bags, and most people were wholly unaware of the fundamental importance of water in making paper. Like so many
resources underwriting the growth of mass consumption in postwar America,
the role of the Floridan Aquifer was largely hidden.

SEEING GROUNDWATER

One of the great challenges associated with groundwater—its use and management—has been its invisibility. Unlike surface water, deep aquifers are difficult to map and understand. As a result, the science of groundwater lagged far behind basic understandings of surface water systems. In fact, it was not until the late twentieth century that scientists developed a firm understanding of the extent and functioning of major regional aquifers such as the Floridan. The inability to visualize and represent such aquifers and their properties surely contributed to their overuse and to the challenges of regulation.[43]

As the science of groundwater hydrology advanced, however, particularly in recent decades with the development of new computer simulation techniques, the improved ability to "see" groundwater has provided a stronger foundation for regulation. Understanding the struggles over groundwater use in coastal Georgia over the last century thus requires some appreciation for how the underlying science has changed and how this has informed new understandings of the resource and a possible basis for new management approaches.

The modern science of groundwater hydrology dates to the middle of the nineteenth century and is often traced to the work of Henry Darcy, a French hydraulic engineer tasked with developing a public water supply for his native city of Dijon.[44] In 1856 Darcy published a report on the city's "public fountains."[45] Buried in one of the appendices to his 680-page report was a simple equation, based on Darcy's field and laboratory observations, intended to capture the basic mechanics of groundwater flow through porous media. Darcy's law, as it has come to be known, has been hailed by succeeding generations of scientists and historians as the foundation for a quantitative understanding of groundwater flow.[46] This new way of seeing groundwater—of visualizing its movement through underground aquifers—would have far-reaching and profound implications for future efforts to map and understand the dynamics of groundwater around the world.

For much of the rest of the nineteenth century, groundwater science (or what was sometimes referred to as hydrogeology) remained a predominantly European enterprise.[47] Scientists across the continent worked with and elaborated on Darcy's research, developing a series of equations and associated concepts to characterize various types of aquifers and their flow.[48] By the end of the century, American scientists working with the recently established U.S. Geological Survey (USGS) began to play a more prominent role, particularly in the effort to understand regional aquifer systems.[49] This coincided with, and was partly driven by, the effort to open up the the arid regions of the western United States to development.[50] Under the leadership of Oscar Meinzer, chief of the USGS groundwater branch from 1912 to 1946, government scientists significantly advanced the field of groundwater hydrology and developed a more systematic approach to regional hydrogeology and the characterization of large aquifers.[51]

Efforts to map and characterize the aquifers in the southeastern United States proceeded in tandem with these efforts, with the USGS sponsoring many of the major scientific reports on the Floridan and other regional aquifers. In 1936, for example, USGS scientist Victor Timothy Stringfield first identified a portion of a large artesian aquifer in Florida.[52] Eight years later, M. A. Warren of the Georgia Geological Survey discovered an extension of the aquifer in southern Georgia.[53] And in 1955, Garald Parker and his USGS colleagues recognized that the various carbonate formations supporting the many artesian wells in Florida were functioning as a single unit, which they named the Floridan Aquifer.[54]

By the mid-1960s, a broader regional conception of the aquifer system was taking shape.[55] Over the next two decades, with the advent of computers and simulation models, scientists were able to represent the multi-state extent of the aquifer and its various formations with much greater precision. This led to the first detailed hydrogeological description of the aquifer throughout the four-state area of Florida, Alabama, Georgia, and South Carolina in 1986 and the first reference to a single "Floridan aquifer system," divided into an upper and a lower Floridan Aquifer.[56] Based on this new characterization, the first regional model of the entire Floridan Aquifer system was developed in 1988.[57] This research in turn provided the basis for the first maps of the cones of depression under areas of high pumping, powerfully representing the impact of development on the aquifer that fed directly into growing concerns about overpumping and saltwater encroachment.[58]

Since the late 1980s, these models and simulations have provided the framework for understanding the aquifer, stimulating further research on the aquifer and the threat of saltwater intrusion.[59] In 2010, based on observations and results from new wells, USGS scientists put forth a revised hydrogeologic framework for the northern coastal area of Georgia and adjacent parts of South Carolina. This framework was developed in part to investigate alternatives to ongoing use of the Upper Floridan Aquifer in the face of saltwater encroachment. The new research showed that the Lower Floridan Aquifer was more extensive in the area than previously assumed, but it also suggested that the Upper and Lower Aquifers were more interconnected than past mod-

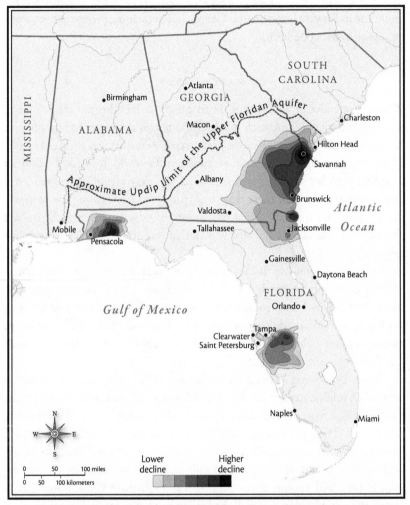

MAP 8.3. Cones of Depression Formed in the Floridan Aquifer
Note: This maps shows cones of depression formed in the Florida under areas of high pumping. Such depressions increase the risk of salt-water intrusion in outlying areas.
Source: Adapted from Peter W. Bush and Richard H. Johnston, *Ground-Water Hydraulics, Regional Flow, and Ground-Water Development of the Floridan Aquifer System in Florida and in parts of Georgia, South Carolina, and Alabama*, U.S. Geological Survey Professional Paper 1403-C (Washington, D.C.: GPO, 1988), plate 6.

els indicated.[60] The implications raised a host of questions about whether the Lower Floridan could indeed provide an alternative source of groundwater for pumping in Savannah and coastal Georgia given ongoing problems with over-pumping in the upper unit.

WATER LORDS

When Savannah city workers dug the first deep wells in the mid-1880s, no one knew that the city, along with much of the rest of the lower coastal plain of Georgia, South Carolina, Florida, and eastern Alabama, was sitting atop one of the most prolific groundwater resources in the world. It would be another hundred years before the Floridan Aquifer was fully identified and named.[61] But everyone knew that these deep wells produced free-flowing, artesian water in significant quantities, that the bounty of what lay beneath the surface was there for the taking, and that was all that was needed for development to proceed.[62]

As Savannah grew, so did its groundwater withdrawals. In the late 1880s, the city drew approximately seven million gallons a day from the aquifer. By 1910, total use had risen to about ten million gallons per day, and by 1935, on the eve of Union Bag's arrival, the city's daily withdrawal had doubled to twenty million gallons. Consequently, the static water level in the city's wells had fallen by some thirty feet.

When Union Bag opened its Savannah mill in 1936, it began pumping around 3.5 million gallons per day. The following year, daily withdrawals at the mill increased to more than seven million gallons a day, as much as the entire city had used fifty years earlier. Five years later, in 1942, the mill was pumping close to eighteen million gallons per day. And by 1955 the mill's daily pumping had climbed to more than twenty-six million gallons—accounting for 40 percent of total withdrawals in the Savannah and Chatham County area.[63] As a result, the water level in area wells had fallen to seventy feet below sea level—a 110-foot drop from the 1880s—creating a cone of depression in the water table under Savannah that reversed the natural eastward flow of the aquifer and began drawing water in from outlying areas.[64]

Not surprisingly, some people began to express concern. In 1955, one observer noted that "Savannah and Chatham County are in a transition or borderline period. For over two centuries, groundwater has been in plentiful supply. We are now crossing over, if we have not already crossed over into, a new, long-term era in which there will be little if any net supply of groundwater in the Ocala formation available for further exploitation, and where a cutback may even be found necessary."[65] The major concern was that the hydraulic gradient created by the cone of depression under Savannah would draw saltwater into the aquifer from coastal areas and contaminate the resource. This was not the first time that such concerns had been raised. As early as 1938, Arthur J. Funk, a Savannah High School physics teacher, who would go on to represent Savannah in the Georgia legislature from 1960 to 1970, warned of the possibility that increased pumping in the area could lead to saltwater intrusion in the aquifer.[66] In 1944, moreover, a report from the Georgia Geological Survey pointed to the potential problems associated with overpumping and argued that twenty-five million gallons per day was the maximum pumping level that could be sustained at Savannah to avoid saline intrusion.[67] At the time, withdrawals were close to double that amount.

Except for the occasional newspaper article, however, there was very little discussion of the groundwater situation for the next two decades. Meanwhile, pumping rates continued to rise. By the late 1950s, there was evidence of saltwater intrusion in Savannah and Brunswick.[68] In 1964, USGS scientists concluded on the basis of new data and Savannah's then-current pumpage rate of sixty-two million gallons per day that saltwater intrusion would begin to significantly affect outlying areas in less than a hundred years. In order to arrest this progression, they urged that the maximum rate of groundwater pumpage in Savannah be limited to forty million gallons per day. Reversing the trend, of course, would require that pumping be reduced significantly below this level.[69]

By 1970, however, pumping in the Savannah area had risen to almost seventy million gallons per day, forcing water levels down to 125 feet below sea level.[70] People were beginning to express alarm. According to Albert N. Cameron of the USGS, "We don't know how much more this aquifer can stand. . . . Using all available data, it is our conclusion that 40 million gallons per day is the maximum amount of water that can be pumped indefinitely from the aquifer, with the present well layout, without lateral movement of salt water from the natural discharge or leakage area." Rock Howard of the Georgia Water Quality Control Board was somewhat more direct: "The Ocala limestone is possibly the largest aquifer in the world," he noted. "But it is a fragile thing, in a certain sense, and a rare thing that ought to be protected." As for the prospect of saltwater intrusion, Howard noted, "It might not happen tomorrow and maybe not for fifty years, but sure as the world it's coming."[71] Not surprisingly, Union Camp had a different perspective on the situation. In spite of mounting evidence of saltwater encroachment in outlying coastal areas such as Hilton Head Island, John E. Ray III, the company's executive vice president, stated that the aquifer had "not even been strained."[72]

The issue was soon thrust onto the national stage when a group of young lawyers and college graduates descended on Savannah in the summer of 1970 to research the connection between industry and the "environmental crisis" in the region. Affiliated with Ralph Nader (and referred to by some in the community as "Nader's Raiders"), the group was led by James Fallows. Much of their attention was directed at the Union Camp mill, by far the largest source of environmental disruption in the area. Along with air and water pollution, groundwater depletion occupied an important part of the group's investigation. In the resulting book, provocatively titled *The Water Lords*, Fallows did not pull any punches in his criticisms of Union Camp. "Of all the abuses it heaps on Savannah," he argued, "Union Camp's arrogant assumption that it can use unlimited amounts of ground water is probably the worst."[73] To remedy the problem, Fallows called for new laws that would force local industries to take a more prudent approach to groundwater use.[74]

The Water Lords heightened concerns about overpumping of groundwater, and it put the environmental crisis in Savannah in a larger, national context. Evoking images of an unaccountable corporation laying waste to public resources, the book provided a searing indictment of the region's wholesale embrace of industrial development at the expense of the environment. In doing so, it tapped into and likely helped to motivate a nascent environmental politics in the region.[75]

Within a year, the Georgia legislature began to debate new regulations to govern groundwater use.[76] The resulting Groundwater Use Act of 1972 established a permitting system for groundwater withdrawals, with a focus on areas of excessive use such as Savannah.[77] But the act, discussed in more detail below, effectively exempted existing uses such as Union Camp's and did nothing to slow or reduce the continued growth of pumping in the area. At the time, there were heated debates regarding when saltwater would reach Savannah if current pumping rates continued, with estimates ranging from decades to centuries.[78] Much of the disagreement stemmed from the fact that the aquifer still had not been fully mapped and modeled. No one actually knew the full extent and nature of the aquifer and its response to ongoing groundwater withdrawals.

Notwithstanding the 1972 legislation and the requirement that large users secure permits, political and business leaders took a strong antiregulatory stance that called for little more than increased study of the problem. Union Camp attorney Thomas Dillon, for example, stated that his company was "of the opinion that present [well] monitoring [by the state] should be continued and perhaps expanded, with action being taken only when and if a problem does develop." Jim Piette, Union Camp's executive vice president, made the point more directly: "We are not in favor of more regulation. We are in favor of analyzing problems." Yet Piette was quick to emphasize that new development could create problems in the future: "We would suggest to anyone coming in here, 'Don't overburden the ground water supply.' . . . It can be abused and probably destroyed." Georgia's governor at the time, George Busbee, who would later join Union Camp's board of directors, fully supported the company's position: "We have an excellent ground water program now. Stronger regulations are unnecessary at this time and could have an adverse effect on industrial development." For regulators such as Leon Ledbetter, director of Georgia's Environmental Protection Division, the implications were clear: "We have no legal authority to preserve ground water for the future. . . Georgia's elected officials do not support the concept of management of groundwater use, only management of misuse."[79]

Despite the flurry of interest in the groundwater issue during the early 1970s, it was largely eclipsed by more pressing concerns with air and water pollution, much of which was created by local pulp and paper mills.[80] But the groundwater issue resurfaced again in the late 1980s, as new data and improved modeling of the aquifer's hydrogeology suggested an increased threat of saltwater encroachment. Making use of the first simulations of the aquifer and the new maps showing the cones of depression that had formed under Savannah and other areas of high pumping, environmental advocates, regulators, and policy makers all began to give the issue more attention. As evidence of saltwater intrusion under Hilton Head Island mounted, moreover, the State of South Carolina threatened to sue the State of Georgia, contending that Georgia's failure to control overpumping in Savannah and Chatham County was destroying the integrity of the aquifer under Hilton Head and other areas of coastal South Carolina.[81] This proved to be an important catalyst for putting the issue back on the policy agenda. As Freddy Vang, executive director of South Carolina's Water Resources Commission, put it: "Either we sit down and solve it in a scientific manner, or we go to the lawyers."[82] In response, Georgia officials scrambled to develop what they referred to as an "interim strategy" to manage the resource over the next ten years as a prelude to a long-term solution.

To support this effort, the USGS, in cooperation with the Chatham County–Savannah Metropolitan Planning Commission, conducted yet another study of the aquifer and its long-term water-supply potential. The results simply confirmed what everyone already knew: there was a deep cone of depression under Savannah (extending some one hundred feet below sea level) that was causing saltwater encroachment at the northern end of Hilton Head Island. Without any specific recommendations and with no mention of major industrial water users, the report concluded, in lackluster fashion, that "the potential of the Upper Floridan Aquifer to supply additional water in the Savannah area is limited under present (1985) hydrologic conditions."[83]

Georgia's Environmental Protection Division (EPD) spent the next five years developing a draft interim strategy to manage the resource in the twenty-four-county area of southern Georgia. In early 1996, EPD submitted a proposal to stakeholders that contained the first "reduced use" scenario calling for a cut in water use, by some twelve million gallons per day.[84] EPD then convened a series of public meetings and eventually received more than four hundred comments on the proposal, many claiming that the proposed reductions would inhibit future economic development in the region. In response, EPD retained several economists from Georgia State University in Atlanta to develop an alternative "non-regulatory" strategy that would be "conducive to economic development." This proposal, which was released in October 1996, recommended that EPD pursue a "rational use" strategy with respect to the aquifer. Noting that the various groundwater models used by state planners indicated that pumping would have to be reduced to almost nothing in order to stop the progression of saltwater into the aquifer, the Georgia State economists argued that pumping should continue or even be expanded until the aquifer salted out. In their view, since any proposed reduction (less than complete cessation) would only delay the onset of contamination, users should simply be charged a fee for pumping—the proceeds from which would go into a "groundwater replacement fund" to develop alternative sources of supply in the future.[85] Their proposal was not well received.[86]

On the other side of the political spectrum, various environmental groups called on EPD to pursue a strategy of "sustainable use"—a course of action that would effectively require reductions of sixty to sixty-five million gallons per day in the Savannah area alone (more than 85 percent of the total) in order to halt the encroachment of saltwater under Hilton Head.[87] Needless to say, the two proposals were about as far apart from each other as possible.

Taking account of the many and varied reactions to its proposal, EPD released its final interim strategy in April 1997, establishing "guidelines for groundwater actions in southeastern Georgia" through 2005, at which point a "final" long-term groundwater management strategy was to be in place. The overall objective, according to the document, was "to STOP THE INTRUSION OF SALT WATER before municipal supply wells on Hilton Head Island, South Carolina and Savannah, Georgia are contaminated, and to prevent an existing salt-water problem at Brunswick, GA from worsening." The strategy also contained new geological information indicating that under pumping conditions of the time—1985, the date to which the USGS models were calibrated— saltwater would reach the center of the cone of depression under Savannah within 120–270 years. Moreover, the report confirmed that only very substantial reductions of sixty million gallons per day or more in Savannah would halt the encroachment. "As long as there is significant pumping in southeast Georgia," the strategy concluded, "salt water intrusion is irreversible."[88]

The means identified for achieving the strategy's objectives, however, seemed woefully inadequate. In addition to water-supply planning and conservation measures in the twenty-four counties of southeastern Georgia, expanded technical investigations of saltwater intrusion, a modification of groundwater permitting, and caps on groundwater use in certain coastal counties, the only reduction called for was ten million gallons per day in Chatham County. Union Camp pledged to provide at least 6.5 million gallons of the total cutback and agreed to a reduction of its groundwater withdrawal permit to 20.1 million gallons per day by the end of 2005.[89] In return, Savannah and Chatham County agreed to double the size of their surface water treatment facility (at a cost of $50 million).

Although this effort to reduce groundwater use clearly represented a departure from past practices, it was obviously a long way from the model of sustainable use that some preferred. But EPD's interim strategy did represent a more formal and forthright recognition of the problem and signaled an effort to establish a meaningful regional planning process. At a minimum, this would provide some political cover in case South Carolina ever followed through with its threatened lawsuit. But the tough choices concerning allocation were put off for the better part of a decade.

As Georgia regulators and local stakeholders worked to develop a long-term plan for the aquifer, evidence mounted of growing saltwater encroachment under Hilton Head and Tybee Island (as well as Brunswick down the coast).[90] In 2006, Georgia's EPD released the "Coastal Georgia Water and Wastewater Permitting Plan for Managing Saltwater Intrusion." The new plan capped withdrawals in Chatham County and southern Effingham County at 2004 levels and required additional reductions of five million gallons per day starting in 2008.[91] By 2010, total municipal and industrial withdrawals in Chatham County (from both the Upper and Lower Floridan Aquifers) were around 54 million gallons per day, close to where they had been in the middle of the twentieth century but still far above what was considered necessary to halt the encroachment of saltwater.[92] The Georgia EPD also imposed a moratorium on new groundwater permits for the Upper Floridan Aquifer in high-use areas, which it then extended to withdrawals from the Lower Floridan Aquifer as evidence accumulated that the two aquifers were interconnected.[93]

The new plan thus appeared to stem groundwater withdrawals, but it was still not enough, and in 2013 South Carolina again threatened to sue Georgia to force further reductions. Georgia's Environmental Protection Division responded in 2015 with a new round of cuts in groundwater withdrawals, including a reduction of 15 million gallons per day by 2025 inside the "red zone" in Savannah and Chatham County.[94] Whether this will be enough to allow the aquifer to recover and to slow saltwater intrusion under Hilton Head and other outlying areas remains to be seen.[95]

LAWS OF DOMINION AND CAPTURE

Perhaps more than anything else, the fundamental problem regarding ground-water use in coastal Georgia over the last century has been the legal status of the resource. Up until the 1970s, there were no clear property rights to ground-water and no regulations governing its use. As in a number of other jurisdictions, groundwater use in Georgia during much of this time was subject to the common law rule of capture—a doctrine that developed in England and was sometimes known as the law of absolute ownership or dominion. Under such a regime, rights to groundwater attached to rights in overlying land. Landowners were essentially free to pump (or "capture") as much groundwater as they desired and to use it however they saw fit.[96]

In one of the few Georgia cases dealing with groundwater, the Georgia Supreme Court made clear in 1909 that the law of absolute ownership applied to all underground waters other than those moving in well-defined subsurface channels or streams.[97] As the court noted,

> The rule seems well settled that "an injury to a subterranean supply of water by lawful acts of an adjacent landowner done within his own premises is, unless the stream is well defined and its existence known or easily discernible, or unless injury is caused by malice, damnum absque injuria [loss or harm for which there is no legal remedy]." . . . The ownership of land extends indefinitely within the bowels of the earth, and the owner has the same exclusive proprietorship in the water which seeps through his soil and collects in the substrata as to that water which falls from the clouds upon the roof of his house and is collected in a cistern until the percolating water becomes a part of a well-defined stream.[98]

Needless to say, the rule of capture did not exactly promote conservation, especially for so-called common-pool resources such as groundwater. In a classic example of the tragedy of the commons, individual landowners had an incentive to extract as much groundwater as they could use, without regard for the impacts of their pumping on other landowners. In the process, they risked collectively undermining the integrity of the resource.[99]

The general lack of legal protections and remedies accorded to neighboring landowners regarding groundwater pumping stemmed in part from the general lack of knowledge regarding groundwater. As the Ohio Supreme Court put the matter in a case from 1861:

> The law recognizes no correlative rights in respect to underground waters percolating, oozing, or filtrating through the earth; and this mainly from considerations of public policy. Because the existence, origin, movement, and course of such waters, and the causes which govern and direct their movements are so secret, occult and concealed, that an attempt to administer any set of legal rules in respect to them would be involved in hopeless uncertainty, and would be, therefore, practically impossible.[100]

Similarly, a Georgia statute from 1863, which is still on the books, declared that because of the difficulty involved in understanding the nature and course of "underground streams," no action for trespass could be brought for any "supposed interference with the rights" of another.[101] Without an ability to visualize or even conceptualize the nature and extent of the resource, in other words, courts and legislatures refrained from trying to define entitlements and manage its use. Although a number of states moved away from the law of absolute ownership to embrace a doctrine of reasonable use during the late nineteenth and twentieth centuries, Georgia's groundwater law remained vague and unsettled for much of the twentieth century.[102]

But as improved understandings of groundwater revealed some of the impacts of overpumping in high-use areas such as Savannah, the legal status of the resource changed. In the 1970s, Georgia began to develop a governance regime more closely aligned with the law governing surface water use in the state, the doctrine of riparian rights, wherein the landowner was entitled to reasonable use of the resource.[103] More importantly, Georgia also established a new groundwater permitting system with passage of the Groundwater Use Act of 1972.[104] The act declared that "the general welfare and public interest require that the water resources of the State be put to beneficial use to the fullest extent to which they are capable, subject to reasonable regulation in order to conserve these resources and to provide and maintain conditions which are conducive

to the development and use of water resources."[105] The act granted authority to
EPD to regulate groundwater use in order to protect against "unreasonable adverse effects" on other users and to abate "salt-water encroachment."[106] Any person seeking to withdraw more than one hundred thousand gallons of groundwater per day was required to obtain a permit from EPD.[107] However, all users
who had been withdrawing groundwater prior to the passage of the act were
granted a permit to meet their "reasonable" needs as existed before passage of
the act, and agricultural users were exempt until 1988.[108] Further, a violation of
the act and its associated regulations was a misdemeanor, with penalties not to
exceed $1,000 and an additional $500 per day per violation.[109]

In effect, the 1972 act locked in the existing pattern of groundwater use and
turned the nebulous "reasonable use" standard into something closer to a prior
appropriation regime.[110] Put another way, for those with large withdrawals,
such as Union Camp and other pulp and paper mills, the decision to grandfather their preexisting withdrawals into new permitted withdrawals marked an
important step toward de facto property rights over those withdrawals. And
for much of the next several decades, Union Camp and other large users had
no problem getting permits for larger and larger withdrawals.

By the 1990s, six pulp and paper mills accounted for 60 percent (216 million gallons per day) of all permitted withdrawals from the Floridan Aquifer in coastal Georgia (360 million gallons per day).[111] These entitlements to
continue pumping served as important bargaining chips in deliberations over
future groundwater use and a transition to surface water. Union Camp, for
example, traded a 6.5 million gallon per day reduction in groundwater withdrawals at its Savannah mill in return for a commitment from Savannah and
Chatham County to double the size of the existing municipal surface water
treatment facility.[112]

As constraints on pumping increased, in other words, existing groundwater permits became more valuable, leading some in the local environmental
community to voice concern. In the view of Becky Shortland of the Georgia
Conservancy, "The paper companies are in a position to be water czars. . . .
We're seeing a definite shift of water rights away from the public to private interests."[113] Another local environmentalist echoed these feelings: "I am very
upset about proprietary water rights. That's a public resource, and I think the
public should have the ability to say who gets it."[114]

But groundwater had never been a public resource in Georgia. The pulp
and paper mills, along with other landowners in the region, had long been free
to pump as much groundwater as they could use. To suggest that the public
had some prior claim on the resource that was now being privatized with the

move to industrial use permits was to ignore the history of the Floridan Aquifer and the limited body of law governing its use. Even the 1972 Groundwater Protection Act's recital of a public welfare and public interest standard as the basis for its permitting regime had limited purchase in the face of the decision to grandfather existing uses and the trivial penalties available for any violations. While the act provided normative support for a more conservation-oriented approach to groundwater use, turning that into an effective and lasting program for good stewardship would take a concerted effort on the part of policymakers, industry stakeholders, and the public.

POLITICS AND GROUNDWATER IN A
WORLD OF CLIMATE CHANGE

Groundwater makes up 98 percent of the freshwater on earth that is not locked in ice sheets and glaciers. It is one of our most important and underappreciated resources. Because it is not visible, because it is so hard to see, so hard to make a part of the places where we live, we tend to take it for granted. Its invisibility leads to neglect, misuse, and waste.[115]

The groundwater crisis in coastal Georgia, as in so many other places around the world, can be viewed as a failure of regulation, a failure of governance, and a failure to value the resource in a manner that will sustain it. Underneath all of these failures, however, is a failure of politics—a failure to recognize collectively that the Floridan Aquifer is a shared resource that will surely be ruined if subjected to a relentless industrial logic of extraction for too long.

Although the politics surrounding groundwater use in southern Georgia have become more sensitive to the damage of overpumping and the need for a long-term transition to sustainable management, the challenges will likely become harder as climate change takes hold. In 1989, just as the groundwater crisis in the region was reaching its peak, the esteemed American ecologist and University of Georgia professor Eugene Odum addressed the issue with his colleague Thomas James in a short report prepared for the Georgia Water Resources Conference:

> Maintaining aquifer levels is especially urgent at this time when droughts are becoming more frequent because of global warming, and the demand for irrigation increases. Improving regulation is part but not all of the answer. Reducing current wasteful use is equally important. Large users such as paper mills should be encouraged to use more surface water, and to recycle water. Conservation of ground-water for domestic, agricultural, and

municipal use should also be stressed. Now is the time to consider various options that are both "carrot" (incentives) and "stick" (regulation), before the situation becomes really critical. Prevention is worth millions of dollars of cure. Georgia's underground water is one of its most valuable resources—more valuable in the long run, than oil.[116]

Climate change will have (and is having) a major impact on coastal Georgia and will surely change the way people in the region think about and use water. And while there is uncertainty in the climate models when it comes to regional impacts over medium-term time scales, if droughts do become more frequent or more severe or both, this will further strain the aquifer and threaten its long-term health. Sea-level rise could also accelerate the process of saltwater intrusion, creating more downward pressure on saltwater entering the aquifer and more points of entry, further changing the saltwater-freshwater interface that Mart Stewart identifies as so important in defining the Georgia coast.[117]

But one thing is certain: the days of unregulated pumping are over. The ability to see the aquifer in new and powerful ways has brought a growing recognition across multiple constituencies and users that the Floridan Aquifer is fragile. At the same time, the political influence of the pulp and paper industry has waned, and a broader environmental politics has emerged in the region, allowing new norms of stewardship and conservation to take hold. All of these will surely be important ingredients in any effort to ensure the long-term sustainability of the aquifer. Without question, the Floridan Aquifer needs more care and protection than it has been getting, but recent efforts to reduce pumping and conserve the resource show that things can change—that people can set to work trying to repair what years of destructive practices have done.

NOTES

Special thanks to Paul M. Pressly and the Ossabaw Island Foundation for the opportunity to participate in the 2016 Coastal Nature, Coastal Culture symposium. Thanks also to symposium participants for feedback and stimulating discussion, to Paul Sutter for editorial direction and suggested revisions, to Dave Owen for comments on an earlier draft, and to the Johns Hopkins University Press for permission to use several paragraphs from my 2015 book, *The Slain Wood: Papermaking and Its Environmental Consequences in the American South*.

1. Peter W. Bush and Richard H. Johnston, *Groundwater Hydraulics, Regional Flow, and Ground-Water Development of the Floridan Aquifer System in Florida and in Parts of Georgia, South Carolina, and Alabama*, U.S. Geological Survey Professional Paper 1403-C (Washington, D.C.: U.S. Geological Survey, 1988), C36.

2. See, for example, ibid., c5.

3. See Richard L. Marella and Marian P. Berndt, *Water Withdrawals and Trends from the Floridan Aquifer System in the Southeastern United States, 1950–2000*, U.S. Geological Survey 1278 (Reston, Va.: U.S. Geological Survey, 2005), 1.

4. See James E. Landmeyer and Peter A. Stone, "Radiocarbon and d13C Values Related to Ground-Water Recharge and Mixing," *Ground Water* 33, no. 2 (1995): 231–32; L. Niel Plummer, "Stable Isotope Enrichment in Paleowaters of the Southeast Atlantic Coastal Plain, United States," *Science* 262, no. 5142 (December 24, 1993): 2017.

5. See David Hurst Thomas, "Deep History of the Georgia Coast," chap. 2 of this volume.

6. See William H. Marquardt, "Shell Mounds in the Southeast: Middens, Monuments, Temple Mounds, Rings, or Works," *American Antiquity* 75, no. 3 (2010): 564–65.

7. E. R. Conant, "History of the Artesian Water Supply at Savannah, Georgia," *Journal of the American Water Works Association* 5, no. 3 (September 1918): 252, 253.

8. Ibid.

9. See S. W. McCallie, *A Preliminary Report on the Artesian Well System of Georgia*, Georgia Geological Survey Bulletin 7 (Atlanta: Franklin Printing and Publishing, 1898).

10. Bush and Johnston, *Ground-Water Hydraulics*, c50.

11. Conant, "History of the Artesian Water Supply at Savannah," 253, 259.

12. See M. A. Warren, "Artesian Water in Southeastern Georgia, with Special Reference to the Coastal Area," *Georgia Geological Survey Bulletin* 49 (1944): 80–88.

13. J. W. Stewart and H. B. Counts, "Decline of Artesian Pressures in the Coastal Plain of Georgia, Northeastern Florida, and Southeastern South Carolina," *Georgia Mineral Newsletter* 11, no. 25 (1958): 26–27.

14. Saltwater encroachment under Brunswick was vertical (upconing) rather than lateral.

15. James Fallows, *The Water Lords: Ralph Nader's Study Group Report on Industry and Environmental Crisis in Savannah, Georgia* (New York: Grossman, 1971).

16. Ga. Code Ann. §§12–5–90 to 12–5–107 (2017).

17. See Charles Seabrook, "Saltwater Contamination Studied; Ga. Firms Face Cuts in Groundwater Use," *Atlanta Journal and Constitution*, September 7, 1991.

18. See Brian Heffernan, "SC Threatens Suit if Water Deal with Georgia Isn't Reached," *Beaufort (S.C.) News*, January 18, 2013; Georgia Department of Natural Resources, Environmental Protection Division, "Georgia EPA Announces Next Phases of Coastal Groundwater Management," press release, June 24, 2015.

19. William Boyd, *The Slain Wood: Papermaking and Its Environmental Consequences in the American South* (Baltimore: Johns Hopkins University Press, 2015).

20. Howard W. Odum, *Southern Regions of the United States* (Chapel Hill: University of North Carolina Press, 1936), 293.

21. The South is hardly distinctive in this respect. Groundwater has not received

much attention from environmental historians generally. But there are notable exceptions. See, for example, John Opie, *Ogallala: Water for a Dry Land* (Lincoln: University of Nebraska Press, 1993); Paul Hirt, Annie Gustafson, and Kelli L. Larson, "The Mirage in the Valley of the Sun," *Environmental History* 13 (July 2008): 482–514. Although he is not a historian, Robert Glennon covers a fair amount of historical ground in *Water Follies: Groundwater Pumping and the Fate of America's Fresh Waters* (Washington: Island Press, 2002). With respect to water and southern environmental history, there is a small but growing body of work. See, for example, Christopher J. Manganiello, *Southern Water, Southern Power: How the Politics of Cheap Energy and Water Scarcity Shaped a Region* (Chapel Hill: University of North Carolina Press, 2015); Craig Colten, *Southern Waters: The Limits to Abundance* (Baton Rouge: Louisiana State University Press, 2014).

22. See Jack P. Oden, "Origins of the Southern Kraft Paper Industry, 1903–1930," *Mississippi Quarterly* 30, no. 4 (1977): 573–74; James I. Pikl Jr., *A History of Georgia Forestry*, Research Monograph 2 (Athens: University of Georgia Bureau of Business and Economic Research, 1966).

23. On timber famine, see Henry Clepper, *Professional Forestry in the United States* (Baltimore: Johns Hopkins University Press, 1971), 136; William Robbins, *American Forestry: A History of National, State, and Private Cooperation* (Lincoln: University of Nebraska Press, 1985), 89–90. On the specific issue of pulpwood supplies, see U.S. Department of Agriculture, *How the United States Can Meet Its Present and Future Pulpwood Requirements*, Dept. Bulletin 1241 (Washington, D.C., Government Printing Office, 1924).

24. See Pikl, *History of Georgia Forestry*, 31. For a more general treatment of industrial recruitment in the South during this period, see James C. Cobb, *The Selling of the South: The Southern Crusade for Industrial Development, 1936–1990*, 2nd ed. (Urbana: University of Illinois Press, 1993).

25. See Southern Pine Association, *Economic Condition in Southern Pine Industry* (Southern Pine Association, 1931), 88; American Institute for Economic Research, *A Report on the Future of the Paper Industry in the Southeastern United States and the Effects on Stumpage Values* (Cambridge, Mass.: American Institute for Economic Research, 1938), 69.

26. Quoted in "Bright Future for Industry," *Savannah Morning News*, October 2, 1936.

27. Thomas D. Clark, *The Greening of the South: The Recovery of Land and Forest* (Lexington: University Press of Kentucky, 1984), chap. 9.

28. For a discussion of early kraft pulp manufacture in the South, see Boyd, *Slain Wood*; Oden, *Development of the Southern Pulp and Paper Industry*; and Jack P. Oden, "Origins of the Southern Kraft Paper Industry, 1903–1930," *Mississippi Quarterly* 30, no. 4 (1977): 565–84. See also William T. Hicks, "Recent Expansion in the Southern Pulp and Paper Industry," *Southern Economic Journal* 6, no. 4 (1940): 440–43; Helen Hunter, "Innovation, Competition, and Locational Changes in the Pulp and Paper Industry: 1880–1950," *Land Economics* 31, no. 4 (1955): 314–27.

29. See Boyd, *Slain Wood*, 7.

30. See Oden, "Southern Kraft Paper Industry", 583. For a discussion of the relationships between increasing scale and locational change in the industry, see Hunter, "Innovation, Competition, and Locational Changes."

31. For specific input numbers, see *Lockwood-Post's Directory of the Pulp, Paper, and Allied Trades* (San Francisco: Miller-Freeman, 1995).

32. "New Industrial Epoch Begins," *Savannah Morning News*, October 1, 1936.

33. "Mayor Praises Savannah Spirit," *Savannah Morning News*, October 2, 1936.

34. Quoted in F. Basil Abrams, "Paper from Georgia Pines," *Atlanta Journal*, February 12, 1933.

35. John Popham, "King Cotton Is Dead in Savannah, the Most Famous of the Old South's Cotton Ports, and the Stately Pine Tree Is the New Ruler," *New York Times*, July 1, 1947.

36. See Boyd, *Slain Wood*, 116–23. See also Alfred Chandler, *The Visible Hand: The Managerial Revolution in American Business* (Cambridge Mass.: Belknap Press of Harvard University Press, 1977), 281–83.

37. "Union Bag and Paper Corp.," *Fortune* 16, no. 4 (1937): 129.

38. See Kenneth W. Britt, "Sulfite Pulping," and George E. Jackson, "Alkaline Pulping," in *Handbook of Pulp and Paper Technology*, ed. Kenneth W. Britt (New York: Reinhold, 1964), 141–65 and 166–200. See also Louis Tillotson Stevenson, *The Background and Economics of American Papermaking* (New York: Harper & Brothers, 1940), 22–26; Nancy Kane Ohanian, *The American Pulp and Paper Industry, 1900–1940: Mill Survival, Firm Structure, and Industry Relocation* (Westport, Conn.: Greenwood, 1993), 185–88; James D. Studley, *United States Pulp and Paper Industry*, U.S. Department of Commerce, Trade Promotion Series 182 (Washington, D.C.: Government Printing Office, 1938), 5–6, 27–28.

39. On the transformative role of the Fourdrinier machine, see Dard Hunter, *Papermaking: The History and Technique of an Ancient Craft* (New York: Knopf, 1947), 340–73; Judith A. McGaw, *Most Wonderful Machine: Mechanization and Social Change in Berkshire Paper Making, 1801–1885* (Princeton: Princeton University Press, 1987), 93–117; Studley, *United States Pulp and Paper Industry*, 5–6.

40. See, for example, Union Camp Corporation, "Artesian Water," Mill Technical Department Report, Savannah, Georgia, November 20, 1968, in possession of author. See also Glenn E. McLaughlin and Stefan Robock, *Why Industry Moves South: A Study of Factors Influencing the Recent Location of Manufacturing Plants in the South* (Kingsport, Tenn.: National Planning Association, 1949), 62; Calvin Hoover and B. U. Ratchford, *Economic Resources and Policies of the South* (New York: Macmillan, 1951), 232–36.

41. Stewart and Counts, "Decline of Artesian Pressures," 26.

42. See Boyd, *Slain Wood*, 228.

43. An early statement on the need for groundwater conservation in the United States pointed to this lack of knowledge as the major impediment to proper management. See Harold E. Thomas, *The Conservation of Groundwater: A Survey of The*

Present Ground-Water Situation in the United States (New York: McGraw-Hill, 1951), 10–11. See also Dave Owen, "Taking Groundwater," *Washington University Law Review* 91, no. 2 (2013): 255.

44. See, for example, Asit K. Biswas, *History of Hydrology* (Amsterdam: North-Holland Publishing, 1970), 308; Jacobus J. de Vries, "History of Groundwater Hydrology," in *The Handbook of Groundwater Engineering*, 2nd ed., ed. Jacques W. Delleur (Boca Raton: CRC Press, 2007), 1–5.

45. The English translation of the French title of the report was "The Public Fountains of the City of Dijon." See R. Allan Freeze, "Henry Darcy and the Fountains of Dijon," *Ground Water* 32 (1994): 23; Craig T. Simmons, "Henry Darcy (1803–1858): Immortalised by his Scientific Legacy," *Hydrogeology Journal* 16 (2008): 1023.

46. Biswas, *History of Hydrology*, at 308; de Vries, *History of Groundwater Hydrology*, 1–5;

47. See T. N. Narasimhan, "Hydraulic Characterization of Aquifers, Reservoir Rocks, and Soils: A History of Ideas," *Water Resources Research* 43, no. 33 (1998): 36–37.

48. Ibid.; Simmons, *Henry Darcy*, 1032–34.

49. See Narasimhan, *Hydraulic Characterization of Aquifers*, 37.

50. See T. N. Narasimhan, "Hydrogeology in North America: Past and Future," *Hydrogeology Journal* 13, no. 7 (2005): 10.

51. See de Vries, *History of Groundwater Hydrology*, 1–15. On Meinzer, see Gerald Meyer, "Oscar E. Meinzer—Father of Modern Groundwater Hydrology in the United States," *Hydrogeology Journal* 3, no. 76 (1995): 76–78; George B. Maxey, "The Meinzer Era of Hydrogeology in the United States, 1910–1940," in *Two-Hundred Years of Hydrogeology in the United States*, ed. Joseph Rosenshein et al., U.S. Geological Survey Open-File Report 86–480 (Reston, Va.: U.S. Department of the Interior, 1986), 45–50.

52. See V. T. Stringfield, *Artesian Water in the Florida Peninsula*, U.S. Geological Survey Water-Supply Paper 773-C (Washington, D.C.: Government Printing Office, 1936).

53. Warren, "Artesian Water in Southeastern Georgia."

54. See Garald G. Parker, *Water Resources of Southeastern Florida*, U.S. Geological Survey Water-Supply Paper 1255 (Washington, D.C.: Government Printing Office, 1955), 3.

55. See V. T. Stringfield, *Artesian Water in Tertiary Limestone in the Southeastern States*, Geological Survey Professional Paper 517 (Washington, D.C.: Government Printing Office, 1966).

56. See James A. Miller, *Hydrogeologic Framework of the Floridan Aquifer System in Floridan and in Parts of Georgia, Alabama, and South Carolina*, U.S. Geological Survey Professional Paper 1403-B (Washington, D.C.: Government Printing Office, 1986).

57. Bush and Johnston, "Ground-Water Hydraulics," C27–33. See also Richard H. Johnston, "Historical Development of Concepts of Regional Groundwater Flow in

the Floridan Aquifer System," in *Hydrogeological Processes in Karst Terranes: Proceedings of the International Symposium and Field Seminar at Antalya, Turkey, 7–17 October 1990*, IAHS Publication 207 (Wallingford, UK: International Association of Hydrological Sciences, 1993), 355.

58. Bush and Johnston, "Ground-Water Hydraulics," C32.

59. See, for example, W. Brian Hughes, Michael S. Crouch, and A. Drennan Park, *Hydrogeology and Saltwater Contamination of the Floridan Aquifer in Beaufort and Jasper Counties, South Carolina, S.C.*, Water Resources Commission Report 158 (Columbia: South Carolina Water Resources Commission, 1989); Reggina Garza and Richard E. Krause, *Water-Supply Potential of Major Streams and the Upper Floridan Aquifer in the Vicinity of Savannah, Georgia*, U.S. Geological Survey Open-File Report 92–629 (Washington, D.C.: Government Printing Office, 1992); Barry S. Smith, *Saltwater Movement in the Upper Floridan Aquifer Beneath Port Royal Sound, South Carolina*, U.S. Geological Survey Open-File Report 91–483 (Columbia, S.C.: U.S. Geological Survey, 1993).

60. Lester J. Williams and Harold E. Gill, *Revised Hydrogeologic Framework of the Floridan Aquifer System in the Northern Coastal Area of Georgia and Adjacent Parts of South Carolina*, USGS Scientific Investigations Report 2010–5158 (Atlanta: U.S. Geological Survey, 2010), 1–2, 36–42, 64–72.

61. During this time, the aquifer was known as the "principal artesian aquifer" and the "Ocala limestone."

62. Conant, "History of Artesian Water Supply at Savannah," 253.

63. For pumpage rates for Union Bag mill and for Savannah and Chatham County, see Stewart and Counts, "Decline of Artesian Pressures," 26–27.

64. Stewart and Counts, "Decline of Artesian Pressures," 28; H. B. Counts and E. Donsky, "Salt-Water Encroachment, Geology, and Ground-Water Resources of Savannah Area, Georgia and South Carolina: A Summary," *Georgia Mineral Newsletter* 12, no. 96 (1959): 100.

65. John M. Henderson, "Water Resources Abundant in Greater Savannah Area," *Savannah Morning News*, December 18, 1955.

66. "Pollution Danger from Sea Water," *Savannah Morning News*, August 15, 1938.

67. Warren, *Artesian Water in Southeastern Georgia*.

68. See Stewart and Counts, *Decline of Artesian Pressures*, 27–31. For a discussion of the groundwater issue in Brunswick, see Martin E. Smith and G. E. Seaburn, "Alternatives for Ground-Water Management in the Brunswick, GA Area," in *Proceedings of the 1997 Georgia Water Resources Conference*, ed. Kathryn J. Hatcher (Athens: University of Georgia, Institute of Ecology, 1997), 434–36.

69. M. J. McCollum and H. B. Counts, *Relation of Salt-Water Encroachment to the Major Aquifer Zones, Savannah area, Georgia, and South Carolina*, U.S. Geological Survey Water-Supply Paper 1613-D (Washington, D.C.: Government Printing Office, 1964). See also M. J. McCollum, "Salt-Water Movement in the Principal Artesian Aquifer of the Savannah Area, Georgia and South Carolina," *Ground Water* 2, no. 4 (1964): 4–8.

70. Figures are from Bill Carpenter, "Sitting on Water, but for How Long," *Savannah Morning News*, November 1, 1970.

71. Quoted in Bill Carpenter, "Aquifer Drain Exceeds Safe Limits", *Savannah Morning News*, July 15, 1970.

72. Quoted in Carpenter, "Sitting on Water."

73. Fallows, *Water Lords*, 121.

74. Ibid., 113–27.

75. See Boyd, *Slain Wood*, chap. 4, for a discussion of environmental politics in Savannah during the 1970s and 1980s.

76. See H. Floyd Sherrod Jr., "The Groundwater Use Act of 1972: Protection of Georgia's Groundwater Resource," *Georgia Law Review* 6 (1972): 709, 710, discussing publicity from *The Water Lords* and response by Georgia legislature.

77. See Ga. Code Ann. § 12–5–97(f); Ga. Code Ann. § 12–5–105. See also "Groundwater Use Act of 1972," *Georgia Law Review* 6 (1972): 976.

78. Fallows, *Water Lords*, used a figure of ten to fifty years, without any references, while USGS predictions from the 1960s put the number closer to four hundred years. See Sherrod Jr., "The Groundwater Use Act of 1972," 716; McCollum and Counts, *Relation of Salt-Water Encroachment to the Major Aquifer Zones*, D25.

79. Quotes from Betsy Neal, O. Kay Jackson, and Shannon Lowry, "Special Series, Ground Water: The Crisis Below," *Savannah Morning News*, reprint, October 26–31, 1980, 12, 16, 15.

80. For information on the pollution caused by Union Camp and the pulp and paper industry more broadly, see Boyd, *Slain Wood*, 149–50, 167–69, 183–89.

81. See Heffernan, "SC Threatens Suit if Water Deal with Georgia Isn't Reached."

82. Quoted in Carrie Teegardin, "The Southeastern Water Wars," *Atlanta Constitution*, June 19, 1991.

83. Garza and Krause, *Water-Supply Potential Major Streams*, 46.

84. Georgia Environmental Protection Division, *Interim Southeast Georgia Groundwater Management Strategy* (Atlanta: Georgia Department of Natural Resources, 1997). For a synopsis, see William Frechette, "Development of an Interim Strategy for Managing Salt Water Intrusion in the Upper Floridan Aquifer of Coastal Georgia," in *Proceedings of the 1997 Georgia Water Resources Conference*, ed. Kathryn J. Hatcher (Athens: University of Georgia, Institute of Ecology, 1997), 427–30.

85. Ronald G. Cummings, Peter Terrebonne, and Gabriel Valdez, *Management Principles for Ground Water with Salt-Water Intrusion: An Analysis of Alternative Policies for Georgia's Upper Floridan Aquifer*, report prepared for Georgia Environmental Protection Division (Atlanta,1996): 14–15.

86. See Jim Morekis, "Troubled Waters," *Creative Loafing Savannah*, December 28, 1996.

87. Ibid.

88. Georgia Environmental Protection Division, *Interim Strategy for Managing Salt Water Intrusion in the Upper Floridan Aquifer of Southeast Georgia* (Atlanta: Georgia Department of Natural Resources, 1997), 1 (emphasis in original), 4–5.

89. Ibid., 1–2, 11.

90. See W. F. Falls et al., *Hydrogeology, Water Quality and Saltwater Intrusion in the Upper Floridan Aquifer in the Offshore Area Near Hilton Head Island, South Carolina and Tybee Island, Georgia, 1999–2002*, U.S. Geological Survey Science Investigations Report 2005–5134 (Reston, Va.: U.S. Geological Survey, 2005); A. M. Foyle et al., "Mapping the Threat of Seawater Intrusion in a Regional Coastal Aquifer-Aquitard System in the Southeastern United States," *Environmental Geology* 43 (2002): 151–59.

91. Georgia Environmental Protection Division, *Coastal Georgia Water and Wastewater Permitting Plan for Managing Saltwater Intrusion* (Atlanta: Georgia Environmental Protection Division, 2006).

92. See Stephen J. Lawrence, *Water Use in Georgia by County for 2010 and Water-Use Trends, 1985–2010*, USGS Open-File Report 2015–1230 (Reston, Va.: U.S. Geological Survey, 2016), 72.

93. See Sarita Chourey and Mary Landers, "State Prohibits New Water Pumping on Georgia Coast," *Savannah Morning News*, May 22, 2013.

94. See Heffernan, "SC Threatens Suit if Water Deal with Georgia Isn't Reached"; Georgia Department of Natural Resources, "Georgia EPD Announces Next Phases of Coastal Groundwater Management," press release, June 24, 2015; Mary Landers, "Water Woes," *Savannah Morning News*, September 27, 2015.

95. In the meantime, new threats to the aquifer have emerged. In particular, an ongoing project managed by the U.S. Army Corps of Engineers to dredge the bottom of the Savannah River as part of an effort to expand the Savannah Harbor could exacerbate the problem of saltwater intrusion. According to some scientists, there are "paleo channels" in the river bottom that cut into the confining layer above the aquifer. If dredging disturbs these channels, it could create new pathways for saltwater contamination of the aquifer. The Army Corps of Engineers environmental impact statement for the project indicates that this a very remote possibility. U.S. Army Corps of Engineers, "Final Environmental Impact Statement for Savannah Harbor Expansion Project, Chatham County, Georgia and Jasper County, South Carolina," July 2012, 4.02.1, U.S. Army Corps of Engineers, Savannah District, http://www.sas.usace.army.mil/Missions/Civil-Works/Savannah-Harbor-Expansion/Final-Environmental-Impact-Statement.

96. A. Dan Tarlock, *Law of Water Rights and Resources* (St. Paul: Thomson Reuters, 2015), 176–80.

97. *Stoner v. Patten*, 132 Ga. 178 (1909).

98. Ibid., 897–98. See also *Saddler v. Lee*, 66 Ga. 45, 47 (1879).

99. It is worth recognizing here how groundwater use (and overuse) has helped us understand common pool resources. See, for example, John R. Wagner, "Water and the Commons Imaginary," *Current Anthropology* 53 (2012): 617. See also Barton H. Thompson Jr., "Tragically Difficult: The Obstacles to Governing the Commons," *Environmental Law* 30 (2000): 249–53, discussing groundwater overdrafting as a problem of commons management.

100. *Frazier v. Brown*, 12 Ohio St. 294, 311 (1861).

101. Ga. Code Ann. § 51–9–8 (2017). See also Joseph W. Dellapenna, "The Law of Water Allocation in the Southeastern States at the Opening of the Twenty-First Century," *University of Arkansas, Little Rock, Law Review* 25 (2002): 41. Dellapenna cites this statute as evidence of the Georgia legislature's embrace of the absolute ownership rule because of a lack of knowledge regarding how groundwater behaved.

102. See Dellapenna, "Law of Water Allocation," 67–68; Craig K. Pendergrast, "Whose Water Is It Anyway? A Survey of Georgia Law on Surface Water and Groundwater Withdrawal Rights," *Proceedings of the 1997 Georgia Water Resources Conference*, ed. Kathryn J. Hatcher (Athens: University of Georgia, Institute of Ecology, 1997), 450; Robert Clark Kates, *Georgia Water Law* (Athens: University of Georgia Institute of Government, 1969), 242.

103. Georgia's riparian rights doctrine is codified at Georgia Code Ann. §§ 85–1301 and 105–1407: "The owner of land through which nonnavigable watercourse may flow is entitled to have the water in such streams come to his land in its natural and usual flow, subject only to such detention and diminution as may be caused by a reasonable use of it by other riparian proprietors." As for judicial interpretation, see *Price v. High Shoals Manufacturing Co.* 132 Ga. 246, 248 (1909): "Every riparian owner is entitled to a reasonable use of the water in the stream.... Every such proprietor is also entitled to have the stream pass over his land according to its natural flow, subject to such disturbances, interruptions, and diminutions as may be necessary and unavoidable on account of the reasonable and proper use of it by other riparian owners.... What is a reasonable use is a question for the jury in view of all the facts in the case." See also Kates, *Georgia Water Law*, 231–32.

104. Modeled on similar laws in North and South Carolina, the legislation was signed into law by Governor Jimmy Carter on April 7, 1972. 1972 Ga. Laws 976, codified at Ga. Code Ann. §§ 12–5–90 to 12–5–107 (2017).

105. Ga. Code Ann. § 12–5–91.

106. Ga. Code Ann. § 12–5–95.

107. Ga. Code Ann. § 12–5–96. See also Julie A. Beberman, "Conversation and Natural Resources," *Georgia State University Law Review* 12 (1995): 53–54.

108. Ga. Code Ann. § 12–5–97(f); Ga. Code Ann. § 12–5–105. For discussion, see Pendergrast, "Whose Water Is It Anyway?," 447–51; Beberman, "Conservation and Natural Resources."

109. Ga. Code Ann. §§ 12–5–106 and 12–5–107.

110. "Prior appropriation" refers to a system of water rights common in the U.S. West under which the first person to appropriate water for a beneficial use secures a right to continue using that amount. These water users are accorded senior water rights and have priority over other, later users. The principle is sometimes referred to as "first in time, first in right." To be sure, the grandfathering of existing groundwater pumping under the 1972 act did not create a detailed system of senior and junior water rights depending on time of first use, but it did give priority to existing users when compared to new users and it did create a de facto property right with the per-

mits. Joseph Dellapenna refers to the permitting system as one of "regulated riparianism" because of the emphasis on reasonable use. See Dellapenna, "Georgia Water Law: How to Go Forward Now?," *Proceedings of the 2005 Georgia Water Resources Conference* (Athens: University of Georgia Institute of Ecology, 2005).

111. The six mills were Rayonier's Jesup mill (76 million gallons per day, hereafter "mgd"), Georgia-Pacific's Brunswick mill (55.5 mgd), Gilman Paper Company's St. Marys mill (40 mgd), Union Camp's Savannah mill (28.5 mgd), Interstate Paper Company's Riceboro mill (13 mgd), and Fort Howard's Rincon mill (3 mgd). The top four mills alone, which held the four largest permits, accounted for 55 percent of the total. Figures are from 1995 permit data from the Georgia EPD. The differences among the largest mills stem primarily from the type of pulping operations. Rayonier, for example, manufactures specialty pulp at its Jesup mill, and Georgia-Pacific makes bleached paper and linerboard at its Brunswick mill. Both processes are much more water-intensive than unbleached kraft pulp production.

112. More recently, the Savannah mill, which was acquired by International Paper as part of its acquisition of Union Camp in 1998, has made a series of voluntary commitments to further reduce its withdrawals.

113. Quoted in Jim Morekis, "A Mighty Thirst," *Creative Loafing Savannah*, January 18, 1997.

114. Environmentalist who prefers to remain anonymous, interview with author, July 30, 1997.

115. Dave Owen, "Taking Groundwater," *Washington University Law Review* 91 (2013): 253, 254–55, 262.

116. See R. Thomas James and Eugene P. Odum, "Trends in Groundwater Levels and Use in Georgia: 1950–1987," *Proceedings of the 1989 Georgia Water Resources Conference* (Athens: University of Georgia, Institute of Natural Resources, 1989), 69.

117. Mart Stewart, "Islands, Edges, and Globe," chapter 1 of this volume.

CHAPTER 9

The Gold Standard

Sunbelt Environmentalism and Coastal Protection

CHRISTOPHER J. MANGANIELLO

On a sunny winter morning in Atlanta, Senator Ronald Adams rose from his seat on the chamber floor beneath the Gold Dome. From the well he voiced support for "the marshlands bill" and read from Sidney Lanier's "well-known" and famous poem "The Marshes of Glynn." "These marshes were beautiful for Sidney Lanier 100 years ago," Adams said. "They are beautiful for us now. Let us save it for our children and our children's children."[1] Lanier had captured Georgia's landscape and culture in verse from the mountains ("Song of the Chattahoochee," 1877), across the piedmont and coastal plain ("Corn," 1875), and to the sea. In "The Marshes of Glynn" (1879), Lanier described a tangle of ubiquitous live oaks, marginal slivers of sandy beach, and a carpet of marsh grasses with deep roots that were flooded by the incoming tides, overflowing the marshes' "million veins." When Adams—a resident of coastal Brunswick in Glynn County—read Lanier's words, he tapped into a culture he shared with his fellow legislators, and thousands of Georgians understood what was at stake on the coast in 1970. They knew why the marshlands bill was necessary.[2]

Reid Harris—also from Brunswick—had introduced the marshlands bill to protect Georgia's coast from unplanned development. The coast and its waterscape are tidally influenced and comprise an arrangement of "outer" and "inner" barrier islands. In the roughly one hundred miles between the Savannah River and the St. Marys River, thirteen "barrier" islands line Georgia's coast. What lies between the islands and the mainland sets Georgia apart from its neighbors: an estimated 378,000 acres of tidal salt marsh—or about one-third of the East Coast's salt marsh—and 12 percent of the East Coast's freshwater tidal marsh.[3] This arrangement of water and land was the result of natural and cultural processes: the ancient flushing of soils from inland to the coast and the fluctuation of sea level on a geologic timescale, plus more recent flushing as a result of land clearing and intensive cultivation by cotton farmers since the nineteenth century. Regardless of history, this arrangement of water and land was important to Harris. His bill had narrowly cleared the state house of representatives in 1969, but languished in the senate chamber until the Coastal Marshlands Protection Act passed unanimously "amid poetry and applause" during the Georgia General Assembly's 1970 session.

Sidney Lanier provided the poetic inspiration to protect a unique waterscape, but a small circle of civic-minded Georgians built the broad coalition responsible for preserving the marsh. Why did the coast matter to these Georgians? University of Georgia professor Eugene P. Odum (1913–2002) was one voice. Odum—soon to be the globally recognized "father of modern ecology"—considered the marsh a "nutrient trap" that turned the space between the barrier islands and mainland into one of the world's most productive nurseries for shrimp, crabs, oysters, finfish, migratory birds, and other aquatic and terrestrial creatures.[4] The estuaries were said to support a $30 million commercial and sport fishery.[5] Bob Hanie, the director of a new environmentally oriented state agency and Garden Club of Georgia leader Jane Hurt Yarn emerged as respected environmental professionals who spoke for the marsh. They interpreted the coastal landscape as an aesthetic masterpiece, a place for rejuvenation, and an escape from the modern world. Those who mobilized in support of coastal wetlands were also simultaneously campaigning alongside Charles Wharton, who led a campaign to protect the Alcovy Swamp's freshwater wetlands in Georgia's piedmont from stream channelization. And there was one more voice. Representative Reid Harris (1930–2010) was aware of the dangers of strip mining and feared it would forever damage the marshlands. As a real estate lawyer, he was also dubious of claims of private ownership of the tidal marsh and its wetlands. This injected a different element—the issue of property rights—into the environmental debate in Georgia. These individuals and their motivations infused public campaigns to save Georgia's wetlands—as natural landscapes and landscapes of ruin—from sprawl and pollution.

Most of the Georgians who lobbied Senator Adams and his colleagues were not commercial fishers or steeped in the science of the marsh. But the voters knew something about the beauty and mystique of the coast's eight major islands: Cumberland, Sapelo, St. Catherines, Ossabaw, Wassaw, Jekyll, St. Simons, and Tybee. Most of Georgia's Golden Isles were owned by "a handful of America's wealthiest families," including the Carnegies (steel), Fords (automobiles), Candlers (Coca-Cola), Reynoldses (tobacco), and Nobels (Life

Savers candy), which made the islands symbols of exclusive leisure and private land conservation. In 1968, five of the largest islands were only accessible by boat and owned by private interests: Cumberland (which would become a National Park Service property in 1972), Sapelo (which the State of Georgia began acquiring in 1969), St. Catherines, Ossabaw (which the State of Georgia would purchase in 1978), and Wassaw (which would become a national wildlife refuge in 1969). The remaining three largest islands were accessible by bridges and causeways, but access remained limited by class and race. Jekyll was privately owned before it became a state park in 1948 with racially segregated motels. St. Simons was a destination for people with the means to own property, and the island was the gateway to the Sea Island Company's most exclusive and polished properties. Finally, Tybee—labeled at times Georgia's "Redneck Riviera"—was home to an eclectic community and "overcrowded Savannah Beach," often awash in the sewage of the namesake industrial city and river.[6] In short, there were specific islands, beaches, and coastal escapes for specific Georgians. In the post–World War II era, these coastal islands continued to evolve into leisure landscapes that promised sunshine, warm temperatures, and water-based outdoor recreation. Visitors and residents, regardless of science, avocation, or socioeconomic status, wanted to experience the beauty of the South's coastline.

This is a story about Georgia's coast, the origins of the Coastal Marshlands Protection Act of 1970, and the beginning of the Sunbelt's modern environmental movement. As in most environmental policy success stories, the effort to preserve coastal marshlands was a reaction to a substantial and real threat: the owners of a subsidiary of Oklahoma-based Kerr-McGee Corporation were eyeing more than seventy thousand acres of Georgia's salt marsh, barrier islands, and offshore seabed, and they had a dual vision to mine phosphate and convert thousands of acres of marsh and wetlands into dry land for homes and golf course communities. The preservation campaign involved a coalition of respected scientists who authored an environmental impact statement before the National Environmental Policy Act existed, state agency staff who challenged Georgia's economic leadership, a legislative champion who risked his career, and a grassroots army of garden club women. In the end, the marsh escaped the phosphate miners' dredge and real estate developers' bulkheads. It would be easy to reduce this collective effort to a simple battle by preservationists to protect an aesthetically pleasing waterscape using ecological arguments. But there was another deep current shaping Sunbelt environmentalism. It was equally important for the State of Georgia to support a vision of property rights that expected owners—including the state itself—to own nature

The Collapse of the Twentieth-Century Georgia Oyster Industry

Oysters have played a vital role on the Georgia coast, serving as a source of food and construction material for coastal inhabitants since prehistoric times. For thousands of years, Native Americans left countless shell middens or waste deposits along the coast, attesting to the importance of oysters in their diets. British, French, and Spanish settlers consumed oysters in significant numbers while using their shells to make tabby, a major construction material for building homes, forts, and workplaces. During the nineteenth century, Georgians used oyster shells as material for roads and footpaths, as fill for wharfs, railway embankments, and lowlands, and as a "sweetener" or fertilizer for agricultural fields.

At the end of the nineteenth century, oysters became Georgia's leading fishery as their consumption by Americans rose dramatically. In earlier times, wealthier people were the only ones who could afford to

Oysterman at Night.
Courtesy of the
Jack Leigh Gallery.

eat them, except in local harvesting areas. When production surged, consumer prices fell dramatically, and oysters became less expensive than beef, poultry, and fish. Harvesting of oyster meat increased from three hundred thousand pounds in 1880 to eight million pounds in 1908. Canneries popped up along the coast, from Brunswick and Darien to Cedar Point and Thunderbolt. One-masted sloops towed small bateaux to the oyster beds, where oysters were harvested at low tide by hand with rakes. The oyster harvesters, largely African Americans, rowed their bateaux back to the sloop and shoveled oysters onto the vessel. The larger canneries used conveyor belts with a steam wash to separate the meat from the shell, while smaller canneries relied on individuals to open each shell. In serving a national market, the canneries, large and small, provided a precarious but important means of subsistence for African American women.

In order for oyster beds to remain healthy, harvesters must return a portion of the shells to their beds so that larvae, known as spat, can attach themselves to old shells and begin their growth. For a long time, fishers and canneries ignored

this reality. Canneries found it profitable to sell the shells for coating coastal roads and driveways and for other purposes, and overfishing hastened the oysters' decline. "Oystermen" ignored the minimal regulations provided by the state, and by the 1930s the oyster industry in Georgia was in rapid decline. It would never recover.

The overharvesting of oysters and destruction of the oyster beds, coupled with the mismanagement of the fishery by the state, led to the collapse of the once-lucrative fishery. At the start of the twenty-first century, only thirty-eight hundred pounds of meat were harvested annually, the lowest level on record, but the state has since taken steps to counter the decline. In 2015, the first oyster hatchery in the state was created at the Shellfish Research Laboratory at the University of Georgia Marine Extension in Savannah. The researchers' aim is to coax wild oysters into spawning, raise the resulting spat in the protective environment of the hatchery, and then, once they reach a certain size, hand them off to commercial oyster farmers from Chatham to Camden Counties. It is a small but promising development.

RANDAL L. WALKER

---

responsibly and in the public's interest. This story, then, is about how a campaign to protect Sidney Lanier's unequaled "marshes of Glynn" set a gold standard for environmentalism in Georgia.

The campaign to protect the marsh was a formative moment for Sunbelt environmentalism. The Sunbelt's movement leaned on multiple constituencies to shape environmental awareness and citizen engagement before the nation's first Earth Day celebration on April 22, 1970. Liberals, scientists, women, students, conservationists, and journalists living in the suburbs of New York, Los Angeles, and Washington, D.C., were not the only groups steering the course of environmentalism in the 1960s and driving such landmark federal legislation of the era as the Wilderness Act (1964), the Wild and Scenic Rivers Act (1968), and the National Environmental Policy Act (1969).[7] So too were southerners.

One additional historical marker requires acknowledgment in this turbulent era of social unrest, political assassinations, and antiwar protest. How the civil rights movement may have influenced the environmental movement remains an open question. While coastal environments mattered to and provided refuge for African Americans before, during, and after the height of civil rights activism, how the mechanics and strategy of these political movements influenced each other prior to the rise of the "environmental justice movement" of the 1990s awaits further study.[8] Julian Bond, cofounder of the Student Nonviolent Coordinating Committee and longtime Georgia state legislator, believed that coastal conservation and pollution were serious issues. However, he thought "public attention given" to those issues was "the result of the so-called 'Establishment' exploiting the issue to take the heat off the civil rights movement."[9] If Bond was right, then Georgia's environmental battles may have provided a convenient distraction from the realities of white flight, black disenfranchisement, and economic inequities.

The story of coastal protection in Georgia does, however, fit within the context of a much larger environmental movement in the United States, and it is an example—not unlike the contemporaneous campaigns to stop the Cross Florida Barge Canal and save the Everglades—of how the national movement played out in the South.[10] Environmental activism in Georgia was geographically decentralized, produced new professional institutions, and had deep roots in the countryside and small cities within hunting, fishing, and farming communities. The fight to save the marsh was as much bottom-up as it was top-down, attracted statewide attention, and hinged on an assumption that the state owned the tidal marsh. In the end, a statewide, nonpartisan coalition of wealthy white landowners, environmental scientists, suburban women, conservative southern politicians, sportsmen, countercultural activists, and others came together to protect Georgia from pollution and sprawl. They started on the coast in the state's iconic marsh, and together they established a new standard for coalition building and community engagement to protect *all* of Georgia's air, land, water, and cultural resources.

THREATS TO THE COAST

In the mid-1960s, threats to the Georgia coast came from multiple sources. Untreated municipal and industrial waste threatened commercial fisheries that had sustained coastal people for generations, including the first St. Catherines Islanders. Georgia's oyster harvest fell from more than eight million pounds in 1908 to fewer than two hundred thousand pounds in 1966. The crab catch fell 50 percent between 1960 and 1966.[11] Tybee Island, site of Georgia's most easily accessible public beach, had degenerated in proportion to the rise of industrial development along the Savannah River in the age before the Clean Water Act (1972). By the mid-1960s, kraft pulp and paper mills, such as those of Union Camp and Continental Can, and chemical operations, such as that of American Cyanamid, were dumping millions of gallons of wastewater into the river each day. This joined the untreated sewage of over one hundred thousand residents because the City of Savannah lacked a sewage treatment plant before 1972. Tybee's "disagreeable smell" was well known, and its beach received by far the lowest scores among a survey of visitors' opinions of the quality of Savannah attractions.[12]

The greatest threat came from developers. In the early 1950s, highway planners in Glynn County declared, "The Rip van Winkle era of Coastal Georgia must pass." It was time, they believed, for a highway down the coast, with causeways to each barrier island, to transform "wild acreage" into subdivisions. These roads would open "Georgia's Golden Coast" to a new wave of "gold miners." Prosperity would follow.[13] In 1965, State Highway Department planners submitted a proposal for an island-hopping "scenic" highway connecting Tybee, Wassaw, Ossabaw, St. Catherines, and Jekyll islands, and running parallel with Interstate 95, which was already under construction on the mainland.[14] Federal investment in the interstate system made coastal development possible as much as interstate construction made the rise of suburbia possible. And Georgia real estate developers were eager to mimic the successes on Charles E. Fraser's Hilton Head Island, South Carolina, and Marco Island, Florida, which seemed to instantly attract tourists and increase the tax base. These land use decisions had drastic ecological implications, not to mention social consequences for poor, minority, and elderly property owners who lost their land to condemnation or who in the future would not benefit from county services but would face rising property taxes.[15]

For many Georgians, the coast seemed to face a wide range of "predators," as described by Atlanta author Betsy Fancher: "foreign chemical manufacturers . . . developers who now have whole recreation cities on the drawing boards; and the back-country politicians who would squander this irrecover-able legacy" for "nightclubs and hamburger stands, filling stations and memo-rial parks."[16] Eugene Odum agreed, using hyperbole when he told a "conserva-tion teach-in" audience: "We're being invaded—the carpet baggers are coming back . . . and we're not prepared [to manage the associated development and environmental impacts]."[17] For Georgians who appreciated the marsh, sandy beaches, waterways, and fisheries, there was much at stake. The coast faced the same challenges of pollution and sprawl evident elsewhere in the country, and it needed protection and voices to speak for it.

AN ORGANIZED ENVIRONMENTAL MOVEMENT IN GEORGIA

The effort to save Georgia's coast and barrier islands from reckless "progress" emerged gradually in the mid-1960s. While many of the key players lived and worked in Atlanta, they relied on decentralized statewide networks of friends and colleagues to inform their thinking and get things done. Addition-ally, new statewide institutions—in government and the nonprofit sector—emerged and cultivated professional staff to identify and respond to environ-mental challenges.

One newcomer to environmentalism was Bob Hanie. In June 1961, the young Georgia native stepped off a plane to begin a new job in East Africa. Robert Edward Hanie (1937–95) was a fifth-generation Georgian, son of a dam-building engineer and Civil War buff. With a freshly minted master's degree in history from the University of Richmond, he was about to begin a two-year stint teaching geology, geography, art, and history at a school on the slopes of Mount Kilimanjaro. His first letter home remarked on the fra-grances, lush wildlife, and interracial exchanges evident in East Africa, the likes of which he had not experienced in Georgia.[18] Hanie became intoxicated by the African cultures and landscapes, and he studied herds of thousands of ze-bras, the flight patterns of Russian cranes, the seasonal habits of ants, and the native peoples' intense and personal interactions with nature. Never at a loss of words and prone to aggrandizement, he became more and more aware of what he described to his mother as the "artificial life with artificial stimulations, ar-tificial responses, and artificial people" that had characterized his experiences in the United States.[19] Although young people in similar situations might have responded to postcolonial Africa likewise, Hanie clearly was highly attuned to his changing awareness of the natural and spiritual world.

When Hanie returned to Georgia in 1963, he was immediately struck by the differences from where he had been in East Africa, including the ubiquity of pollution, violence, and limits of racial exchanges. In contrast to the "sweet smell of life" in Africa, he found a "sensory leukemia" and what seemed to be "the bleeding corpus of a sick nation."[20] While Hanie considered the United States sick in comparison to Africa, he had contracted hepatitis while abroad. His plans to pursue a doctorate in history at Duke University were put on hold because of his lingering illness, and he returned home to teach at a local high school.

Hanie's return to Atlanta coincided with the rise of the modern environmental movement and professionalism in Georgia. James Mackay (1919–2004), then a congressman serving suburban Atlanta's Decatur community, launched a series of constituent meetings labeled "Panels for Progress." Hanie and Mackay connected and together decided to move beyond the highly decentralized national groups like the Audubon Society (founded in 1905) and National Wildlife Federation (1935). Mackay did not envision a politically engaged organization like the Sierra Club (1892) where "archdruid" David Brower's direct advocacy to save the Colorado River from dams cost the nonprofit organization its Internal Revenue Service tax-free status in 1966. And Mackay later expressed lack of interest in using lawsuits to resolve environmental problems as the Environmental Defense Fund (1966) did.[21] While Georgia's hook and bullet crowd—through the Georgia Wildlife Federation (1935) and Izaak Walton League (1954)—was central to the rise of a modern environmental movement in the state, Mackay envisioned something different. He was inspired by another example—the Western Pennsylvania Conservancy (1932)—to establish a statewide organization that addressed more than fish, birds, or single issues and that might acquire property for conservation. Mackay's new statewide organization, in Hanie's typically embroidered wording, would seek to "understand and guard the total environment."[22] Mackay obtained a grant from the national office of the Nature Conservancy (1951) to fund a six-month salary for Hanie to get the new organization, the Georgia Conservancy, up, running, and registered as a nonprofit in 1967.[23] In an article that introduced the group's first and only employee to fledgling members of the Georgia Conservancy, Mackay astutely described Hanie: "If you ever want to see someone who is really on fire about something, that's Bob Hanie."[24] Hanie organized the group's first annual meeting in 1967 and started monthly awareness-raising excursions to unique areas such as the undammed Chattooga River before it was designated a national wild and scenic river and Panola Mountain before the granite outcrop became a state park.[25]

The early work of the Georgia Conservancy coincided with the formative

months of a new state agency, the Georgia Natural Areas Council. Beginning
in 1961, Charles Wharton (1924–2004), a prominent naturalist and professor of biology at Georgia State College, demonstrated that many "splendid areas" in Georgia had recently been destroyed. While the state already managed
parks and the federal government protected national forests, Wharton urged
the state government to more actively protect its valuable natural areas, and he
provided evidence that other states had done so. State leaders, including two
future governors—Jimmy Carter and Zell Miller—embraced Wharton's idea,
and they toured other states to see how their governments identified and managed natural areas. Convinced that many private landowners felt no obligation
to protect valuable natural areas and would not do so on their own, Wharton
and his allies believed that the state had a responsibility to create an inventory
of unique areas, recommend private properties for acquisition, and work with
landowners to conserve them.[26] In 1966, Representative Robert H. Farrar, a
Decatur resident and second-generation member of a coastal hunting and
fishing club along the Altamaha River, sponsored legislation drafted by Wharton to establish a new state agency, the Georgia Natural Areas Council, to ac-
complish these tasks and advise state leaders and legislators on environmental
matters.[27]

The council's advisory board—appointees who included the directors of
four state agencies plus four academics from state and private colleges and
universities—defined the council's mission and found a leader for the organization. Many of the board members were already familiar with Hanie,
and Wharton argued at the council's first board meeting that a doctorate in
ecology was not essential for the job. He suggested that someone like Bob
Hanie—a twenty-nine-year-old with a master's degree in history—could be in
charge. Hanie beat out the other finalist. With an annual salary of nine thousand dollars, a secretary, and an empty office, Hanie began work in September
1967 after his contract with the Georgia Conservancy ran out. Launching a
new government agency without a blueprint, Hanie had significant freedom.
To get started, he formed alliances with county foresters, county soil conservation district representatives, members of regional planning commissions,
and professors of the natural sciences to help him identify archaeological sites,
stands of important trees, scenic rivers, wetlands, and other "natural areas" of
Georgia that deserved attention and protection—for example, "river swamp,"
"beach and dune communities," and "salt marsh." The council and the Georgia
Conservancy provided critical institutional capacity for the state's emerging
environmental movement.[28]

As he traveled the state building relationships, perhaps the most powerful and influential contact Hanie made was with Jane Hurt Yarn (1924–95). Yarn emerged from Atlanta's garden club culture to become one of the state's leading environmental activists and later President Carter's key environmental advisor. Ensuing debates over the fate of Cumberland Island's proposed development, Harris's marshlands bill, and metropolitan air and water pollution issues prompted influential garden club members in Atlanta like Yarn to speak for the environment. Like Hanie, Yarn's passion for environmental issues had roots in East Africa: she had witnessed British efforts to conserve wildlife and habitats in Kenya. Unlike Hanie, she had substantial personal wealth, and as the wife of a successful plastic surgeon (Charles Yarn) she had access to many of Atlanta's leaders. If Hanie was somewhat of a countercultural visionary, Yarn was a strategically minded high-society type with a thick address book. Like many women of her era, her social network revolved around garden clubs, but atypically she thought these organizations abounded with women whose talents were being "wasted."[29] Through the Habersham Garden Club, a suburban Atlanta group, Yarn created an "Emergency Committee" that devoted every meeting on its 1968–69 calendar to environmental issues. The clubwomen read Stewart Udall's *Quiet Crisis*—which offered a critical interpretation of the nation's booming post-1945 economic success juxtaposed with descriptions of "vanishing beauty" and environmental degradation.[30] They also studied strip mining and investigated the work of "destructive government agencies" such as the Soil Conservation Service and its channelization of streams and wetlands throughout the state (and nation) to improve drainage and reduce flooding.[31] Yarn also joined the Nature Conservancy's board in 1969. Then, in 1970, after internal conflict within the Georgia Conservancy over advocacy strategy, donor relations, and tax-exempt status, she established Save Our Vital Environment (SAVE) as the first dedicated "environmental lobbying organization in the state." When Yarn met Hanie early in 1968 to discuss the growing threats to Georgia's marsh, she had promised him that her "informed and enthusiastic ladies" would lobby to protect it.[32] According to Reid Harris, Yarn's mobilization of the Federated Garden Clubs of Georgia members, the media, and others to speak for the coast was crucial to passage of the marshlands bill in 1970.[33]

Hanie's whirlwind tour of the state took him to Ossabaw Island, where he met Clifford and Eleanor Torrey "Sandy" West, the island's owners until 1978. One dominant question affecting the fate of the Golden Isles concerned how the older generations of the West, Torrey, Reynolds, Carnegie, and other families could preserve their privileges as island owners and share their property with a new generation of heirs in the face of development pressures. Sandy West's parents, whose wealth was connected to breakthroughs in the plate glass industry and the founding of a large chemical company, had purchased the island in its entirety in 1924. They had built an impressive mansion and enjoyed the island's seclusion for decades as a winter retreat, and Sandy would live there until moving off the island in May 2016 at age 103.[34] At the time of Hanie's visit, the Wests were negotiating the island's future with other family members who wanted to develop the island, and the pair was actively looking for ways to keep Ossabaw undeveloped. Hanie urged the Wests to generate more publicity about their concerns. With Hanie's help, Atlanta journalists Betsy Fancher and Andrew Sparks generated numerous newspaper and magazine articles about the Georgia coast and presented issues essentially from the environmentalists' point of view.[35]

Georgians like Hanie, Yarn, Wharton, and the Wests were clearly attuned to pollution and sprawl before a single new threat emerged and transformed these various efforts into something that caught the attention of politicians and mobilized a greater number of Georgia's citizens. In these crucial days for the environmental history of the Georgia coast, any one of several issues or threats might have brought these emerging leaders and organizations together to speak for Georgia's islands. One threat did: plans to turn Georgia's coastal marshlands into dumping grounds for strip miners.[36]

THE PHOSPHATE CRISIS OF 1968

The search for phosphate minerals along the Atlantic coastal plain has a long history, dating to mines established in the late nineteenth century in South Carolina and Florida to supply fertilizer to farmers. The issue intensified in the mid-1960s, as political leaders such as Atlanta mayor William Hartsfield took an interest in developing the state's mineral resources. In 1965, for instance, one consultant promised an insatiable market for phosphates, then used in insecticides, dental cements, detergents, and other products. According to another report, Florida was supplying 75 percent of the U.S. market's phosphates, which were mostly for the manufacture of agricultural fertilizer.[37] In 1966, mining firms began securing options to purchase land on Little Tybee and Cabbage Islands. Events culminated later that year when a subsidiary of the Oklahoma-based Kerr-McGee Corporation announced the discovery of what it called one of the biggest phosphate deposits ever, located about forty feet below the waters off of Wassaw Island. The company began discussing extraction plans and assured local residents that it would "preserve and beautify" the area, and that phosphate mining should raise no concern among "fish, game, and anti-pollution supporters."[38]

Over the next year and a half, the company tried to keep its specific plans secret, which may have intensified the ensuing controversy. In May 1968, Kerr-McGee submitted an application to the Georgia Mineral Leasing Commission signaling the company's interest in submitting a bid for mineral leases covering a portion of seventy-two thousand acres of state-owned underwater land and barrier islands. Most alarming to conservationists and members of the Georgia Conservancy, the company had its eyes on potential phosphate beds under the open water off of Wassaw, Ossabaw, and St. Catherines Islands. Even though the company had no prior experience in phosphate mining, and open-water subsurface phosphate mining had never been attempted, it was clear that the company planned to mine phosphate from the coastal seafloor, even more than one hundred feet below the ocean surface. Then they would dump millions of tons of exhumed sea-bottom onto Georgia's marshes and barrier islands. The company planned to use the overburden—the leftover dredged material—to expand the landmass of the Georgia coast, beginning with an expansion of Little Tybee Island. The master plan called for beaches and communities built atop "new land"—piles of dredged material—complete with golf courses, condominiums, canals, and marinas.[39] If carried out, these plans would have turned the region into a series of bulkhead communities like those found throughout southern Florida in places like Marco Island and Miami. Unsurprisingly, many state officials, especially those from coastal counties, were very interested in the economic potential of this huge project. Kerr-McGee officials speculated that the mining would generate fifteen hundred jobs with a $10 million annual payroll.[40]

The mining proposal immediately mobilized activists throughout the state to save Georgia's Golden Isles and hundreds of thousands of acres of marshlands from destruction. Bob Hanie was unequivocal: "WE MUST HAVE A PUBLIC HEARING!," he wrote in a mass mailing.[41] The new Georgia Conservancy sent a campaign appeal on June 3, 1968, asking members to write letters, sign petitions, and support scientific studies.[42] Eugene Odum asserted that he "had every reason to believe that extensive pollution, damage to sport and commercial fisheries, [and] reduction of potential protein food sources" would result from mining. Furthermore, the state was "setting a dangerous precedent" by agreeing "to sell special privileges involving vast estuaries which belong to the

FIGURE 9.1. Marco Island, Florida, in the 1970s.
Photo for the U.S. Environmental Protection Agency by Flip Schulke.
Courtesy of National Archives and Records Administration.

people of Georgia."[43] Odum spoke for Georgia Conservancy members and others, opposing the project with ecological, economic, and public trust arguments.

The Kerr-McGee mining proposal also highlighted the expertise of professional scientists other than Odum. These included Fred Marland, Tom Linton, Jim Henry, and other researchers at the University of Georgia Marine Institute facility on Sapelo Island who were researching and publishing papers on oceanography, marsh ecology, estuarine science, and related disciplines. They all embraced new and active roles as public citizens, but Odum stood out. Author of the first ecology textbook—*The Fundamentals of Ecology*—in 1953, he possessed a keen ability to translate complex scientific information into a language that inspired a wide readership. His research on the movement of nutrients and energy through a variety of "edge" environments—in old fields in South Carolina and coral reefs in the South Pacific Ocean—also became a central basis of the defense of the marsh.[44] People around the state learned of the notion of "ecology" for the first time, especially as it applied to coastal, barrier island, and estuarine environments.

Virtually every activist and journalist who spoke on the issue referred directly or indirectly to Odum's lessons on the importance of marshlands. For example, the *Atlanta Constitution* directly channeled Odum's science and more, writing, "If it were just a question of Georgia's industrial growth, we would have no reservations about the project. But this is not just a question of economics; it also involves ecology—the relationship of living things to their environment."[45] Odum's lesson on "marshbanks"—that estuarine and marsh ecosystems are depositories of energy for the food chain—also resonated. Odum called the coast among the most fertile natural areas of the world, and many routinely mentioned his claim that marshlands were among "the most valuable" ecosystems in the world, more valuable than even the richest farmland to society as a whole.[46] In 1968, Odum argued that "the potential yield of meat from [the] estuaries is greater on a per acre basis than is possible by land animal husbandry. Accordingly, the Georgia tidelands must be considered as potentially among the most productive of the state's agricultural landscapes."[47] Odum—like other scientists across the country—was no longer a detached, objective observer. He had become an environmental activist and spokesperson with credentials.[48]

Meanwhile, Georgia's regulatory institutions did not sit idly. R. S. "Rock" Howard, the director of the Water Quality Control Board, stressed the risks dredging posed to groundwater supplies.[49] Howard predicted that dredging would pierce the layer of bedrock separating fresh groundwater from saltwater and hasten saltwater intrusion that could prove devastating for the hundreds of thousands of coastal Georgians who still relied on wells and the Floridan Aquifer for their drinking water.[50] George T. Bagby, the Georgia Game and Fish Commission director, jumped headlong into the fray. The fishing and hunting community was critical to the rise of southern environmentalism and coastal protection. The Game and Fish Commission's monthly magazine, *Georgia Game and Fish*, published many editorials and letters opposing the phosphate mining proposal. In September 1968, officials hosted public hearings in Atlanta and Savannah to allow citizens to assess the pros and cons of the mining. At one such meeting, Bagby warned that Kerr-McGee was like a wolf "masquerading in sheep's clothing," an outside company unwilling to reveal its true motives and ready to "feast at our expense."[51] Georgia's regulatory agencies were setting a high bar, and they exercised considerable autonomy without being fully captured by the politics of economic development.

Many conservationists and environmentalists were simply uncomfortable with the unknown technological and environmental risks associated with the project. The *Savannah Morning News*, for instance, editorialized that the burden of proof remained with Kerr-McGee, while Darien activist William Haynes stressed that better mining methods would emerge in the future and that "meanwhile the phosphate will still be there."[52] Kerr-McGee engineers thought they could develop a technological system to dike and dewater large sections of coastal waterways prior to removing phosphate from deep below the ocean floor. Observers did not think this was realistic. Kerr-McGee, however, referred to its experiences in the oil and gas industry. In the Gulf of Mexico, it was written, "technology did not lead to major discoveries offshore; rather, big discoveries, using basic technology, stimulated the spending on new technologies to [fully] develop [oil and gas fields]." The oil and gas industry adapted to environmental conditions with new technologies because it foresaw an outcome worth the risk and great cost.[53] But Georgia was not the Gulf of Mexico, and phosphate was not oil. Georgia's activists, scientists, and public officials thought the marsh—an inherently and historically unstable tidal environment—was simply incompatible with the industrial development Kerr-McGee proposed.

As noted above, the company's untested mining process aimed to remove overburden and use it as fill to build new land. In order for the company to produce an anticipated three million tons of concentrated phosphate yearly, approximately 43.5 million cubic yards of watery earth would be exhumed. Approximately 7 percent would become phosphate concentrate, and 93 percent would be available for building bulkhead communities. Once the phosphate was isolated from the concentrate, any remaining colloidal clays would be pumped out to sea. The preliminary processing plant on Little Tybee would "wash" phosphate out of the sediment, and the washing would require up to 1.5 million gallons of freshwater per day from the Savannah River. For all of this, it was proposed, the state would only receive a rental fee of three dollars per acre for areas with known phosphate reserves as stipulated in the lease agreement.[54]

Conservationists, environmentalists, and regulators agreed that Kerr-McGee's proposal was unsound. The public hearings held in Atlanta and Savannah in 1968 allowed all interested parties—from grassroots to professional—a chance to speak up. The pressure was widespread to protect the marsh. In the words of one participant's letter to Governor Lester Maddox, "In this united and immediate response by the people of the Georgia coast in defense of the natural resources, you have witnessed an amazing phenomenon. You should be proud of your fellow Georgians."[55] In general, the dominant themes included expressions that Kerr-McGee, as an out-of-state entity, did not have Georgians' futures in mind, that commercial and recreational shrimping and fishing along the Georgia coast could not withstand the predicted devastation, and that taxpayers would be giving away state property with little compensation.

One study dove deeply into the issue. The 1968 *Report on Proposed Leasing of State Owned Lands for Phosphate Mining in Chatham County, Georgia* was essentially a proto-environmental impact statement as requested by Governor Maddox. Since the subsequent passage of the National Environmental Policy Act in 1970, federal agencies have been required to evaluate the environmental, social, and economic effects of major construction projects seeking federal permits. These reviews, commonly referred to as environmental impact statements or environmental assessments, are subject to an interagency environmental review process and public comment. But in 1968, the *Report* did not incorporate public comments and was not evaluated by state or federal agencies. The *Report*, published in November that year, was completed by a committee of five university-based scientists, including Eugene Odum. As in a modern environmental review, the party proposing the activity—in this case, Kerr-McGee—provided the bulk of the drilling data, mining practices information, and economic projections to the committee.

The committee's goal was to "develop a reasonable projection or concept of mining, ore processing and land fill operations" of the type Kerr-McGee might conduct if the state accepted its bid. With that goal in mind, and as in the sort of environmental impact study that would soon become common, the committee analyzed the technical aspects of the proposed action, considered the "physical and biological" effects of the proposed operations, performed a cost-benefit analysis of mining, and completed a cultural resources study. Based on this analysis, the committee concluded that Georgia lacked the necessary public policy, regulatory framework, and institutions to adequately steward state resources on the coast. According to the committee, Kerr-McGee's mining proposal could technically be implemented but illustrated what massive policy gaps existed. At a time when scientists in other communities in the United States were beginning to take a stand to address air pollution, groundwater contamination from failed septic systems, and sprawl, the committee concluded, "There is time now in Coastal Georgia, before great damage is done, to look ahead and apply a reasonable, realistic approach to the use and enjoyment of this rich and beautiful environment."[56]

Given the clear opposition by members of the public, the General Assembly, and other public officials to the Kerr-McGee proposal, and given the findings published in *Report on Proposed Leasing of State Owned Lands for Phosphate Mining*, the state's Mineral Leasing Commission denied Kerr-McGee's bid to mine twenty-five thousand acres. Despite this rejection, the interconnected issues of mining, uncontrolled development, and pollution on the coast were not dead. This was just an early battle in the war to protect Georgia's marshlands from incompatible development. By all indications, the marshes' future lay in the hands of a broad coalition that was now asserting itself.

MARSHLANDS CONFERENCE

Many of the people who would prove most influential in efforts to protect the Georgia coast came together at "The Future of the Marshlands" conference in October 1968. Bob Hanie organized the event and invited ecologists, oceanographers, owners of barrier islands and large portions of marshland property, politicians, and visionaries in the emerging national environmental movement to participate.[57] While citizens around the state had mobilized against Kerr-McGee's phosphate mining proposal in a reactive, defensive way, the marshlands conference was supposed to be grounded in science and offer proactive solutions to the mounting problems facing the Georgia coast.

The event took place in the ballroom of the opulent and exclusive Cloister Hotel on Sea Island. Ingram Richardson, a successful businessman and co-owner of Little Cumberland Island, introduced the proceedings by citing the work of Hanie, Odum, and Wharton in forging a coalition of "what might be called an ecological-homogeneity" among those who had a stake and expertise in the fate of the Georgia islands.[58] Hanie came next to the stage, and charged the conferees to not act like "yellow-crested conservationist nuthatchers, who after wailing, feel better and go home having done nothing." Echoing the recommendations from the *Report on Proposed Leasing of State Owned Lands for Phosphate Mining*, Hanie treated the gathering as a call for action because "the future will come planned and responsible or bashed and wrecked."[59]

State legislator Reid Harris argued that the time had arrived to address the critical issue of determining who held title to marshland properties. Harris, a real estate lawyer from Brunswick, had been interested in damages caused by surface mining in the state, and in early 1968 he had cosponsored and helped pass the Surface Mining Land Use Act, a bill that brought some modest regulations to Georgia's kaolin and marble mines.[60] He told the marshlands conference audience, including the island landowners, that they might have been misinformed in thinking that the tidal marshes adjacent to the islands and mainland could be privately owned. Most "may be owned by the state," he asserted.[61] For Harris and the conference attendees, the main objective remained finding a solution for the long-term protection of the marshes of Glynn.

HARRIS'S MARSHLANDS BILL

The marshlands conference ultimately helped mobilize support for Harris's state bill to spare Georgia's coastal marsh and barrier islands from reckless development.[62] Harris presented House Bill 212 in January 1969, beginning a fourteen-month legislative project. Passing the bill would prove far more difficult than defeating Kerr-McGee's request to lease underwater mining rights. After all, the bill would limit many potential plans for economic development on the Georgia coast, not just those of a single company.

The first incarnation of House Bill 212 established a two-tier process for entities seeking to dredge and fill in the marsh. First, applicants would need to obtain a permit from local city or county governments, and, second, a new state agency would have the authority to approve or deny the permit. Harris faced pushback from county governments and business interests that did not want to limit development on private property. In response, Harris eliminated the creation of a new state agency, and he inserted language stating that development in the marsh could proceed if property owners could prove they held legal title (and title insurance) to the marshland they wished to develop and the local government approved of the project.[63] This version of the bill cleared a house committee and passed the full house by a 98–30 vote. Because the bill faced continued opposition, it failed to move through the senate during the 1969 session.

Nearly all of the political, economic, and industrial leaders in Harris's own district staunchly opposed the bill. In the words of scientist Fred Marland—who helped write the bill—it had "many more enemies (including Harris's own father, a prominent businessman in the coastal Georgia city of Brunswick), than friends."[64] Opponents of the bill, identified by one of Harris's supporters as "money interests," included the Brunswick–Glynn County Chamber of Commerce, the Brunswick Central Labor Council, Brunswick–Golden Isles Committee of 100, the Brunswick–Golden Isles Chamber of Commerce, Glynn County Real Estate Board, the Georgia Business and Industry Association, the Brunswick Pulp and Paper Company, Hercules Inc., the Sea Island Company, Seaboard Construction Company, and the Brunswick County Real Estate Board. They generally made the same arguments: that the bill would control development on private property or usurp local control and "home rule." Local governments, such as the city of Brunswick, wanted to retain responsibility for evaluating proposals for development in the marsh.[65] While opponents did indeed stall the bill, they could not kill it.

Throughout the remainder of 1969, Harris shepherded the bill through an interim salt marsh study committee and at least seven public hearings. After the 1970 legislative session began, the bill was amended to more closely resemble its first iteration. Then constituents barraged their legislators, in support of the bill. According to Senator Al Holloway, he received more mail regarding HB 212 than on "all other issues" in his decade in the state legislature. Holloway believed the letters he received were sincere but unknowledgeable. In his opinion, the majority of the letters "came because somebody like the local garden club president called up a bunch of her friends and asked them to write."[66] Regardless of the letter writers' knowledge, Holloway conceded: "a majority of the people of Georgia want some control of the marshes."[67]

After a long legislative struggle stretching over two sessions of the General Assembly, the Coastal Marshlands Protection Act passed "amid poetry and applause and without a dissenting vote." The act created a Coastal Marshlands Protection Agency with the power to implement the act and protect Georgia's 378,000 acres of coastal marshlands. The new agency was empowered to vet proposals to alter state-owned salt and brackish marshlands, issue permits for such activities, and enforce compliance with the act.[68] The agency was required to post public notices soliciting public comment on pending applications and provide public hearings. Additionally, any permitted construction had to be completed within two years of an application's approval.

Harris's legislation hinged on a major assumption: that the state owned the tidal marsh. Harris arrived at this conclusion based on history and basic property law. Prior to the American Revolution, the king of England owned the colonial tidelands in the public trust, meaning that the tidal areas were open to the general public unless the king made specific land grants to individuals. After the American Revolution, all of the king's land transferred to the colonial governments and eventually to the United States to be managed in the public's interest. The only exceptions would be any of the king's specific land grants.[69] Nonetheless, before and after final passage of the marshlands protection bill in 1970, opponents continued to argue that it would control development on private property or usurp local control and "home rule." As a counterpoint, Harris, state attorney general Arthur K. Bolton, and others "expressed strong doubts" about people who claimed to own tidal marsh, because the titles were "so unclear." Furthermore, they believed that "the state itself may lay claim to a major portion of the marshlands."[70] As such, the bill was poised to do two things: protect the marsh from massive dredging projects and ensure that the state regulated state property on the public's behalf.

A little more than one month after Harris's marshlands protection bill passed, the attorney general's office weighed in on this specific public owner-ship issue. The attorney general issued a March 17, 1970, "Position Paper Re-lating to the Georgia Coastal Marshlands" that stated that "the marshlands of Georgia are not susceptible to private exploitation or conservation without re-gard to the common-law trust purposes to which these lands have long been dedicated." Furthermore, "In the unlikely event that one should establish a ti-tle to marshland, such person could not use the property in such a way as to impede the public right of enjoyment" unless the original grant provided for exclusive private use.[71] In other words, the marsh belonged to the state, and the state had an obligation to manage the resource and protect public use of the resource.

It was still unknown whether the business-friendly governor would veto the bill as he had threatened to do. Ten days after the attorney general's posi-tion paper was published, the bill remained on the governor's desk unsigned. March 27, 1970, was the last opportunity for Governor Maddox to act. If he did nothing, the bill would become law. On March 27, Harris, Odum, Yarn, Howard, Bagby, and Senator Holloway were all summoned to the governor's office by Maddox's executive secretary, Zell Miller. With everyone in the room, Maddox explained that it was a controversial bill, that he had had a lot of con-versations about it, and that he had received enough letters of support to fill three barrels. In the end, conceding to legislative and constituent pressure, he signed the bill, establishing the Coastal Marshlands Protection Act. Maddox reportedly passed out pens to those present and then tossed other pens over his shoulder, indicative of his frustration.[72]

CONCLUSION

I have stood on the edge of the North American continent on the rocky Atlan-tic shore in Maine, on the sandy barrier islands of Massachusetts, New York, Delaware, Maryland, Virginia, and North Carolina, and in Florida's mangrove thickets. There is nothing quite like walking the edges of Fort McAllister State Park or Wormsloe State Historic Site, cycling around Jekyll Island, or sitting at Musgrove Plantation to experience the marshes of Glynn and Georgia. The region with the closest aesthetic to that of Georgia's coast is perhaps the Ches-apeake Bay. It is easy to understand why Georgia's assemblage of water and land spoke to Sidney Lanier. I am grateful the marsh does not resemble the bulkhead communities I have found throughout Florida and thankful that the Georgia shrimp fishery continues to exist.

The campaign to protect Georgia's marshlands set a benchmark for future

FIGURE 9.2. "Morning Marsh." More than 378,000 acres of tidal salt marsh, or about one-third of the East Coast's salt marsh, have been protected since 1970 by the Coastal Marshlands Protection Act. Photo by Diane Kirkland.

citizen engagement and showed a new way to think about environmental protection. Activists built an infrastructure and professionalized environmentalism. According to a Georgia Conservancy history, the campaign to protect the marsh "was the first time [Georgians] sent state agencies a massive number of letters on any environmental issue."[73] Environmental leaders developed and deployed tactics—securing a legislative champion, mobilizing grassroots activists, and working with the media—that would be used in subsequent environmental campaigns to stop Soil Conservation Service stream channelization projects and to save the Flint River from dams and the Chattahoochee River from sewer lines. A broad coalition rallied with the intent to protect a beautiful and unique waterscape forever. Saving the coast was not a proactive environmental campaign; most are not. Georgians identified key issues recognized by their counterparts elsewhere in the country. Pollution and sprawl were national problems that required local solutions because, in the end, all politics is local.

The campaign to protect the marsh also changed the way people interpreted property ownership on the coast. While it was indeed a campaign to protect the coast's unique beauty, and ecological arguments mattered, there were more fundamental questions at play: Would the marsh's fate be determined by a few property owners—namely industrial interests in Brunswick and Savannah— and their claims to the marsh? Or would the marsh live on as property protected by the state for all the people of Georgia, including those dependent upon it, like subsistence and commercial fishers. In the end, the state did not support a vision of "anything goes" property rights. Instead, it accepted a role to protect the marsh while expecting property owners—including itself—to own nature responsibly. Property rights are a product of the laws we write and can rewrite—they are dynamic. In the words of Eric T. Freyfogle, a property rights and environmental law professor, "It is possible to reshape ownership norms so that private property continues to provide its many benefits even as we expect owners to use their lands in responsible ways."[74] Even Eugene Odum understood this, though in slightly different terms: "The question is not who owns it (coastal area) but who's responsible for it."[75] Today the marsh is protected by the State of Georgia in the public trust. Moving forward, the health of the marsh and the coast and all that live there will fall heavily upon private property owners and their land use decisions. There is reason to be optimistic that private property owners will increasingly support environmental campaigns after fully understanding how a robust regulatory regime ultimately protects their properties and investments.

The Coastal Marshlands Protection Act protected the marsh—big dredging machines will never go to work here—but the law alone will not save the marsh. Today's threats to the marsh are individual property owners' efforts to build as close as possible to the marsh (even in it), mega-docks over a thousand feet long, bulkheads, stormwater runoff, and water pollution from elsewhere (e.g., nitrates and other fertilizers from residential and agricultural lands). The marshlands act asks Georgians to think big, to stand at the marsh's edge as Sidney Lanier did but with their backs to the ocean of cordgrass. Landward is where the fate of the marsh can be found. What happens in the forests, in agricultural operations, and at the "modern logistics" mega-sites along the state's inland rivers, creeks, and streams affects the coast. What happens in the Blue Ridge Mountain, piedmont, and coastal plain headwaters affects the coast.

Odum and his professional colleagues used the watershed as a category of analysis and scientific study for decades. For nearly forty years scientists measured "the behavior of the water itself," the sediment loads, erosion rates, or what surface water did to the land in a watershed. These experiments primarily measured water quantity and quality based on human-induced disturbances. What these experiments ignored was what the water passed through and what pollutants the water might pick up prior to entering a stream course. As such, water problems were not always contained within the riverbanks but originated above the banks. "In other words, it's what happens on the land, not what happens in the river" that matters, according to Odum.[76] He and his colleagues honed their energy flows thesis in the marsh, but Odum applied those findings on a much broader scale and thought like a watershed. While Reid Harris correctly stated years after the Coastal Marshlands Protection Act was implemented that the legislative intent never included protection of the uplands adjacent to the marsh, his scientific mentors could not so easily separate upland, coastal, and river basin ecology.[77] History tells us that the marshlands act protected one part of the whole—the marsh, but it also tells us to look upstream to the other part to ensure that the marsh and the whole system remains resilient in the face of global climate change.

The influence of the arts and sciences that made the marshlands act possible now looks like a relic. When Senator Adams referred to Lanier's "The Marshes of Glynn" during the floor debate of Harris's House Bill 212, he illustrated one reason why saving the marsh was easy. In 1970, nearly every grown adult who attended primary school in Georgia had probably memorized Lanier's lyrical homage to the coast.[78] When Rock Howard of Georgia's Water Quality Control Board, a Savannah native, was asked to review an early version of Harris's bill, he recommended "that the term 'wetlands' be dropped in favor of the designation 'marshes,' a term we use commonly and about which poetry is written."[79] Because many Georgians knew the poem, they identified with the coast and the Golden Isles even if they had not visited the place. And because they identified with the coast, they knew at a basic level what was at stake and why they had to speak for the marsh that had so clearly spoken to Sidney Lanier. Today, we should all be grateful for what Georgia's Sunbelt environmentalists accomplished and recognize that there is still work to do to ensure that the marsh, and everything that feeds it, survives.

NOTES

I thank Paul Pressly, Chris Curtis, and Mark Finlay's family for graciously providing me with access to Mark's unpublished Ossabaw manuscript. After reading the manuscript I realized that Mark had already covered a lot of the ground and history of the Coastal Marshlands Protection Act I wanted to cover and had used many of the same sources I was beginning to uncover. This chapter is based on a portion of Mark's manuscript and research regarding the act's history. I am grateful for the opportunity to advance Mark's labor and contributions to Georgia's coastal environmental history.

1. *Atlanta Constitution*, February 7, 1970, clipping in Reid Harris Papers related to the Coastal Marshlands Protection Act, Richard B. Russell Library for Political Research and Studies, University of Georgia Libraries, Athens, Georgia, hereafter Harris Papers.

2. *Brunswick News*, February 6, 1970, clipping in Harris Papers.

3. Leslie Edwards, Johnathan Ambrose, and L. Katherine Kirkman, *The Natural Communities of Georgia* (Athens: University of Georgia Press, 2013), 512, 567, 579.

4. University System of Georgia Advisory Committee for Mineral Leasing, *Report on Proposed Leasing of State Owned Lands for Phosphate Mining in Chatham County, Georgia* (n.p., 1968), Appendix C, "Environmental Effects," page C-6, hereafter, *Report on Proposed Leasing*.

5. *Savannah Morning News-Evening Press*, June 30, 1968, and *Atlanta Constitution*, January 30, 1970, both clippings in Harris Papers.

6. *Savannah Morning News*, January 18, 1970; "A Weekend on Georgia's 'Redneck Riviera,'" *Savannah Morning News*, August 2, 1998.

7. For the best answers to the question "where did modern environmentalism come from and who shaped it?," see Christopher C. Sellers, *Crabgrass Crucible: Suburban Nature and the Rise of Environmentalism in Twentieth-Century America* (Chapel Hill: University of North Carolina Press, 2012); Adam Rome, *The Genius of Earth Day: How a 1970 Teach-In Unexpectedly Made the First Green Generation* (New York: Hill and Wang, 2013); Robert D. Lifset, *Power on the Hudson: Storm King Mountain and the Emergence of Modern Environmentalism* (Pittsburgh: University of Pittsburgh Press, 2014); and Cody Ferguson, *This Is Our Land: Grassroots Environmentalism in the Late Twentieth Century* (New Brunswick, N.J.: Rutgers University Press, 2015).

8. Andrew W. Kahrl, *The Land Was Ours: African American Beaches from Jim Crow to the Sunbelt South* (Harvard University Press, 2012); Eileen Maura McGurty, "From NIMBY to Civil Rights: The Origins of the Environmental Justice Movement." *Environmental History* 2, no. 3 (1997): 301–23.

9. *Atlanta Journal Constitution*, February 9, 1970, clipping from Harris Papers.

10. Jack Davis, *An Everglades Providence: Marjory Stoneman Douglas and the American Environmental Century* (Athens: University of Georgia Press, 2009), part 3; Steven Noll and David Tegeder, *Ditch of Dreams: The Cross Florida Barge Canal and the Struggle for Florida's Future* (Gainesville: University of Florida Press, 2009), chap. 6.

11. John L. Raulerson, "Where Have All the Oysters Gone?," in *The Future of the Marshlands and Sea Islands of Georgia: A Record of a Conference Convened by the Georgia Natural Areas Council and the Coastal Area Planning and Development Commission*, ed. David S. Maney, Frederick C. Marland, and Clifford B. West (Georgia

Natural Areas Council and the Coastal Area Planning and Development Commission, 1970), 70–71, hereafter *Future of the Marshlands.*

12. Adolph Sanders, *Tourism Development in the Coastal Empire of Georgia* (Athens: Bureau of Business and Economic Research and Institute of Community and Area Development, University of Georgia, 1968); Charles D. Clement, *The Georgia Coast: Issues and Options for Recreation* (Athens: University of Georgia, College of Business Administration, 1971), I-3–I-5; and James M. Fallows and Ralph Nader, *The Water Lords: Ralph Nader's Study Group Report on Industry and Environmental Crisis in Savannah, Georgia* (New York: Grossman Publishers, 1971).

13. Quote from the Scenic Highway Committee of the Commissioners of Roads and Revenue, Glynn County, *The Challenge of Georgia's Coast: A Realistic Analysis of Present Highway Problems, Undeveloped Resort Facilities, and a Blueprint for Unlocking the Golden Coast of Georgia* (1950), in Mary R. Bullard, *Cumberland Island: A History* (Athens: University of Georgia Press, 2003), 264–65.

14. *Savannah Morning News*, March 19, 1965, and July 3, 1966.

15. Anne W. Simon, *The Thin Edge: Coast and Man in Crisis* (San Francisco: Harper & Row, 1978), 78–80; Kahrl, *Land Was Ours*. Two Gullah Geechee communities established by former African slaves—Harris Neck and Sapelo Island's Hog Hammock—have challenged inequitable and unjust treatment by county tax accessors and the federal government.

16. Betsy Fancher, *The Lost Legacy of Georgia's Golden Isles* (New York: Doubleday, 1971), 209.

17. *Atlanta Constitution*, January 30, 1970, clipping from Harris Papers.

18. Robert Hanie to Mother, Daddy, and Charlie, July 16, 1961, box 14, Georgia Natural Areas Council, State Parks and Historical Sites (of the Georgia Dept. of Natural Resources collection), 30–8–43, Georgia Archives, Morrow, Georgia, hereafter GNAC files.

19. Robert Hanie to Mother, January 12, 1963, in Robert Hanie, *Letters from Tanganyika*, unpublished collection in possession of the Hanie family. This is one of dozens of letters in this typed collection that shed light upon Hanie's intellectual and personal journey.

20. Robert Hanie vita, personal papers of Wynne Coplea, Springfield, Illinois; Betsy Fancher, "Profile of Bob Hanie," draft of magazine article, 1969 or 1970, box 6, GNAC files; "Celebrate Life, Naturalist Says," *Macon News*, April 9, 1970, in box 14, GNAC files.

21. James A. Mackay, "Memorandum from Chairman of the Legal Committee to Members," January 4, 1971, Alma Toevs Walker, MS 2696, University of Georgia Libraries, Hargrett Rare Book and Manuscript Library, Athens.

22. Rome, *Genius of Earth Day*, 47–56; Sellers, *Crabgrass Crucible*, 253; Robert H. Claxton, *A History of the Georgia Conservancy, 1967–1981* (Atlanta: Georgia Conservancy, 1981), 7–10; Christopher J. Manganiello, *Southern Water, Southern Power: How the Politics of Cheap Energy and Water Scarcity Shaped a Region* (Chapel Hill, University of North Carolina Press, 2015), 174–76.

23. Letter from Robert E. Hanie, to Dr. H.S. Alden, May 13, 1967, box 7, GNAC files.

24. *Georgia Conservancy Quarterly* 1, no. 1 (Winter 1968): 1, clipping in box 16, James A. Mackay papers, Manuscript, Archives, and Rare Book Library, Emory University, hereafter Mackay Papers.

25. James A. Mackay speech, January 20, 1978, box 15, and James A. Mackay speech, February 28, 1992, both in Mackay Papers.

26. Robert Hanie, executive director, Georgia Council for the Preservation of Natural Areas, to Mr. Vann, January 7, 1969, box 3, GNAC.

27. House Bill 304, "State Council for the Preservation of Natural Areas," March 10, 1966; "Committee Report on Natural Areas (S.R. 161)," and Council For the Preservation of Natural Areas, "Organizational Meeting," November 10, 1966, all in box 12, Collection 25–1–8, Department of Game and Fish–Commissioner's Office–Assistant Director's Subject Files, Georgia Archives, Morrow, Georgia, hereafter GAF files; Robert Hanie to Edward Roberts, January 29, 1968, box 14, GNAC files; *History of Fort Barrington Club* (Decatur, Ga.: Bowen Press, 1958).

28. Council For the Preservation of Natural Areas, "Organizational Meeting," November 10, 1966; "Minutes" of April 17, 1967; and "Minutes" of August 14, 1967—all in box 12, GAF files. See also Andrew Sparks, "Bob," article draft written in June 1968, presumably never published, box 22, Andrew H. Sparks Papers, Mss. 2777, Hargrett Rare Book and Manuscript Library, Athens, Georgia, hereafter Sparks Papers.

29. Andrew Sparks, "The Housewife and Egg Island," *Atlanta Journal Constitution Magazine*, November 2, 1969.

30. Sellers, *Crabgrass Crucible*; Rome, *Genius of Earth Day*.

31. "Environmental Syllabus" for the Habersham Garden Club, 1969–70, box 12, GNAC files.

32. Georgia Women of Achievement Honorees, "Jane Hurt Yarn," https://www. georgiawomen.org/jane-hurt-yarn; Michael L. Jordan, "Jane Hurt Yarn (1924–1995)," *New Georgia Encyclopedia*, August 20, 2013, http://www.georgiaencyclopedia.org/ articles/geography-environment/jane-hurt-yarn-1924–1995; "Agenda for Dogwood District Emergency Committee Meeting," May 14, 1969, box 12, GNAC files; Merle Schlesinger Lefkoff, "The Voluntary Citizens' Group as a Public Policy Alternative to the Political Party: A Case Study of the Georgia Conservancy" (PhD diss., Emory University, 1975), 30, 159. I thank Tally Sweat for lunch and sharing personal stories about Jane Yarn and Bob Hanie; she was the only person I found in Georgia's conservation and environmental community who knew Hanie personally.

33. Reid W. Harris, *And the Coastlands Wait: How a Small Group of Legislators, Scientists and Concerned Citizens Helped Save 500,000 Acres of the World's Most Productive Area* (St. Simons Island, Ga.: Reid W. Harris, 2008), 52.

34. For basic biographical information on the Torrey and West families, see Arthur Pound, *The Salt of the Earth: The Story of Captain J. B. Ford and the Michigan Alkali Company, 1890–1940* (Boston: Atlantic Monthly, 1940); Ann Foskey, *Ossabaw*

Island (Charleston, S.C.: Arcadia Press, 2002); Ann Hardie, "The Old Lady of Ossabaw," *Atlanta Magazine*, March 2011, http://www.atlantamagazine.com/great-reads/ossabaw-sandy-west.

35. Eleanor Torrey West to Roman Jakobson, May 6, 1968, box 6, Roman Jakobson Papers, Institute Archives and Special Collections, MIT, Cambridge, Massachusetts. Other examples of these publicity efforts include Andrew Sparks, "Georgia's Wild Coast ... Can't It Be Saved?" *Atlanta Journal Constitution Magazine*, November 24, 1968; Betsy Fancher, "Keeping the Tapestry Whole" *Atlanta Magazine*, December 1969, 89.

36. Danyel Goldbarten Addes, "The Length, Breadth, and Sweep of Marshland Protection in Georgia: Protection Afforded by Georgia's Coastal Marshland Protection Act and Coastal Nonpoint Source Program" (master's thesis, University of Georgia, 2012); Harris, *And the Coastlands Wait*, 17–23; Charles Seabrook, *The World of the Salt Marsh: Appreciating and Protecting the Tidal Marshes of the Southeastern Atlantic Coast* (Athens: University of Georgia Press, 2012), 170–77.

37. Louis H. Dixon, "New Program of Mineral Exploration in South Georgia, Progress Report 1," Georgia State Division of Conservation, April 1965, box 43, Ms. 558, William B. Hartfield Papers, Manuscripts, Archives, and Rare Book Library, Emory University, Atlanta; James W. Furlow, "Stratigraphy and Economic Geology of the Eastern Chatham County Phosphate Deposit," *Geological Survey Bulletin*, no. 82 (1969): 5.

38. *Savannah Morning News*, November 30, 1966.

39. *Savannah Morning News*, August 7, 1968.

40. *Savannah Morning News*, May 25, 1968, clipping from Harris Papers.

41. Robert Hanie, n.d. [ca. May–June 1968], "IMPORTANT: RE DREDGING OF THE GEORGIA SALT MARSHES," box 13, GAF files. See also *Atlanta Constitution*, May 25, 1968.

42. Lynn Hill to Members of the Georgia Conservancy, June 3, 1968, box 70, Ashantilly Press Papers, Mss. 3395, Hargrett Library, Athens, Georgia, hereafter Ashantilly Papers.

43. *Atlanta Constitution*, June 14, 1968, clipping from Harris Papers.

44. Joel B. Hagen, *An Entangled Bank: The Origins of Ecosystem Ecology* (New Brunswick: Rutgers University Press, 1992), 126; Betty Jean Craige, *Eugene Odum: Ecosystem Ecologist and Environmentalist* (Athens: University of Georgia, 2001).

45. *Atlanta Constitution*, May 28, 1968, clipping from Harris Papers.

46. Odum's own language on "marshbanks" is found in "A Proposal for a Marshbank and the Strategy of Ecosystem Development for the Estuarine Zone of Georgia," in *Future of the Marshlands*, 74–85. For others' use of this notion, see J[im] M[orison], "Preserve Marshes Now!" *Georgia Game & Fish* 3, no. 12 (December 1968): 2, 20; Fred Marland to George T. Smith, February 18, 1969, box 1, Harris Papers.

47. *Report on Proposed Leasing*, Appendix C, "Environmental Effects," page C-6.

48. Rome, *Genius of Earth Day*, 20–29.

49. The Executive Reorganization Act of 1972 created the Department of Natural

Resources (DNR) and also abolished the Water Quality Control Board and replaced it with the Georgia Environmental Protection Division (EPD), which is housed within the DNR.

50. *Atlanta Journal Constitution*, June 16, 1968, clipping from Harris Papers.

51. Statement, and Draft of Statement, to be delivered at public hearing in Atlanta, September 16, 1968, box 13, GAF. Bagby's draft statement was more aggressive than his actual statement and published remarks. In the draft, he promised that he would not allow "one shovel" of ocean floor to be removed. See also George T. Bagby, "Phosphates $100 Million Giveaway," *Georgia Game & Fish* 3, no. 11 (November 1968): 2, 15, 16.

52. William G. Haynes to Robert G. Stephens Jr., September 19, 1968, box 70, Ashantilly Papers.

53. Tyler Priest, "Extraction Not Creation: The History of Offshore Petroleum in the Gulf of Mexico," *Enterprise and Society*, June 2007, 227–67.

54. *Savannah Morning News*, August 7, 1968, clipping from Harris Papers.

55. William G. Haynes to Lester Maddox, October 7, 1968, box 70, Ashantilly Papers; Fred C. Marland interview with Mark Finlay, December 2, 2012.

56. *Report on Proposed Leasing*, 19.

57. Hanie to Conferees, September 18, 1968, Eugene Odum Papers, UGA 97–045, University Archives, Hargrett Rare Book and Manuscript Library, University of Georgia, Athens, hereafter Odum Papers.

58. Ingram H. Richardson, introduction to *Future of the Marshlands*, 2–5.

59. Robert Hanie, "The Yellow Submarine," in *Future of the Marshlands*, 6–14.

60. Harris, *And the Coastlands Wait*, 17–23; Charles Seabrook and Marcy Louza, *Red Clay, Pink Cadillacs and White Gold: The Kaolin Chalk Wars* (Marietta, Ga.: Longstreet Press), 96–98.

61. Reid W. Harris, "The Proposed Georgia Coastal Wetlands Conservation Act of 1969," in *Future of the Marshlands*, 51–54.

62. Seabrook, *World of the Salt Marsh*, 172–73.

63. *Atlanta Constitution*, February 21, 1969.

64. Fred Marland to Eugene P. Odum, February 4, 1969, Odum Papers.

65. See correspondence in Harris Papers, folders 7 and 13, including Forest P. Jones to Reid Harris, February, 3, 1970.

66. *Atlanta Constitution*, February 9, 1970, clipping from Harris Papers.

67. *Atlanta Constitution*, February 7, 1970, clipping from Harris Papers.

68. James E. Kundell and J. Alec Little, "Management of Georgia's Marshlands under the Coastal Marshlands Protection Act of 1970," in *Proceedings of the Fifteenth Annual Conference on Wetlands Restoration and Creation, May 19–20, 1988* (Plant City, Fla.: Hillsborough Community College), 158–60.

69. Harris, *And the Coastlands Wait*, 49–50.

70. *Savannah Morning News*, January 20, 1970.

71. Courtney W. Stanton, "Position Paper Relating to the Georgia Coastal Marshlands," approved and issued on March 17, 1970 by Attorney General Arthur K. Bolton, and *Atlanta Constitution*, March 17, 1970, both from Harris Papers.

72. Harris, *And the Coastlands Wait*, 113; Bill Ship, "Developers Set Their Sights on Coast," *Athens Banner Herald*, December 10, 2006.

73. Claxton, *History of the Georgia Conservancy*, 18.

74. Eric T. Freyfogle, "Owning Nature, Responsibly," in *Imagination and Place: Ownership*, ed. Kelly Barth (Lawrence, KS: Imagination and Place Press, 2010), 177.

75. *Savannah Morning News*, January 20, 1970, clipping from Harris Papers.

76. Eugene P. Odum, "The Watershed as an Ecological Unit," box 1, Odum Papers; Wayne T. Swank, Judith L. Meyer, and Deyree A. Crossley, Jr., "Long Term Ecological Research: Coweeta History and Perspectives," in *Holistic Science: The Evolution of the Georgia Institute of Ecology (1940–2000)*, ed. Gary W. Barrett and Terry L. Barrett (Ann Arbor: Sheridan Books, 2001); Eugene P. Odum, typescript of an audio recording of remarks before the Cuyahoga River Watershed Symposium panel "Gaps in the Watershed—Knowledge, Communication, Application, Management," November 1, 1968, box 1, Odum Papers.

77. Brief of Amicus Curiae, Reid W. Harris in Support of the Respondents, regarding *Center for a Sustainable Coast, Georgia River Network and Satilla Riverwatch Alliance v. Coastal Marshlands Protection Committee, Georgia Department of Natural Resources, and Point Peter, LLLP*, Petition No. S07C1745, April 2008, Harris Papers.

78. I thank Dorinda Dallmeyer for this lesson.

79. R. S. Howard Jr. to Leon Kirkland, January 14, 1969, Harris Papers.

CHAPTER 10

"The Majestic Scene East-ward"

Sense of Place in the Literature of the Georgia Coast

JANISSE RAY

Since colonist Peter Gordon penned his first impressions of the Georgia coast in 1732, volumes have been written about a swath of lowcountry along the southern Atlantic, between the Savannah and St. Johns Rivers, and an archipelago of wind-beaten and water-buffeted islands strung out like oblong golden beads along it.[1] The Georgia coast is a stunning place, filled with strange and mysterious environments, clairvoyant beauty, and a splendid diversity of life-forms, and these features have inspired a body of literature known for an emotional attachment to land and landscape. The literal place and the experience of place there have shaped a unique and often tragic literature, and much can be learned about Georgia's coastal nature through the lens of its body of literary work.

Peter Gordon's description of the Georgia coast upon his arrival, as it turns out, is among the first in recorded history.[2] Gordon was one of 114 settlers who left England via the River Thames in November 1732 on the ship *Anne* and disembarked some two months later in what would become their new home, "His Majesty having by Royall Charter granted that tract of land lying between the rivers, Savannah and Altamaha, and now distinguished by the name of Georgia," as Gordon wrote. King George II had granted a charter for the new colony, named after him, based on a proposal by General James Edward Oglethorpe to allow prisoners whose only crime was debt to begin anew. Gordon, who became bailiff and "Conservator of the Peace" in the new colony, traced in his journal his voyage from England with Oglethorpe and details of the colony's establishment. The *Anne* landed briefly at Charles Town, South Carolina, then proceeded to Beaufort, from which its passengers continued south in "periagores," small sailboats. On February 1, 1732, Oglethorpe and a group of the colonists anchored and climbed Yamacraw Bluff near the site of present-day Savannah.

Gordon depicts the land as a kind of wall, a barrier through which the colonists will have to pass. "The country all round us was a continued forrest," he wrote in his journal, "and nothing to be seen but wood and water."[3] Fear can be read in Gordon's description of the flatness, but also opportunity. Something in humans loves the blank slate, the unwritten scroll, the narrative waiting to be told. With these words the literature of the Georgia coast began.

The boundaries of the Georgia coast are fluid, inexact, and ever-changing. Exactly where does such a place begin and end, given the movement of sand, the deposition of sediment, the ancient coastline, and the now-rising seas? For the sake of exactness, we use the northerly and southerly lines of two rivers, the Savannah and the St. Marys, which, although fluctuating, separate Georgia from bordering states at their mouths. In terms of east and west, the coastline involves the whole—the places where water and land meet currently, where they met in the past, and where they will meet in the future. The past informs the present, the present informs the future, and in the end everything affects everything else.

Wherever humans gather to live, we begin to tell stories about place. These stories form a collective narrative from which a culture takes shape, with "culture" defined as a cache of stories that explain the way of life of a group of people—behaviors, symbols, beliefs, survival mechanisms—and that are passed between inhabitants and between generations.

The stories of the Georgia coast, of course, stretch back at least five thousand years to the first humans who slipped though ancient maritime forests and brackish marshes, through pine flatwoods and cypress swamps.[4] Until the early eighteenth century the narratives of these people were, as far as we can discern, mostly unwritten, with centuries of storytellers and culture-makers reliant on the human mind as a tablet. Development of paper birthed literature, and the printing press heralded the industrialization of the book, offering the potential for longer shelf life and wider audiences, thus the dissemination of culture. The literature of the Georgia coast, then, is necessarily modern and also aristocratic, a manufacture of people who could write and who could read, since certain factions—including the uneducated poor, indentured servants, and slaves—were denied access to literacy.

I am looking at a sense of place in the writings of the Georgia coast, interested in the environment's impression on its written culture. I believe that unlettered Native peoples, slaves, and other illiterate people possessed a sense of place—we all do, to one degree or another—and that they contributed monumentally to Georgia's coastal culture, no matter that their names and often their stories were lost in the wreckage of history. Pieces of who they were and what they experienced and what they thought were gathered up by the storytellers, and elements of what they knew and believed crept into the work of writers. In some cases, writers captured entire stories from oral traditions and folk literature. The lived history of all who were inextricably linked with the particularities of this place, even unlettered people, informed its letters, which happens to be my focus here.

First I would like to define what I mean by "a sense of place" and explore how it might manifest in a writer and his or her work. Thinkers of myriad disciplines for decades now have attempted to define the human response and relationship to place. American geographer J. B. Jackson, looking at how natural forces shape the human environment, writes that a sense of place is one of the ways in which we identify the peculiar characteristics of a land and its inhabitants.[5] Geographer Yi-Fu Tuan speaks of "topophilia," the link between a person and a place that is often described as love.[6] In a similar way cultural anthropologists and environmental psychologists talk of the human-nature bond as "place attachment." More simplistically, poet Richard Wilbur defines a sense of place as a "fusion of human and natural order, and a peculiar window on the whole," and he went a step further to affirm, "A place is a piece of the whole environment that has been claimed by feelings."[7]

Georgia colonists, many of whom made the long journey for the chance to own a parcel of land, were in general trained to think of place as a piece of the whole environment claimed by a deed, and surely the principle of property as home remains current today. Rather than ownership or even tenancy, which define our relationship to place in economic terms, literary scholar Harold P. Simonson posited in 1989 that "a sense of place" entails being owned by land: one belongs to a place.[8] Residence is not a matter of property but embeddedness.

In studying the idea of place as it relates to literature, we think first of regionalism. The concept of "regionalism" in literature broadly connotes not only differences between specific regions of a country but also similarities *within* these regions.[9] Literary scholars use the term "local color" to refer to a movement in literature that began after the Civil War in work focusing on unique aspects of regions of the United States. Then, a century later, in conjunction with the environmental movement, the term "sense of place" began to show up in literary critiques. Sense of place, contrary to regionalism or local color, implies that a narrator, character, or writer understands the land not as a

political or cultural construct but as an ecological one. The place is an ecosystem within ecosystems. The term "sense of place," then, is only as old in common usage as the popularization of the concept of "ecology," which surged in
the 1960s, bringing with it the genre of "nature-writing" or "place-based writing."

Though all three terms—"sense of place," "local color," and "regionalism"—
spring from the same concept, the latter two tend to be linked to symboliza-
tion of a place only for a time, until that symbolism overshadows the reality
of the place that then ceases to be seen and experienced freshly and clearly.
"Regionalism would imply," poet William Stafford told the literary critic Lars
Nordstrom, "that the writer is deliberately exaggerating the localness of the
material. . . . A sense of place would be different, I think, because you would
not be deliberately exploiting or making hay out of the exoticness of the material; you would just be in the material, just be using what is natural to you
in your kind of life."[10] Magnolia blossoms and burning crosses, sweet tea and
mint juleps, tradition and family, typify the South. But the South is much
more complex.[11] Even now, we do ourselves a huge disservice to continue to
mythologize the South as a place of hospitality and manners; of paternalism
toward people of color; of farming communities; of innocent, salt-of-the-
earth agrarians; of coastal purity. The coast specifically symbolizes a place to
start anew, to re-create, to slow down; but the coast is so much more. Symbol-
ization obscures the complexity of the human experience and obstructs fresh
responses to the tragedies and trials of our time.

Poet Gary Snyder came to refer to this literary movement as "new regionalism." As Snyder said to Nordstrom, "What I am calling the new regionalism
starts very precisely from sense of place, rejects the necessity for an American
identity at all, renames the continent, renames the localities, erases political
boundaries, extends the time back."[12] We can dial time backward, as Snyder
proposed, until we reach an epoch that predates humans. But the human experience is necessary for our conceptualizations of nature, others argue. "The
concept of natural process is an idea that is useful only if one perceives human-
ity as part of it," writes landscape architect Michael Hough.[13] Wallace Stegner too writes, "So I must believe that, at least to human perception, a place is
not a place until people have been born in it, have grown up in it, lived in it,
known it, died in it—have both experienced and shaped it."[14]

I interpret sense of place as the experience of the human body in a landscape, the effect of the real environment on one's emotional landscape, the
intersection of the human heart with the natural world. The model for the
concept could be parallel lines, perhaps parallel narrative arcs between a geog-

raphy and a life. Sense of place involves conscious (as well as unconscious) cognition of the characteristics that make a particular space unique. I want to look at how a sense of place might manifest in a person.

Sometimes our birth gives us what poet and essayist Wendell Berry calls "nativity" with the land. "Some have the luck to be born, and to remain," Richard Wilbur writes, "in country which is continuous with their personalities; others ramble about until they can say at last, like Brigham Young, 'This is the place.'"[15] In this survey I address sense of place as it develops in a newcomer.

Beyond nativity, at its most elemental a sense of place begins in the eye, with visual calculation of the superficial—scenery—both of the sublime and the ordinary. As Hough says, "Natural scenery has a powerful influence on our perception of places."[16] Therefore, the first impressions of the Georgia immigrants offer fascinating perspectives. A year after Peter Gordon described a wall of wood and water, Baron Philipp Georg Friedrich von Reck accompanied the first band of Salzburgers to Georgia. The Salzburgers were German-speaking Protestants who had been expelled from predominantly Catholic Austria. King George II had felt enough sympathy for these refuge-seekers to offer them asylum in the new territory. Von Reck too kept a journal and in March 1733 he wrote, "God blessed us this Day with the Sight of our Country, our wish'd-for Georgia, which we saw at ten in the Morning, and brought us unto the Savannah River." He described the river in as painstaking detail as he could muster. "This River is in some Places broader than the Rhine, and from 16 to 25 Foot deep; and abounds with Oysters, Sturgeon, and other Fish. Its Banks were cloathed with fresh Grass; and a little beyond were seen Woods, old as the Creation; resounding with the Musick of Birds, who sing the Praise of their Creator."[17] His comparison of the new with the familiar is an attempt to comprehend and categorize his surroundings: the Savannah is like the Rhine.[18] The place is both fresh and ancient, and he conjures in it the divine, likely because his faith can remain a constant in the face of so much change.[19] Preoccupation with visual perception—scenery—is necessary when one has not spent time in a place. And although we Americans are particularly inflamed by scenery, some modern environmentalists avow that scenery limits real understanding and connection to a place, scenery being cursory and superficial. "The preoccupation with scenery as visual enjoyment is an expression of society's dissociation from nature and the processes that shape the land and its scenic variety," writes Hough.[20]

Fascination with scenery, in the eyes of a place-based thinker, is eclipsed by a desire for tell narratives, complete with epiphanies. This represents an inhabitant's quest for meaning: only through lived experience can deeper understandings of and in a place begin to develop. "No place is a place," Stegner declares, "until things that have happened in it are remembered in history, ballads, yarns, or monuments."[21] As nature writer and literary critic John Tallmadge writes, "A place is nothing more than a space with a story, and the basic question in all nature writing is, 'What happened here?'"[22]

Things began to happen to early writers on the Georgia coast. Peter Gordon reported the lived experience of his first storms, which had to have been a bit shocking. "The rains were very frequent and very severe," he wrote.[23] Other writers likewise noted the storms, including one Benjamin Ingham, who arrived in Georgia in 1736. Twenty-three years old, he had been a member of John and Charles Wesley's Methodist group at Oxford, and he had assumed clerical and educational duties for their mission. On January 25, ensconced in the new colony, Ingham wrote, "Towards evening we had a terrible Storm, which lasted several hours. I observ'd it well, and truly I never Saw any thing hitherto so solemn and majestic. The Sea Sparkled and Smoak'd as if it had been on fire; the Air darted forth Lightening, and the wind blew so fierce that You could scarce look it in the face and draw your Breath."[24]

First a writer sees a place. Then he or she begins to experience life there. The third stage of developing a sense of place involves scholarship—of the soils, the archaeology, the history, the weather, and, most important, the natural history. Natural history, as Hough points out, "tells us about things we cannot see, as well as those we can."[25] It tells us about things we cannot see from a distance or without patient observation. Natural history allows us to move beyond superficial understanding and beyond lived experience, relying on science to plunge deeper into layers of meaning and the interrelatedness of all biota. The oystercatcher needs the oyster, which depends on microorganisms, which need the spartina in the marsh. The white-tailed deer depend on the passionflowers, which need native bees, which require cavities in sand. The diamondback rattlesnake relies on the beach mice, which survive on seeds, which need soil and water, which we all depend on—a lovely, brutal web. Wendell Berry says, "One cannot act well or beneficently in a place until one has understood its nature, precedent to human intention." This nature Berry terms "the genius of a place."[26] Through inquiry we begin to understand the genius loci, or spirit of a place.

Perhaps the most useful and revelatory account of this three-step response to place comes in *A Voyage to Georgia Begun in the Year 1735*, by Francis Moore, who was in the company of forty families chosen to settle Frederica. On March 18, 1736, sailing from Savannah down the coast, Moore described the scenery: "The Land seem'd high about the Middle. . . . It look'd pleasant, the Beach being white Sand, the Woods lofty, and the Land hilly."[27] Then things began to happen: "After Mr. Oglethorpe was gone to Savannah, most of the Colony went ashore upon Peeper Island [this is Cockspur, in the mouth of the Savannah], where I found an Eagle's Nest on a Fir-tree; we cut it down, and found an Egg in it, in which was a young Eagle."[28] Moore's natural history, as with the writings of most early European explorers and settlers, begins with lists of flora and fauna, a documentation for which his work as storekeeper and recorder perhaps prepares him: live oak, water oak, laurel, bay, cedar, gum, sassafras, pines, fox grape, deer, rabbits, "Rackoons" ("a Creature something like a Bedger, but somewhat less, with a bushy Tail like a Squirrel, tabbied with Rings of brown and black"), wild turkeys, partridges, turtledoves, "the red Bird, or Virginia Nightingale," "the mocking Bird," "the Rice-Bird," "the common English Wild Goose," mallards, teal, "a Hooping Crane," "Poor Jobs," hawks, "the Land and the Sea Eagle," pelicans, cormorants, alligators, rattle-snakes, "the Black, the Red, and the Chicken Snake," and so on.[29]

But Moore was more than a list maker. He exhibited a passion for natural history and was curious, observant, and disciplined in his note taking. "I have seen several of these Snakes which were kill'd at Frederica," Moore wrote, "the largest above two Yards long, the Belly white, and the Back of a brown Co-lour; they seem to be of the Viper Kind, and are of a strong Smell, somewhat like Musk. The Rattles are Rings at the End of their Tails of a horny Substance; these shaking together make a Noise, which with their strong musky Smell gives Cautious People Notice where they are."[30]

He continued: "I observed here a kind of long Moss I had never seen before; it grows in great Quantities upon the large Trees, and hangs down 3 or 4 Yards from the Boughs; it gives a noble, ancient and hoary Look to the Woods; it is of a whitish green Colour, but when dried, is black and like Horse-hair." Thus the Georgia coast becomes Place of Rattlesnakes and Place of Spanish Moss, and it becomes Place of Fox Squirrels: "There are great Numbers of Squirrels of different Sizes, the little Kind the same as in England, a lesser than that, not much bigger than a Mouse, and a large grey Sort, very near as big as a Rabit, which those who are accustomed to the Country say, eats as well." And the Georgia coast was Place of Buffalos: "The Island abounds with Deer and Ra-bits; there are no Buffaloes in it, though there are large Herds of them upon the Main."[31]

By far the greatest recorders of natural history during the era of European settlement were father-and-son duo John and William Bartram. Born in Pennsylvania in 1699, John Bartram was drawn to botany even as a child, and as a young man he began to collect native American plants and to transplant them to his farm, then to ship specimens to botanists in Europe. He is credited with introducing many New World plants, including Venus flytrap, kalmia, fringe tree, and umbrella magnolia, to horticulture. To find new plants, he journeyed farther and farther afield. Between July 1, 1765, and April 10, 1766, he traveled with his son William on a botanical exploration of the new territories. In his subsequent book, *Diary of a Journey through the Carolinas, Georgia, and Florida*, John Bartram recorded what he found. On October 1, 1765, he wrote, "This days rideing was very bad thro bay swamps, tupelos both sorts, & Cypress in deep water, some of which on the borders was very full of brush & bryers, yet got safe through all. This days Journey of 20 mile was all low flat ground, the highest piney ground seldom above 3 or 4 foot perpendicular above the swamps . . . we saw several dear, 2 or 3 together both young & ould, & several turkeys." And so his account goes. He makes long lists: A dwarf oak with long, shining leaves. A winter oak with little oval leaves. Water oak and white oak. Papaws. "Chinkapins." "Fine flowering shrubs beside the great magnolia." "Red & purple berried bay & umbrella." Maple. "Alcea florideana." Sassafras. "Cornus." "Mirtle." Pines. Hop hornbeam. "A shrub like the dogwood." "Liquid amber." "Persimons." "Cephalanthus." "Two kinds of Ash." "A rare tupelo with large red acid fruite called limes, which is used for punch."[32]

Years later, William Bartram, whom John's journal refers to as "Billy," retraced their earlier path. William left Philadelphia in 1773 on a journey that would last four years and take him through eight southern colonies, resulting in the epic volume we know today as *Bartram's Travels* (first published in 1791). Its writing is floral, soaring, painstaking, its achievement monumental. Of especial interest are his keen perceptions of the Georgia coast, a set of "fine islands," as he called them. One of my favorite scenes from *Travels* is a brief anecdote. "At length I doubled the utmost south point of St. Simon's, which forms the north cape of the south channel of the great river Alatamaha," the account began. "The sound, just within this cape, forms an excellent bay, or cove, on the south end of the island, on the opposite side of which I beheld a house and farm, where I soon arrived." Bartram followed a line of beehives along an avenue and found the good man of the house reclining on a bearskin, spread under the shade of a live oak, smoking his pipe. The planter's servant brought the traveler a bowl of honey and water, then served a repast of venison. Bartram wrote: "Our rural table was spread under the shadow of Oaks, Palms, and Sweet Bays, fanned by the lively salubrious breezes wafted from the spicy groves. Our music was the responsive love-lays of the painted nonpareil, and the alert and gay mockbird; whilst the brilliant hummingbird darted through the flowery groves, suspended in air, and drank nectar from the flowers of the

FIGURE 10.1. William Bartram (1739–1823)
by Charles Willson Peale, ca. 1808.
Courtesy of Independence National Historic Park.

yellow Jasmine, Lonicera, Andromeda, and sweet Azalea." The prose is poetic and ecstatic, evidence of an impressive diction and a tremendous joie de vivre. But perhaps the ecstasy is derived from the brandy in the honey-water. Bartram continues: "But yet, how awfully great and sublime is the majestic scene east-ward! The solemn sound of the beating surf strikes our ears; the dashing of yon liquid mountains, like mighty giants, in vain assail the skies; they are beaten back, and fall prostrate upon the shores of the trembling island."[33]

So much of American sensibility has focused on westward expansion and the new frontier. Tutored into colonizers and capitalists was the idea of a new place with unlimited resources and unbridled potential, and so much of American culture has followed this design, all the way to the grandeur of the Rocky Mountains and the trophy of the Pacific Ocean. In this passage, instead of praising westward motion and vision, Bartram gazes east, toward the Atlantic Ocean, where things began in colonial America, and he gazes everywhere. This is what a place needs from its inhabitants—to look downward, to the ground, and to look around.

Out of reverence for the Bartrams' work, naturalist Francis Harper, sometimes accompanied by his brother Roland, studied the father-and-son travelers during the first half of the twentieth century and retraced their routes. Francis published naturalist's annotated editions of both John's *Diary* and William's *Travels*, adding more layers of understanding to the ecology of the region and to the body of place-based literature of the Georgia coast.[34]

In examining this literature, we find that some elements have a particular effect on writers, and top among these is Georgia's stunning and extensive salt marshes. Elder Bartram wrote about a "very extensive salt marsh all covered with salt water at high tides."[35] Younger Bartram observed in greater detail: "There is a large space betwixt this chain of seacoast-islands and the main land, perhaps generally near three leagues in breadth; but all this space is not covered with water: I estimate nearly two-thirds of it to consist of low salt plains, which produce Barilla, Sedge, Rushes, etc. and which border on the main land."[36]

Over seventy years after William Bartram traversed what I'll call Place of Saltmarsh, in December 1838 Frances Anne Kemble, known as Fanny Kemble, an accomplished British actress, accompanied her husband, Pierce Mease Butler, to the Sea Islands. Two years before, Butler had inherited his grandfather's land holdings and other property, including hundreds of slaves. Kemble was morally opposed to slavery. During the winter of 1838–39, Kemble faithfully kept a diary, which would be published in 1863 as *Journal of a Residence on a Georgian Plantation in 1838–1839.* "I should like the wild savage loneliness of the far away existence if it were not for the one small item of 'the slavery,'" she wrote. That "small item" contributed to a marital separation in 1845 and divorce in 1849. Kemble writes of her first walk on "the island," which apparently was one of the small islands in the mouth of the Altamaha: "After this I got out of the vicinity of the settlement, and pursued my way along a narrow dyke—the river on one hand, and on the other a slimy, poisonous-looking swamp, all rattling with sedges of enormous height, in which one might lose one's way as effectually as in a forest of oaks."[37]

I remember the first time I myself saw the salt marsh. I was a child driving with my family to Brunswick. We reached the place where Highway 341 first crosses a salt creek, Burnett, and its attendant marsh. My father, who had studied with wonderful teachers in the public school system of Appling County and who had been made to memorize poetry, quoted a beautiful couplet about the marsh. It had the name of the county—Glynn—in it. I saw the landscape from the moving car as an endless sweep of spiky grass, a landscape wholly different from any that I had known. Over the years of my life I have learned that the scenic salt marsh is full of secret life, populated as it is with marsh periwinkles, mud snails, air-breathing coffeebean snails, mud fiddler crabs, purple marsh crabs, oysters, and ribbed mussels. Higher in the marsh, clapper rails build cup-shaped nests of grasses and sedges in clumps of vegetation above the high-tide line. They soften their nests with fine strips of grass, often build ramps leading into them, and sometimes even erect canopies overhead. The seaside sparrow, a bird so closely connected to the salt marsh that its abundance indicates the health of the system (and already the subspecies "dusky" is extinct), walks around gleaning soft-bodied spiders and sedge seeds. Sand fiddlers and wharf crabs scurry about.

In 1847 Francis Robert Goulding (1810–81), son of Presbyterian minister Thomas Goulding of Liberty County, Georgia, began work on a popular juvenile novel that was published in 1852. It was called *The Young Marooners on the Florida Coast*. Although most of the action takes place near Tampa Bay, the book's child sailors journey southward through the Sea Islands. The writing is vivid and beautiful: "On the first day of September the voyagers approached some placid-looking islands, tasseled above with lofty palmettos, and varied beneath with every hue of green, from the soft colour of the mallow to the sombre tint of the cedar and the glossy green of the live oak."[38] In the preface to a later edition of the novel, Goulding admitted to a desire to impart a sense of place: "There were many *facts in nature* which I wished to communicate." Another of his books was *Sapelo, or, Child-Life on the Tidewater*, published in 1870. Although Goulding was born in coastal Georgia, he spent much of his life away from it.

On March 13, 1853, the British novelist William Makepeace Thackeray, author of *Vanity Fair* and a prodigious lecturer, arrived by steamer to Georgia. What he reported was a little less glowing than descriptions by others who had come before. He wrote in a letter to his daughters that Savannah "is approached by a red muddy river like the Nile with great swampy stretches of gray flats, lying to the right and left negro houses here and there, and groves of darkling cedars and now and again palmetto-trees sprouting up. Along the red river you see white steamers padeling flinging out great rolling banners of smoke, or across the stream shoot black canoes with black rowers and black passengers, and then you come to a quay with a hundred ships."[39] Thackeray saw black rowers, black canoes, darkling cedars, smoke, and mud.

John Muir, a Scottish-born naturalist who would later fall in love with the

American West, found the Sierra Club, and help establish a number of national parks, explored the southern territories in late 1867. He wrote, in his beguiling *A Thousand-Mile Walk to the Gulf*, ecstatically and brilliantly of the landscape through which he passed. In early October, in the delta of the Savannah River, he wrote: "Am made to feel that I am now in a strange land. I know hardly any of the plants, but few of the birds, and I am unable to see the country for the solemn, dark, mysterious cypress woods which cover everything. The winds are full of strange sounds, making one feel far from the people and plants and fields of home. Night is coming on and I am filled with indescribable loneliness. Felt feverish; bathed in a black, silent stream; nervously watchful for alligators."[40]

He too commented on Spanish moss, writing, "Toward evening I came to the country of one of the most striking of southern plants, the so-called 'Long Moss' or Spanish Moss [Tillandsia], though it is a flowering plant and be-longs to the same family as the pineapple [Bromelworts]. The trees hereabouts have all their branches draped with it, producing a remarkable effect." He also described the salt marshes that so sublimely represent the landscape of the Georgia coast, "belonging more to the sea than to the land; with groves here and there, green and unflowered, sunk to the shoulders in sedges and rushes; with trees farther back, ill defined in their boundary, and instead of rising in hilly waves and swellings, stretching inland in low water-like levels."[41]

In 1878 Nathaniel H. Bishop's *Voyage of the Paper Canoe* was published. Bishop was a corresponding member of the Boston Society of Natural History and the New York Academy of Sciences. During 1874–75 Bishop floated a small canoe twenty-five hundred miles from Quebec to the Gulf of Mexico. Bishop's writing is lovely, melodic and fluid. Consider this line: "The fish sprang from the water as I touched it with my light oars." On March 9, 1875, he noted the salt marshes: "The bright sunlight played with the shadows of the clouds upon the wide marshes, which were now growing green with the warmth of returning spring." And he wrote, "One of the sudden tempests which frequently vex these coastal waters arose, and drove me to a hammock." Coming there upon "cabins of two or three families of negroes," he continued, "I waded to my knees in the mud before the canoe could be landed, and, as it stormed all night, I slept on the floor of the humble cot of the negro Echard Holmes."

So far in this survey, the picture painted is by far that of the traveler forming incipient impressions and then moving on. However, the sense of place developed after a month or years in a locale is not the sense of place of decades, and the sense of place of decades is not that of generations. I don't say this because

I come from generations of South Georgia colonizers. I say it as a traveler, having seen many landscapes, experienced them, made lists and sketches of their wildflowers and birds, meandered their trails, sized up their people—and departed a stranger, a dilettante. History is like soil, with strata of knowledge from bedrock to topsoil. The traveler represents the duff on the forest floor, blowing away, leaving trace minerals. The inhabitant deteriorates into the humus of the place.

Because memory is the vessel for stories, some of them are contained for a while before being passed around and down, cultural intelligence that moves from person to person, ancestor to heir. In other words, some stories are cultural exchange, while other stories are heritage. Some disappear. New stories form, and those likewise get exchanged, passed down, or lost. Whether the storyteller is aware of it or not, contained within all of the new stories are the generations and layers of old ones, making the culture richer and more fertile.

I have discussed three stages of a sense of place. I believe that a sense of place, in order to be fully formed, highly developed, and most useful to literature, involves a fourth requisite. This is settling down, what Hough calls a "stability and sense of investment in the land because one's wellbeing and survival depend on it."[42] It is a commitment, fidelity, the "permanence" of which historian and author Buddy Sullivan speaks.[43] If a person is transported to a novel landscape long after birth, a sense of that place can occur because of sights, experiences, and education, and this sense deepens with the accumulation of time spent there. Time allows inhabitants, if they are lucky, to become, as Wallace Stegner wrote in his famous essay "The Sense of Place," "lovers of known earth, known weathers, and known neighbors both human and nonhuman," and thus native.[44]

Charles Colcock Jones is perhaps the first writer of settlement-era Georgia who spent most of his life in the place. Born in 1804 in Liberty County, he attended seminary and became a Presbyterian missionary and professor. Jones wrestled with the moral dilemma of slavery and solved the problem in his own mind by becoming a "benevolent slaveholder" and a "Christian slaveholder" until the Civil War removed his source of wealth. He published *Catechism of Scripture Doctrine and Practice* (1837), *The Religious Instruction of the Negroes in the United States* (1842), and *A History of the Church of God* (1867). His work is not place-based in the strict sense of the adjective but is worth mentioning because he lived and died in this place.

His son, Charles Colcock Jones Jr. (1831–93), was also a writer and became a historian of renown. He attended Princeton and Harvard, where he obtained a law degree. He served as mayor of Savannah starting in 1860 but moved to New York following the war. In 1877 he returned south, this time to Augusta. His works include *Historical Sketch of the Chatham Artillery* (1867), *Antiquities of the Southern Indians, Particularly of the Georgia Tribes* (1873), *The Siege of Savannah in December, 1864* (1874), *The Dead Towns of Georgia* (1878), and *History of Georgia* (1883). Toward the end of his life, Jones became fascinated with folklore. Joel Chandler Harris's dialect tales of Uncle Remus were enjoying great popularity as local color. Harris contacted Jones, seeking stories for his second book, and over the next five years, Jones collected fifty-seven oral narratives that he published in 1888 in the book *Negro Myths of the Georgia Coast*. It was reprinted by the University of Georgia Press in 2000 as *Gullah Folktales from the Georgia Coast*. Thus some of the unwritten narratives have been folded into the written culture. The same is true of *Slave Songs of the United States*, a collection of spirituals published in 1867.[45] Likewise *Slave Songs of the Georgia Sea Islands*, by Lydia Austin Parrish, wife of famed American painter Maxfield Parrish, who wintered and died on St. Simons Island, a now-classic anthology of sixty folk songs from descendants of slaves, first published in 1942.[46]

A contemporary of the younger Jones, Sidney Lanier (1842–81), Macon-born attorney, musician, composer, and poet, wrote what is arguably the most famous ode to the coast, a magnificent poem beloved by the schoolchildren of Georgia for a century, "The Marshes of Glynn." The poem was inspired by visits to Brunswick in the 1860s and 1870s.

> And what if behind me to westward the wall of the woods stands high?
> The world lies east: how ample, the marsh and the sea and the sky!
> A league and a league of marsh-grass, waist-high, broad in the blade,
> Green, and all of a height, and unflecked with a light or a shade,
> Stretch leisurely off, in a pleasant plain,
> To the terminal blue of the main.

> Oh, what is abroad in the marsh and the terminal sea?
> Somehow my soul seems suddenly free
> From the weighing of fate and the sad discussion of sin,
> By the length and the breadth and the sweep of the marshes of Glynn.

Within this poem we see again the idea of the untrammeled west—and the writer, against all cultural movement westward—looking east. Lanier is swimming upstream. "The world lies east," he says, which can be read to mean, "Look around. Stay home. This place is good—more than good, actually. This place is divine." Lanier proceeds to use the language of grandeur, language re-

FIGURE 10.2. Sidney Lanier (1842–81).
Courtesy of Hargrett Rare Book and Manuscript Library,
University of Georgia Libraries.

served for western vistas, for the eastern coast: "length" and "breadth" and "sweep." This is "ample," he says.

I return to Stegner's audacious thoughts about place: "No place is a place until it has had a poet. . . . No place, not even a wild place, is a place until it has had that human attention that at its highest reach we will call poetry."[47] If we believe this, then we can say that the Georgia coast was not a place until Sidney Lanier came to visit.

Following Lanier, Conrad Aiken (1889–1973) was the first Georgia writer to win a Pulitzer Prize, in 1930, for his *Selected Poems*. Aiken spent the first eleven years and last eleven years of his life in Georgia—Savannah, specifically—but his writing rarely took up homeland as a subject or theme. Daniel Whitehead Hicky (1900–76), who made the shortlist for a Pulitzer Prize in

1941, was a poet likened to Lanier in theme. Although he lived in Atlanta most of his adult life, his collection *Wild Heron* was written largely in the Golden Isles.

One of the most interesting writers of the coast was a woman born in Charleston, West Virginia, in 1916, a woman who fell in love with the Golden Isles on a visit in 1961 during a book tour and who would spend the rest of her life researching and telling its stories in fiction startlingly faithful to real life. Eugenia Price was a woman smitten with a place, a love borne out in book after book. Her most famous is a trilogy of historical novels: *The Beloved Invader* (1965), *New Moon Rising* (1969), and *Lighthouse* (1972). She wrote, "Sit down, sit down, if you can find a place. Try this chair by the window, where you can behold our glorious sunset over our glorious marsh."[48] Price died on St. Simons Island in 1996.

Other writers, with varying degrees of being place-based, should be mentioned: black activist and resettlement agent Tunis Campbell, with his *Sufferings of the Rev. T. G. Campbell and His Family in Georgia* (1877); Savannah-born Flannery O'Connor, whose work is distinctly inland; John Berendt with his *Midnight in the Garden of Good and Evil*; James Kilgo, Jack Leigh, Alan Campbell, and John Lane, and their *Ossabaw: Evocations of an Island*; Buddy Sullivan, with many modern environmental histories, including *Early Days on the Georgia Tidewater* and *A Georgia Tidewater Companion*; St. Simons Island resident Tina McElroy-Ansa, whose books center around the make-believe town of Mulberry, Georgia, which is similar to the Macon of her childhood; Taylor Schoettle and Mallory Pearce and their naturalist guides; and Anthony J. Martin and his *Life Traces on the Georgia Coast*.

The Georgia coast, like the rest of the country, was colonized by displaced persons, and we Americans have been loathe to take the motion out of ourselves. The settling of America—its colonization—was almost immediately followed by what Wendell Berry calls "the unsettling of America."[49] The process of abandoning a country for another country, and countryside for countryside, is well established. For a brief century or two we endured (or enjoyed) a period of agrarian landedness, but that era has ended, and we Americans have become, for the most part, a placeless and thus homeless people. "Nothing in our history has bound us to a plot of ground as feudalism once bound Europeans," writes Stegner.[50] Four-fifths of us now live in cities, not close to the land at all. Fewer of us are getting out in the nature that is left. We have seen, in the words of Richard Louv, the last child in the woods. We live in places, of course, and travel between them, but most of us have few real connections to the landscape. Our ties are financial, or human, or by default—we are kept in a place because we find ourselves there. We urge restlessness in our children: if they are to be successful, they should leave the places where they are born and reared, because to stay put is to fail. We do not know the texture and fertility of the soil, and frosts harden and melt upon non-native grasses without our ken. A certain arrangement of clouds means little, if anything, and even the common names of the birds and insects and reptiles are lost.

We humans are biological, absolutely dependent on the earth for survival—suckling babes at the breast of earth—and I believe that we lose part of our humanness when we lose our engagement to place. I believe that it is essential to know and understand the cycles of seasons, moons, weather, tides, and all the things that connect us to the thousands of generations that were here before there were cell phones and global positioning systems and birdsong computer applications. Therefore, the highest and best use for a piece of land is its natural processes, on which we're all dependent for health and life.

The South has been hard-hit environmentally, and the Georgia coast is no exception. The area of natural forest across the South has declined from 356 million acres in colonial times to about half that today. Fourteen ecosystems across the South have declined to occupy only 2 percent of their original range. By 1995, 99 percent of the longleaf pine forests of the coastal plain were gone. There are more threatened ecosystems in the South than any other region of the country. Half of the forested wetlands—swamps and marshes—of the South have been lost.

People are attracted to coastlines, but rampant and unregulated development destroys them. Jekyll Island, for example, is under constant pressure from challenges to its state-granted protection, and some parts of the island have become unrecognizable to me in my lifetime. Preserving wilderness on Cumberland Island is a recurring battle. Up and down the coast, Georgia's salt marshes are continually assaulted—dozed and filled for road projects, for houses, for docks. "On the Georgia coast the environmentalist never sleeps." In the hands of planners and developers, our places change so fast that our memories fall away, leaving us on shifting sands, longing for lifeways some of us never knew, a perplexing nostalgia. Our places look more and more homogenous. Our stories stop making sense. Culture disintegrates.

Georgians, like all southerners, have long been typified as devotees of place. Our qualities are said to include reverence for history and a strong and implacable sense of our geography, two themes that course through our literature. Yet what happens if the essence of our coastal landscape vanishes? What happens to our sense of place and our culture and thus our identity? Does our culture become entirely urban, streetwise, irreverent, disloyal, speechless? Does it turn its back on family, history, and land? Does the literature, as Reynolds Price suggested, consist of "bad poems and novels full of neon light on wet asphalt, unshaven chins, scalding coffee at four a.m.?" Is this the danger, that we lose a defining culture (that served to shape our literature, having also been shaped by it) and so must, through our literature, reinvent ourselves?

American culture since colonization has focused on opportunity and abundance, the new frontier always ahead. Half a millennium has passed since Europeans first laid eyes on the continent. Now all our frontiers save the internal ones have been crossed. It is time we settled down. It is time to be domestic, to pay attention to our home places. It is time as a country and as a region to grow up.

During the long environmental history of the Georgia coast, many peoples have called it home: Native Americans, colonizers, imperialists, plantation owners, slaves and freedpeople, wealthy industrialists, nature lovers and environmentalists, wilderness-savers, fishers and millworkers, loggers and pulpers, and more. Somehow, through all the waves of settlement, we have managed on the Georgia coast to save a great deal of its essence, its character, its nature. It is time to have a deeply honest conversation about what has made and continues to make this place a good home and to address what we love as part of our policy making.

It is time to become scholars of the incredible and magnificent Georgia coast, to listen to its stories, and to write them down. The environmental history of the coast is written in its literature, and much remains unstated. I believe that we can create a literature in which we can clearly see the Georgia coast as the remarkable and inimitable place that it is, and this will be a literature of caretaking, recognizing that the coast has sustained centuries of human inhabitants. The coast has weathered groundswells and trends, upsurges and impulses. Likewise it has withstood dearth and deficits, shortcomings and imperfections. My hope is that we cultivate, in our lives and in our literature, a sense of place and a reverence so profound that we protect the Georgia coast, with its spectacular ecological richness, its dramatic and sensuous beauty, and its extraordinary history.

NOTES

1. The term "archipelago" here is used in the sense, "a sea in which there are islands" (*Oxford English Dictionary* [1971], s.v. "archipelago").

2. Luca Vázquez de Ayllon visited the Georgia coast in 1526, and Franciscan missions were established in the late sixteenth century, including Mission Santa Catalina de Guale in 1580.

3. Peter Gordon, "Journal of Peter Gordon," *Our First Visit in America: Early Reports from the Colony of Georgia, 1732–1740* (Savannah, Ga.: Beehive Press, 1974), 16.

4. The story of human habitation along the Georgia coast stretches much farther back than five thousand years. David Hurst Thomas at the Coastal Nature, Coastal Culture symposium reported that canoes eight thousand years old have been found in Florida. It should be noted that the coastline of Georgia eight thousand years ago was at Gray's Reef, located sixteen miles east of Sapelo and now sixty to seventy feet underwater. "Older human occupations are, of course, still farther out (and more deeply underwater)—many have been found off Florida," said Thomas.

5. John B. Jackson, *Discovering the Vernacular Landscape* (New Haven, Conn.: Yale University Press, 1984).

6. "Topos" + "philia" = love of place.

7. Richard Wilbur, introduction to *A Sense of Place: The Artist and the American Land*, by Alan Gussow (San Francisco: Friends of the Earth, 1972), 27.

8. Harold P. Simonson, *Beyond the Frontier: Writers, Western Regionalism, and A Sense of Place* (Fort Worth: Texas Christian University Press, 1989), 174.

9. Anne E. Rowe, "Regionalism and Local Color," Documenting the American South, University Library, University of North Carolina, http://docsouth.unc.edu/southlit/regionalism.html.

10. Lars Nordstrom, *Theodore Roethke, William Stafford, and Gary Snyder: The Ecological Metaphor as Transformed Regionalism* (Uppsala, Sweden: Uppsala University, 1989), 16.

11. The region must also exist as a subset of the whole, which especially in the South introduces a set of painful politics. In many ways the postwar local color movement was a reaction against the Civil War, which established nationalism over regionalism (and also the onslaught of a capitalistic society, which was already destroying local identities and local resources in favor of national economic expansionism).

12. Nordstrom, *Theodore Roethke, William Stafford, and Gary Snyder*, 16.

13. Michael Hough, *Out of Place: Restoring Identity to the Regional Landscape* (New Haven, Conn.: Yale University Press, 1990), 32.

14. Wallace Earle Stegner, "The Sense of Place," in *Where the Bluebird Sings to the Lemonade Springs* (New York: Random House, 1992), 201.

15. Wilbur, *A Sense of Place*, 25.

16. Hough, *Out of Place*, 19.

17. Baron Von Reck and J. M. Bolvius, "An Extract of the Journals of Mr. Commissary von Reck and of the Reverend Mr. Bolzius," in *Our First Visit in America: Early Reports from the Colony of Georgia, 1732–1740*, ed. Trevor Richard Reese (Savannah, Ga.: Beehive Press, 1974), 46.

18. Likely Von Reck borrowed this comparison from Oglethorpe, who used it in the pamphlet that he published in order to build support for a debtor's colony in Georgia.

19. Trevor Richard Reese, introduction to *Our First Visit in America*, ix. Gordon's, Von Reck's, and others' stories of early European settlement of the Georgia coast are

collected in this wonderful volume. As British historian and scholar Reese writes in the foreword, the book "contains useful and interesting narrative and commentary on the founding periods of the new colony."

20. Hough, *Out of Place*, 24.

21. Stegner, "The Sense of Place," 3.

22. John Tallmadge, "Writing as a Window into Nature," in Claire Walker Leslie, John Tallmadge, and Tom Wessels, *Into the Field: A Guide to Locally Focused Teaching* (Great Barrington, Mass.: Orion Society, 1999), 24.

23. Gordon, "Journal of Peter Gordon," 16.

24. Benjamin Ingham, "Mr. Ingham's Journal of His Voyage to Georgia," in Reese, ed., *Our First Visit in America*, 173.

25. Hough, *Out of Place*, 26.

26. Berry, *Standing by Words*, 156.

27. Francis Moore, *A Voyage to Georgia Begun in the Year 1735* (London: Ludgate-Street, 1744), 50.

28. Ibid., 92–93.

29. Ibid., 55–60.

30. Ibid., 122–23.

31. Ibid., 108, 120.

32. John Bartram, *Diary of a Journey through the Carolinas, Georgia, and Florida from July 1, 1765 to April 10, 1766*, annotated by Francis Harper (Philadelphia: American Philosophical Society, 1942), 42.

33. William Bartram, *Travels through North and South Carolina, Georgia, East and West Florida, the Cherokee Country, the Extensive Territories of the Muscogulges, or Creek Confederacy, and the Country of the Chactaws; Containing an Account of the Soil and Natural Productions of Those Regions, Together with Observations on the Manners of the Indians* (1791), electronic ed., Documenting the American South, University Library, University of North Carolina, 2001, http://docsouth.unc.edu/nc/bartram/bartram.html, hereafter William Bartram, *Travels*.

34. More than two centuries after William Bartram's journey, Dorinda G. Dallmeyer, an environmental ethicist, University of Georgia professor, and nature writer, compiled a new edition of *Travels*, which is in part reflections "acknowledging the debt Southern nature writers owe the man called the 'South's Thoreau.'" William Bartram, *Bartram's Living Legacy: The "Travels" and the Nature of the South*, ed. Dorinda G. Dallmeyer (Macon, Ga.: Mercer University Press, 2010), xi.

35. John Bartram, *Diary of a Journey through the Carolinas, Georgia, and Florida, from July 1, 1765, to April 10, 1766*, 53.

36. William Bartram, *Travels*.

37. Frances Anne Kemble, *Journal of a Residence on a Georgian Plantation in 1838–1839*, edited by John Anthony Scott (1961; repr., Athens: University of Georgia Press, 1984), 18.

38. Francis Robert Goulding, *Young Marooners on the Florida Coast* (Philadelphia: William S. Martien, 1852), 16.

39. Jane Lightcap Brown, "From Augusta to Columbus: Thackeray's Experiences in Georgia, 1853 and 1856," *Georgia Historical Quarterly*, Fall 1983, 307.

40. John Muir, *A Thousand-Mile Walk to the Gulf* (Boston: Houghton Mifflin, 1916), 13.

41. Ibid., 13, 17.

42. Hough, *Out of Place*, 35.

43. Buddy Sullivan, Coastal Nature Coastal Culture symposium, February 2016, Savannah, Georgia.

44. Stegner, "Sense of Place," 1.

45. William Francis Allen, Charles Pickard Ware, and Lucy McKim Garrison, *Slave Songs of the United States* (1867), electronic ed., Documenting the American South, University Library, University of North Carolina, 2000, http://docsouth.unc.edu/church/allen/allen.html.

46. Lydia Austin Parrish, *Slave Songs of the Georgia Sea Islands* (New York: Creative Age Press, 1942).

47. Stegner, "Sense of Place," 3.

48. Eugenia Price, *The Beloved Invader* (Nashville, Tenn.: Turner Publishing Company, 1965), 29.

49. Wendell Berry, *The Unsettling of America: Culture and Agriculture* (San Francisco: Sierra Club Books, 1977).

50. Stegner, "Sense of Place," 4.

CONTRIBUTORS

ELLIOT H. BLAIR is assistant professor at the University of Alabama. He is an anthropological archaeologist whose research focuses on the early colonial and Late Mississippian periods in the Southeast. He is coauthor of *The Beads of St. Catherines*.

WILLIAM BOYD is professor of law, John H. Schultz Energy Law Fellow, and director of the Laboratory for Energy and Environmental Policy Innovation at the University of Colorado, Boulder. He is the author of *The Slain Wood: Papermaking and its Environmental Consequences in the American South*.

DORINDA G. DALLMEYER is director of the Environmental Ethics Certificate Program, College of Environmental Design, University of Georgia. She is author of numerous articles and chapters and coauthor of *Altamaha: A River and Its Keeper* and *Bartram's Living Legacy: The Travels and the Nature of the South*.

S. MAX EDELSON is associate professor of history at the University of Virginia. He is the author of *Plantation Enterprise in Colonial South Carolina* and *The New Map of Empire: How Britain Imagined America before Independence*. He is codirector of the University of Virginia Early American Seminar at Monticello and director of MapScholar, an online platform for map history visualization.

BARBARA FERTIG is professor of history at Georgia Southern University–Armstrong Campus and a specialist in African American life in the Georgia Lowcountry. She has studied the Pin Point community, conducting oral history interviews and researching its connections to the islands.

EDDA L. FIELDS-BLACK, a specialist in early and precolonial African history and the African diaspora, is associate professor of history at Carnegie Mellon University. She is the author of *Deep Roots: Rice Farmers in West Africa and the African Diaspora*, and she is currently working on a historical study on the Gullah Geechee.

CHRISTOPHER J. MANGANIELLO is the water policy director at Chattahoochee Riverkeeper. He previously worked for Georgia River Network and taught at the University of Georgia and Georgia Gwinnett College. He is the author of *Southern Water, Southern Power: How the Politics of Cheap Energy and Water Scarcity Shaped a Region*.

TIYA MILES is the Mary Henrietta Graham Distinguished University Professor at the University of Michigan, where she teaches in the departments of American Culture, History, Afroamerican and African Studies, Native American Studies, and Women's Studies. She is the author of four history books: *The House on Diamond Hill: A Cherokee Plantation History*; *Ties That Bind: The Story of an Afro-Cherokee Family in Slav-*

ery and Freedom; *Tales from the Haunted South*; and *The Dawn of Detroit: A Chronicle of Slavery and Freedom in the City of Straits*. She has also written a novel, *The Cherokee Rose*.

ROBERT B. OUTLAND III teaches history at Louisiana State University. He is the author of *Tapping the Pines: The Naval Store Industry in the American South*, winner of the Charles A. Weyerhaeuser Award for superior scholarship in forest and conservation history.

PAUL M. PRESSLY is director emeritus of the Ossabaw Island Education Alliance, a partnership between the Georgia Department of Natural Resources, the Ossabaw Island Foundation, and the Board of Regents of the University System of Georgia. He is author of *On the Rim of the Caribbean: Colonial Georgia and the British Atlantic World*.

JANISSE RAY is a poet, writer of literary nonfiction, and environmental activist. She is the author of *Ecology of a Cracker Childhood* and *Drifting into Darien: A Personal and Natural History of the Altamaha River*, among other works. She is a member of the Georgia Writers Hall of Fame.

SARAH ROSS is president of the Wormsloe Foundation, director of the Wormsloe Institute for Environmental History, and director of the University of Georgia Center for Research and Education at Wormsloe.

MATTHEW C. SANGER is assistant professor of anthropology and codirector of the public archaeology program at Binghamton University, State University of New York. His forthcoming book is titled *The Making of Place in the Archaic Coastal American Southeast*.

CHARLES SEABROOK is a columnist and writer for the *Atlanta Journal-Constitution*. His columns include a long-running series titled *Wild Georgia*. He is the author of *The World of the Salt Marsh*, among other works.

MART A. STEWART is professor of history at Western Washington University. He is the author of *"What Nature Suffers to Groe": Life, Labor, and Landscape on the Georgia Coast, 1680 to 1920*. He has published widely on environmental history, he is the founding editor of Flows, Migrations, Exchanges, a book series at the University of North Carolina Press, and he has been involved in cooperative teaching and research projects in Vietnam and Cambodia. He was a forester in an earlier career.

PAUL S. SUTTER is professor of history and chair of the History Department at the University of Colorado Boulder. He is the author of *Driven Wild: How the Fight against Automobiles Launched the Modern Wilderness Movement* and *Let Us Now Praise Famous Gullies: Providence Canyon and the Soils of the South*, and he is coauthor of *The Art of Managing Longleaf: A Personal History of the Stoddard-Neel Approach*. He is also the series editor of Weyerhaeuser Environmental Books, published by the University of Washington Press.

DREW A. SWANSON is associate professor of history at Wright State University. He is the author of *Remaking Wormsloe Plantation: The Environmental History of a Low-country Landscape* and *A Golden Weed: Tobacco and Environment in the Piedmont South*. He worked as a farmer and a natural resource manager before turning to academia.

DAVID HURST THOMAS is curator of anthropology at the American Museum of Natural History and founding trustee of the National Museum of Indian History. He is the author of numerous books, monographs, and scientific articles, including *Skull Wars: Kennewick Man, Archaeology, and the Battle for Native American Identity* and *St. Catherines: An Island in Time*. He has conducted archaeology on St. Catherines Island for more than forty years.

RANDAL L. WALKER is associate professor at the University of Georgia and retired director of Marine Extension Services, the School of Marine Programs.

ALBERT G. WAY is associate professor of history at Kennesaw State University and editor of *Agricultural History*. He is the author of *Conserving Southern Longleaf: Herbert Stoddard and the Rise of Ecological Land Management* and coauthor of *The Art of Managing Longleaf: A Personal History of the Stoddard-Neel Approach*.

VIRGINIA STEELE WOOD was the naval and maritime history reference librarian at the Library of Congress for thirty-two years. Her publications include the award-winning *Live Oaking: Southern Timber for Tall Ships*.

INDEX

Reck, Georg Philipp Friedrich von, 313

Reconstruction, 190, 216, 224, 225, 248

Reid, Whitelaw, 185, 186, 187, 199

Religious Instruction of the Negroes in the United States (C. C. Jones), 321

Remoussin, Louis, 135

Report on Proposed Leasing of State Owned Lands for Phosphate Mining, 295, 296

Republican Party, 224

Reynolds family, 12, 280, 289

rice, 29, 104, 105, 106; "abundance of fine Rice Land," 103; cultivation of, 13, 29, 30, 126, 141; culture of, 12, 141; diseases of, 126, 143; as export crop, 43, 104, 105; plantations, 41–42, 128, 137, 143; technology from West Africa, 183; and tidal "pitch," 42. *See also* African Americans; indigo; plantations; Sea Island cotton

Richardson, Ingram, 296

riparian rights doctrine, 276n103

Robert and Harold; or, The Young Marooners on the Florida Coast (Goulding), 31–32, 319

Roberts, Nancy, 163, 164, 166; *Georgia Ghosts*, 163

Robinson Crusoe (Defoe), 31, 32

Rockefeller, William, 232

Roebling, John, 209

Roebling, Washington, 209

Roosevelt, Theodore, 228

Rose, Willie Lee, 4

rule of capture, 264–65

Russell, Tom, 134

saltwater encroachment, 262, 263, 266. *See also* Floridan Aquifer; Savannah; Union Camp

saltwater intrusion, 247, 256, 259

Salzburgers (German Protestant refugees), 40, 100, 106, 213, 313

Sanger, Matthew C., 65

San Miguel de Gualdape, 69, 70, 82; and New Andalucia, myth of, 82; possible location of in Georgia, 69. *See also* Ayllón, Lucas Vásquez de; Florida

Santa Catalina de Guale, 14. *See also* Mission Santa Catalina de Guale

Sapelo; or, Child-Life on the Tidewater (Goulding), 319

Sapelo Island, 7, 188, 280, 281; sound, 41, 219; post–Civil War, 34, 35, 113, 192; protections, 7; tourist literature of, 178

Sapelo Island Marine Institute, 38

Sapelo Island National Estuarine Research Reserve, 38

Sargent, Charles S., 221

Savannah, 35, 101, 107, 196, 258, 260, 310; as America's "Most Haunted City," 160; city of, 246, 252, 285; colonial town of, 14, 15, 28, 100, 106; ghost tours in, 159–60; Industrial Committee of, 252; industry of, 301; "Map of the County of Savannah," 99; papermills of, 176, 246, 247, 285, 301; port of, 43, 104, 217, 319; post–Civil War, 178, 185, 189; saltwater intrusion and, 259, 262; slavery in, 154, 163, 183; "View of Savannah" (Gordon), 99. *See also* Floridan Aqui-

fer; Georgia; Oglethorpe, James Edward; Union Camp

Savannah (Georgia Writers' Project), 194

Savannah Beach, 281

Savannah Morning News, 249, 293

Savannah Press, 190

Savannah Pulp and Paper Laboratory, 252

Savannah Republican, 27

Savannah River: land holdings along, 67, 109, 114, 195; and setting a boundary, 279, 309, 310; —, in colonial era, 93, 94, 96, 97, 100, 111; —, in "New Purchase" land, 114; —, in royal charter, 309, 310; as water source, 243, 294. *See also* Georgia; groundwater crisis; Savannah

Savannah Town, 96

Savannah Wildlife Refuge, 105

Savannah Yacht Club, 191

Save Our Marshes Committee, 41

Save Our Vital Environment, 289

Schottle, Taylor, 324

Scott paper company, 176

Seaboard Construction Company, 297

Seabrook, Charles, 45

Sea Island, 7, 16

Sea Island Company, 281, 297

Sea Island cotton: cultivation of, 141, 179, 181, 182, 190; plantations, 128, 143; post–Civil War, 192; qualities of, 29–30, 184. *See also* African Americans; indigo; plantations; rice; slaves

Sea Islands, 75, 36, 319; blacks on, 125, 143; and global climate change, 46; Sea Island chain, 81; southern, 93, 102, 103. *See also* Golden Isles

sea level rise, 46, 47, 48, 267, 268

Sea Pines Plantation, 2, 5, 7

Searle, R. W., map of colonial Georgia, 100–101

second-growth forest, 248, 252

Sedeno, Antonio, 74, 75

Segura, Juan Baptista de, 75

Selected Poems (Aiken), 323

sense of place: and Americans, 324; definition of, 23, 24, 311; loss of, 325, 326; and regionalism, 311–12; and sense of "settling down," 321, 325; stages in developing sense of place, 314. *See also* landscape, coastal, descriptions of

Serres, Michel, 24

Seven Years' War, 107, 111

Sharpley, Richard, *The Darker Side of Travel*, 158

shellfishing, 60, 61, 62, 63, 65, 66

Shellfish Research Laboratory, 283

shell middens and rings, 25, 61, 62, 64, 65

Sherman, William Tecumseh, 34, 37, 196; Field Order No. 15, 34, 192; march of, 177, 185, 187, 196. *See also* Civil War

Sherman's March: A Meditation on the Possibility of Romantic Love during an Era of Nuclear Weapons Proliferation (McElwee), 37

Shipyard Creek, 106

Shortland, Becky, 266

ENVIRONMENTAL HISTORY AND
THE AMERICAN SOUTH